RADIANT

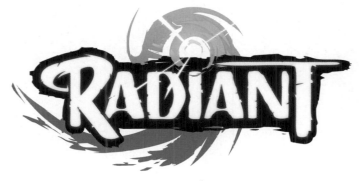

TONY VALENTE

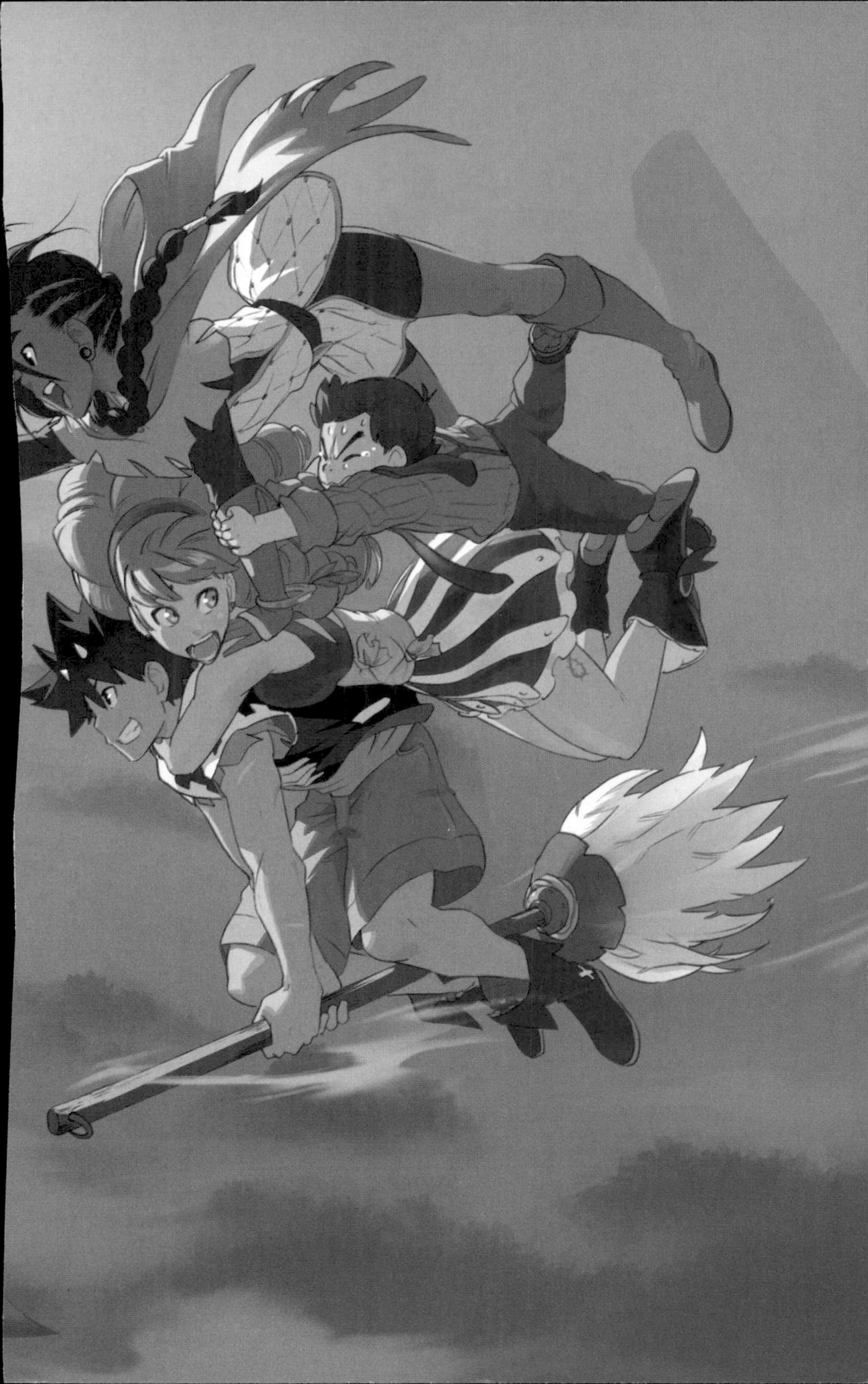

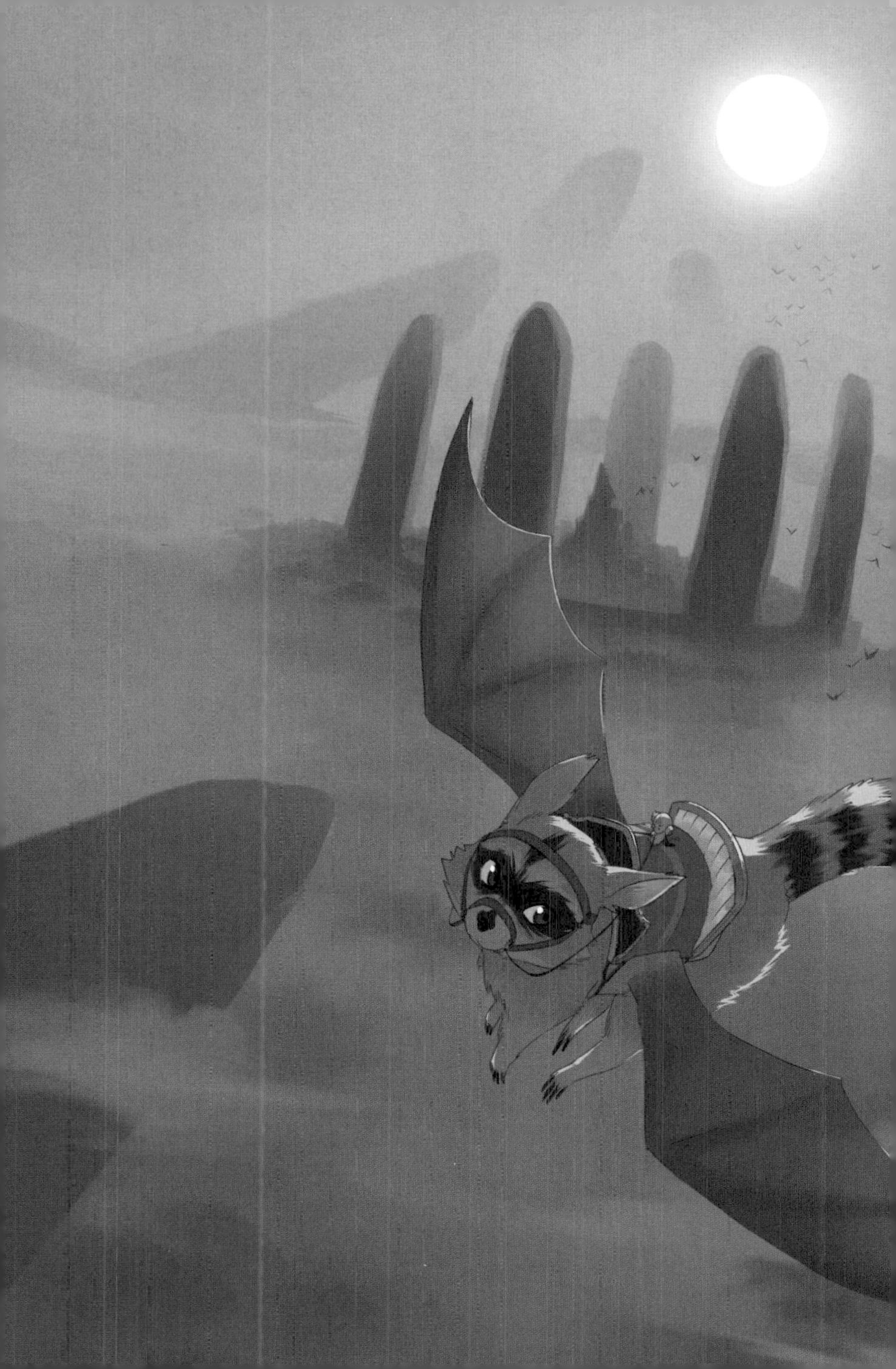

CONTENTS

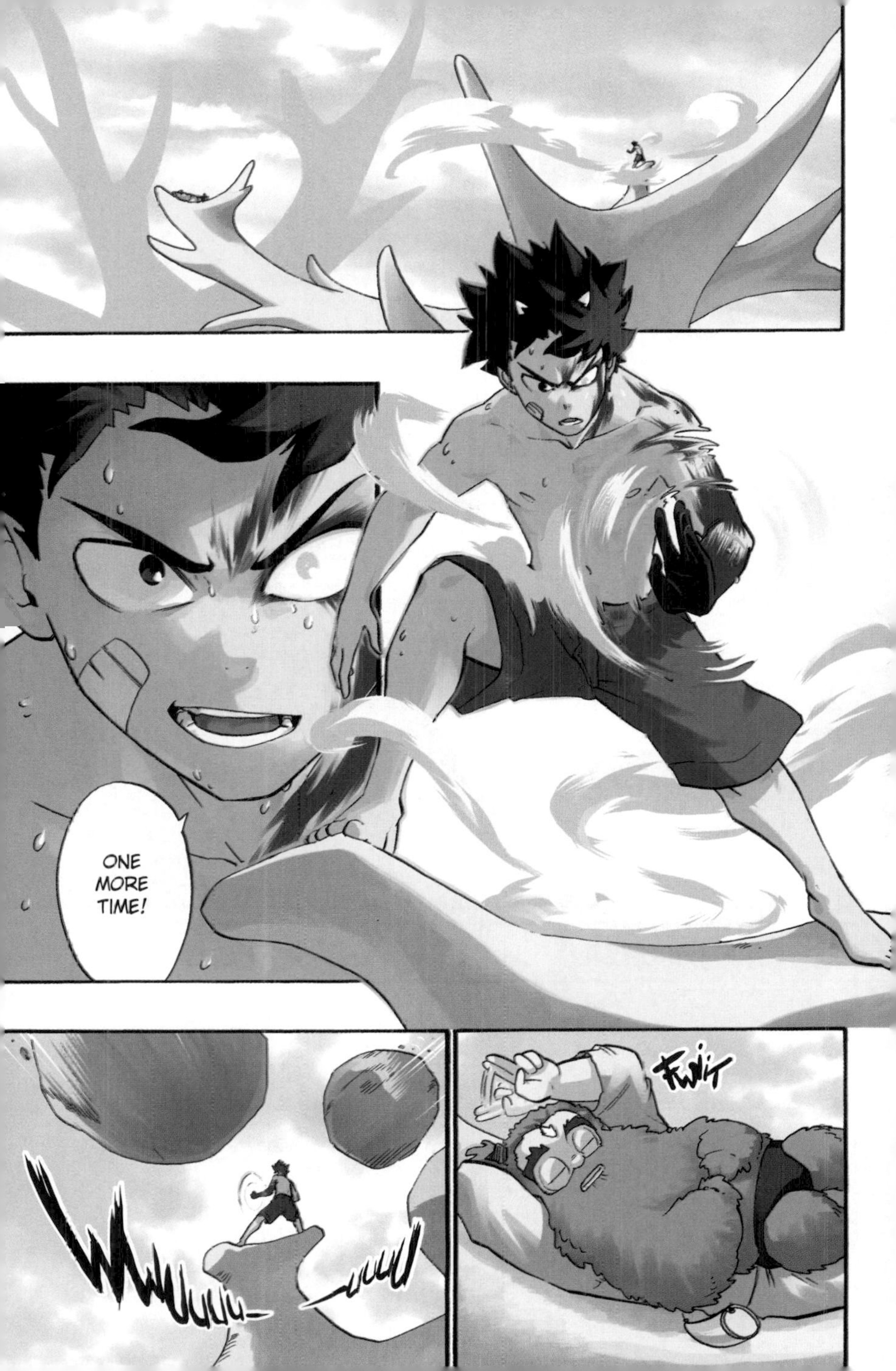
ONE MORE TIME!
FWIT
WHUUUU-UUUU

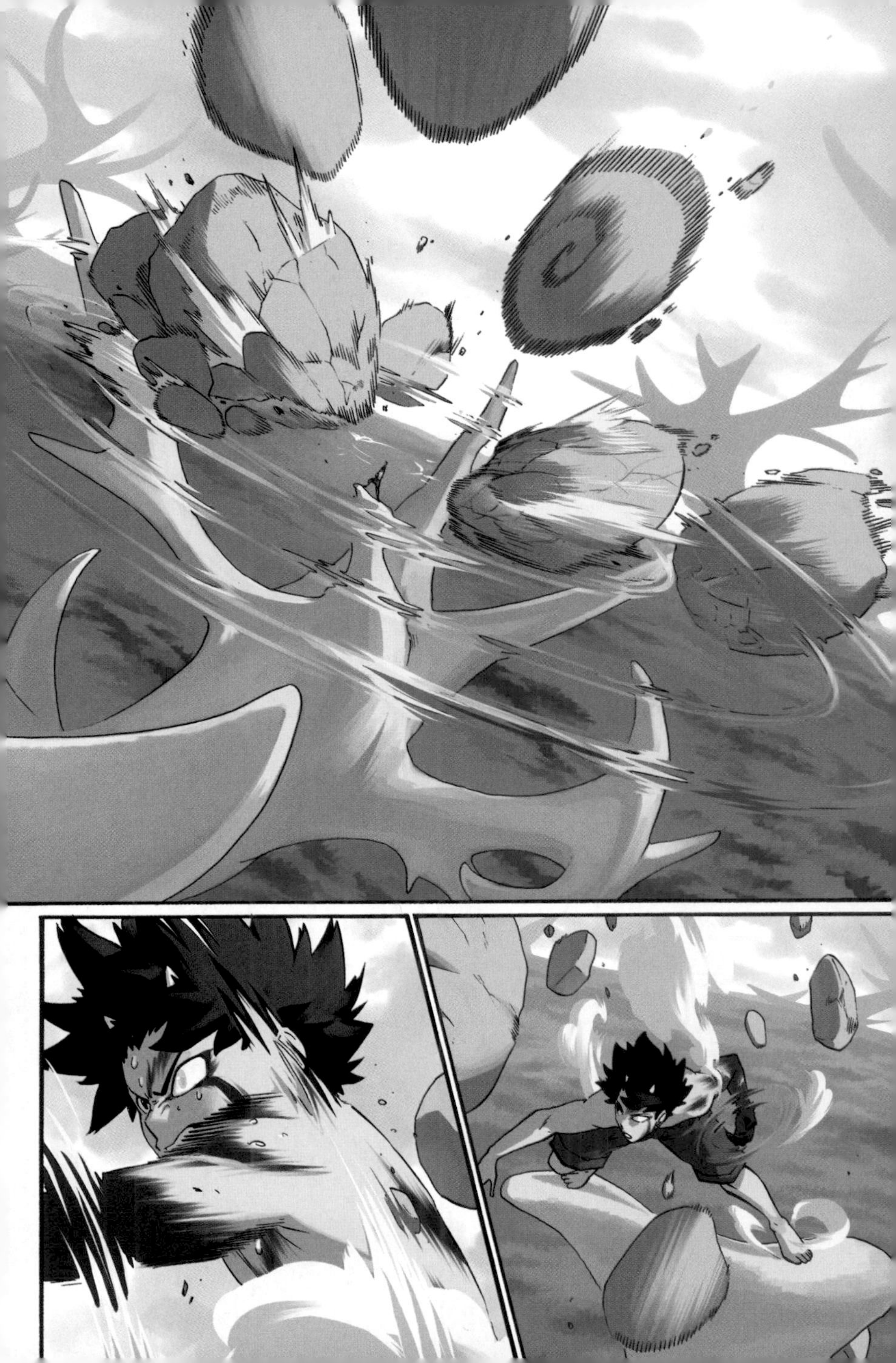

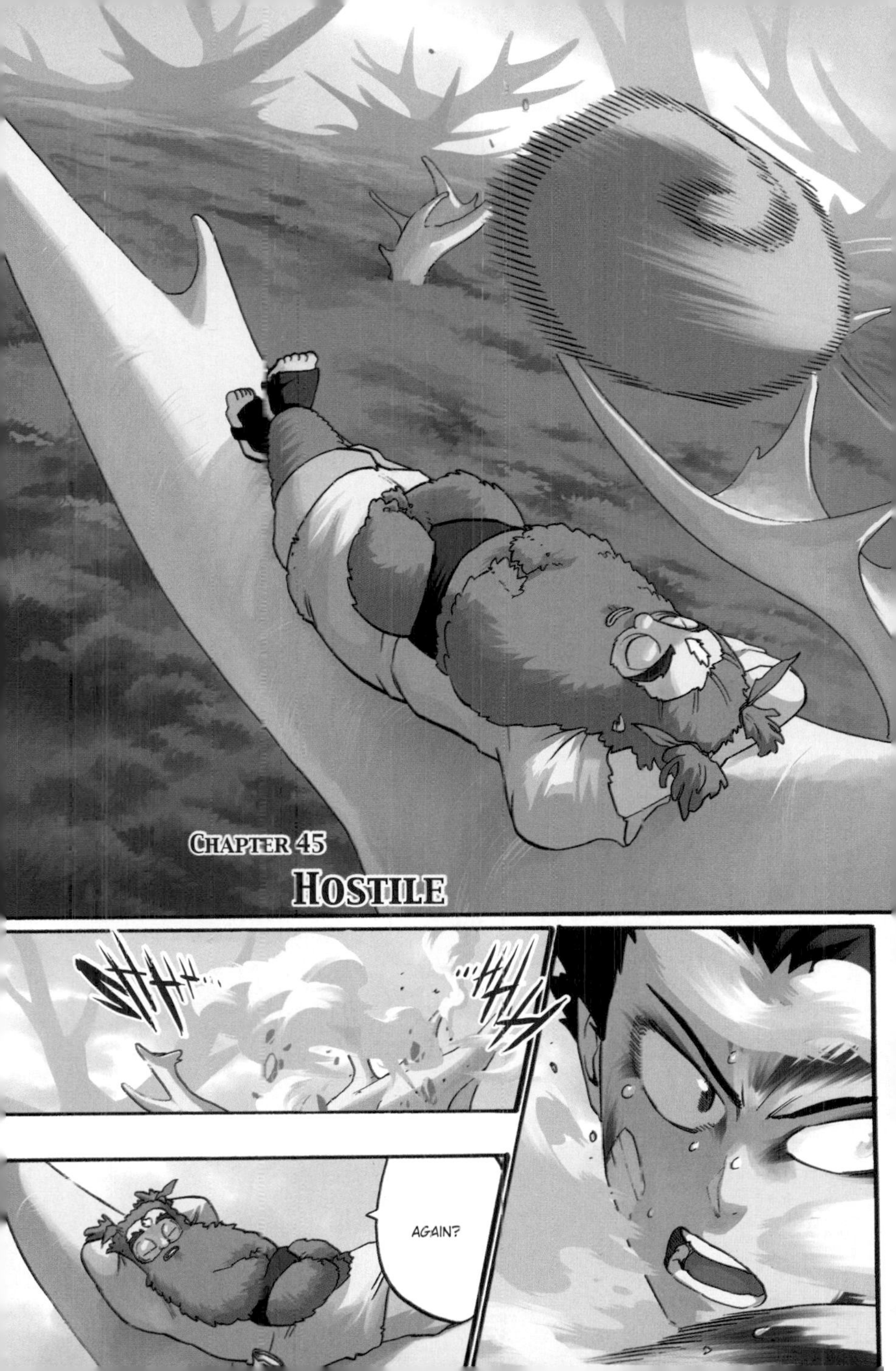
Chapter 45
Hostile
Again?

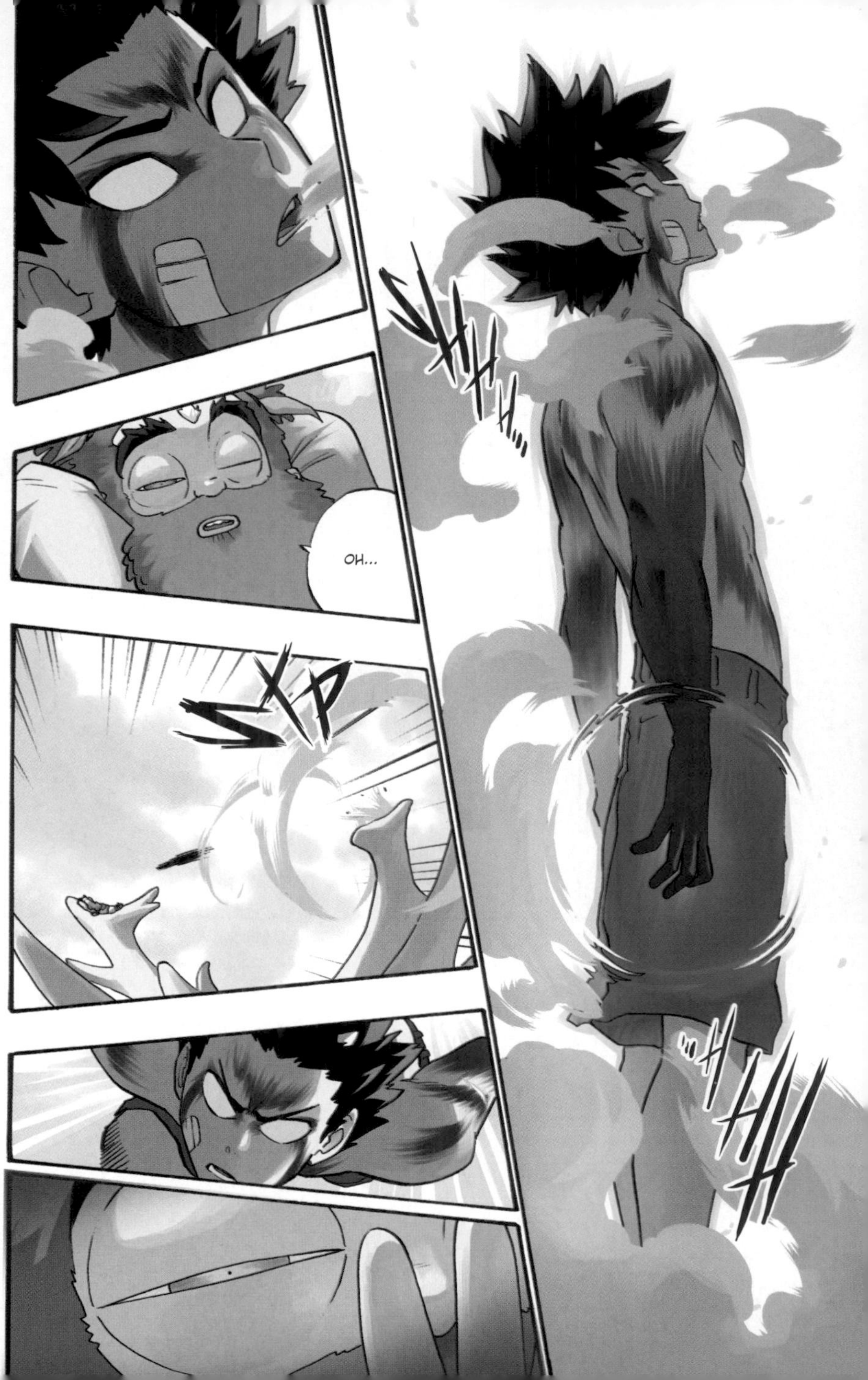
SHHHH...
...HHHHH
OH...

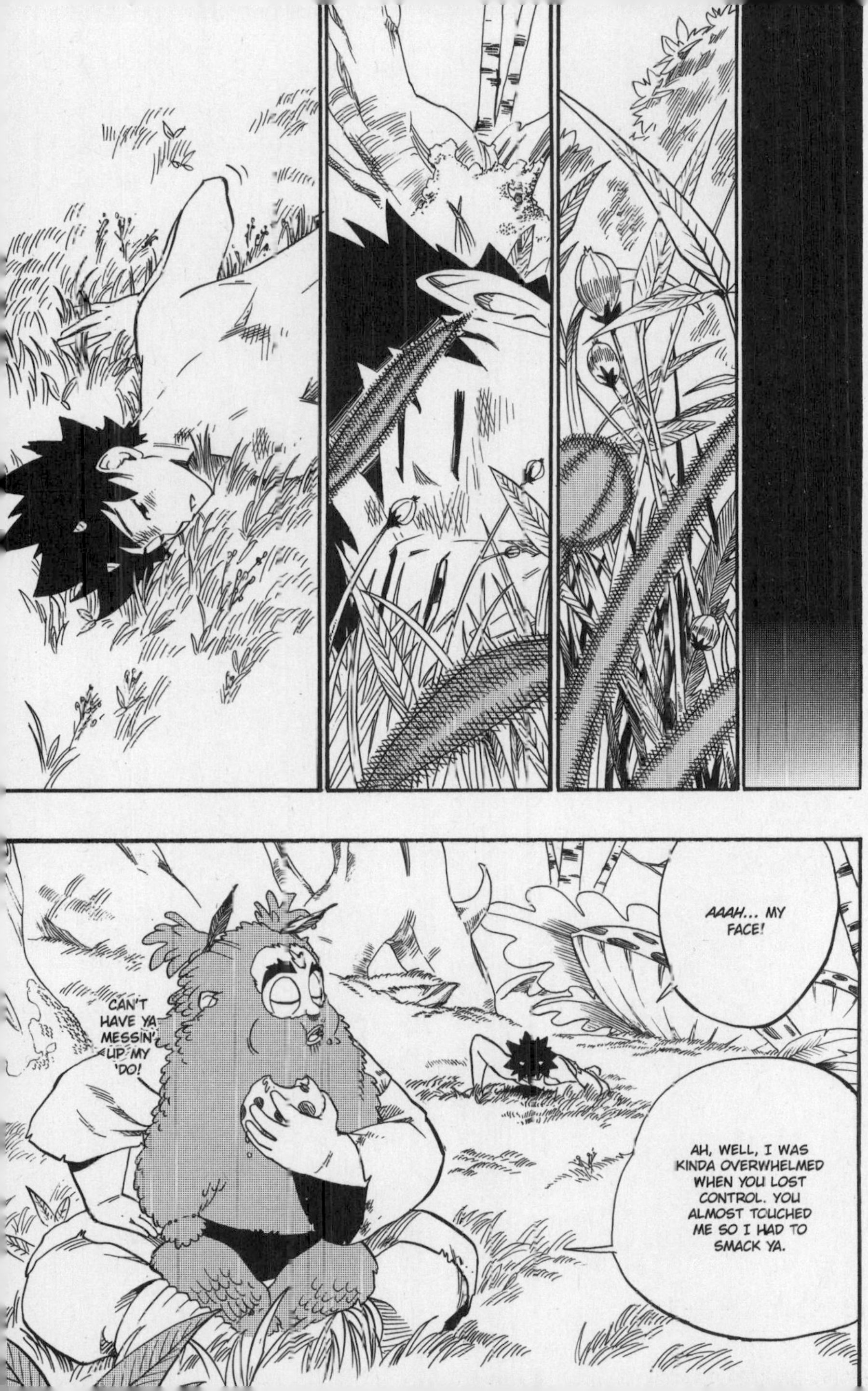
AAAH... MY FACE!
AH, WELL, I WAS KINDA OVERWHELMED WHEN YOU LOST CONTROL. YOU ALMOST TOUCHED ME SO I HAD TO SMACK YA.
CAN'T HAVE YA MESSIN' UP MY 'DO!

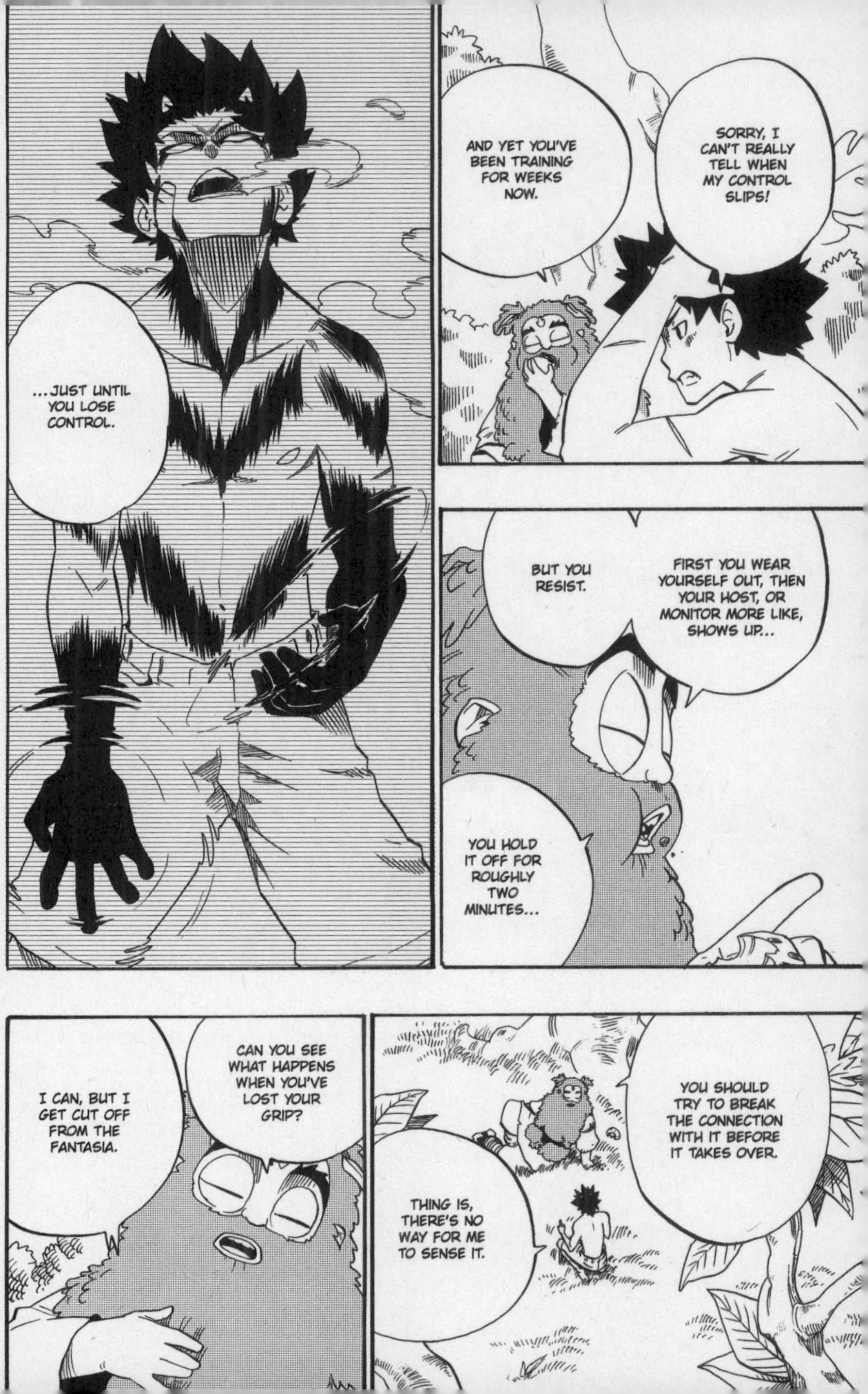
SORRY, I CAN'T REALLY TELL WHEN MY CONTROL SLIPS!
AND YET YOU'VE BEEN TRAINING FOR WEEKS NOW.
FIRST YOU WEAR YOURSELF OUT, THEN YOUR HOST, OR MONITOR MORE LIKE, SHOWS UP...
BUT YOU RESIST.
YOU HOLD IT OFF FOR ROUGHLY TWO MINUTES...
...JUST UNTIL YOU LOSE CONTROL.
YOU SHOULD TRY TO BREAK THE CONNECTION WITH IT BEFORE IT TAKES OVER.
THING IS, THERE'S NO WAY FOR ME TO SENSE IT.
CAN YOU SEE WHAT HAPPENS WHEN YOU'VE LOST YOUR GRIP?
I CAN, BUT I GET CUT OFF FROM THE FANTASIA.

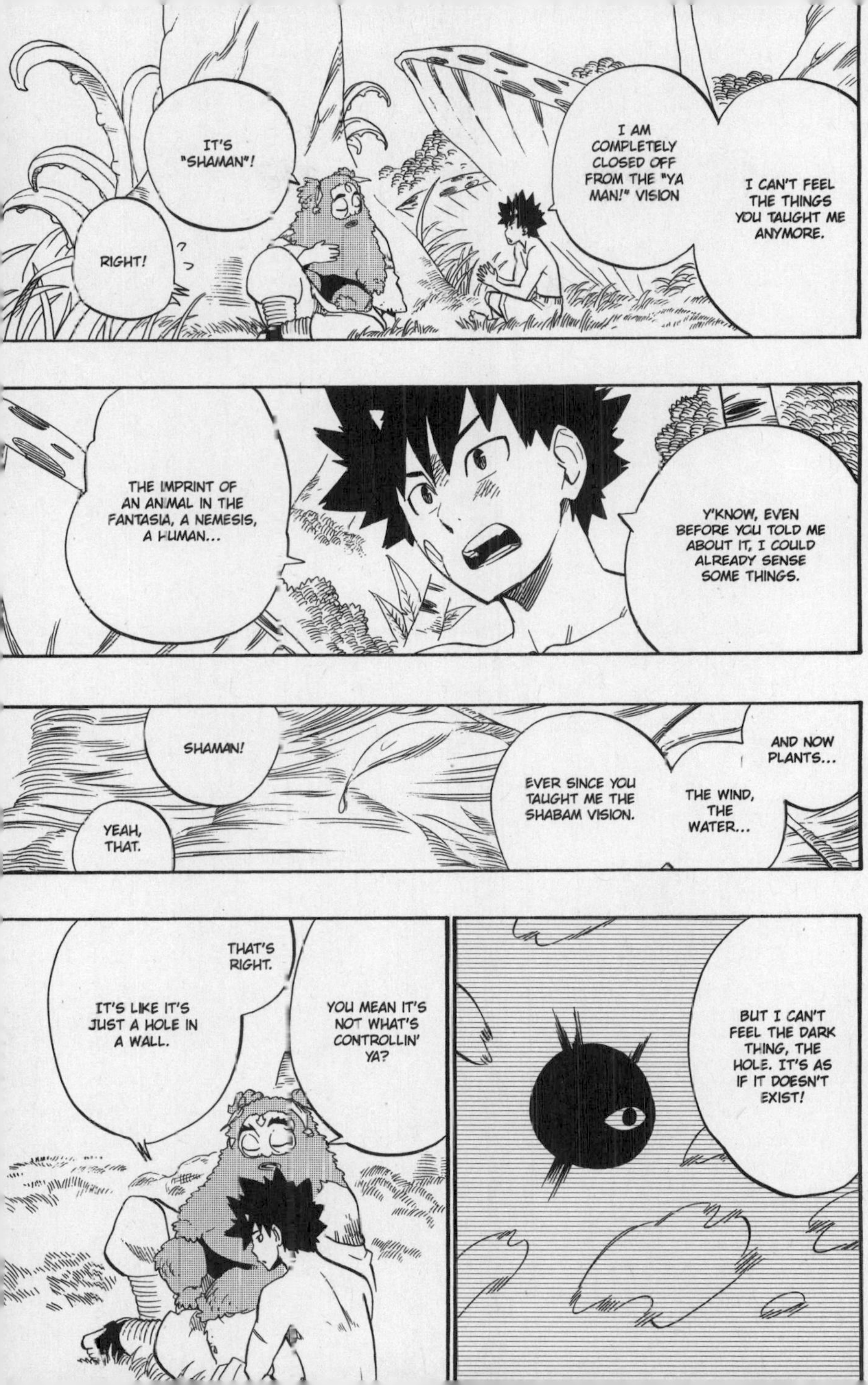
I CAN'T FEEL THE THINGS YOU TAUGHT ME ANYMORE.
I AM COMPLETELY CLOSED OFF FROM THE "YA MAN!" VISION
IT'S "SHAMAN"!
RIGHT!
Y'KNOW, EVEN BEFORE YOU TOLD ME ABOUT IT, I COULD ALREADY SENSE SOME THINGS.
THE IMPRINT OF AN ANIMAL IN THE FANTASIA, A NEMESIS, A HUMAN...
AND NOW PLANTS...
THE WIND, THE WATER...
EVER SINCE YOU TAUGHT ME THE SHABAM VISION.
SHAMAN!
YEAH, THAT.
BUT I CAN'T FEEL THE DARK THING, THE HOLE. IT'S AS IF IT DOESN'T EXIST!
YOU MEAN IT'S NOT WHAT'S CONTROLLIN' YA?
THAT'S RIGHT.
IT'S LIKE IT'S JUST A HOLE IN A WALL.

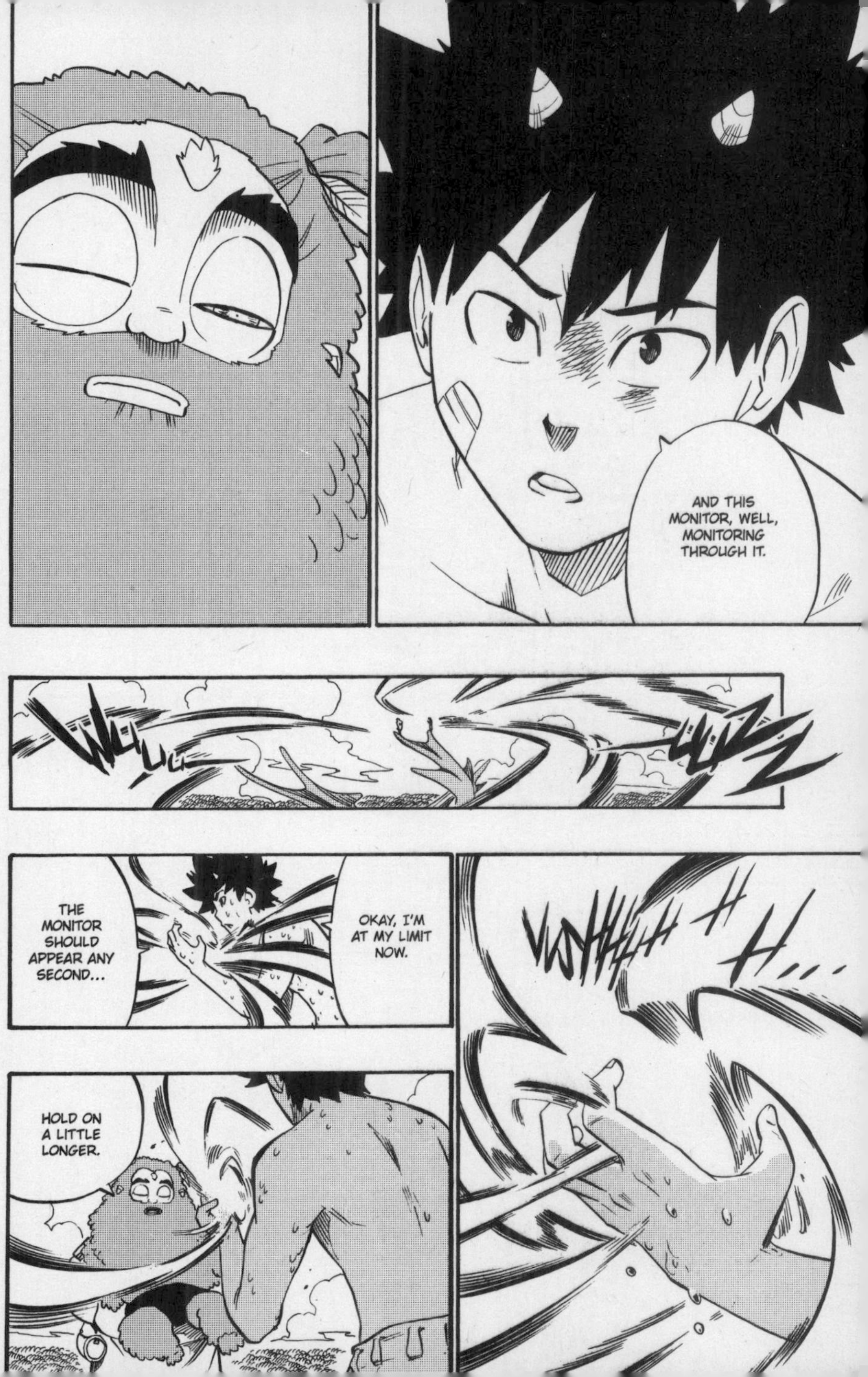
AND THIS MONITOR, WELL, MONITORING THROUGH IT.
OKAY, I'M AT MY LIMIT NOW.
THE MONITOR SHOULD APPEAR ANY SECOND...
HOLD ON A LITTLE LONGER.

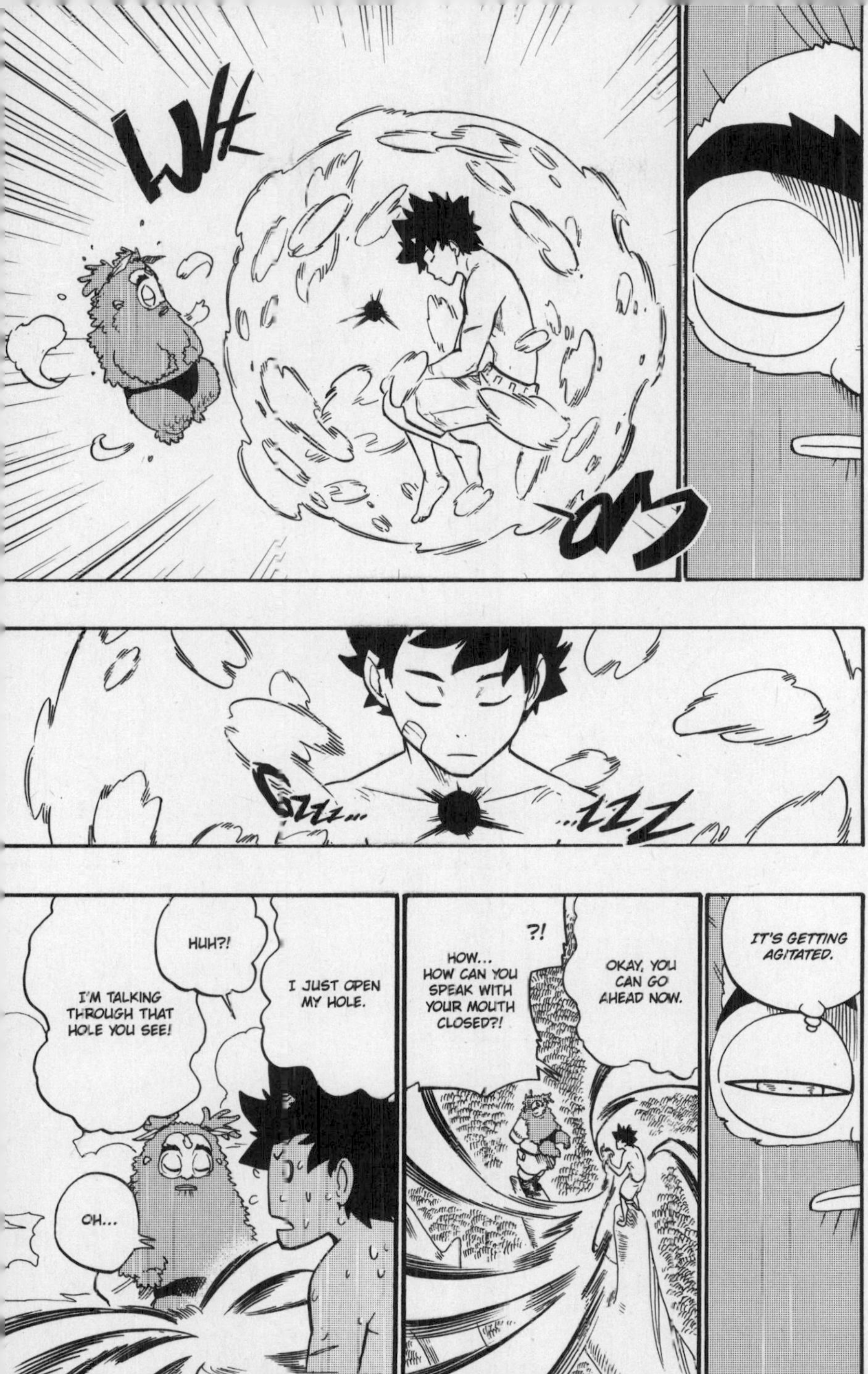
GZZz...
...ZZZ
IT'S GETTING AGITATED.
OKAY, YOU CAN GO AHEAD NOW.
?!
HOW... HOW CAN YOU SPEAK WITH YOUR MOUTH CLOSED?!
I JUST OPEN MY HOLE.
HUH?!
I'M TALKING THROUGH THAT HOLE YOU SEE!
OH...

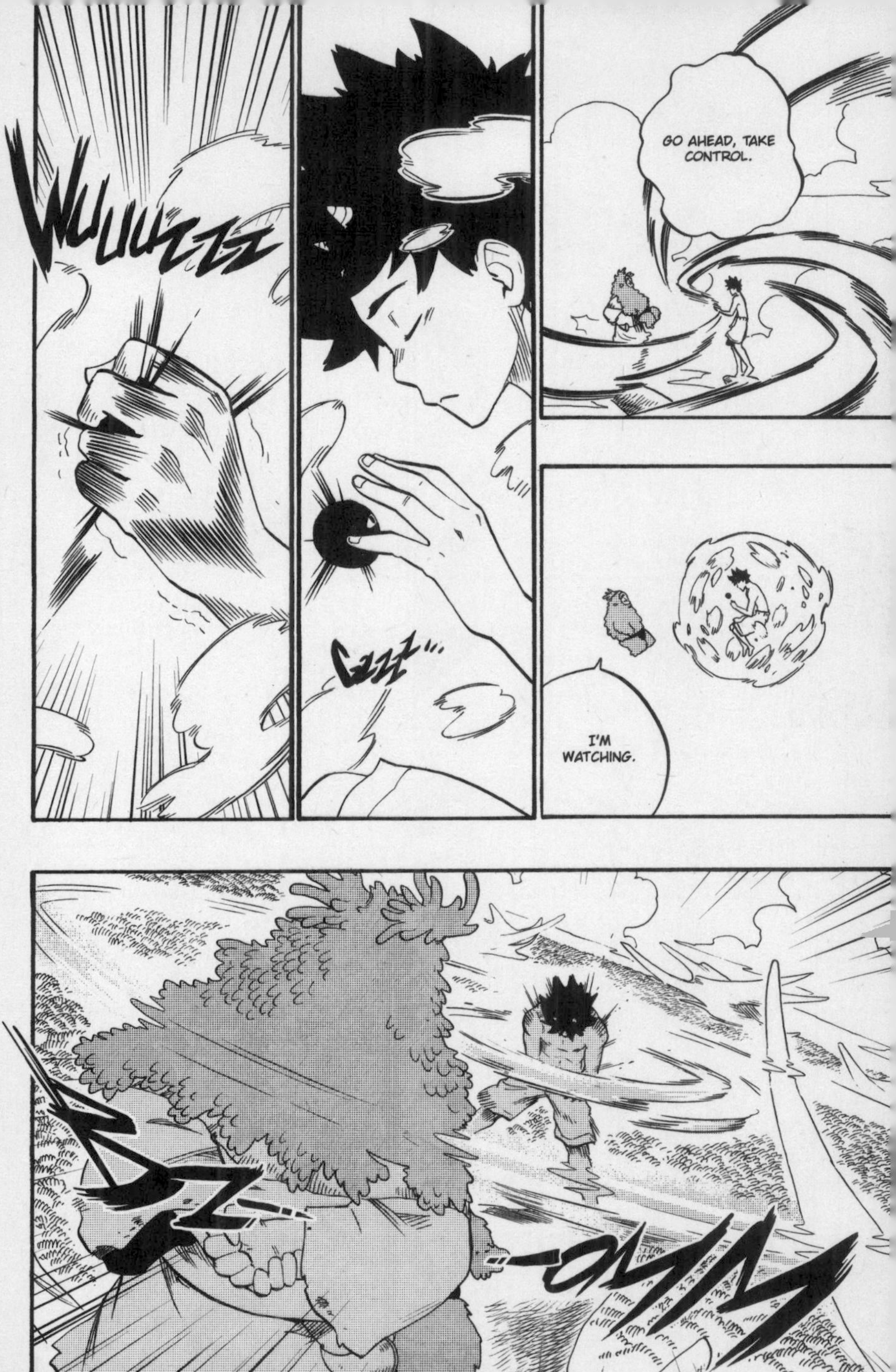
GO AHEAD, TAKE CONTROL.
I'M WATCHING.

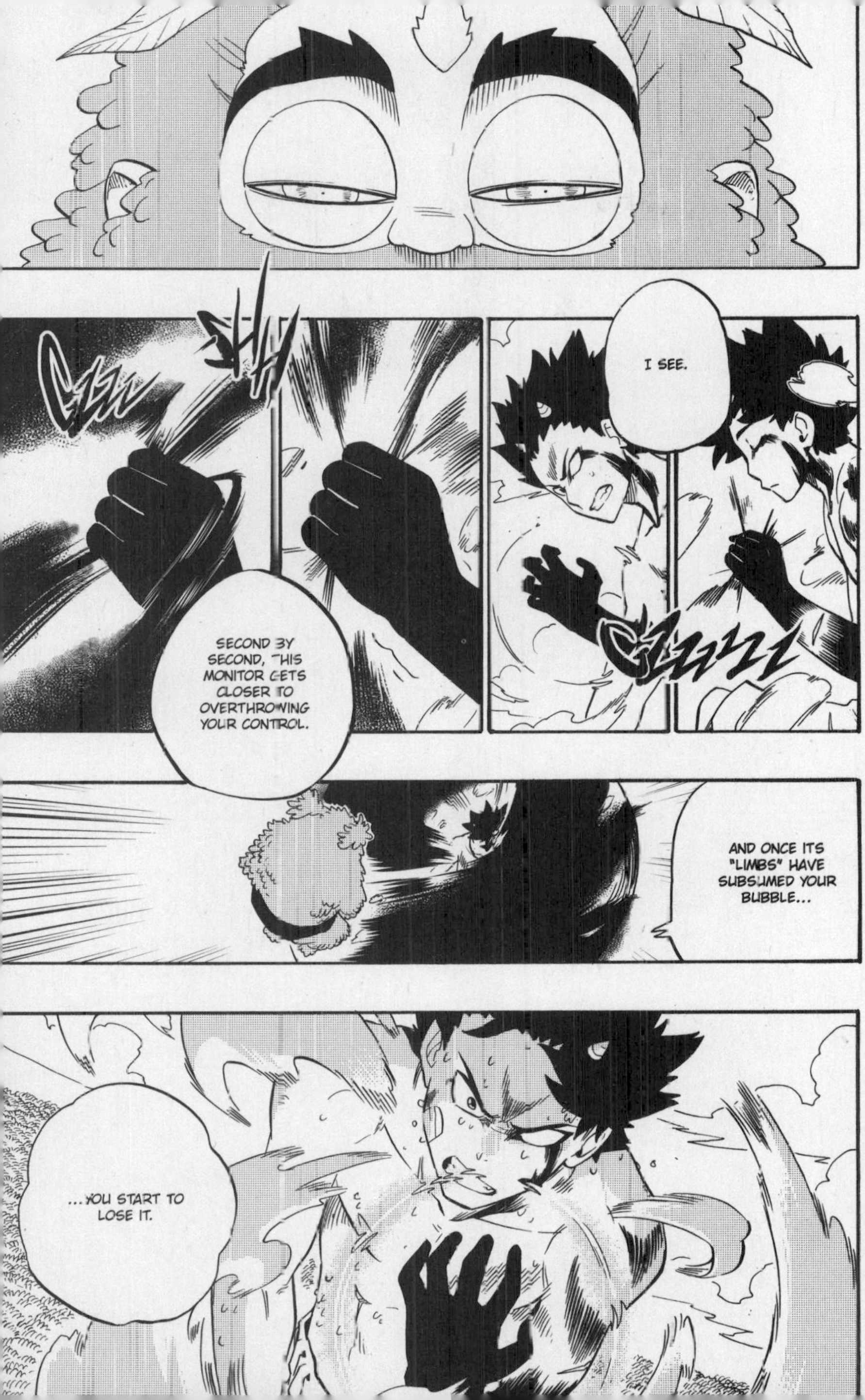
I SEE.
SECOND BY SECOND, THIS MONITOR GETS CLOSER TO OVERTHROWING YOUR CONTROL.
AND ONCE ITS "LIMBS" HAVE SUBSUMED YOUR BUBBLE...
...YOU START TO LOSE IT.

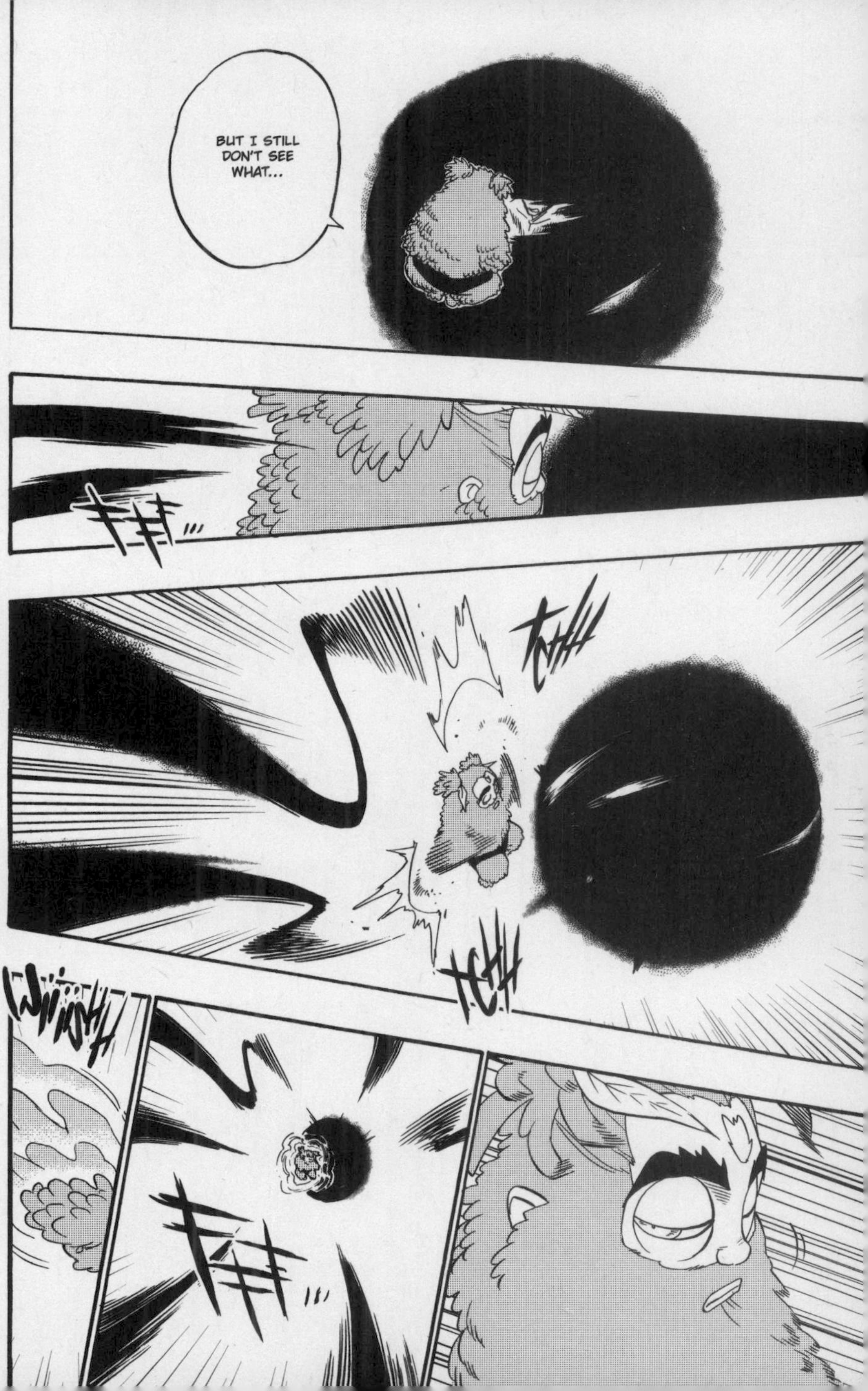
BUT I STILL DON'T SEE WHAT...
TCHH
TCHH

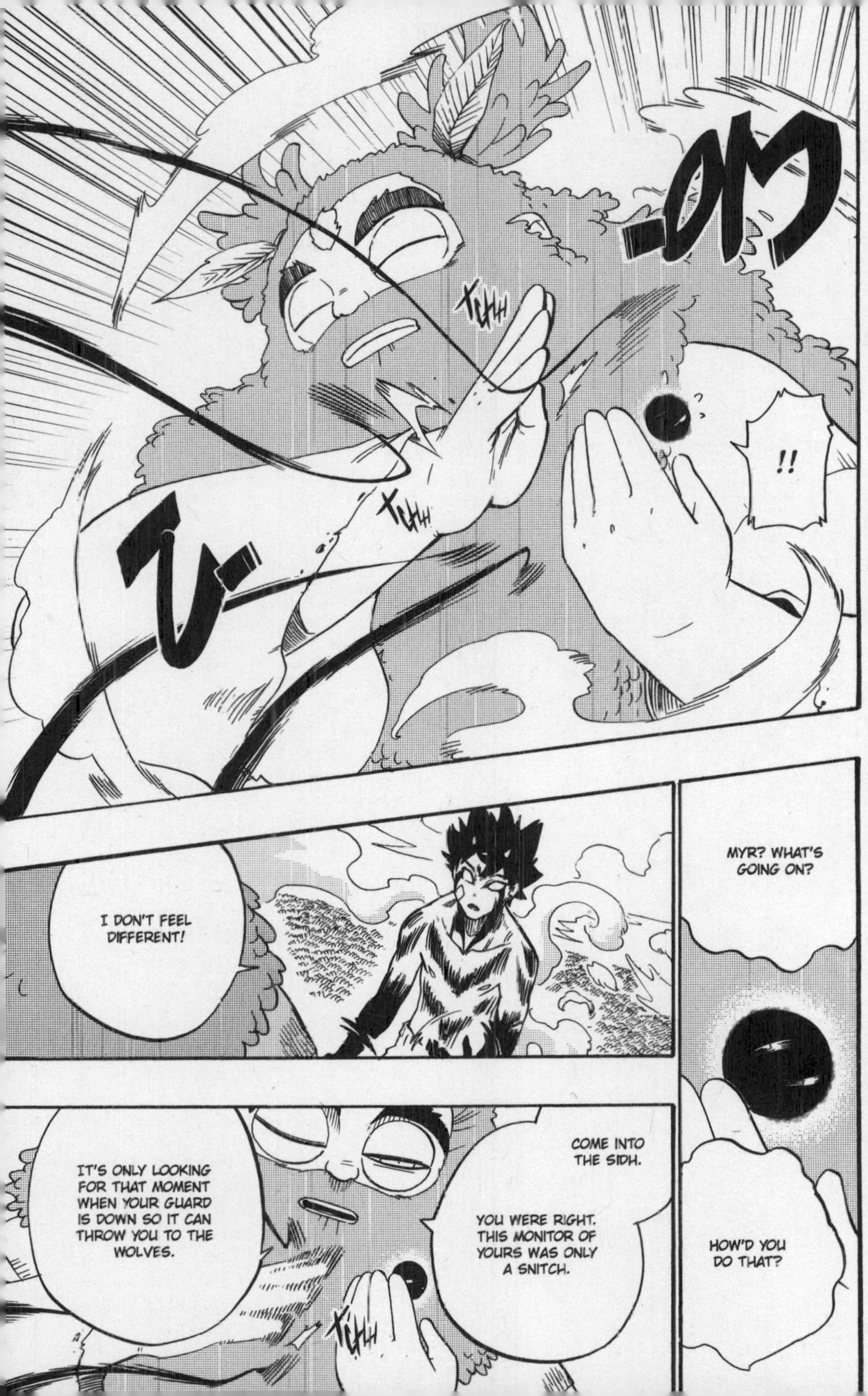
!!
MYR? WHAT'S GOING ON?
HOW'D YOU DO THAT?
I DON'T FEEL DIFFERENT!
COME INTO THE SIDH.
YOU WERE RIGHT. THIS MONITOR OF YOURS WAS ONLY A SNITCH.
IT'S ONLY LOOKING FOR THAT MOMENT WHEN YOUR GUARD IS DOWN SO IT CAN THROW YOU TO THE WOLVES.

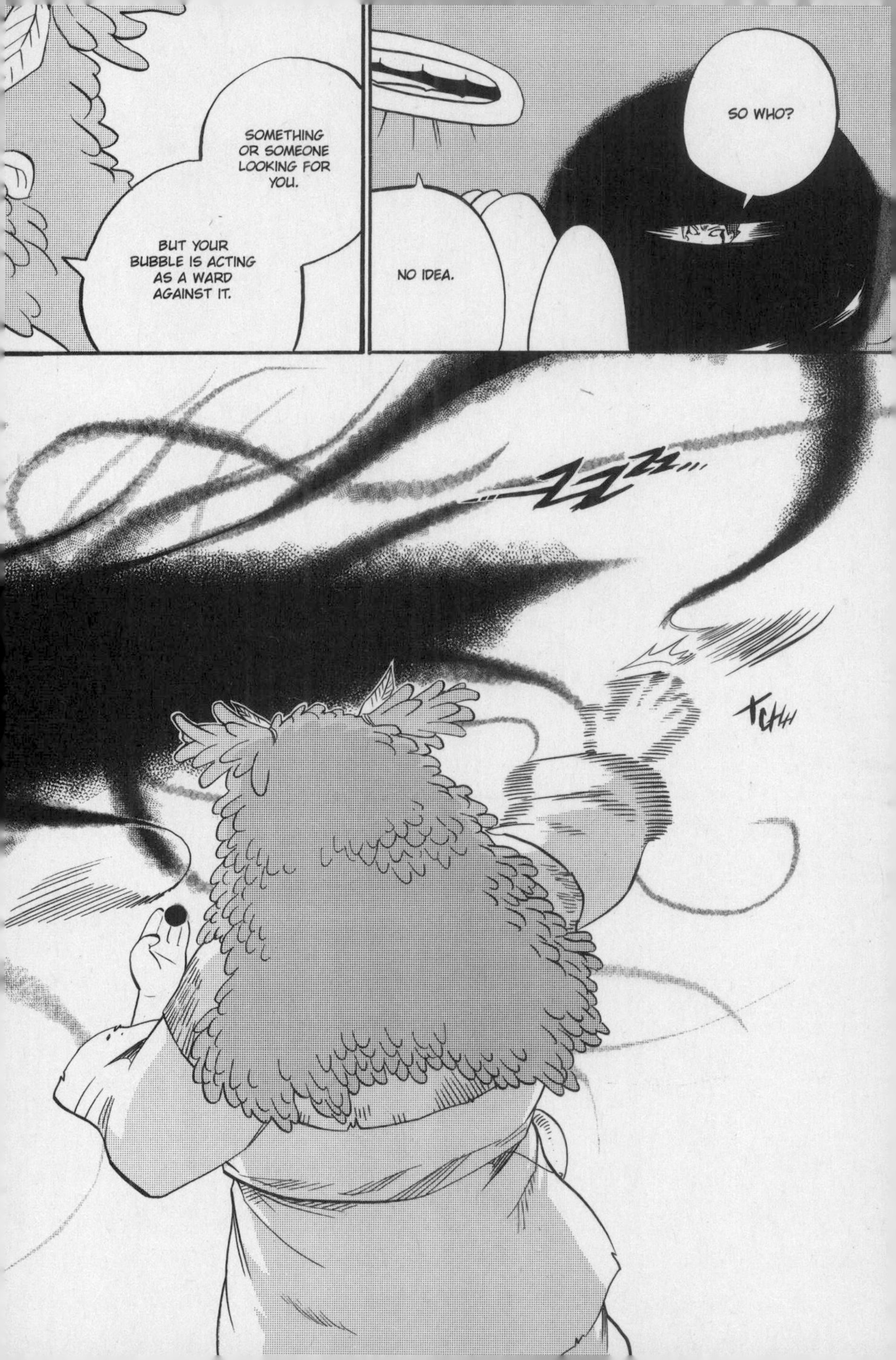
SO WHO?
NO IDEA.
SOMETHING OR SOMEONE LOOKING FOR YOU.
BUT YOUR BUBBLE IS ACTING AS A WARD AGAINST IT.
ZZZZ...
TCHH

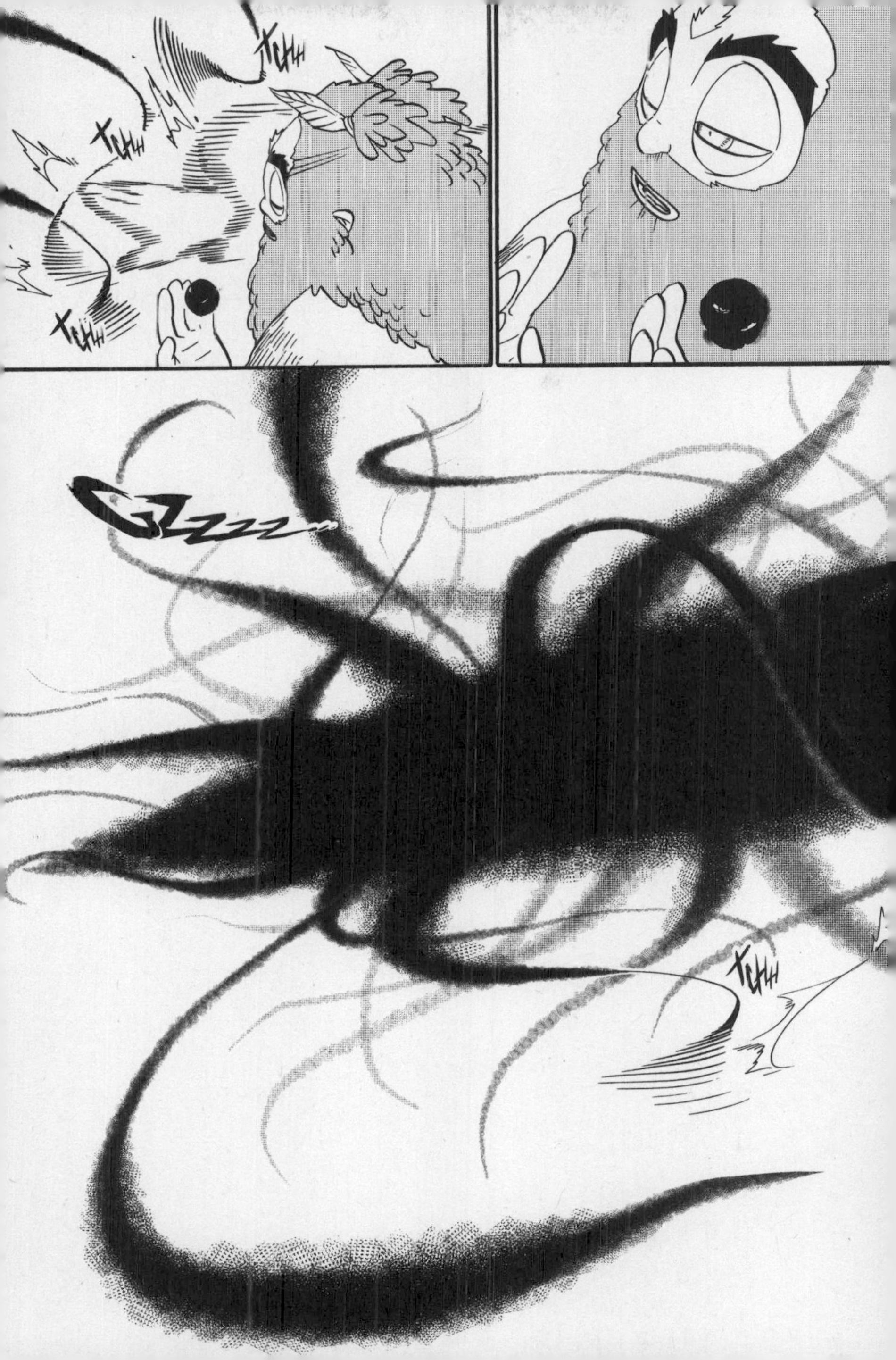
TCHH
TCHH
TCHH
GZZZZZ
TCHH

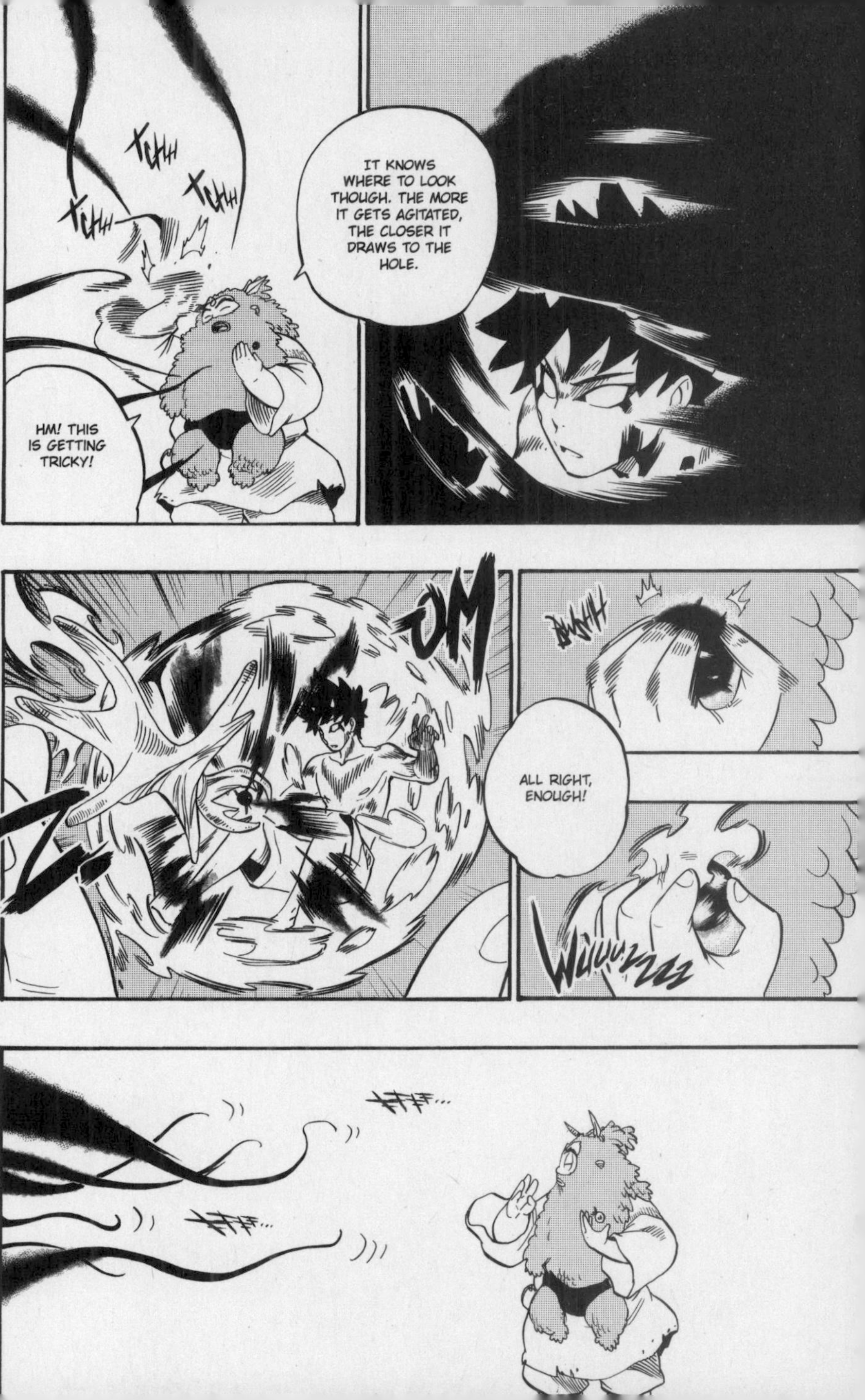
IT KNOWS WHERE TO LOOK THOUGH. THE MORE IT GETS AGITATED, THE CLOSER IT DRAWS TO THE HOLE.
HM! THIS IS GETTING TRICKY!
ALL RIGHT, ENOUGH!

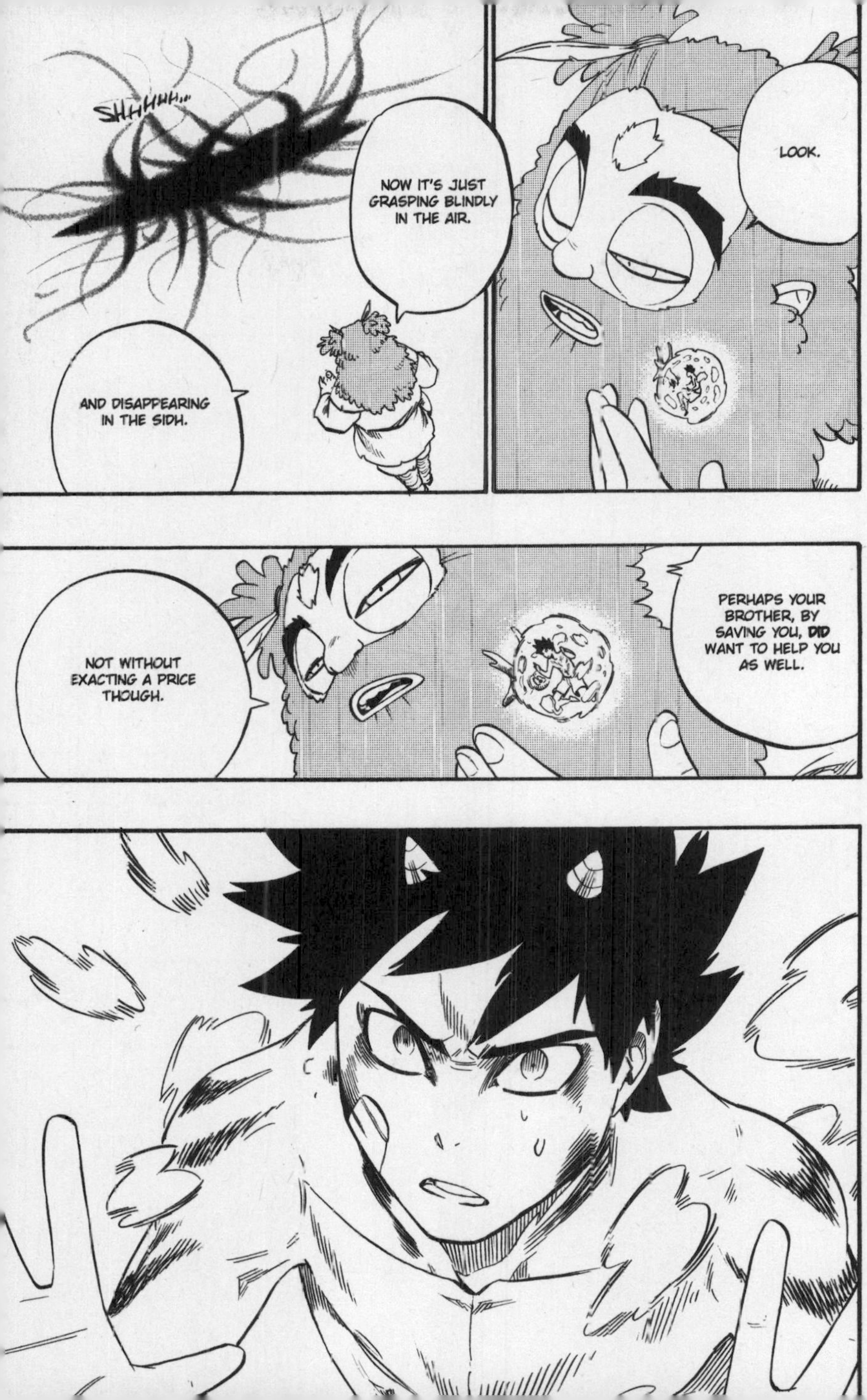
LOOK.
NOW IT'S JUST GRASPING BLINDLY IN THE AIR.
SHHHHH...
AND DISAPPEARING IN THE SIDH.
PERHAPS YOUR BROTHER, BY SAVING YOU, **DID** WANT TO HELP YOU AS WELL.
NOT WITHOUT EXACTING A PRICE THOUGH.

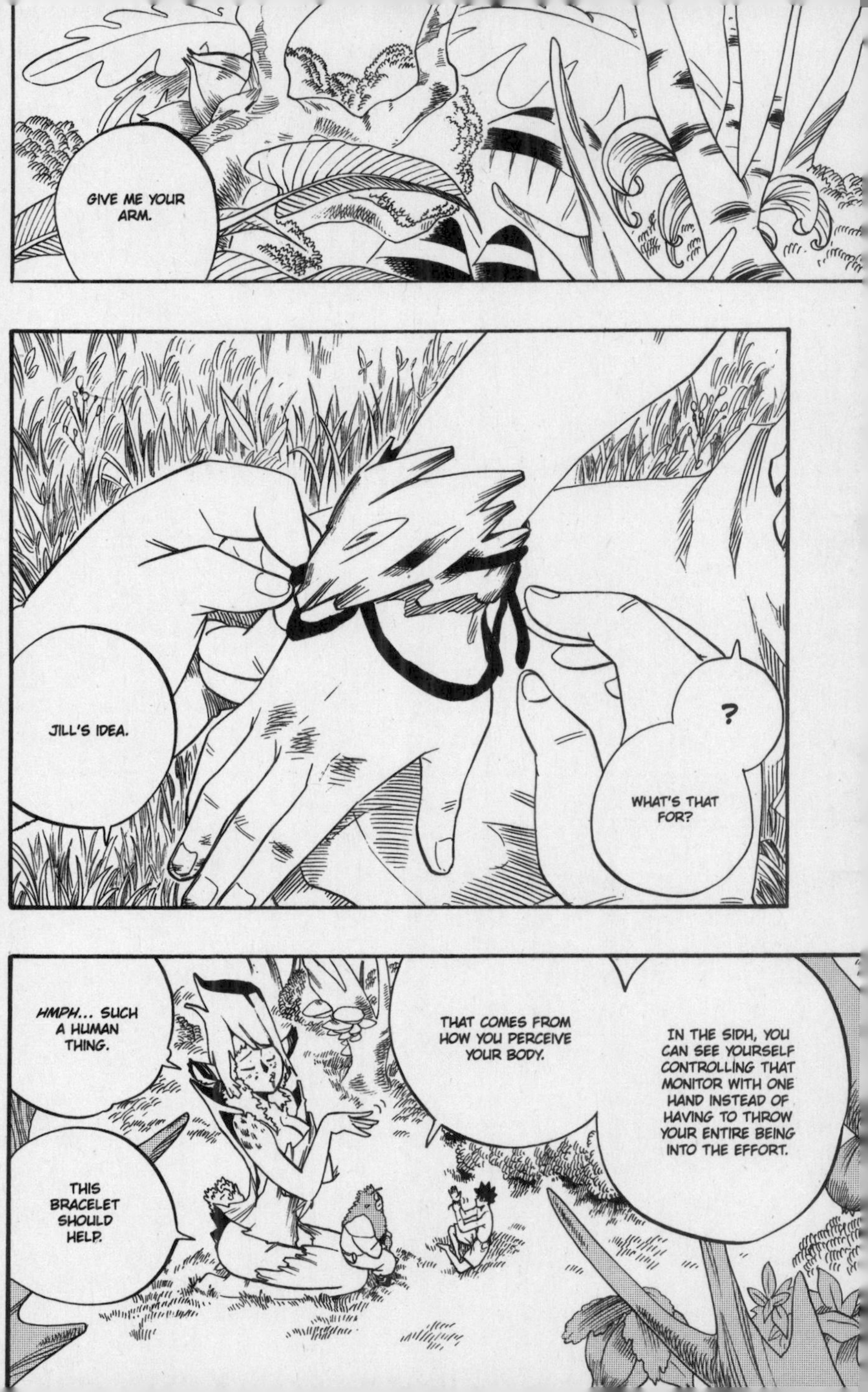
GIVE ME YOUR ARM.
?
WHAT'S THAT FOR?
JILL'S IDEA.
IN THE SIDH, YOU CAN SEE YOURSELF CONTROLLING THAT MONITOR WITH ONE HAND INSTEAD OF HAVING TO THROW YOUR ENTIRE BEING INTO THE EFFORT.
THAT COMES FROM HOW YOU PERCEIVE YOUR BODY.
HMPH... SUCH A HUMAN THING.
THIS BRACELET SHOULD HELP.

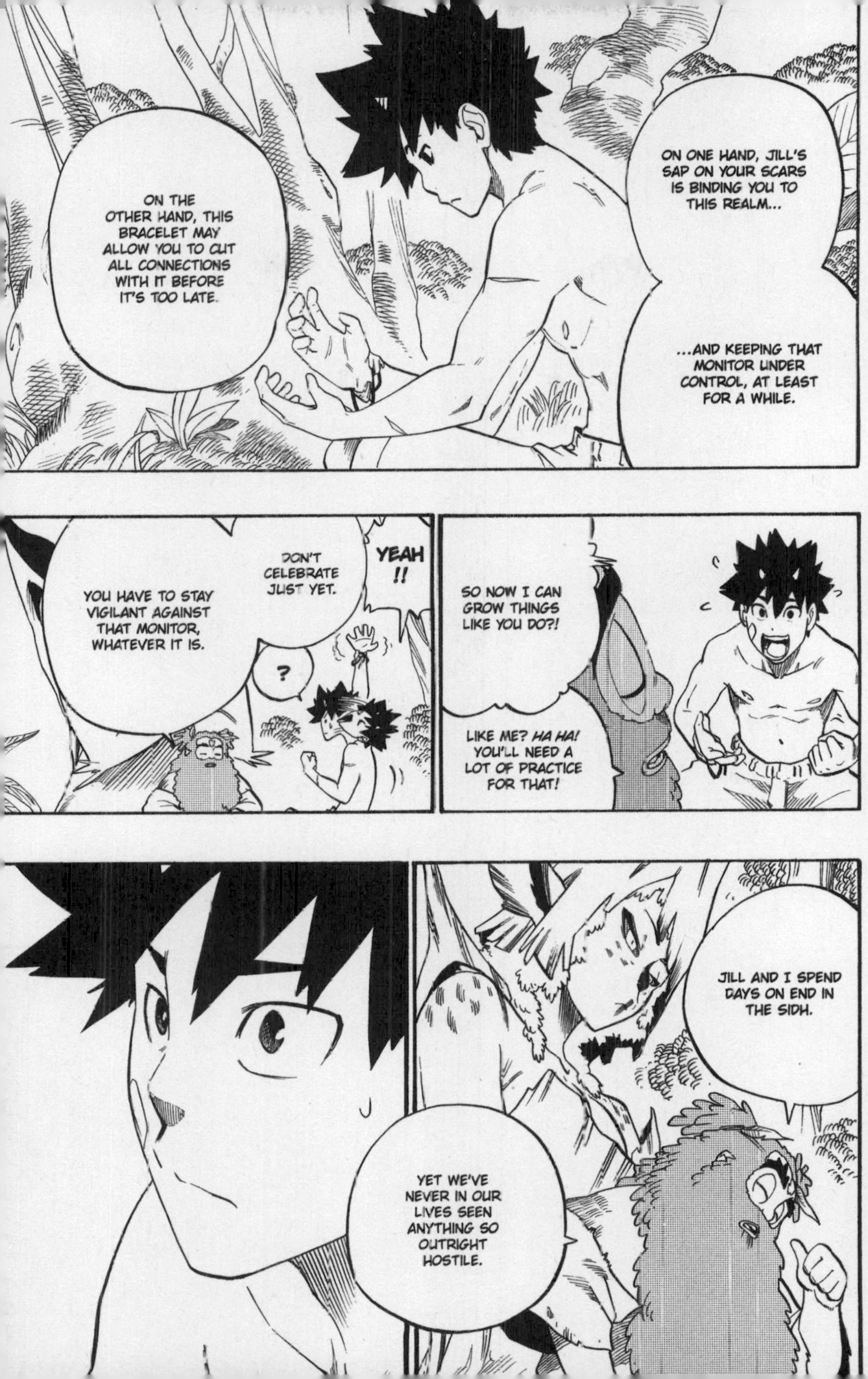
ON ONE HAND, JILL'S SAP ON YOUR SCARS IS BINDING YOU TO THIS REALM...
...AND KEEPING THAT MONITOR UNDER CONTROL, AT LEAST FOR A WHILE.
ON THE OTHER HAND, THIS BRACELET MAY ALLOW YOU TO CUT ALL CONNECTIONS WITH IT BEFORE IT'S TOO LATE.
SO NOW I CAN GROW THINGS LIKE YOU DO?!
LIKE ME? *HA HA!* YOU'LL NEED A LOT OF PRACTICE FOR THAT!
YEAH !!
DON'T CELEBRATE JUST YET.
?
YOU HAVE TO STAY VIGILANT AGAINST THAT MONITOR, WHATEVER IT IS.
JILL AND I SPEND DAYS ON END IN THE SIDH.
YET WE'VE NEVER IN OUR LIVES SEEN ANYTHING SO OUTRIGHT HOSTILE.

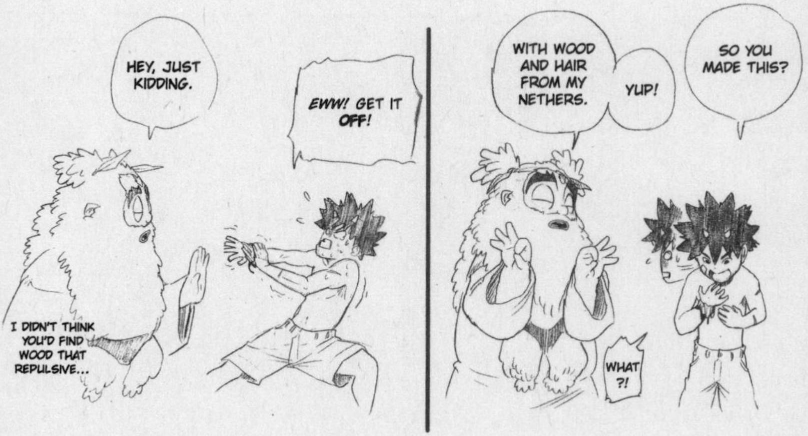
SO YOU MADE THIS?
YUP!
WITH WOOD AND HAIR FROM MY NETHERS.
WHAT?!
EWW! GET IT OFF!
HEY, JUST KIDDING.
I DIDN'T THINK YOU'D FIND WOOD THAT REPULSIVE...

Chapter 46
Improvise!

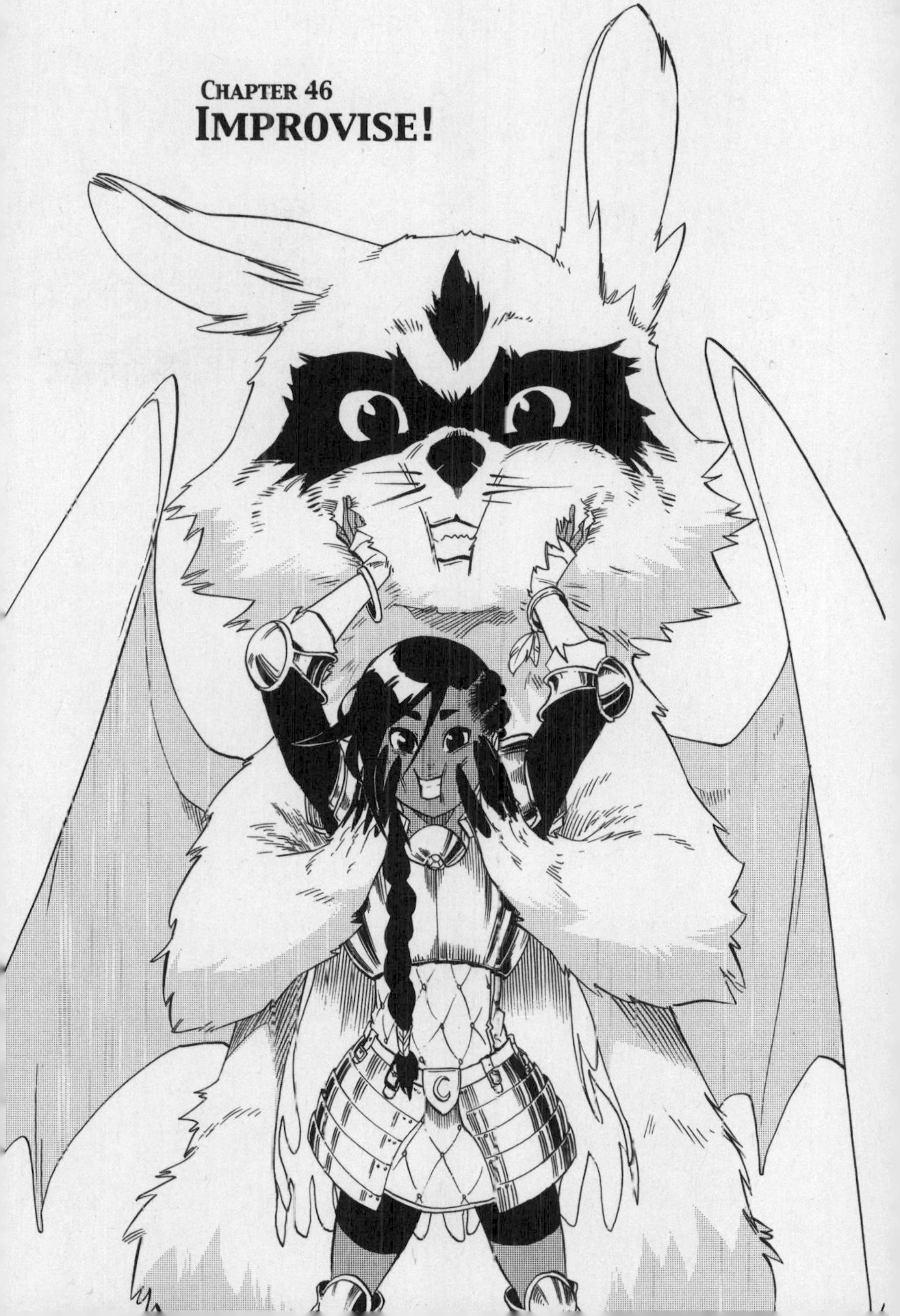

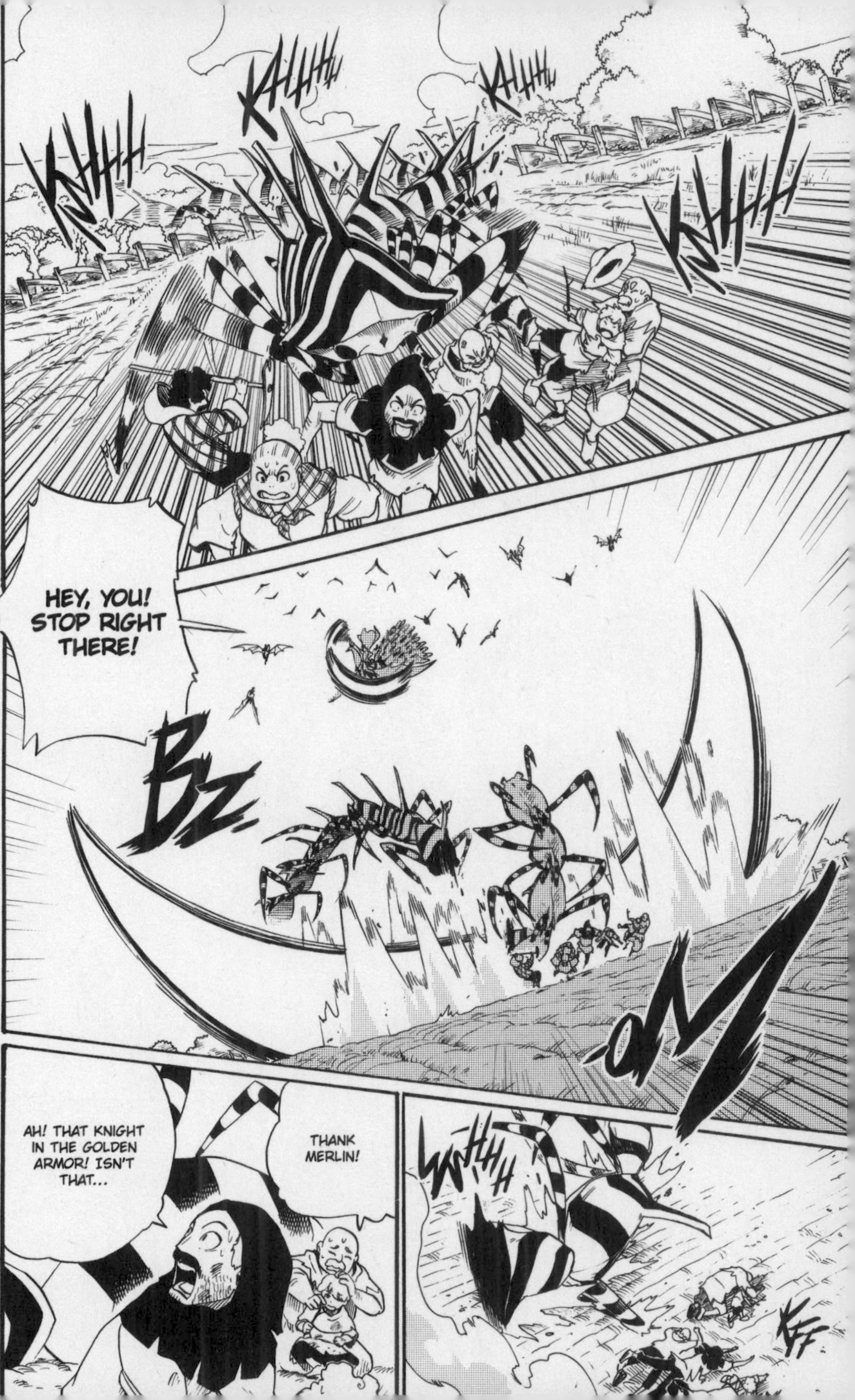
HEY, YOU! STOP RIGHT THERE!
BZ
THANK MERLIN!
AH! THAT KNIGHT IN THE GOLDEN ARMOR! ISN'T THAT...

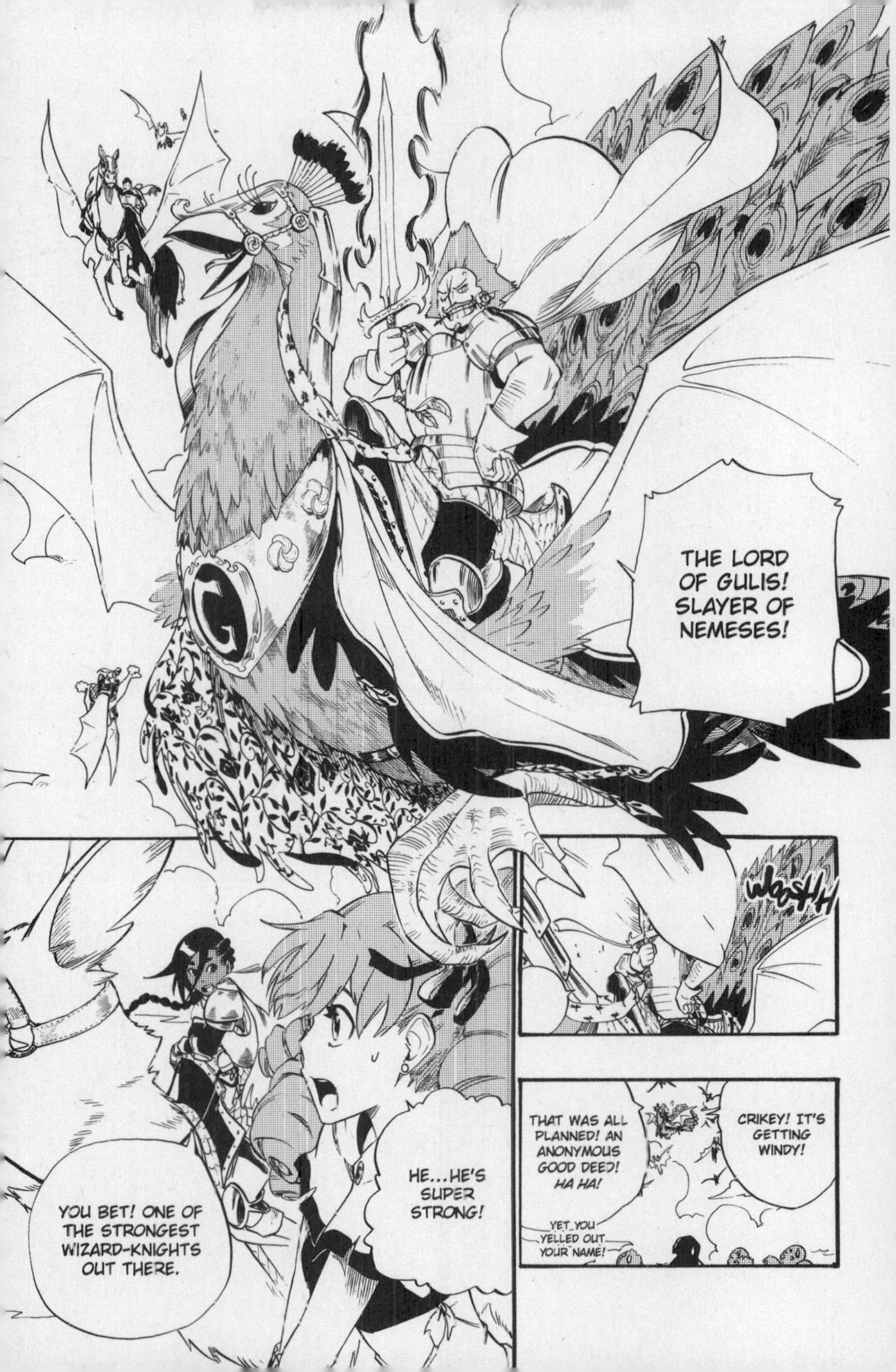
THE LORD OF GULIS! SLAYER OF NEMESES!
WOOSHH
CRIKEY! IT'S GETTING WINDY!
THAT WAS ALL PLANNED! AN ANONYMOUS GOOD DEED! HA HA!
YET YOU YELLED OUT YOUR NAME!
HE...HE'S SUPER STRONG!
YOU BET! ONE OF THE STRONGEST WIZARD-KNIGHTS OUT THERE.

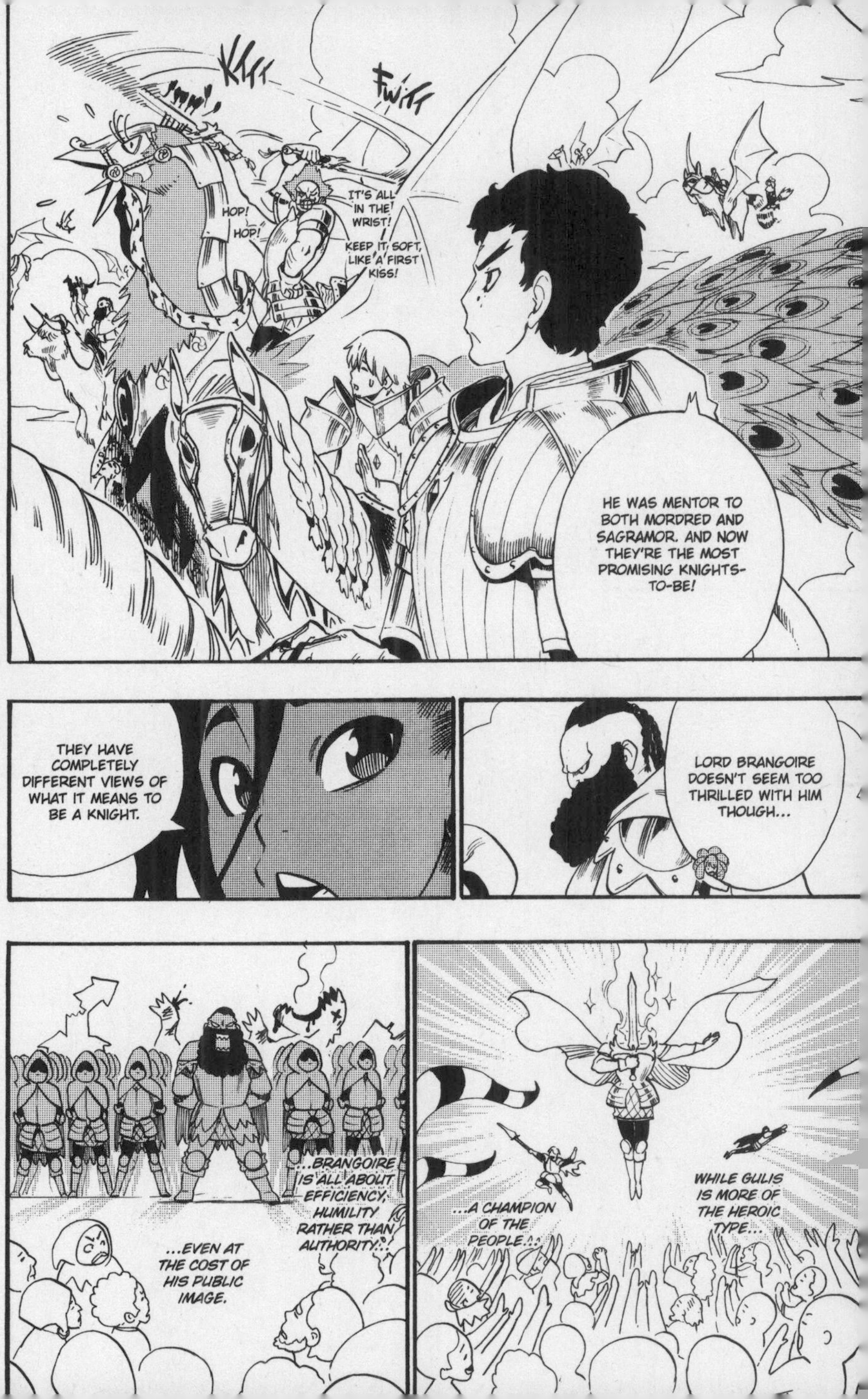
FWIFF
HOP!
HOP!
IT'S ALL IN THE WRIST!
KEEP IT SOFT, LIKE A FIRST KISS!
HE WAS MENTOR TO BOTH MORDRED AND SAGRAMOR. AND NOW THEY'RE THE MOST PROMISING KNIGHTS-TO-BE!
LORD BRANGOIRE DOESN'T SEEM TOO THRILLED WITH HIM THOUGH...
THEY HAVE COMPLETELY DIFFERENT VIEWS OF WHAT IT MEANS TO BE A KNIGHT.
WHILE GULIS IS MORE OF THE HEROIC TYPE...
...A CHAMPION OF THE PEOPLE...
...BRANGOIRE IS ALL ABOUT EFFICIENCY. HUMILITY RATHER THAN AUTHORITY...
...EVEN AT THE COST OF HIS PUBLIC IMAGE.

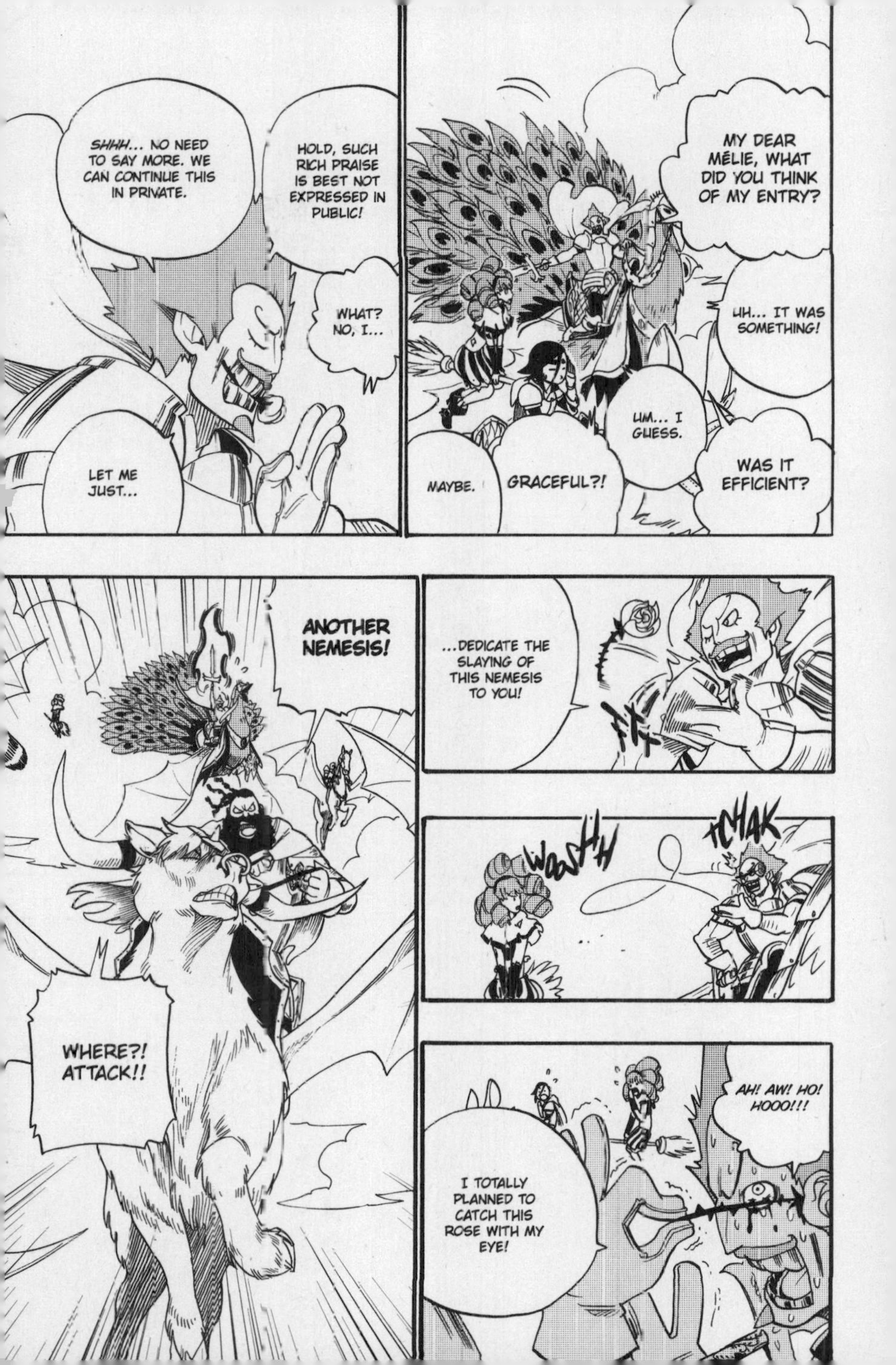
MY DEAR MÉLIE, WHAT DID YOU THINK OF MY ENTRY?
UH... IT WAS SOMETHING!
WAS IT EFFICIENT?
UM... I GUESS.
GRACEFUL?!
MAYBE.
HOLD, SUCH RICH PRAISE IS BEST NOT EXPRESSED IN PUBLIC!
SHHH... NO NEED TO SAY MORE. WE CAN CONTINUE THIS IN PRIVATE.
WHAT? NO, I...
LET ME JUST...
...DEDICATE THE SLAYING OF THIS NEMESIS TO YOU!
TCHAK
WOOSHH
AH! AW! HO! HOOO!!!
I TOTALLY PLANNED TO CATCH THIS ROSE WITH MY EYE!
ANOTHER NEMESIS!
WHERE?! ATTACK!!

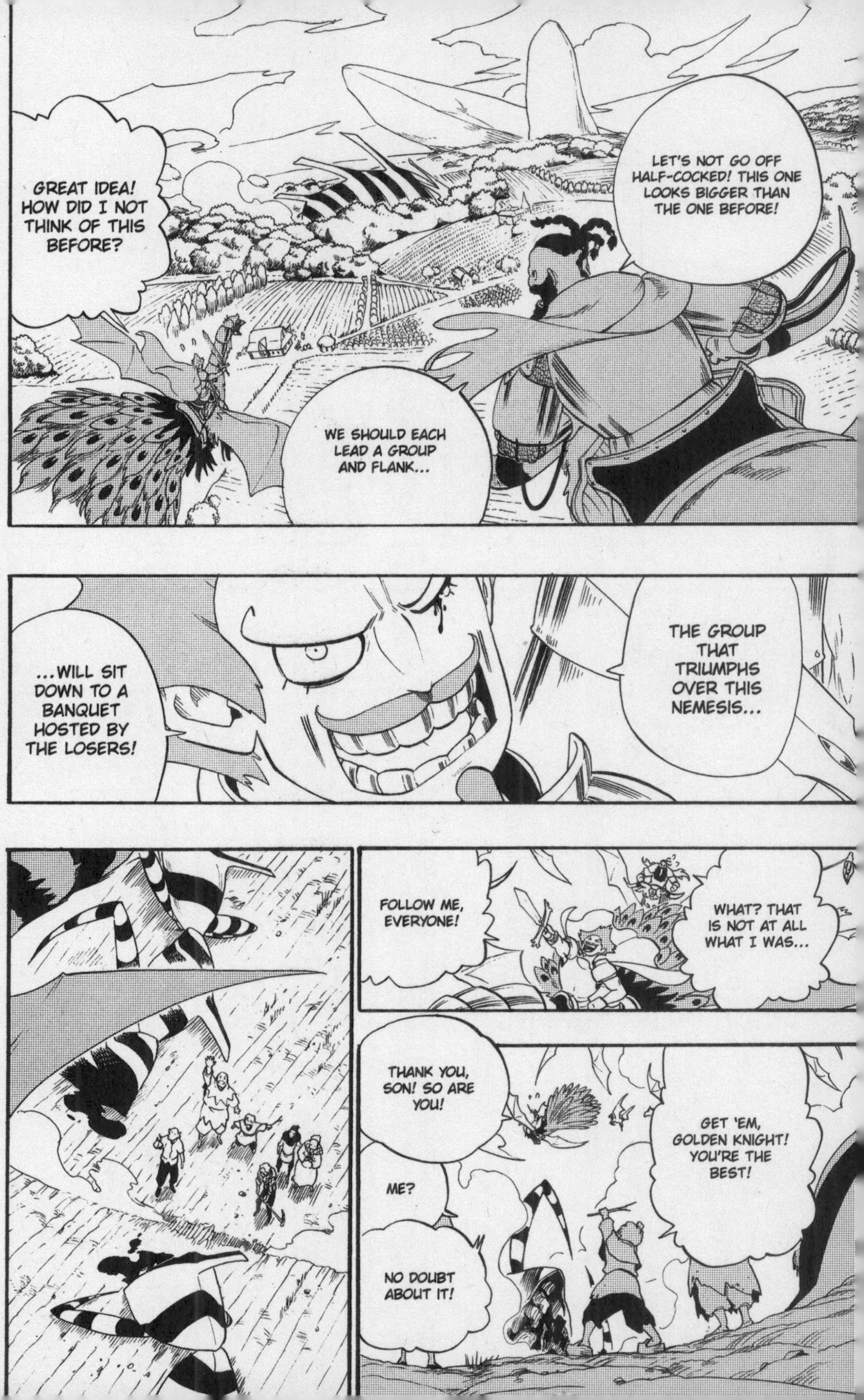
LET'S NOT GO OFF HALF-COCKED! THIS ONE LOOKS BIGGER THAN THE ONE BEFORE!
WE SHOULD EACH LEAD A GROUP AND FLANK...
GREAT IDEA! HOW DID I NOT THINK OF THIS BEFORE?
THE GROUP THAT TRIUMPHS OVER THIS NEMESIS...
...WILL SIT DOWN TO A BANQUET HOSTED BY THE LOSERS!
FOLLOW ME, EVERYONE!
WHAT? THAT IS NOT AT ALL WHAT I WAS...
GET 'EM, GOLDEN KNIGHT! YOU'RE THE BEST!
THANK YOU, SON! SO ARE YOU!
ME?
NO DOUBT ABOUT IT!

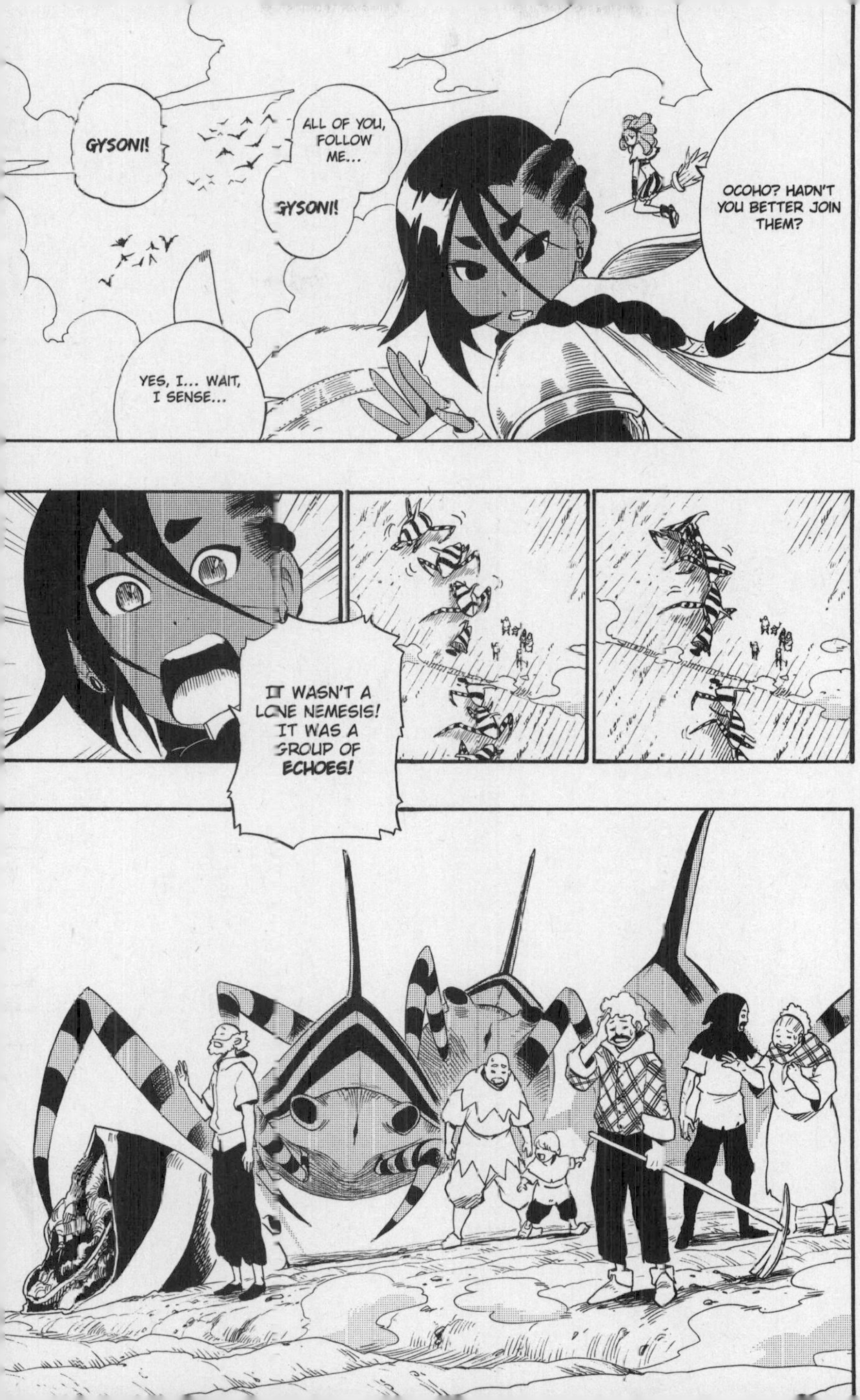
OCOHO? HADN'T YOU BETTER JOIN THEM?
ALL OF YOU, FOLLOW ME...
GYSONI!
GYSONI!
YES, I... WAIT, I SENSE...
IT WASN'T A LONE NEMESIS! IT WAS A GROUP OF ECHOES!

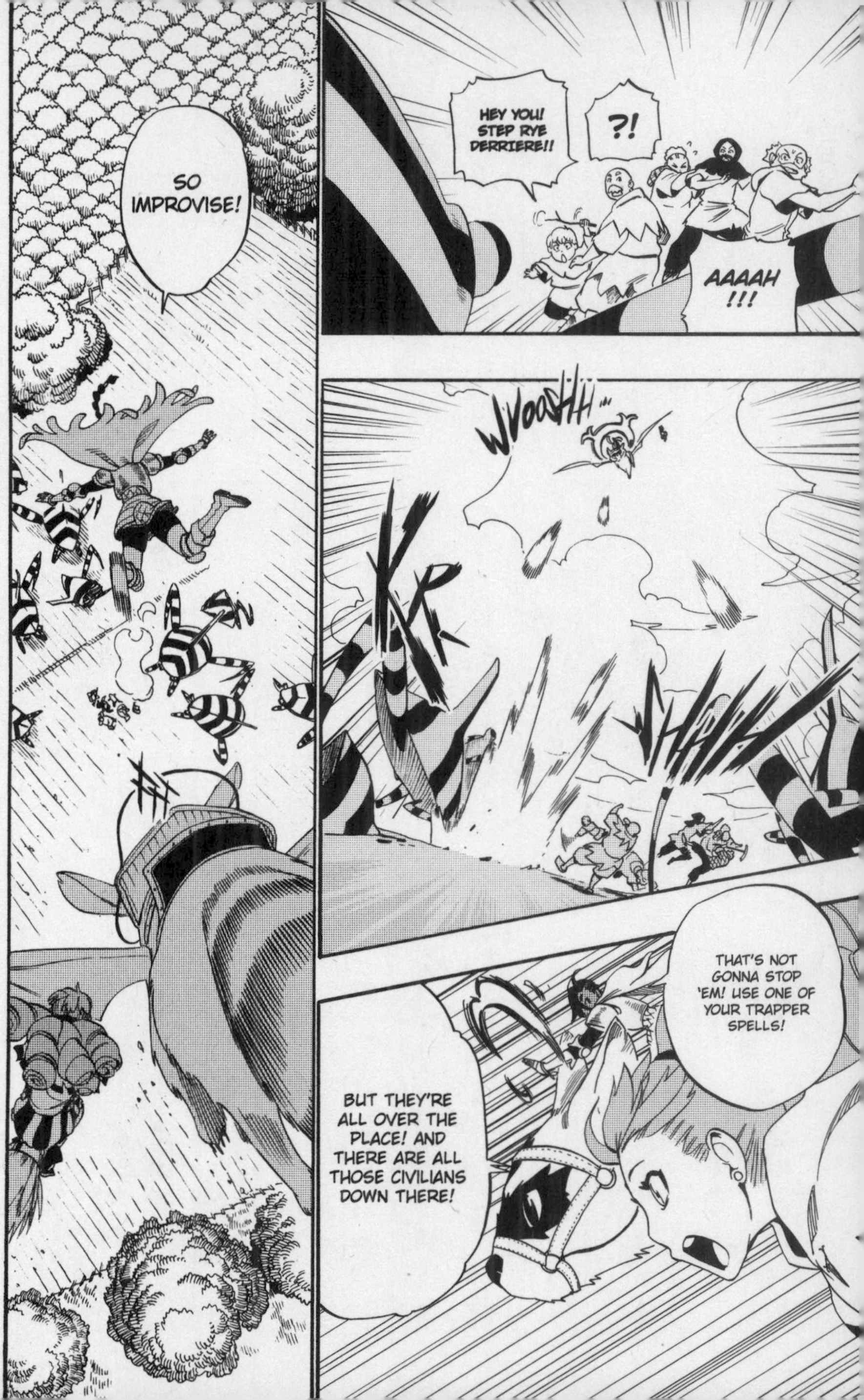
?!
HEY YOU! STEP RYE DERRIERE!!
AAAAH !!!
WVOOSHHH...
THAT'S NOT GONNA STOP 'EM! USE ONE OF YOUR TRAPPER SPELLS!
BUT THEY'RE ALL OVER THE PLACE! AND THERE ARE ALL THOSE CIVILIANS DOWN THERE!
SO IMPROVISE!

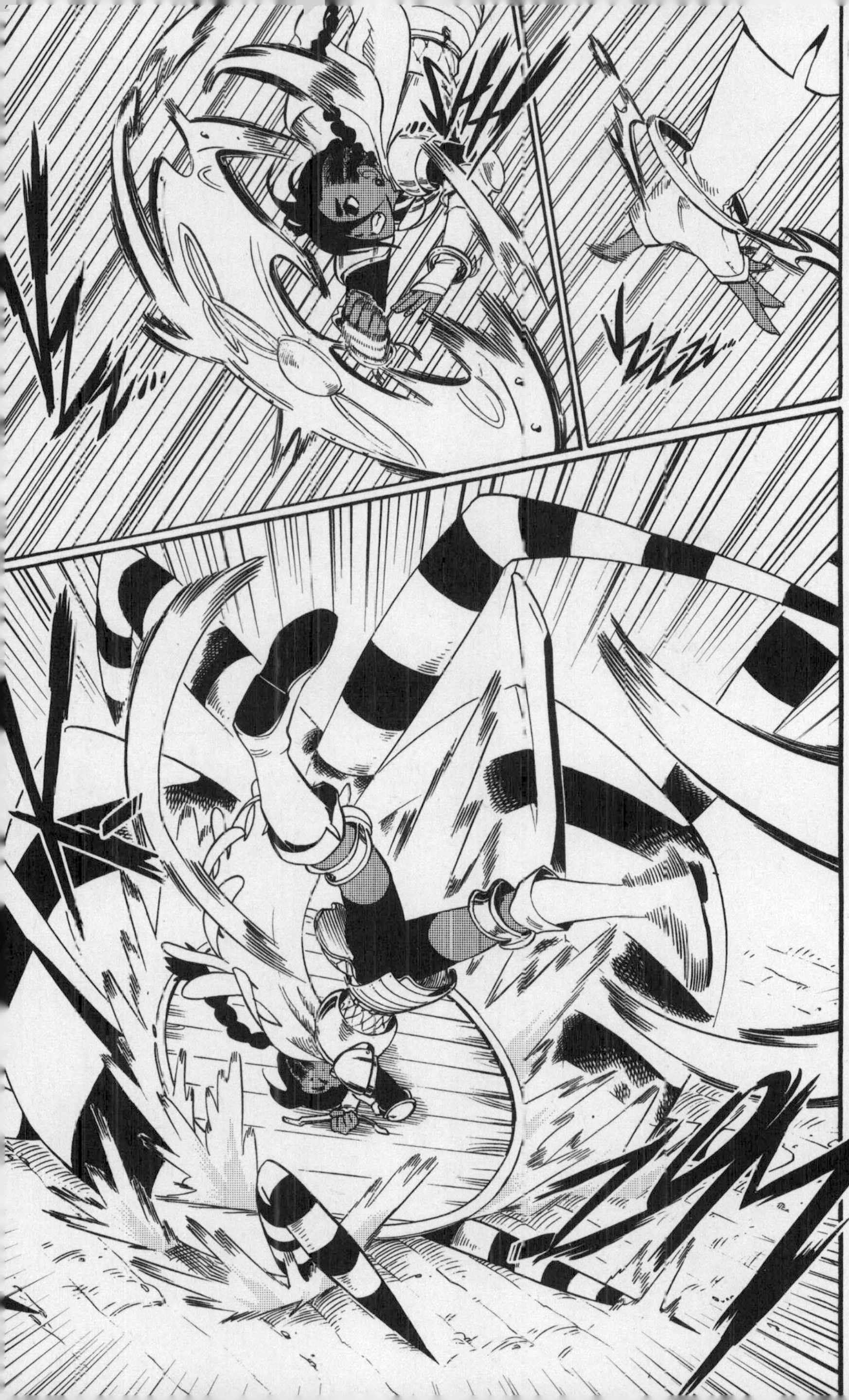

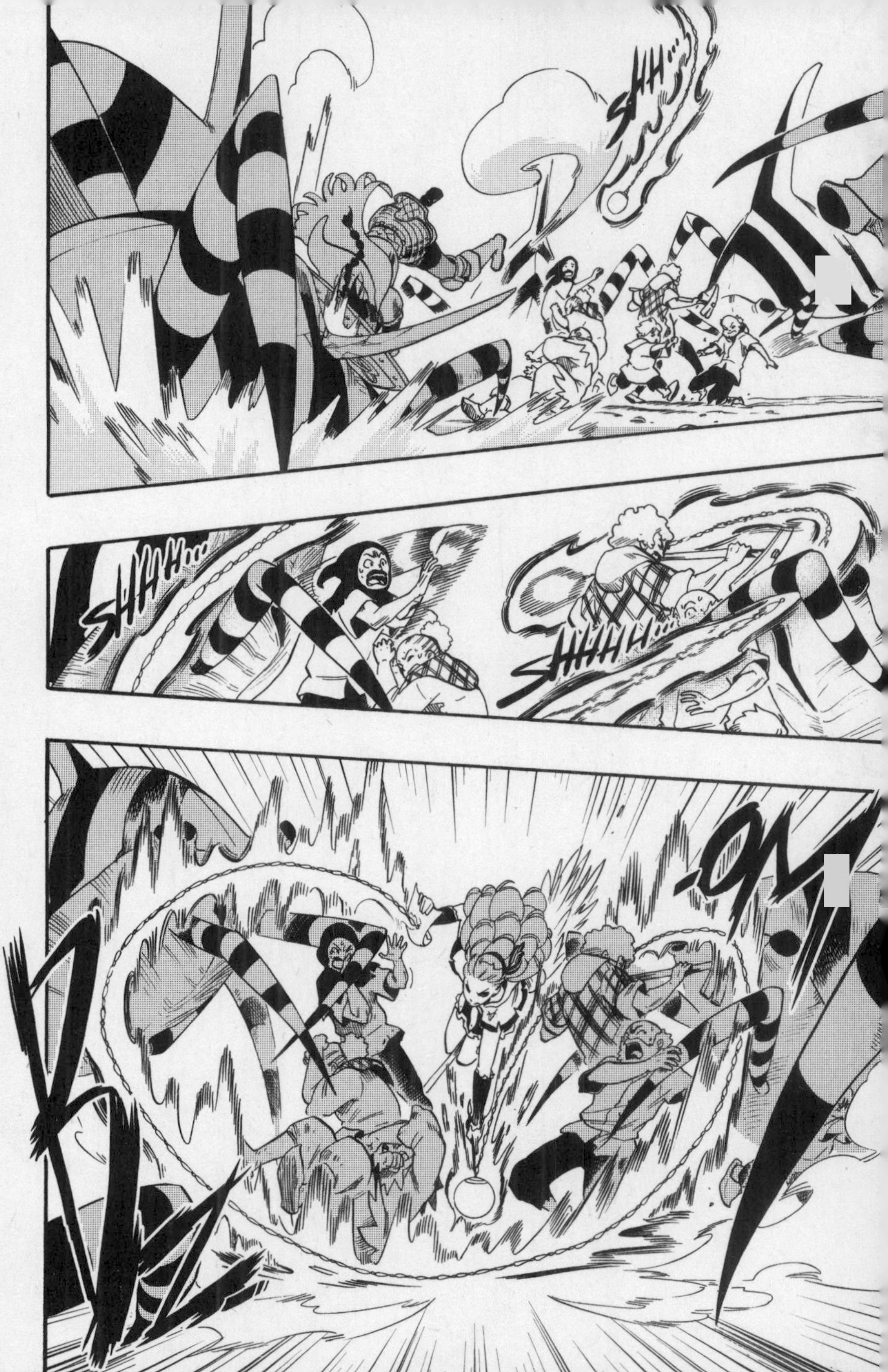
SHH...
SHHHH...
SHHH...
-OM

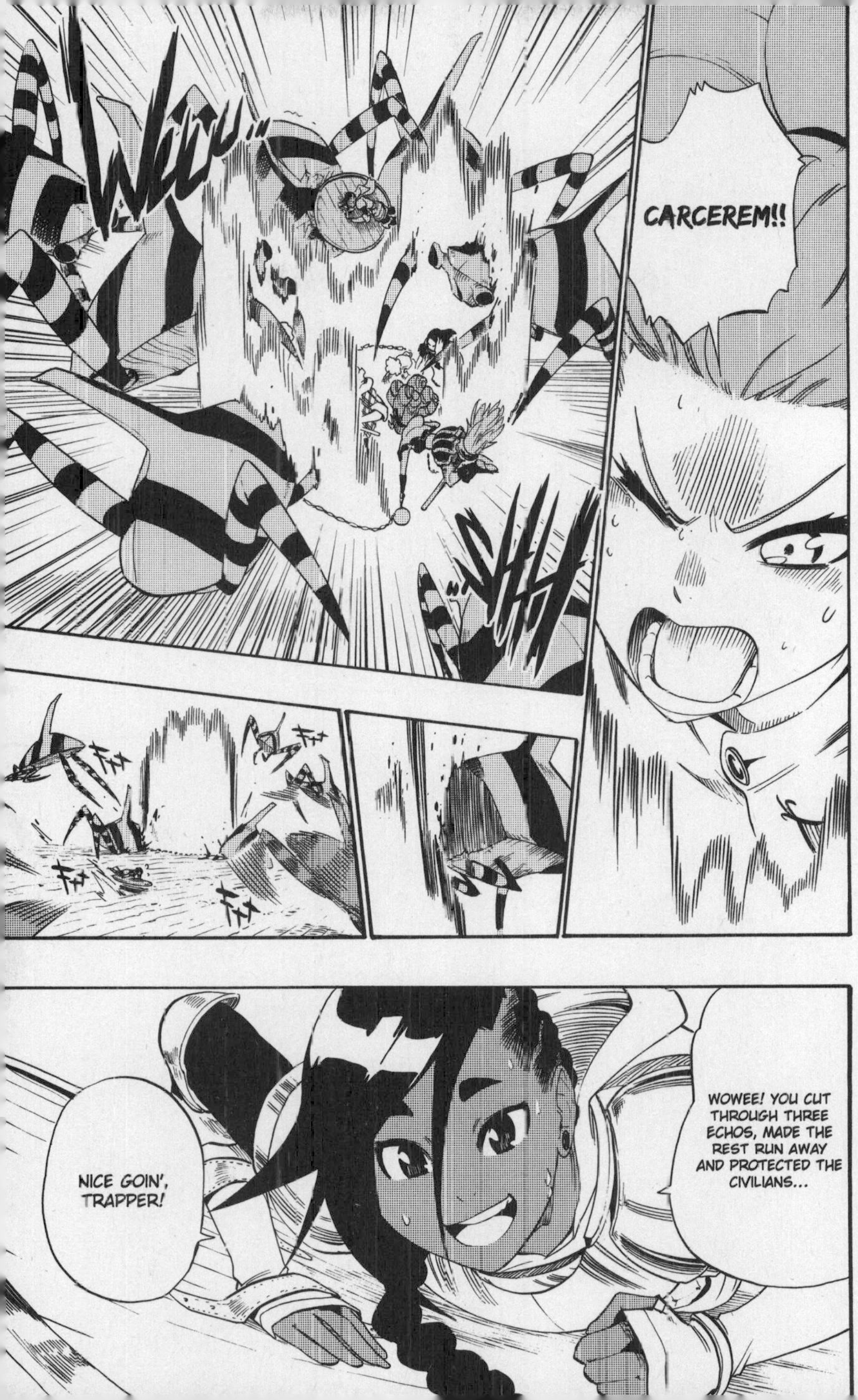
CARCEREM!!
WOWEE! YOU CUT THROUGH THREE ECHOS, MADE THE REST RUN AWAY AND PROTECTED THE CIVILIANS...
NICE GOIN', TRAPPER!

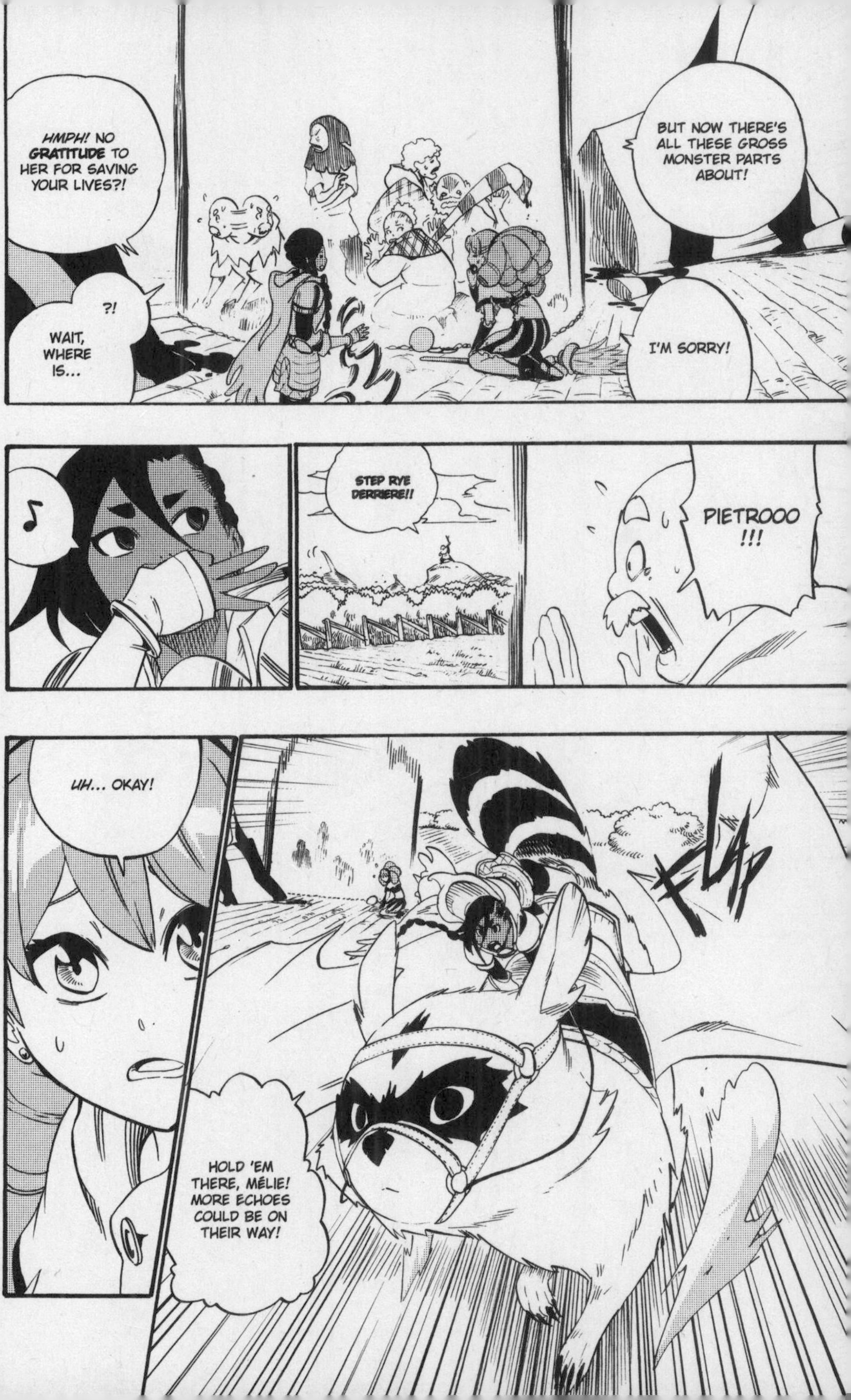
BUT NOW THERE'S ALL THESE GROSS MONSTER PARTS ABOUT!
I'M SORRY!
HMPH! NO **GRATITUDE** TO HER FOR SAVING YOUR LIVES?!
?!
WAIT, WHERE IS...
PIETROOO !!!
STEP RYE DERRIERE!!
♪
FLAP
HOLD 'EM THERE, MÉLIE! MORE ECHOES COULD BE ON THEIR WAY!
UH... OKAY!

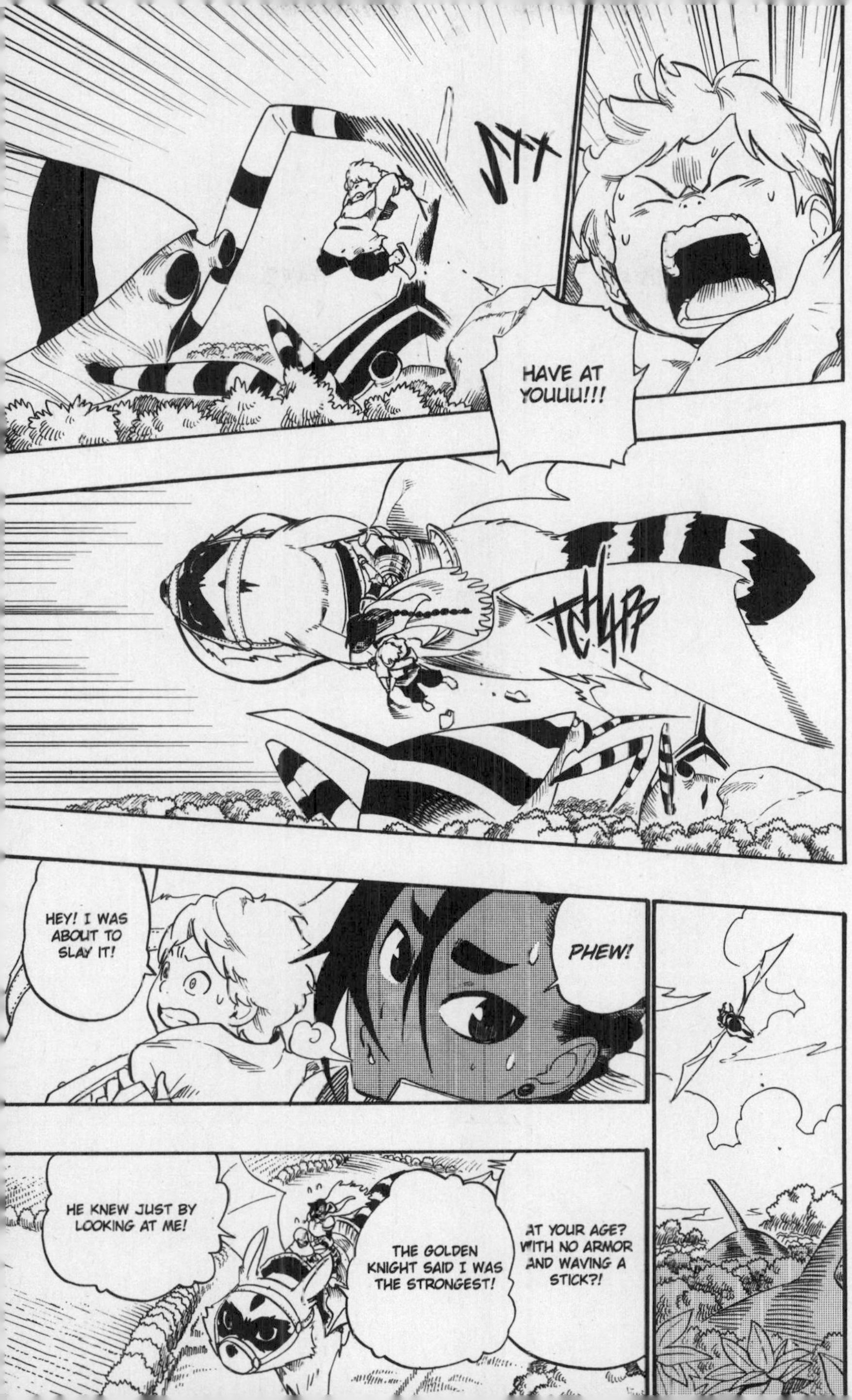
HAVE AT YOUUU!!!
PHEW!
HEY! I WAS ABOUT TO SLAY IT!
AT YOUR AGE? WITH NO ARMOR AND WAVING A STICK?!
THE GOLDEN KNIGHT SAID I WAS THE STRONGEST!
HE KNEW JUST BY LOOKING AT ME!

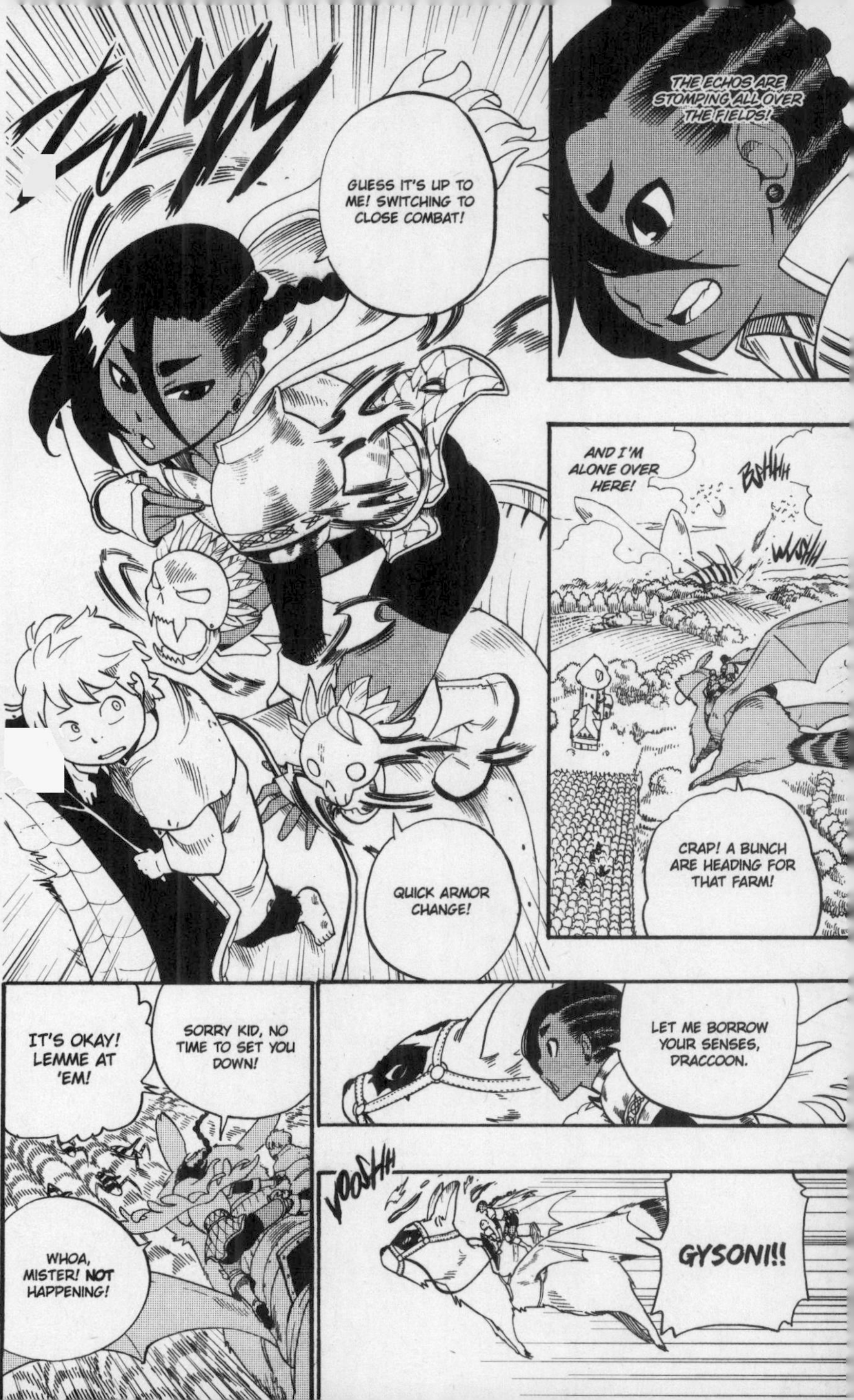
THE ECHOS ARE STOMPING ALL OVER THE FIELDS!
BSHHH
AND I'M ALONE OVER HERE!
WUSHH
CRAP! A BUNCH ARE HEADING FOR THAT FARM!
GUESS IT'S UP TO ME! SWITCHING TO CLOSE COMBAT!
QUICK ARMOR CHANGE!
LET ME BORROW YOUR SENSES, DRACCOON.
GYSONI!!
VOOSHH
SORRY KID, NO TIME TO SET YOU DOWN!
IT'S OKAY! LEMME AT 'EM!
WHOA, MISTER! NOT HAPPENING!

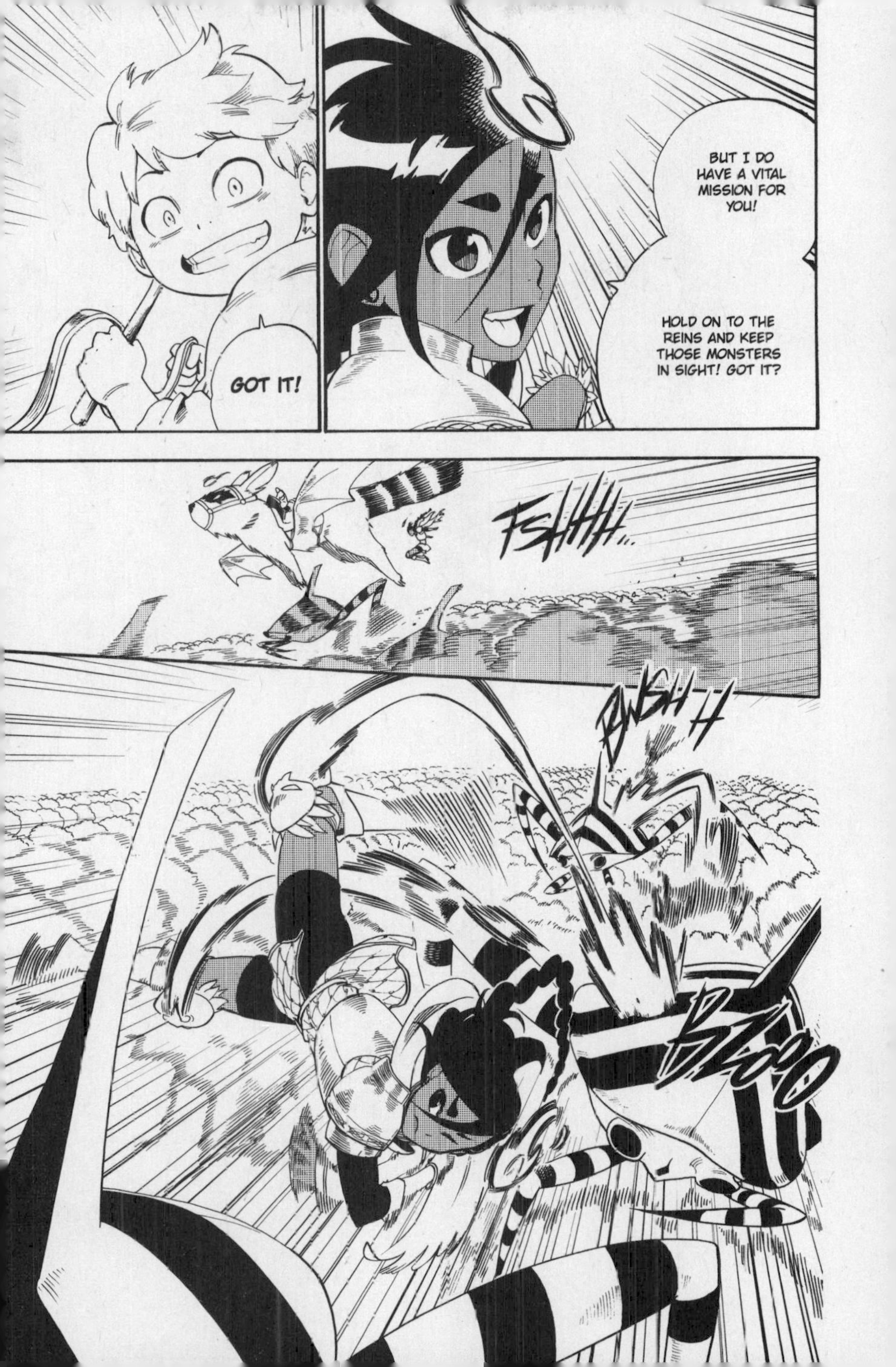
BUT I DO HAVE A VITAL MISSION FOR YOU!
HOLD ON TO THE REINS AND KEEP THOSE MONSTERS IN SIGHT! GOT IT?
GOT IT!
FSHHHH..
BWSHH
BZOOO

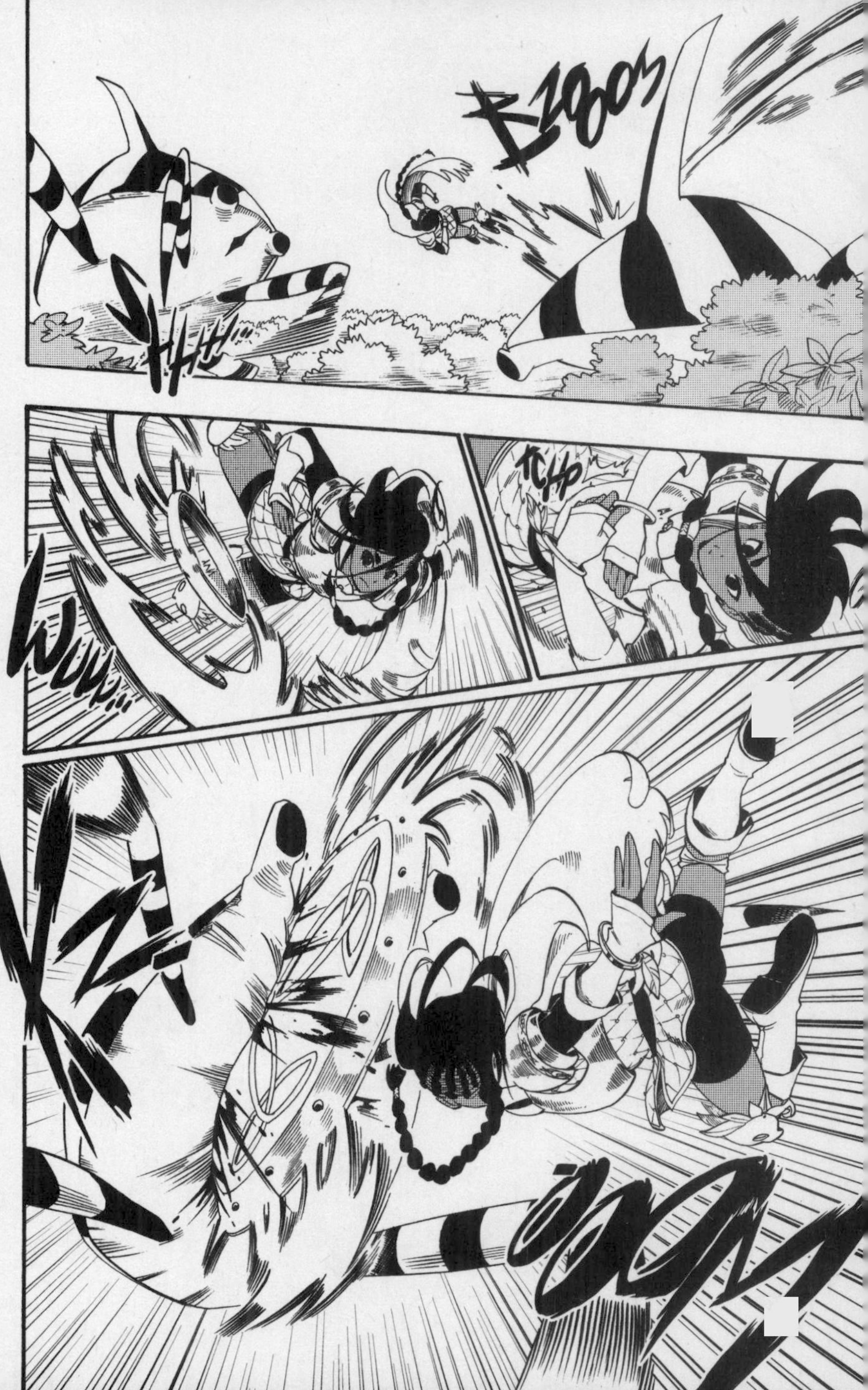
SHHH...
TCHP

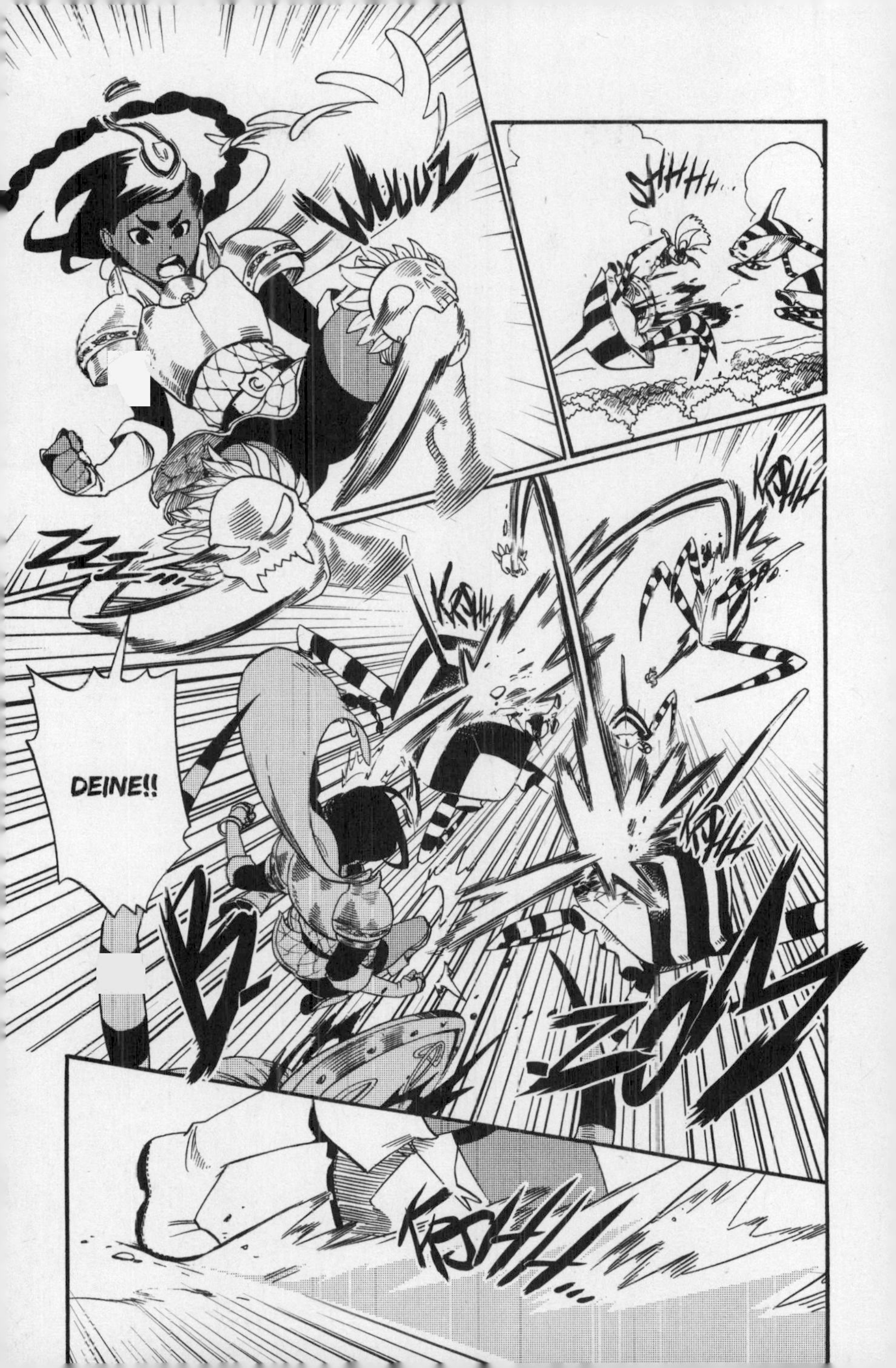
SHHHH...
WUUUZ
ZZZZ...
KRSHH
KRSHH
KRSHH
DEINE!!
KRSHH...

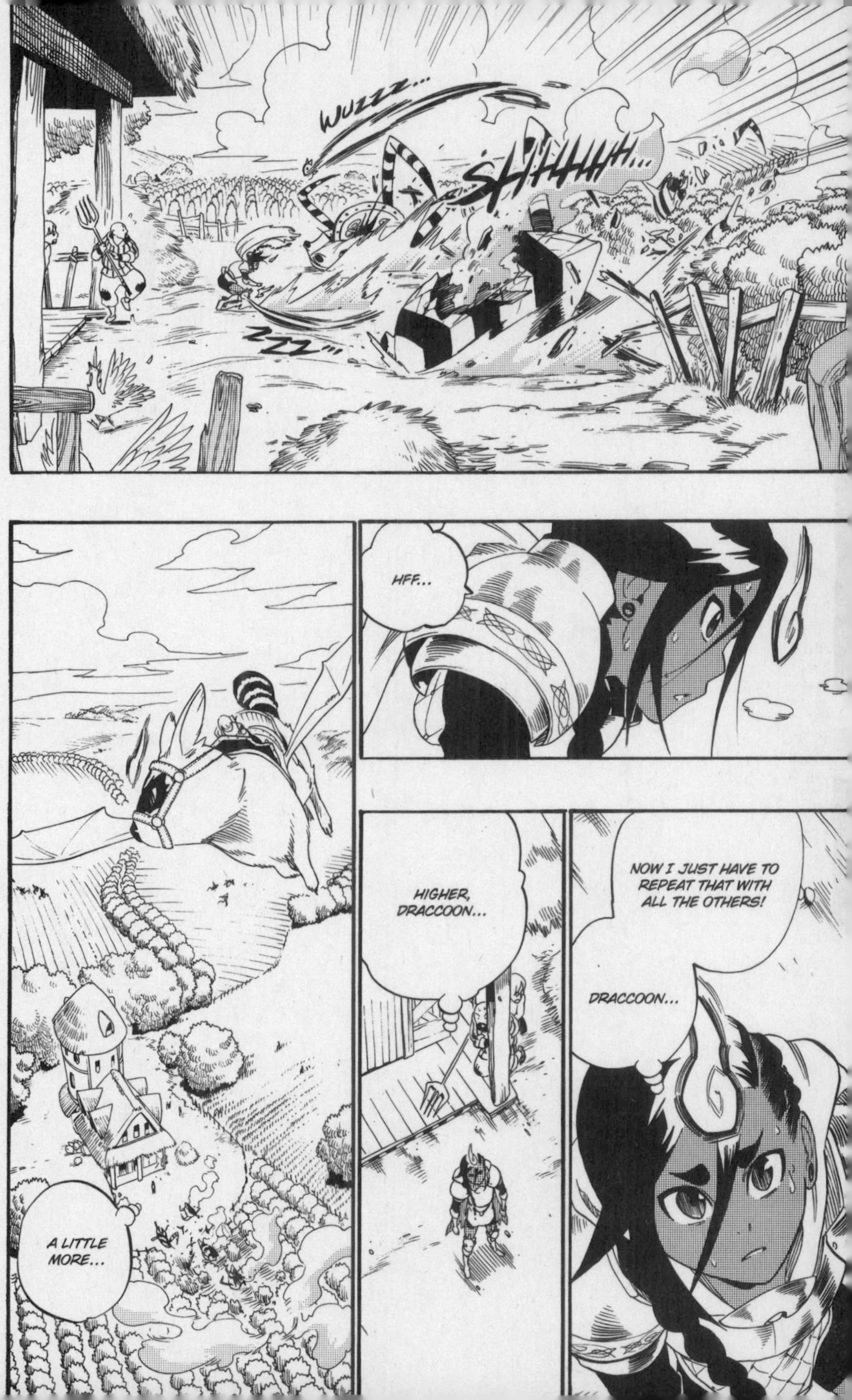
WUZZZ...
SHHHHHH...
ZZZ...
HFF...
NOW I JUST HAVE TO REPEAT THAT WITH ALL THE OTHERS!
DRACCOON...
HIGHER, DRACCOON...
A LITTLE MORE...

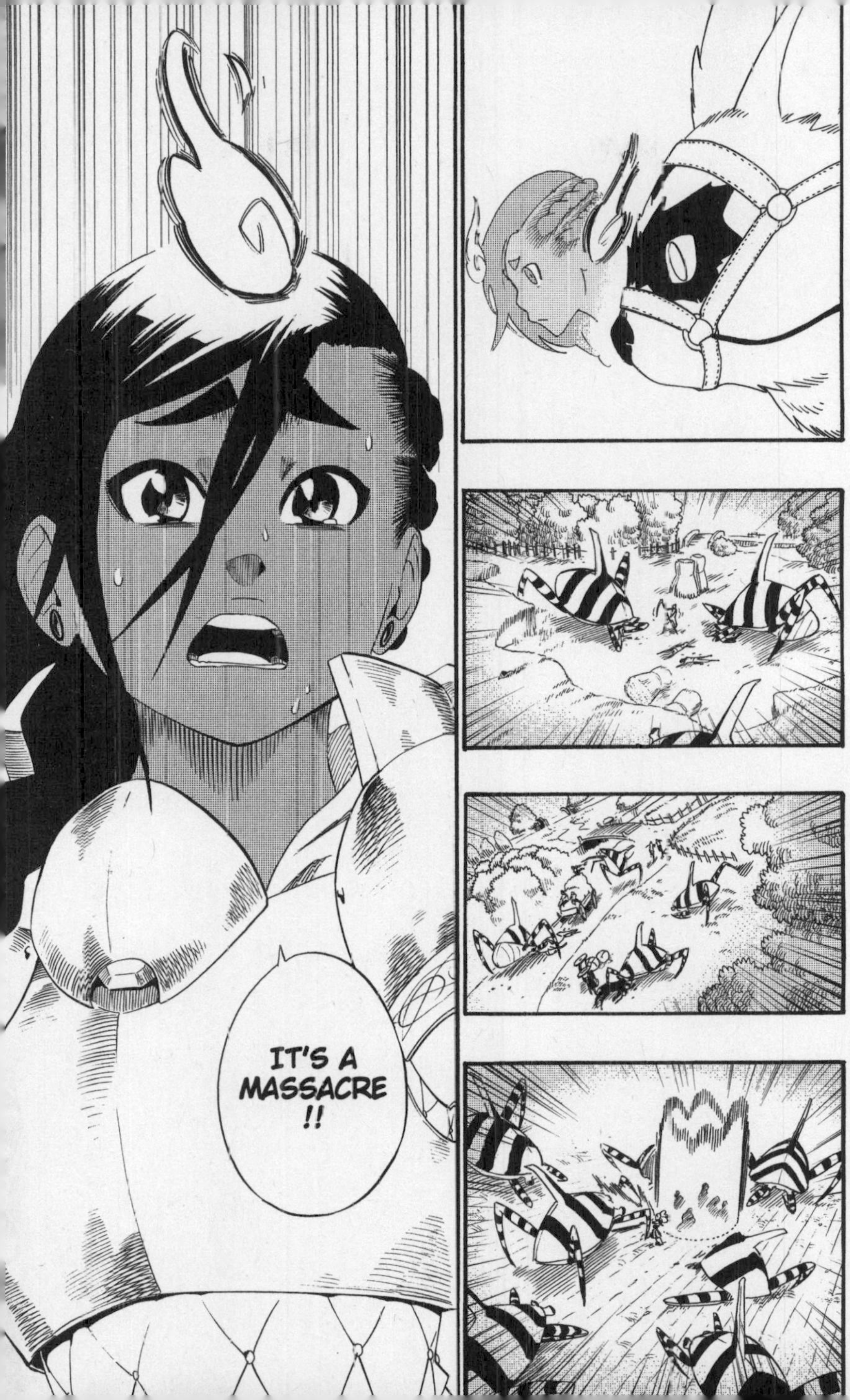
IT'S A MASSACRE !!

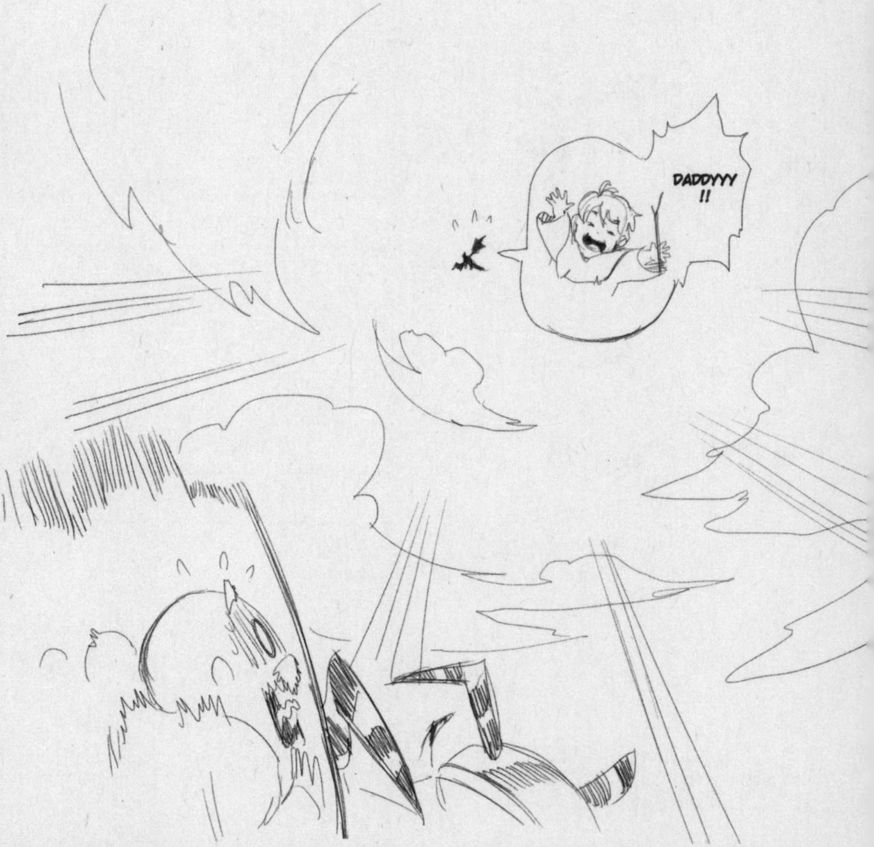
DADDYYY !!

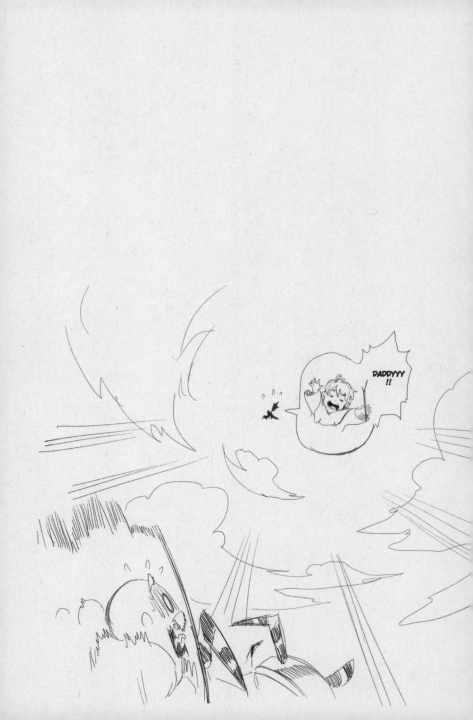

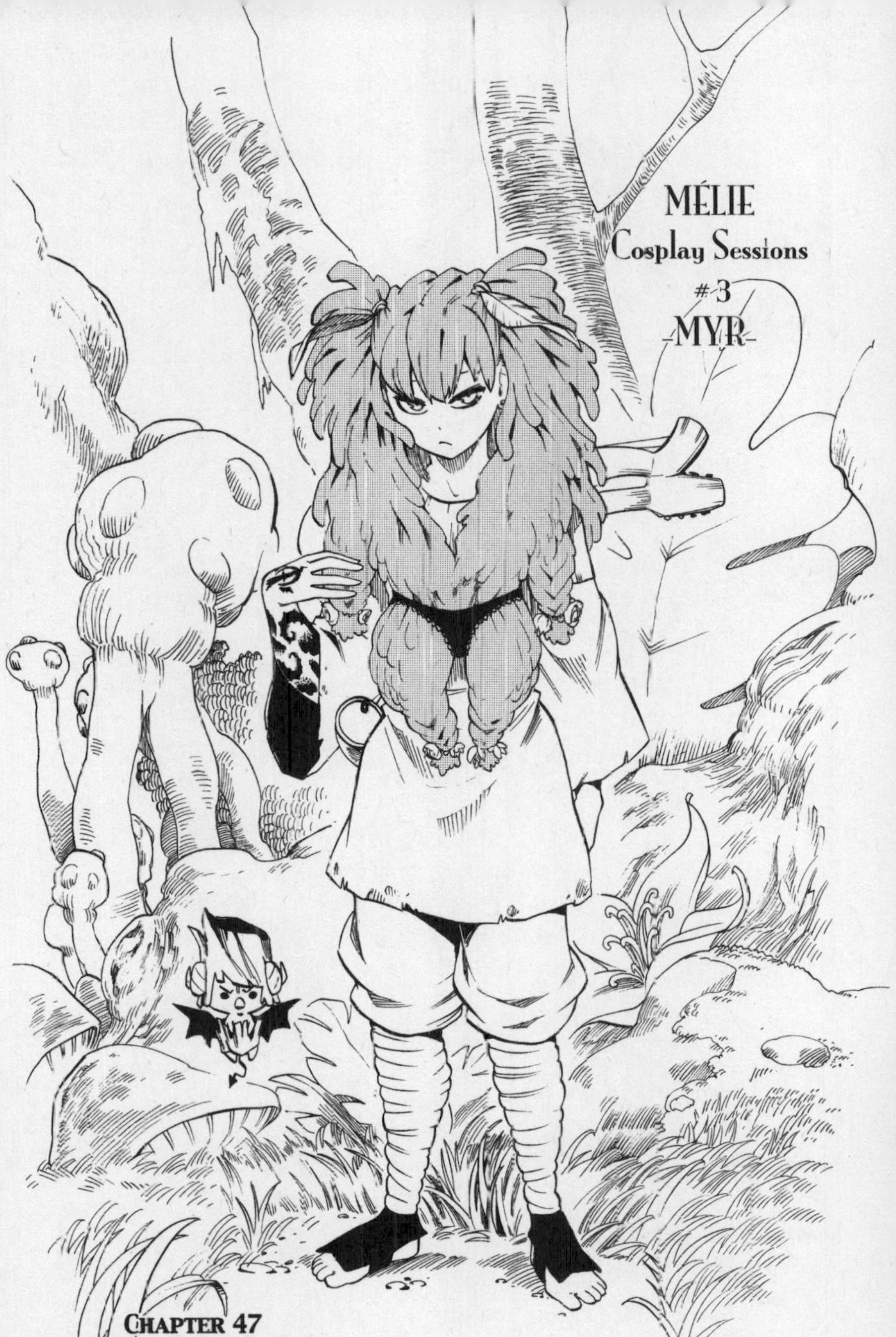
MÉLIE
Cosplay Sessions
#3
-MYR-

Chapter 47
Gysoni

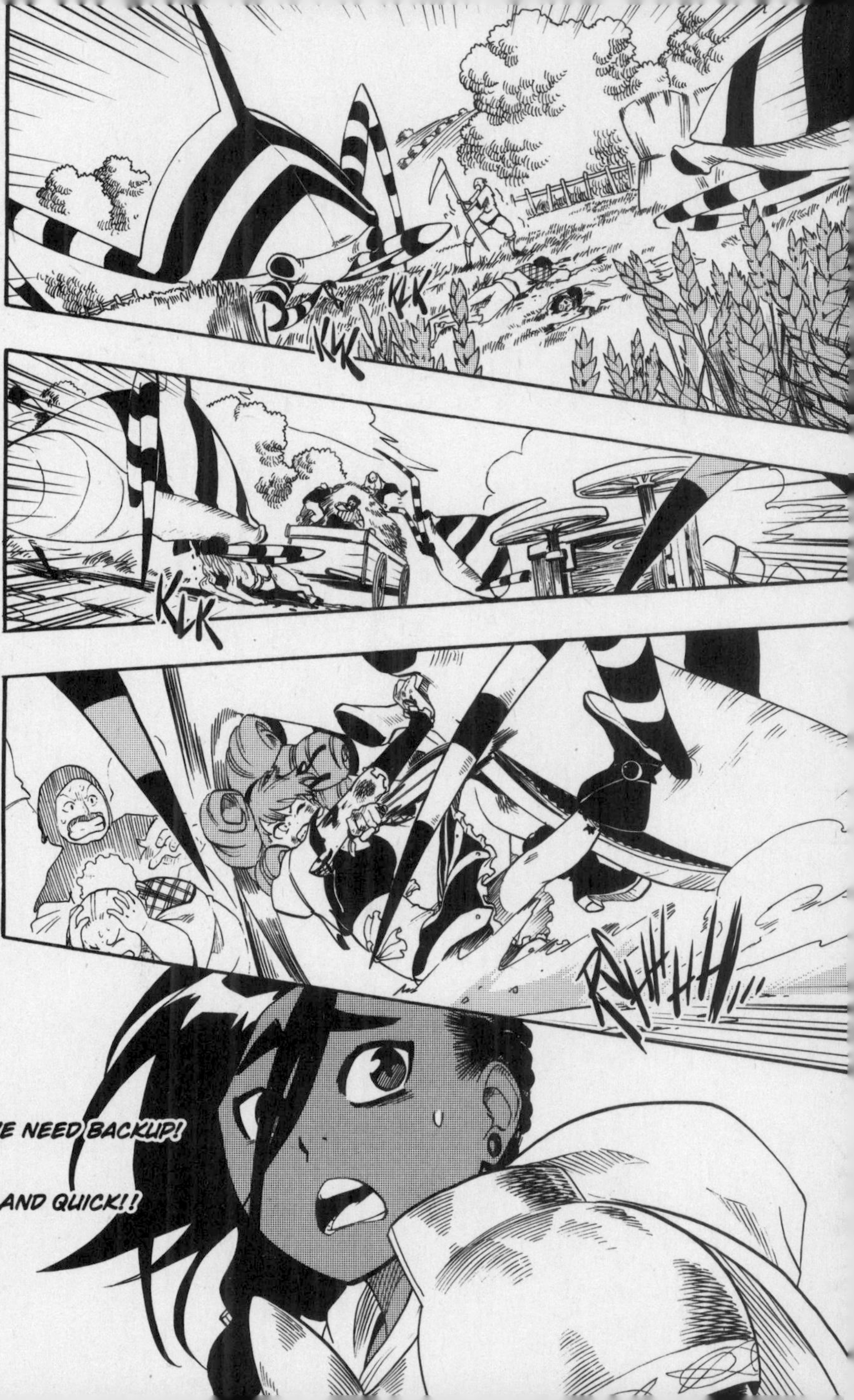
KLK
KLK
KLK
WE NEED BACKUP!
AND QUICK!!

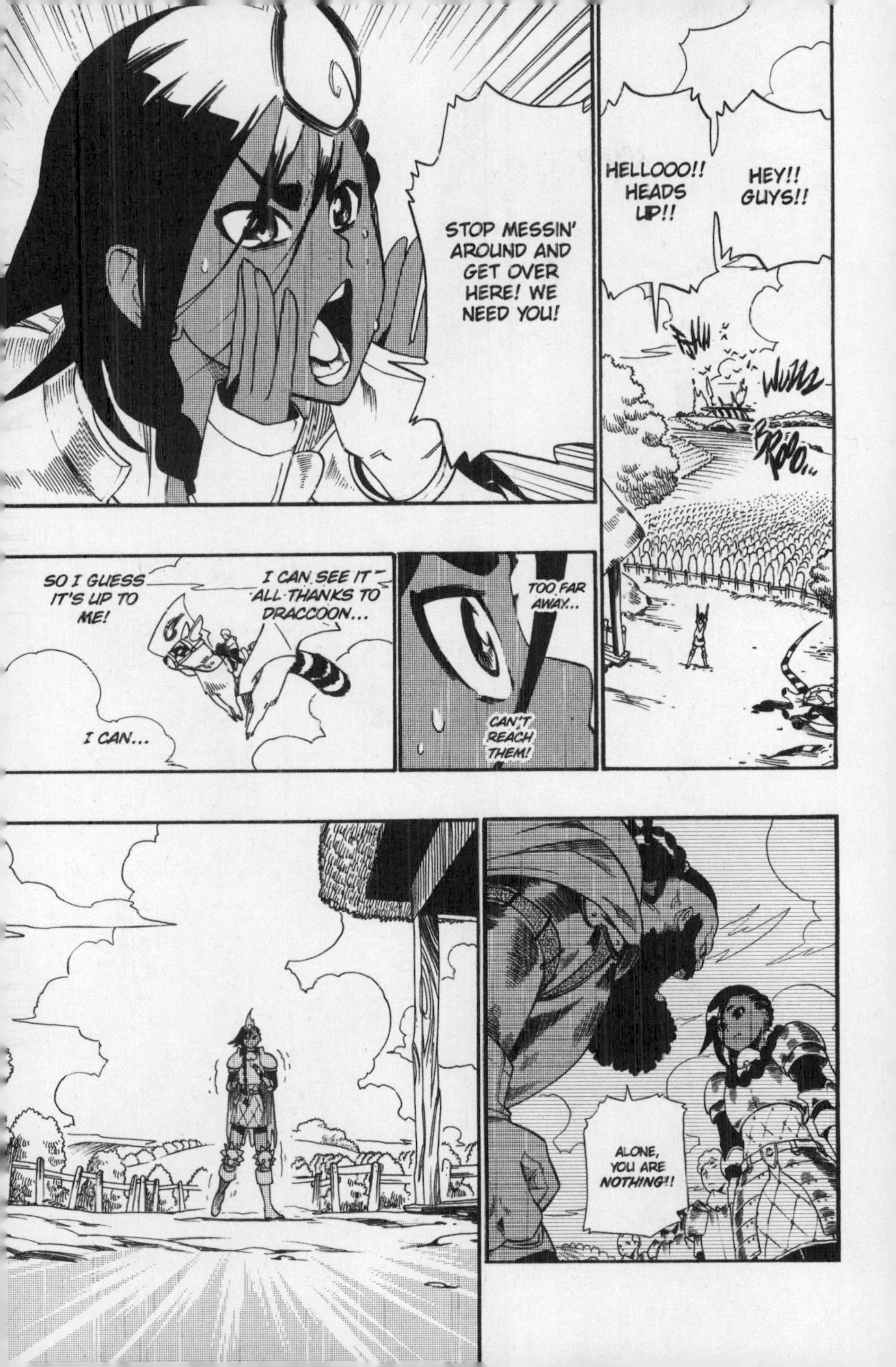
HEY!! GUYS!!
HELLOOO!! HEADS UP!!
WUZZ
BROLO..
STOP MESSIN' AROUND AND GET OVER HERE! WE NEED YOU!
TOO FAR AWAY...
CAN'T REACH THEM!
I CAN SEE IT ALL THANKS TO DRACCOON...
SO I GUESS IT'S UP TO ME!
I CAN...
ALONE, YOU ARE NOTHING!!

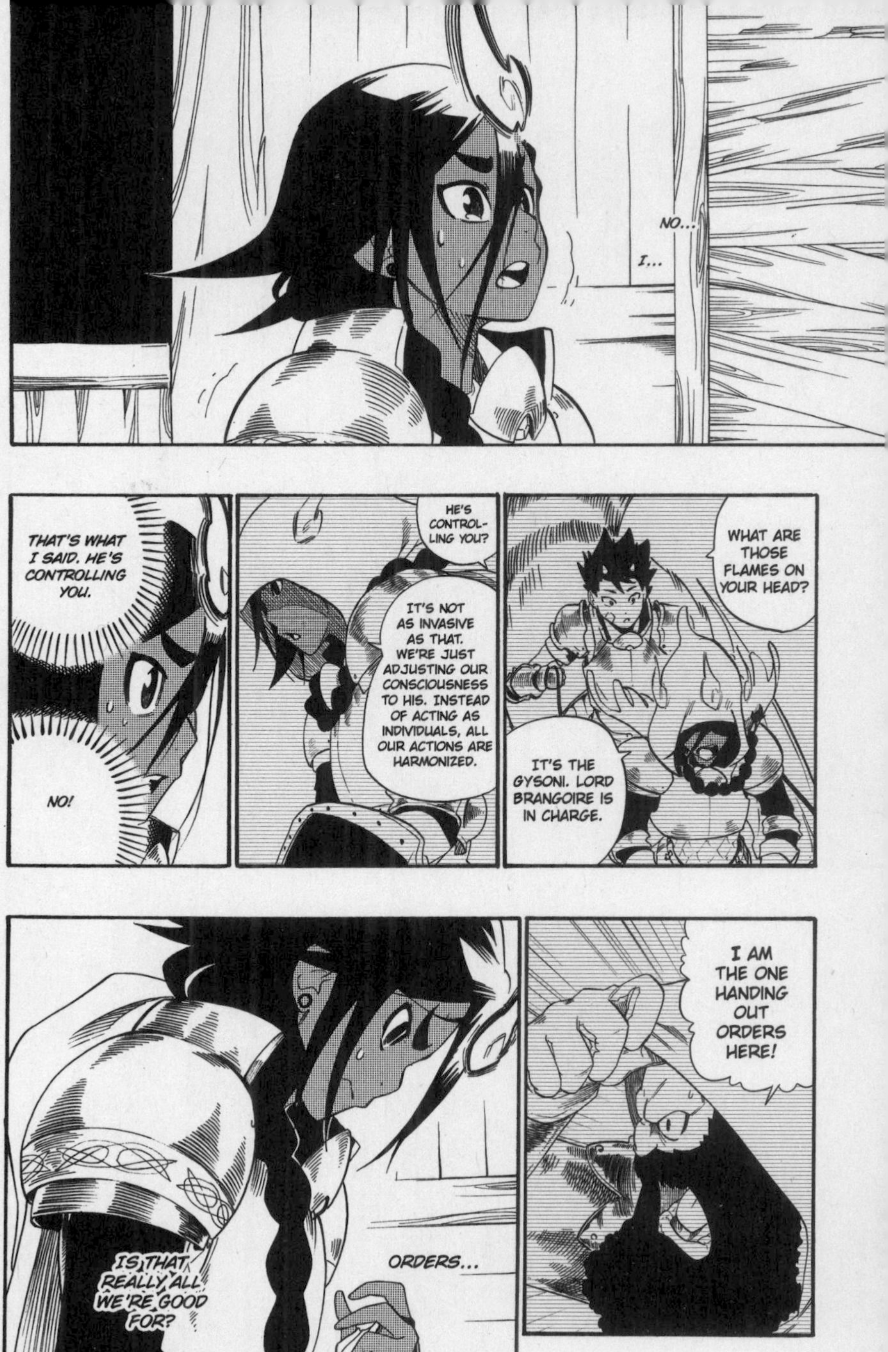
NO...
I...
WHAT ARE THOSE FLAMES ON YOUR HEAD?
IT'S THE GYSONI. LORD BRANGOIRE IS IN CHARGE.
HE'S CONTROLLING YOU?
IT'S NOT AS INVASIVE AS THAT. WE'RE JUST ADJUSTING OUR CONSCIOUSNESS TO HIS. INSTEAD OF ACTING AS INDIVIDUALS, ALL OUR ACTIONS ARE HARMONIZED.
THAT'S WHAT I SAID. HE'S CONTROLLING YOU.
NO!
I AM THE ONE HANDING OUT ORDERS HERE!
ORDERS...
IS THAT REALLY ALL WE'RE GOOD FOR?

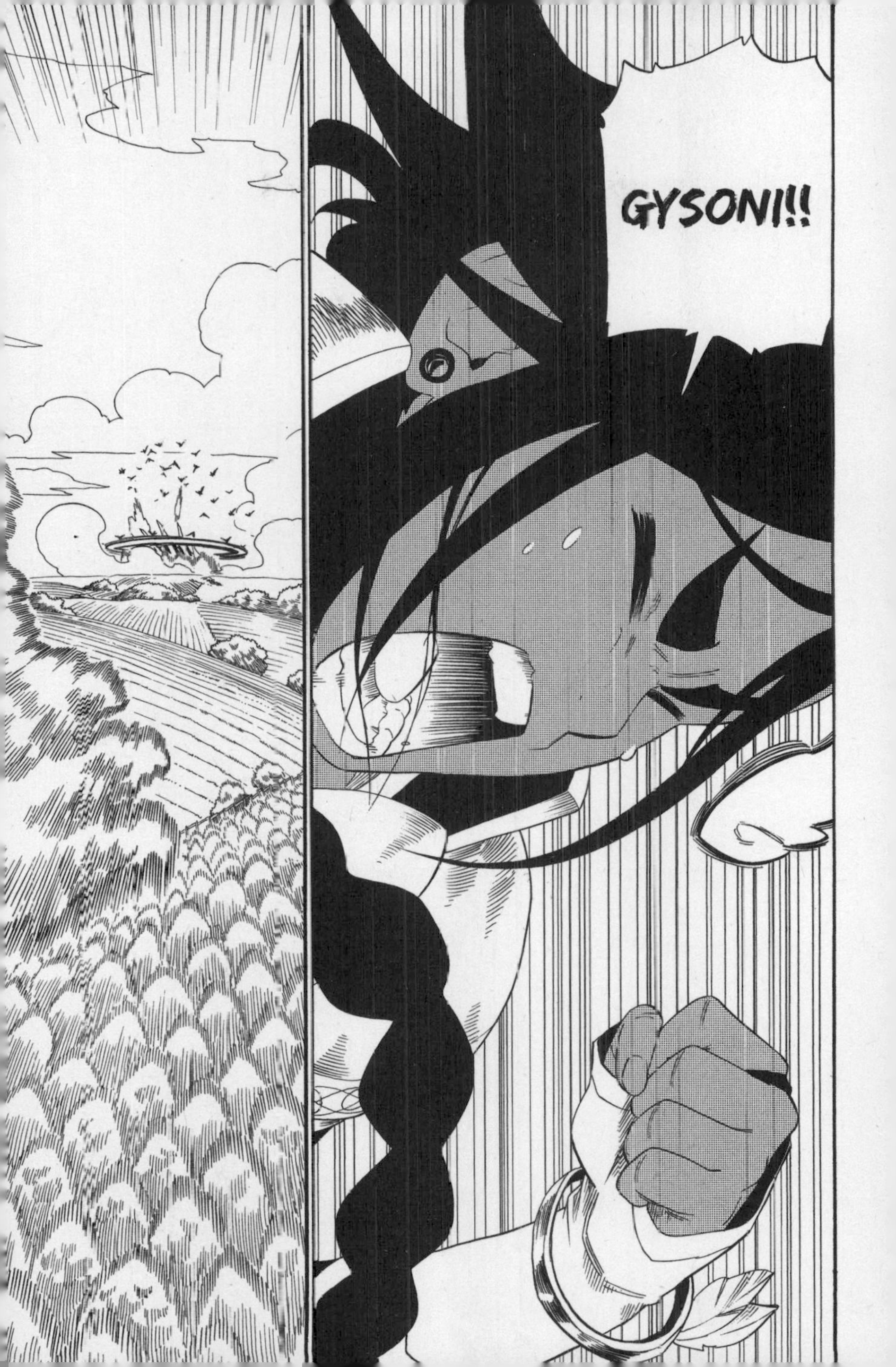
GYSONI!!

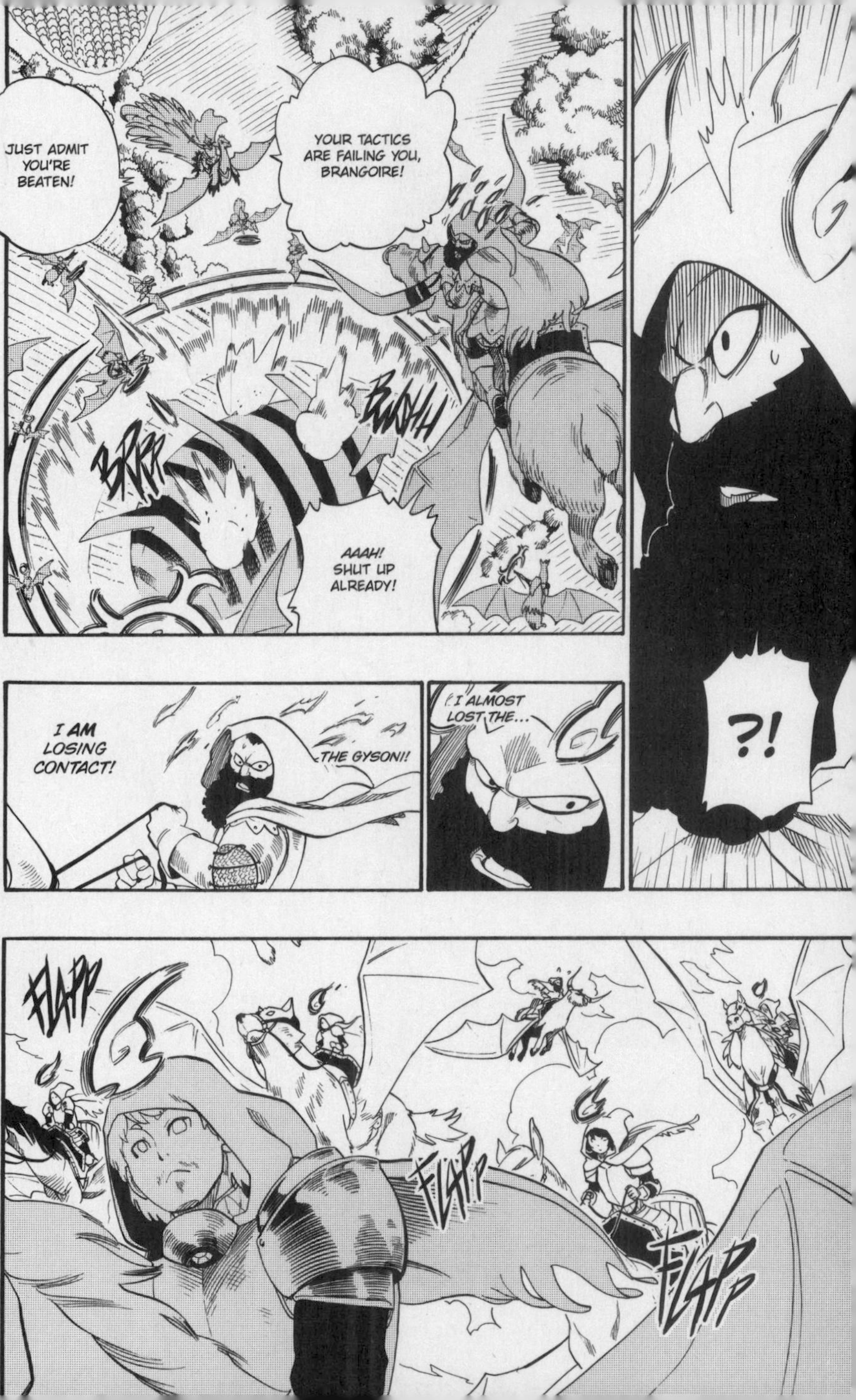
?!
YOUR TACTICS ARE FAILING YOU, BRANGOIRE!
JUST ADMIT YOU'RE BEATEN!
BWOHH
BRRR
AAAH! SHUT UP ALREADY!
I ALMOST LOST THE...
THE GYSONI!
I AM LOSING CONTACT!
FLAPP
FLAPP
FLAPP

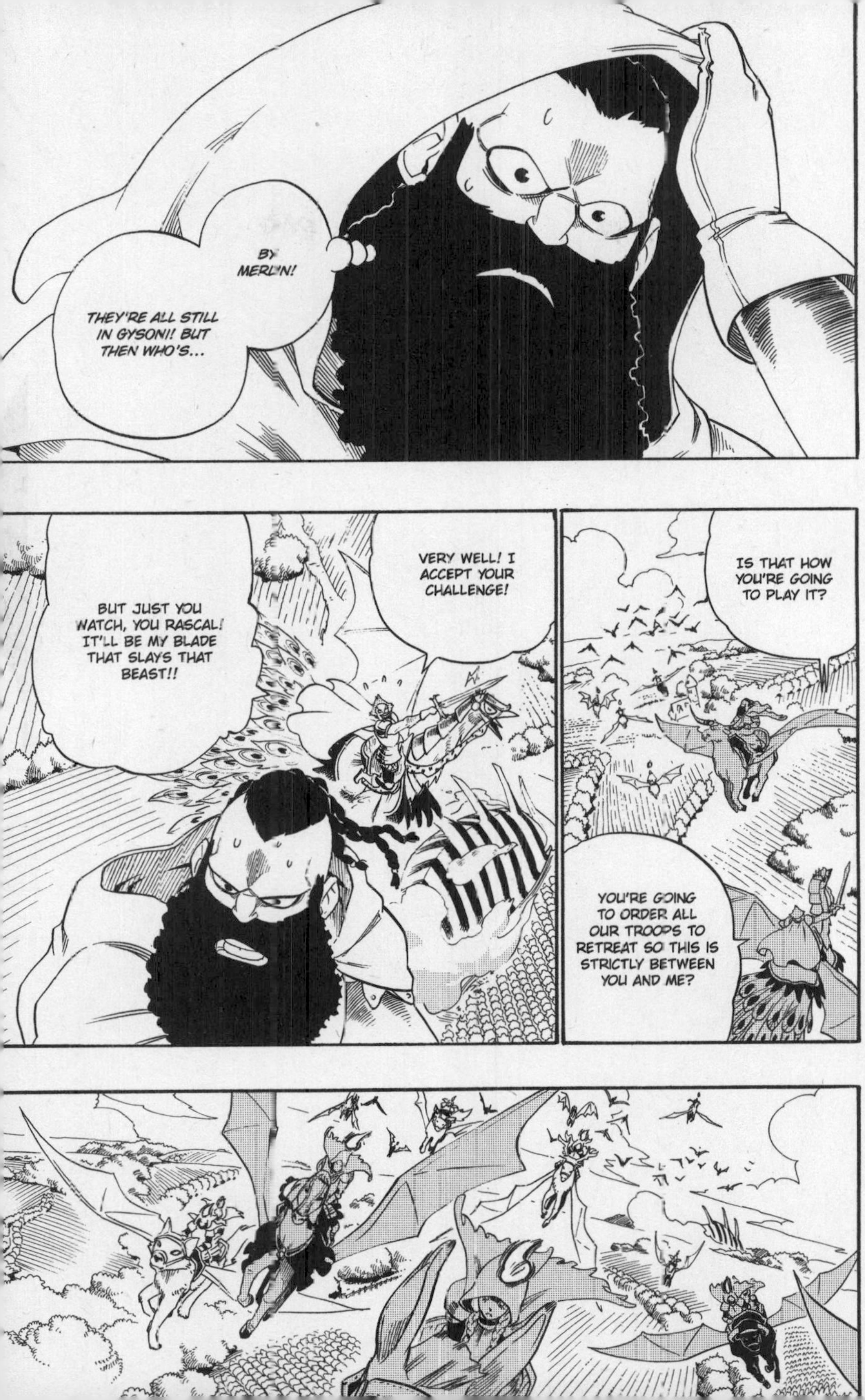
BY MERLIN!
THEY'RE ALL STILL IN GYSON!! BUT THEN WHO'S...
IS THAT HOW YOU'RE GOING TO PLAY IT?
YOU'RE GOING TO ORDER ALL OUR TROOPS TO RETREAT SO THIS IS STRICTLY BETWEEN YOU AND ME?
VERY WELL! I ACCEPT YOUR CHALLENGE!
BUT JUST YOU WATCH, YOU RASCAL! IT'LL BE MY BLADE THAT SLAYS THAT BEAST!!

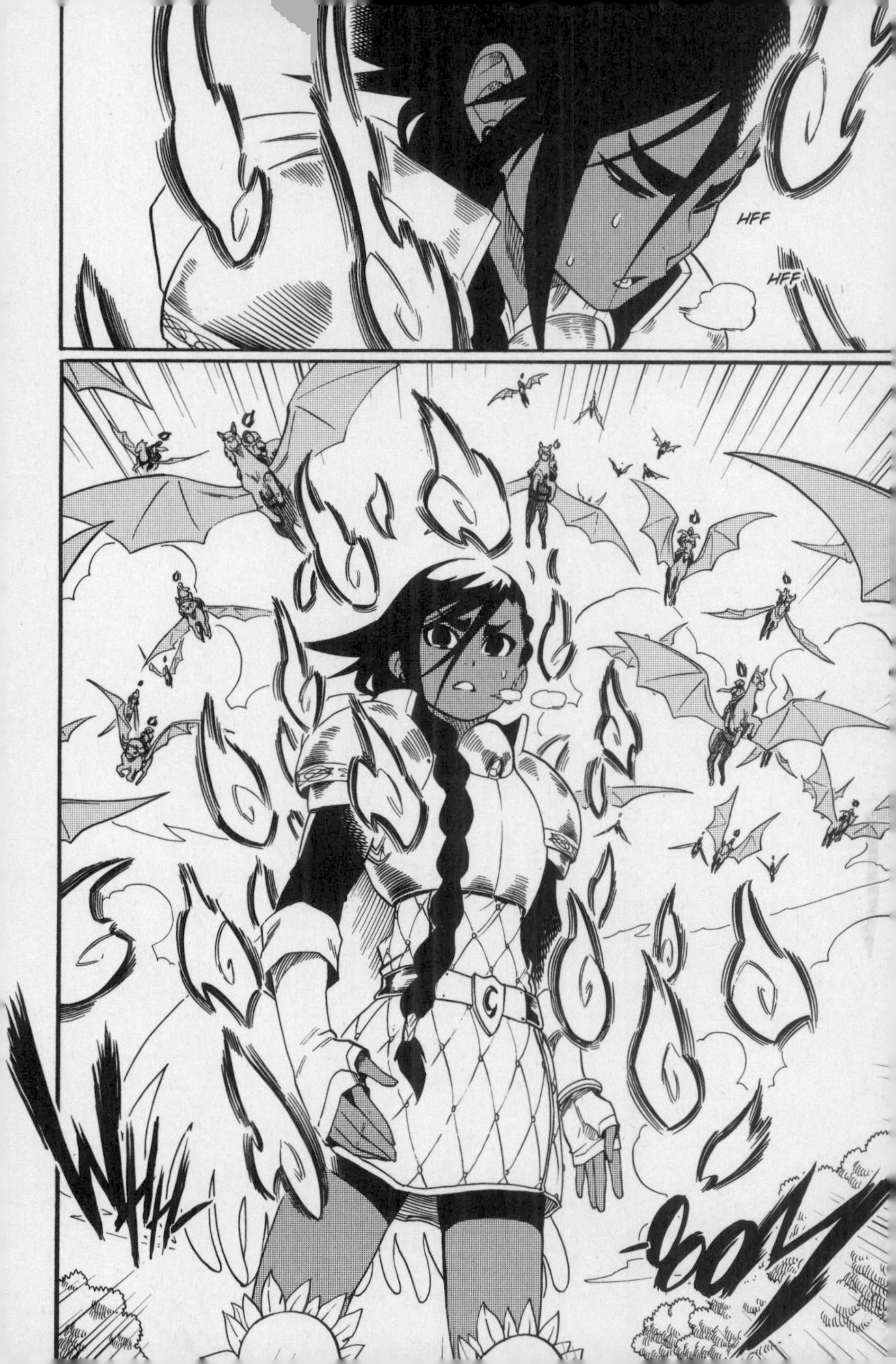
HFF
HFF
BOOM

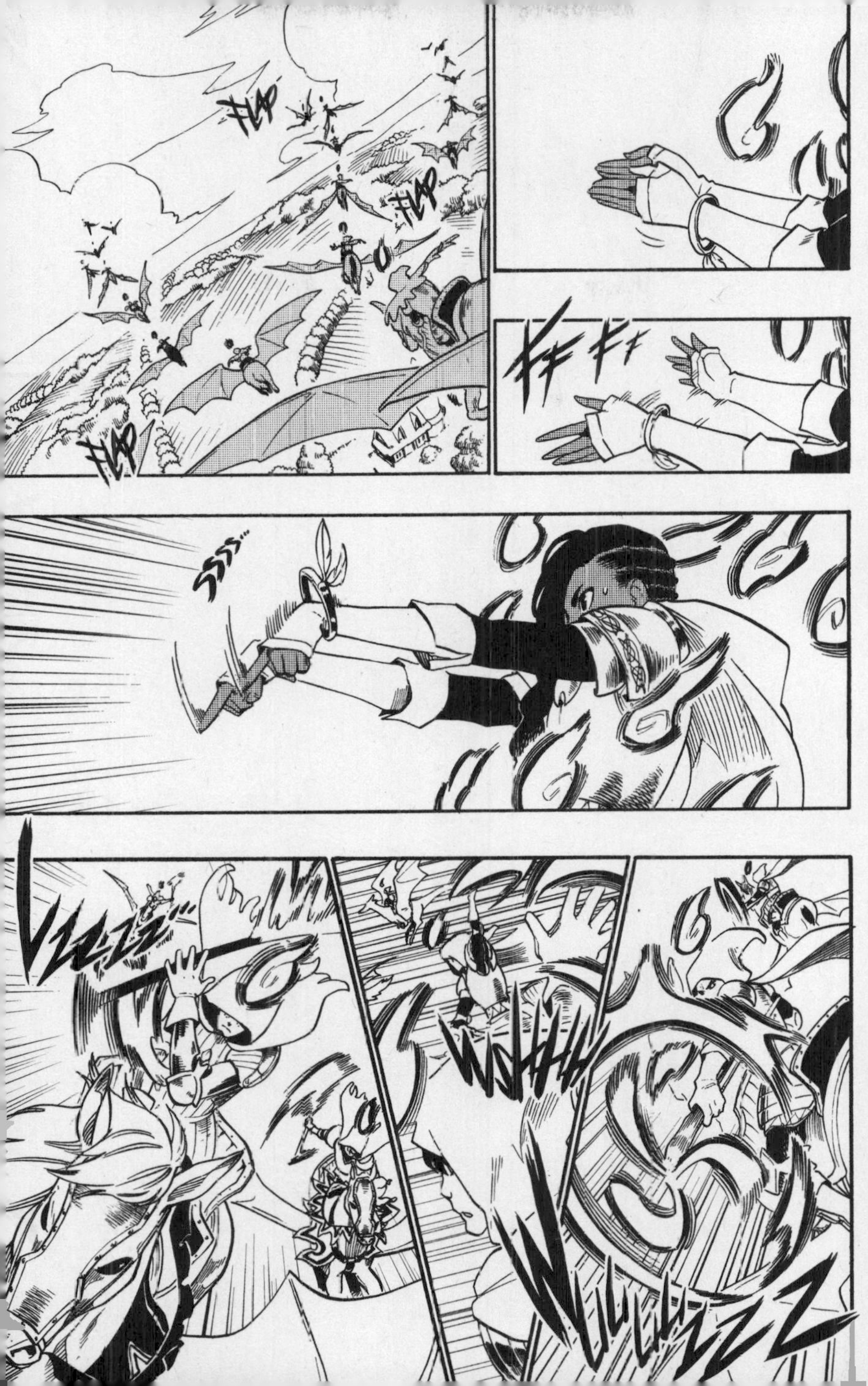
FLAP
FLAP
FLAP
WSHHH
VZZZZZ

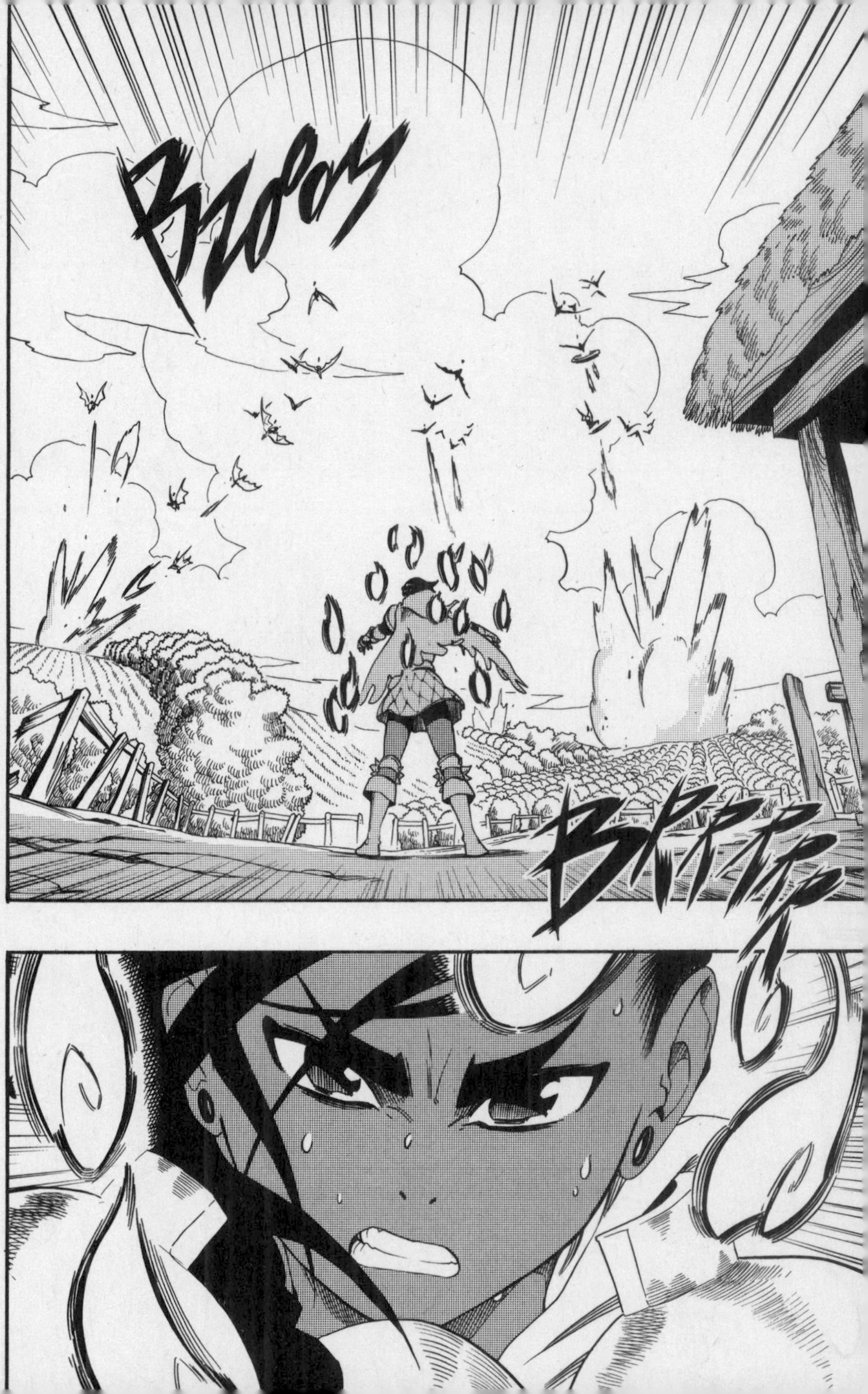

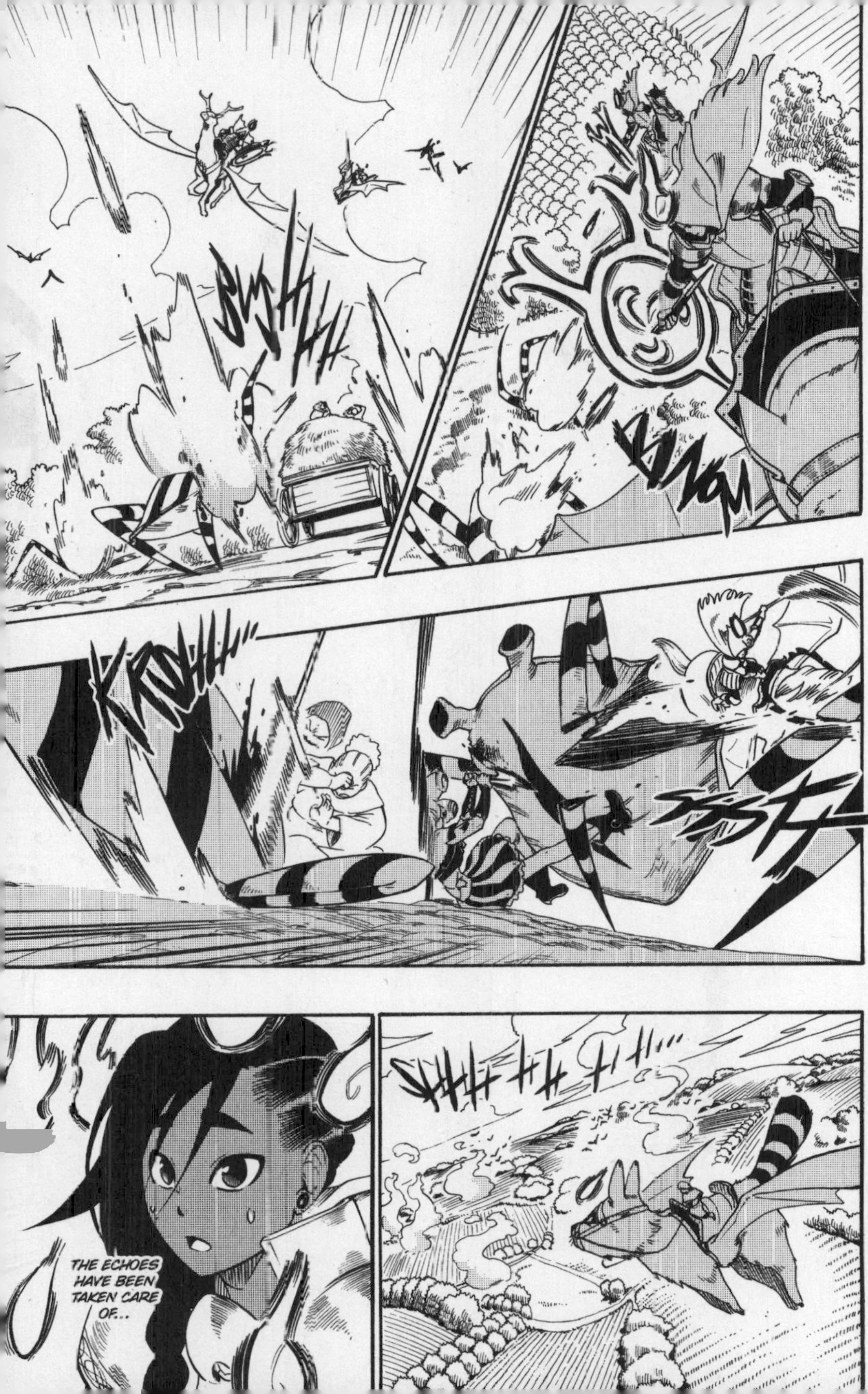
THE ECHOES HAVE BEEN TAKEN CARE OF...

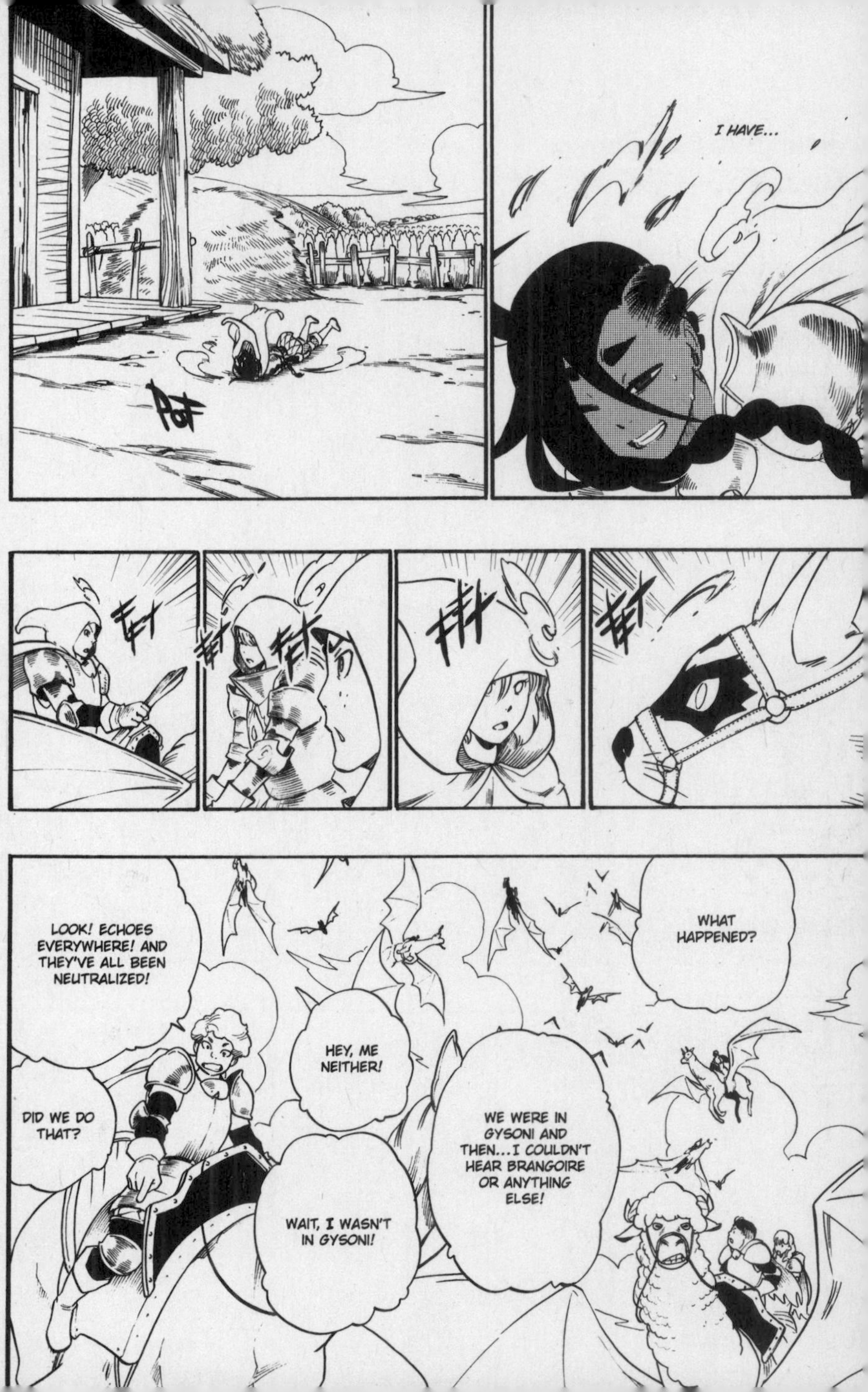
I HAVE...
POF
WHAT HAPPENED?
WE WERE IN GYSONI AND THEN...I COULDN'T HEAR BRANGOIRE OR ANYTHING ELSE!
HEY, ME NEITHER!
WAIT, I WASN'T IN GYSONI!
LOOK! ECHOES EVERYWHERE! AND THEY'VE ALL BEEN NEUTRALIZED!
DID WE DO THAT?

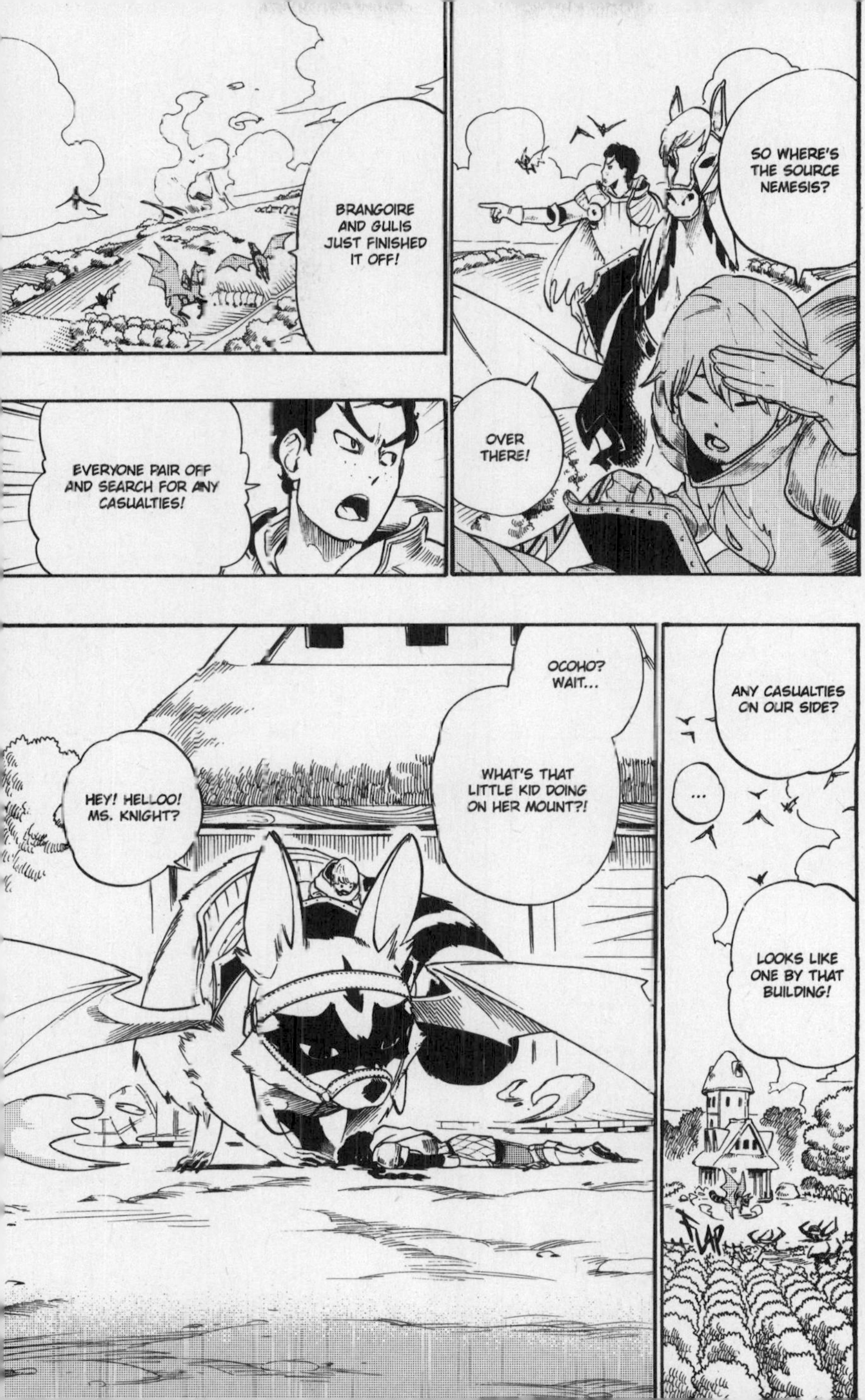
SO WHERE'S THE SOURCE NEMESIS?
OVER THERE!
BRANGOIRE AND GULIS JUST FINISHED IT OFF!
EVERYONE PAIR OFF AND SEARCH FOR ANY CASUALTIES!
ANY CASUALTIES ON OUR SIDE?
...
LOOKS LIKE ONE BY THAT BUILDING!
FLAP
OCOHO? WAIT...
WHAT'S THAT LITTLE KID DOING ON HER MOUNT?!
HEY! HELLOO! MS. KNIGHT?

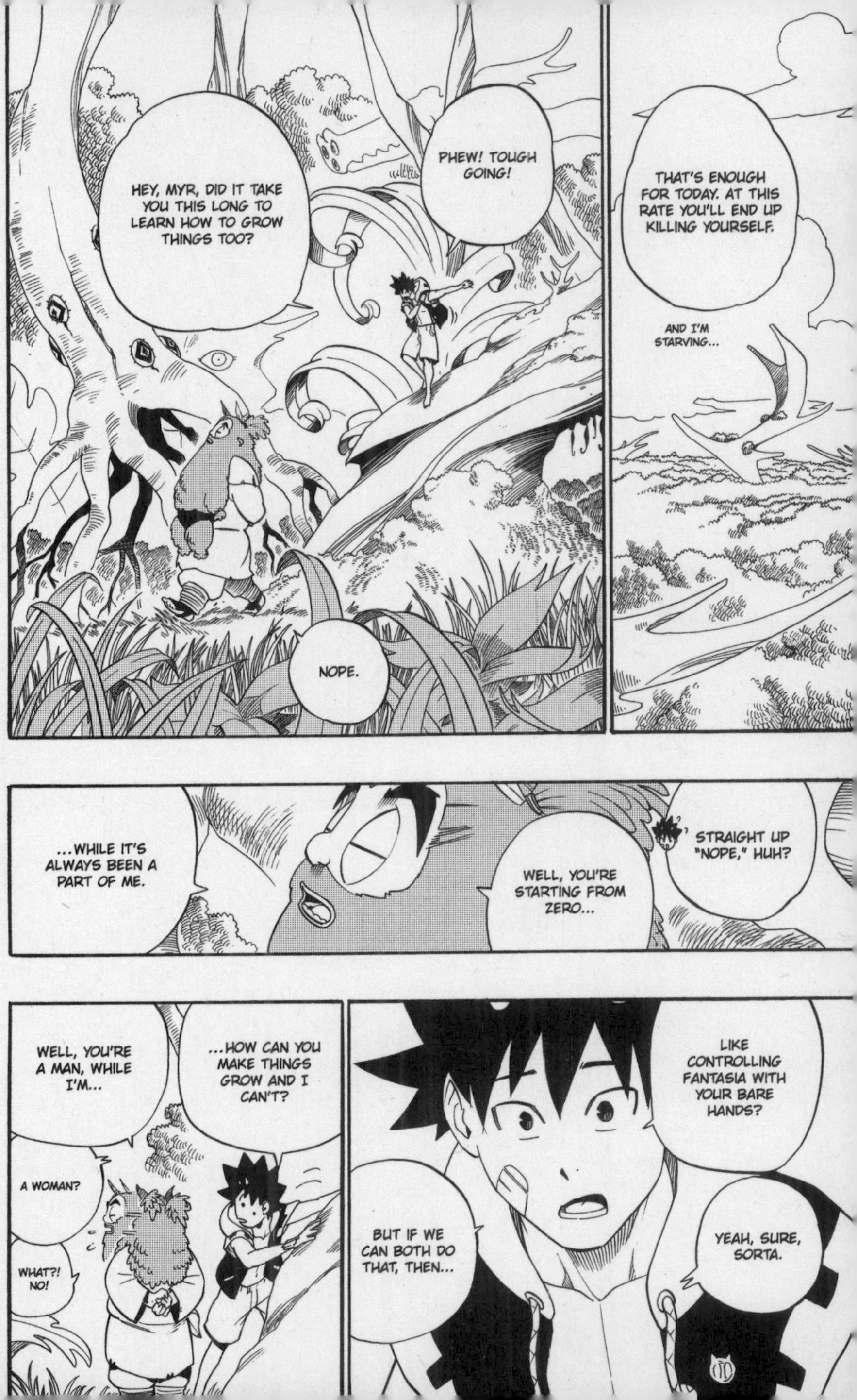
THAT'S ENOUGH FOR TODAY. AT THIS RATE YOU'LL END UP KILLING YOURSELF.
AND I'M STARVING...
PHEW! TOUGH GOING!
HEY, MYR, DID IT TAKE YOU THIS LONG TO LEARN HOW TO GROW THINGS TOO?
NOPE.
STRAIGHT UP "NOPE," HUH?
WELL, YOU'RE STARTING FROM ZERO...
...WHILE IT'S ALWAYS BEEN A PART OF ME.
LIKE CONTROLLING FANTASIA WITH YOUR BARE HANDS?
YEAH, SURE, SORTA.
BUT IF WE CAN BOTH DO THAT, THEN...
...HOW CAN YOU MAKE THINGS GROW AND I CAN'T?
WELL, YOU'RE A MAN, WHILE I'M...
A WOMAN?
WHAT?! NO!

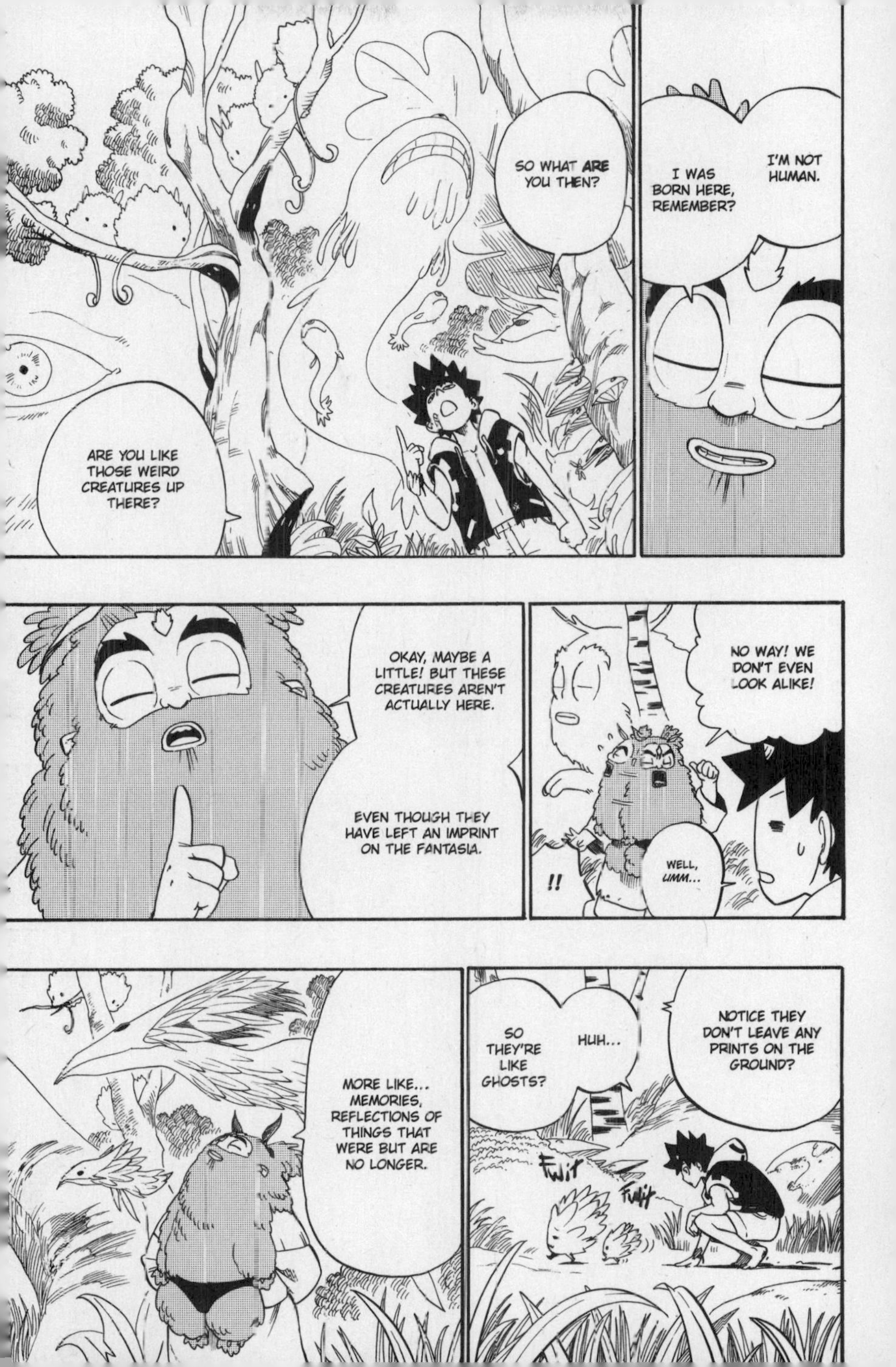
I'M NOT HUMAN.
I WAS BORN HERE, REMEMBER?
SO WHAT ARE YOU THEN?
ARE YOU LIKE THOSE WEIRD CREATURES UP THERE?
NO WAY! WE DON'T EVEN LOOK ALIKE!
WELL, UMM...
!!
OKAY, MAYBE A LITTLE! BUT THESE CREATURES AREN'T ACTUALLY HERE.
EVEN THOUGH THEY HAVE LEFT AN IMPRINT ON THE FANTASIA.
NOTICE THEY DON'T LEAVE ANY PRINTS ON THE GROUND?
HUH...
SO THEY'RE LIKE GHOSTS?
FWIT
FWIT
MORE LIKE... MEMORIES, REFLECTIONS OF THINGS THAT WERE BUT ARE NO LONGER.

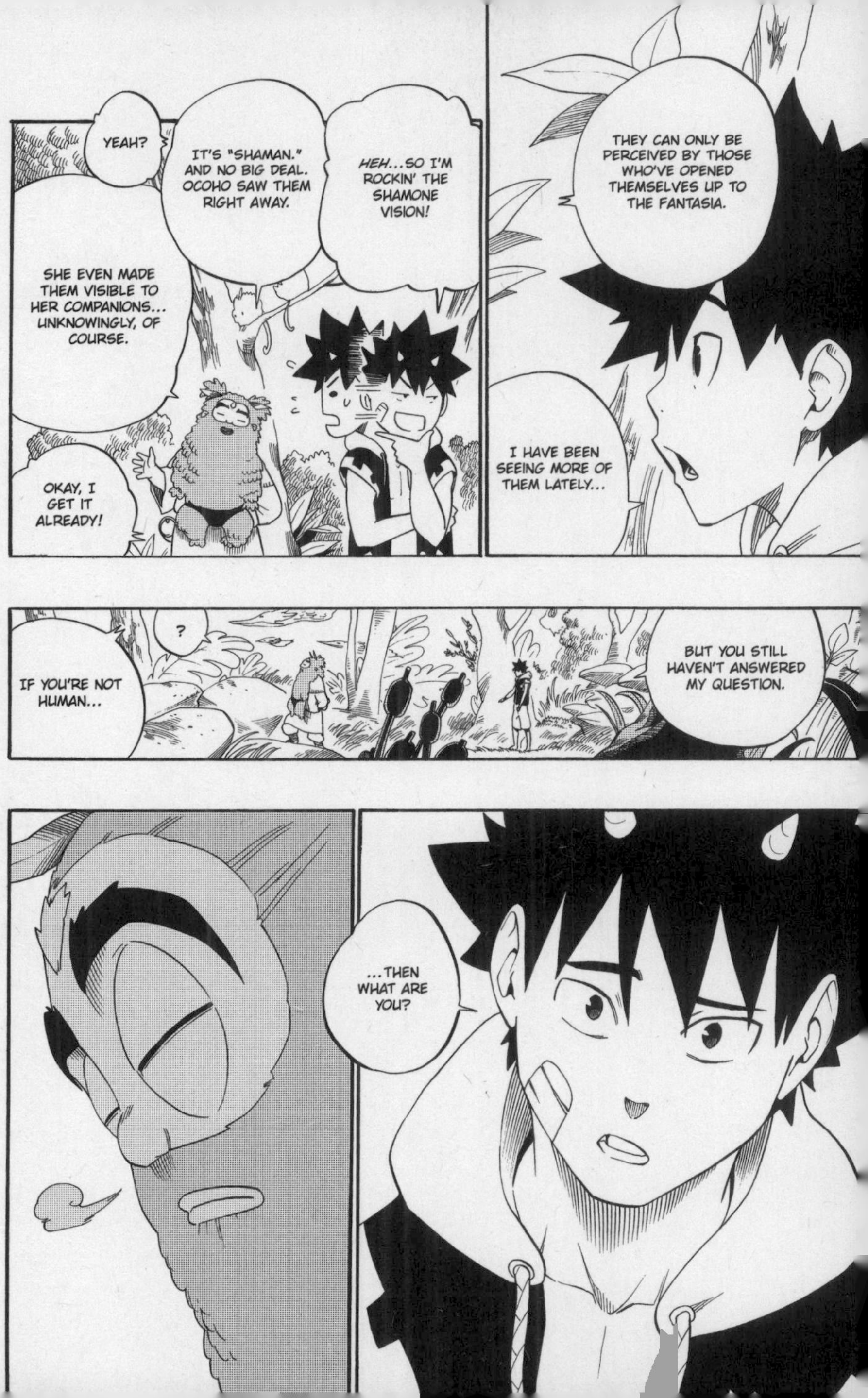
THEY CAN ONLY BE PERCEIVED BY THOSE WHO'VE OPENED THEMSELVES UP TO THE FANTASIA.
I HAVE BEEN SEEING MORE OF THEM LATELY...
HEH...SO I'M ROCKIN' THE SHAMONE VISION!
IT'S "SHAMAN." AND NO BIG DEAL. OCOHO SAW THEM RIGHT AWAY.
YEAH?
SHE EVEN MADE THEM VISIBLE TO HER COMPANIONS... UNKNOWINGLY, OF COURSE.
OKAY, I GET IT ALREADY!
BUT YOU STILL HAVEN'T ANSWERED MY QUESTION.
?
IF YOU'RE NOT HUMAN...
...THEN WHAT ARE YOU?

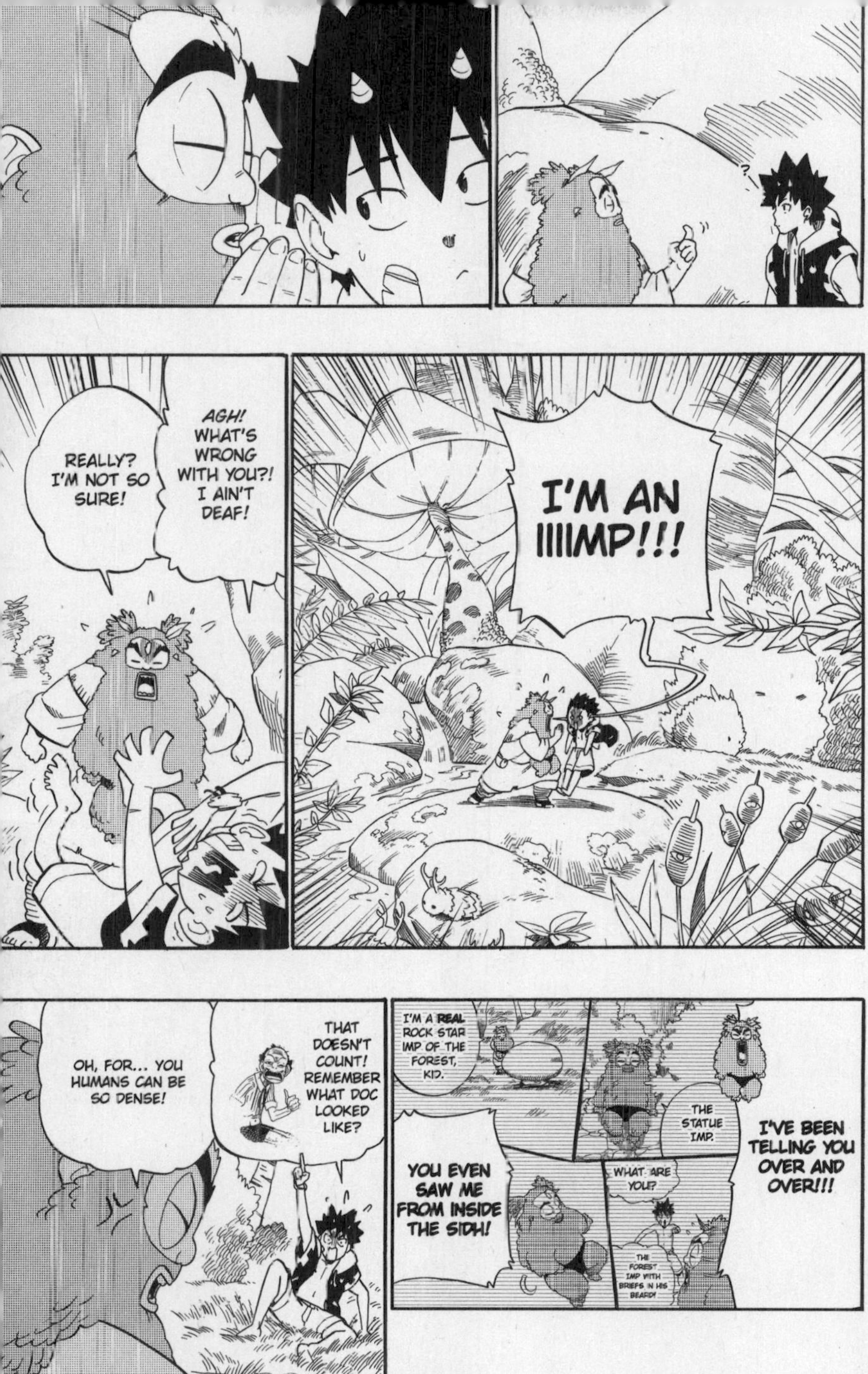
?
I'M AN IIIIMP!!!
AGH! WHAT'S WRONG WITH YOU?! I AIN'T DEAF!
REALLY? I'M NOT SO SURE!
I'VE BEEN TELLING YOU OVER AND OVER!!!
THE STATUE IMP.
I'M A REAL ROCK STAR IMP OF THE FOREST, KID.
WHAT ARE YOU?
THE FOREST IMP WITH BRIEFS IN HIS BEARD!
YOU EVEN SAW ME FROM INSIDE THE SIDH!
THAT DOESN'T COUNT! REMEMBER WHAT DOC LOOKED LIKE?
OH, FOR... YOU HUMANS CAN BE SO DENSE!

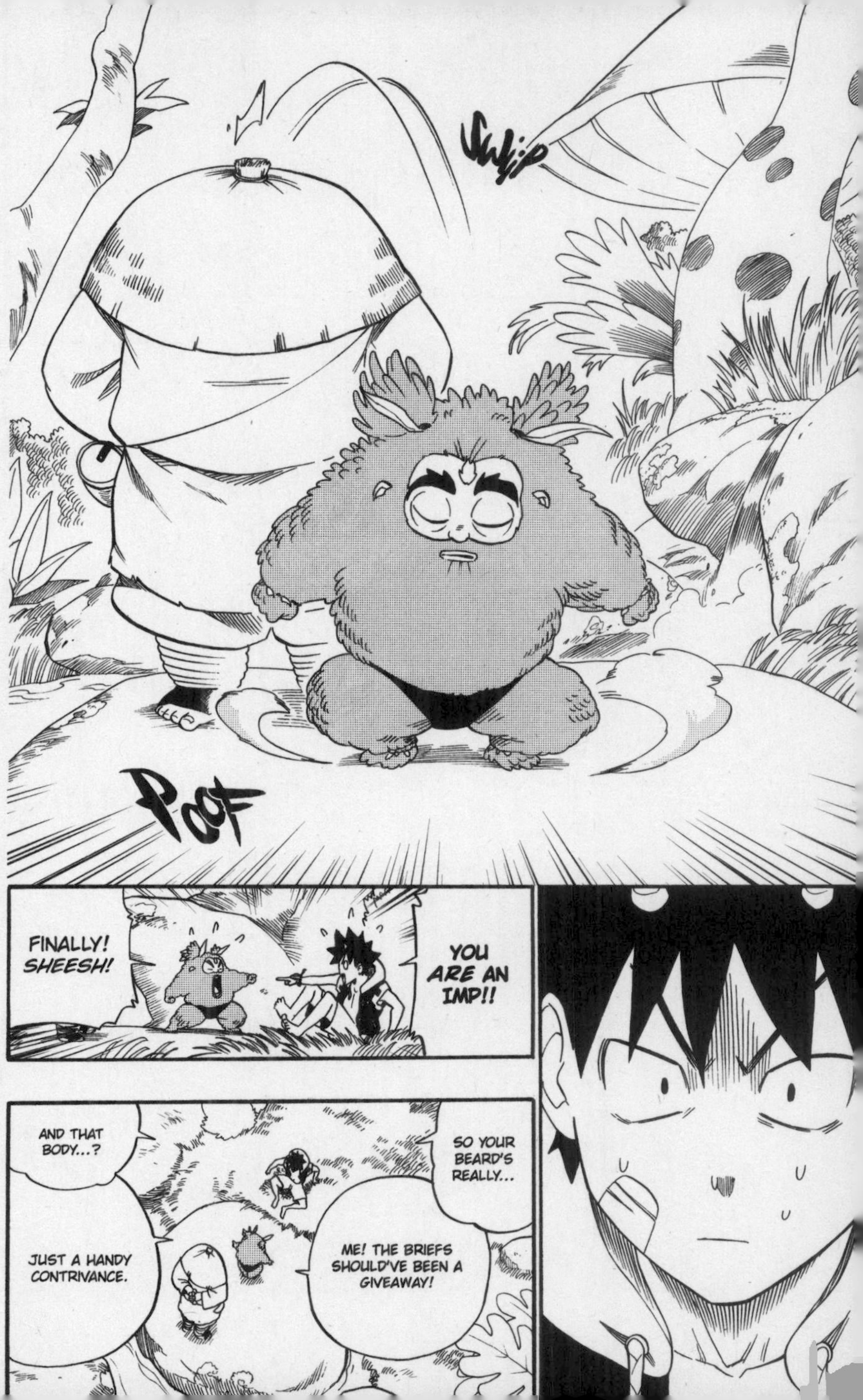
SWHIP
POOF
YOU ARE AN IMP!!
FINALLY! SHEESH!
SO YOUR BEARD'S REALLY...
AND THAT BODY...?
ME! THE BRIEFS SHOULD'VE BEEN A GIVEAWAY!
JUST A HANDY CONTRIVANCE.

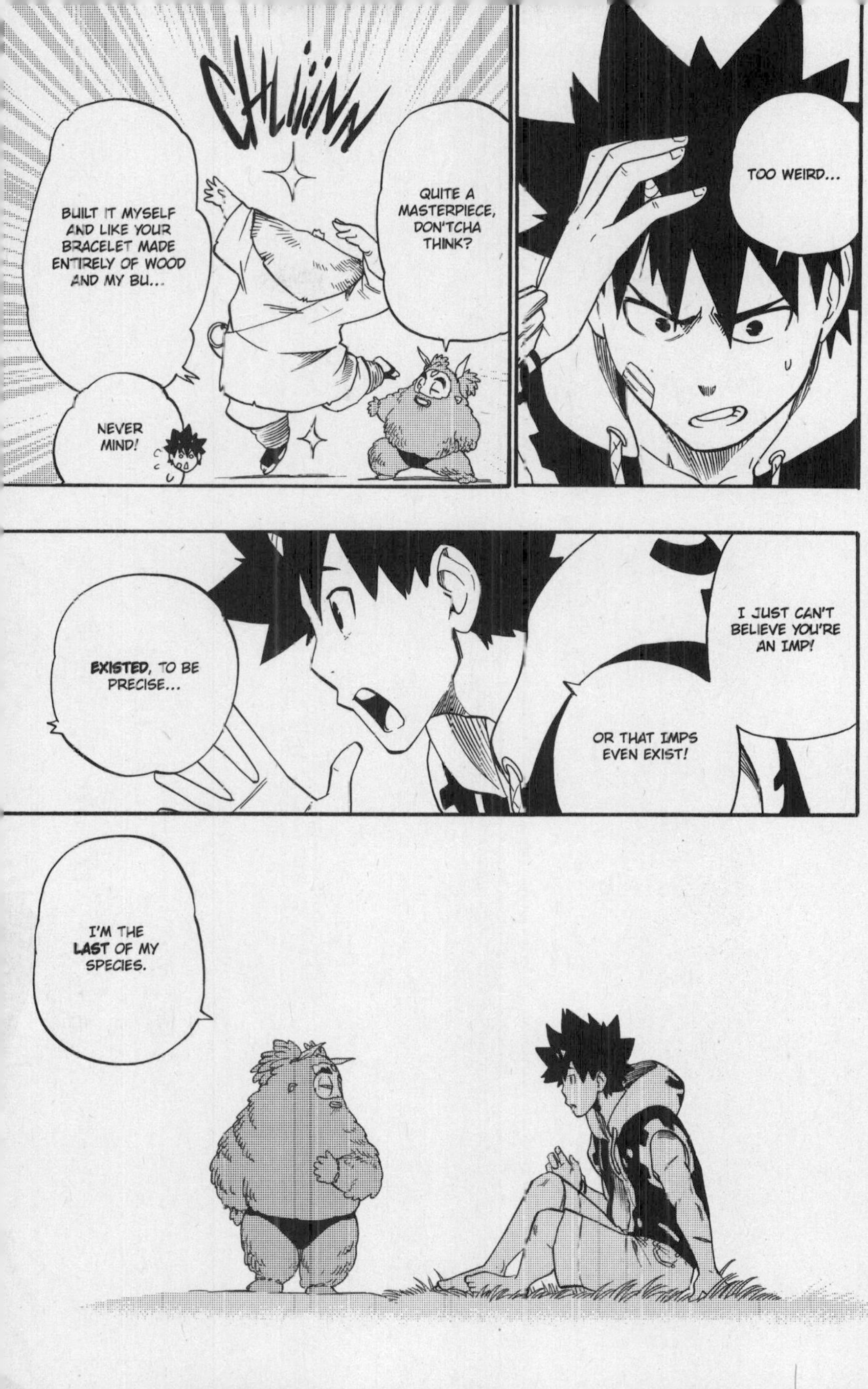
TOO WEIRD...
QUITE A MASTERPIECE, DON'TCHA THINK?
CHLIINN
BUILT IT MYSELF AND LIKE YOUR BRACELET MADE ENTIRELY OF WOOD AND MY BU...
NEVER MIND!
I JUST CAN'T BELIEVE YOU'RE AN IMP!
OR THAT IMPS EVEN EXIST!
EXISTED, TO BE PRECISE...
I'M THE **LAST** OF MY SPECIES.

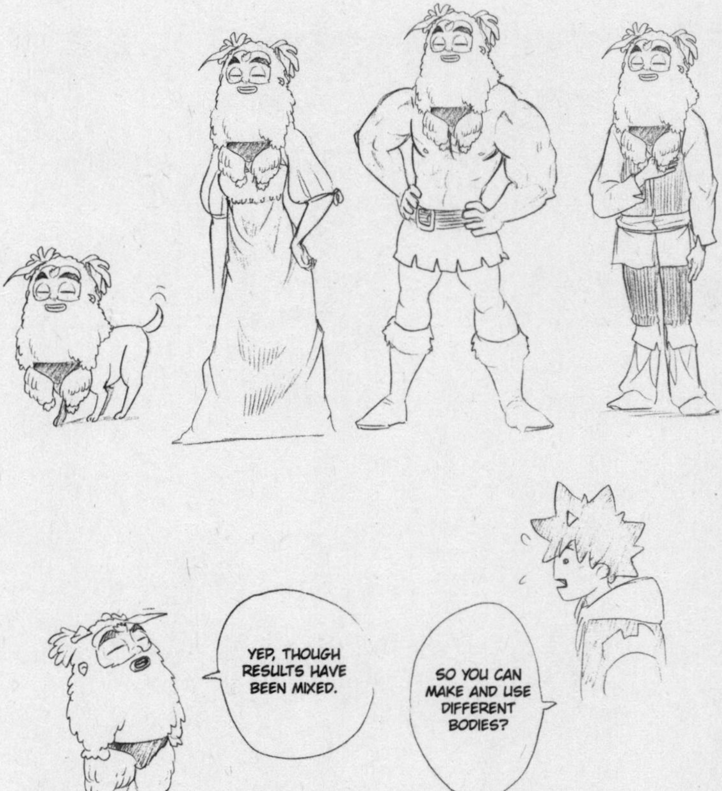
SO YOU CAN MAKE AND USE DIFFERENT BODIES?
YEP, THOUGH RESULTS HAVE BEEN MIXED.

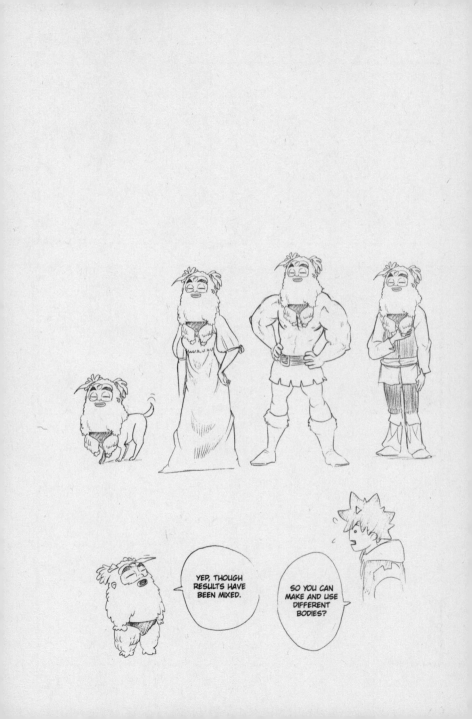

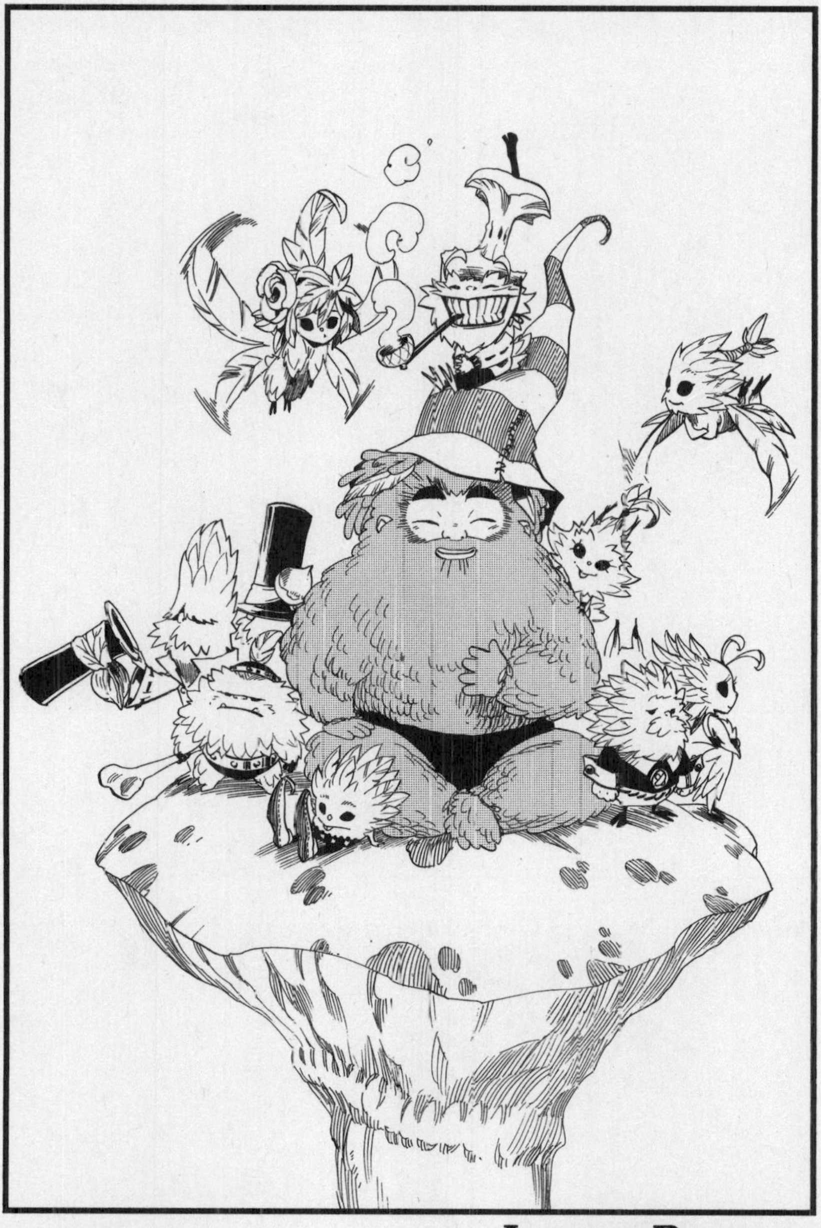

Chapter 48

Little People

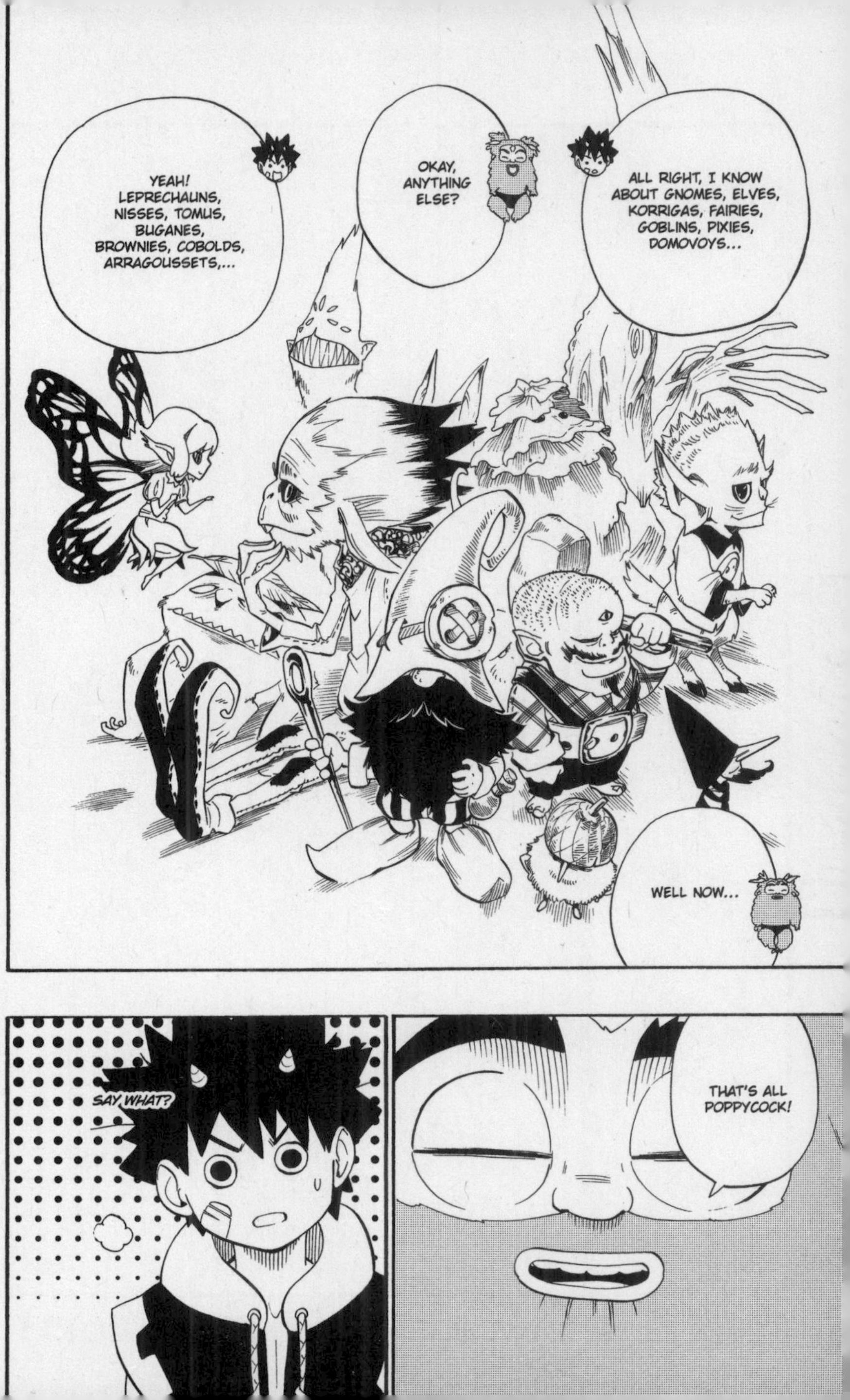
ALL RIGHT, I KNOW ABOUT GNOMES, ELVES, KORRIGAS, FAIRIES, GOBLINS, PIXIES, DOMOVOYS...
OKAY, ANYTHING ELSE?
YEAH! LEPRECHAUNS, NISSES, TOMUS, BUGANES, BROWNIES, COBOLDS, ARRAGOUSSETS,...
WELL NOW...
THAT'S ALL POPPYCOCK!
SAY WHAT?

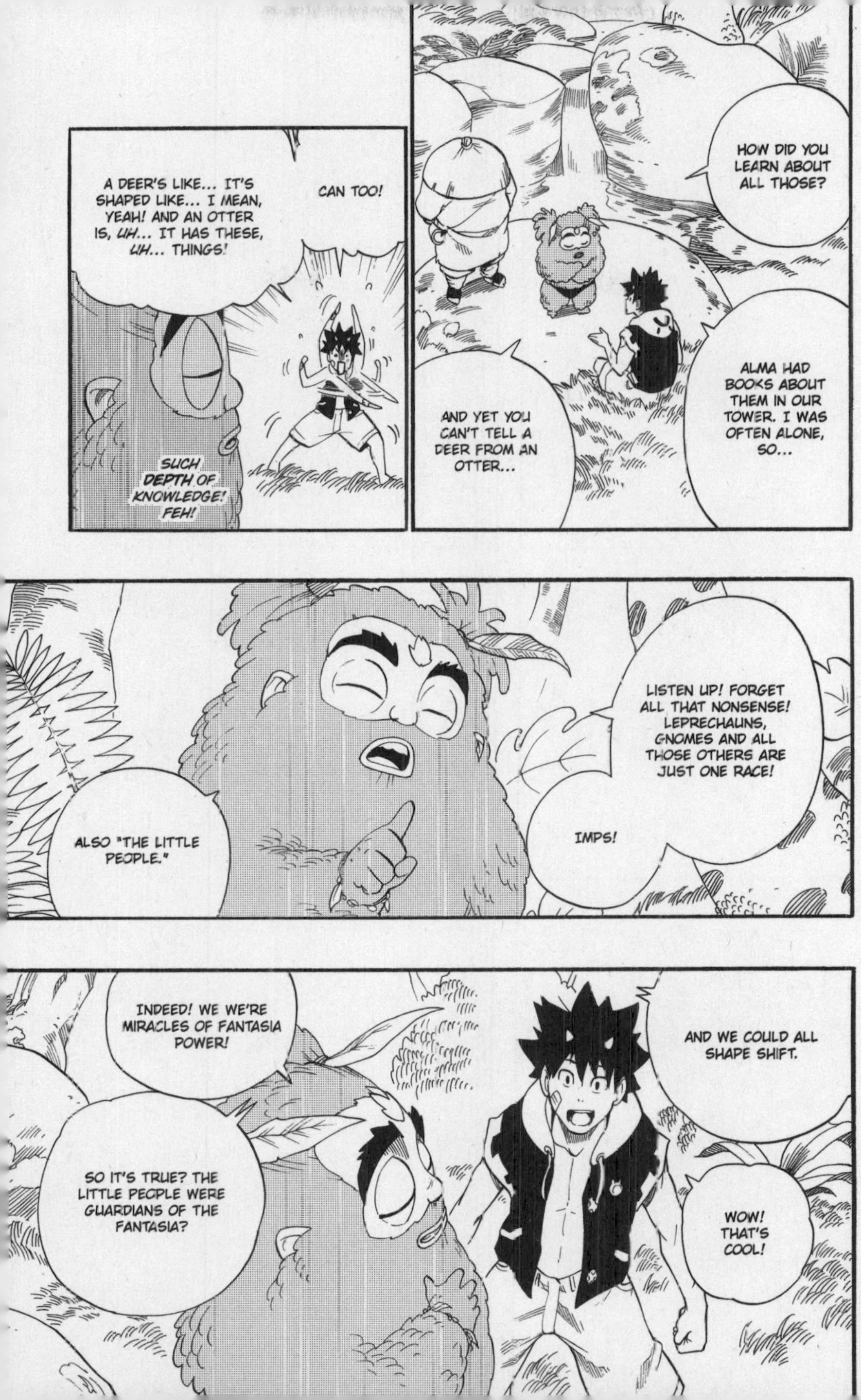
HOW DID YOU LEARN ABOUT ALL THOSE?
ALMA HAD BOOKS ABOUT THEM IN OUR TOWER. I WAS OFTEN ALONE, SO...
AND YET YOU CAN'T TELL A DEER FROM AN OTTER...
CAN TOO!
A DEER'S LIKE... IT'S SHAPED LIKE... I MEAN, YEAH! AND AN OTTER IS, *UH*... IT HAS THESE, *UH*... THINGS!
SUCH **DEPTH** OF KNOWLEDGE! FEH!
LISTEN UP! FORGET ALL THAT NONSENSE! LEPRECHAUNS, GNOMES AND ALL THOSE OTHERS ARE JUST ONE RACE!
IMPS!
ALSO "THE LITTLE PEOPLE."
AND WE COULD ALL SHAPE SHIFT.
INDEED! WE WE'RE MIRACLES OF FANTASIA POWER!
WOW! THAT'S COOL!
SO IT'S TRUE? THE LITTLE PEOPLE WERE GUARDIANS OF THE FANTASIA?

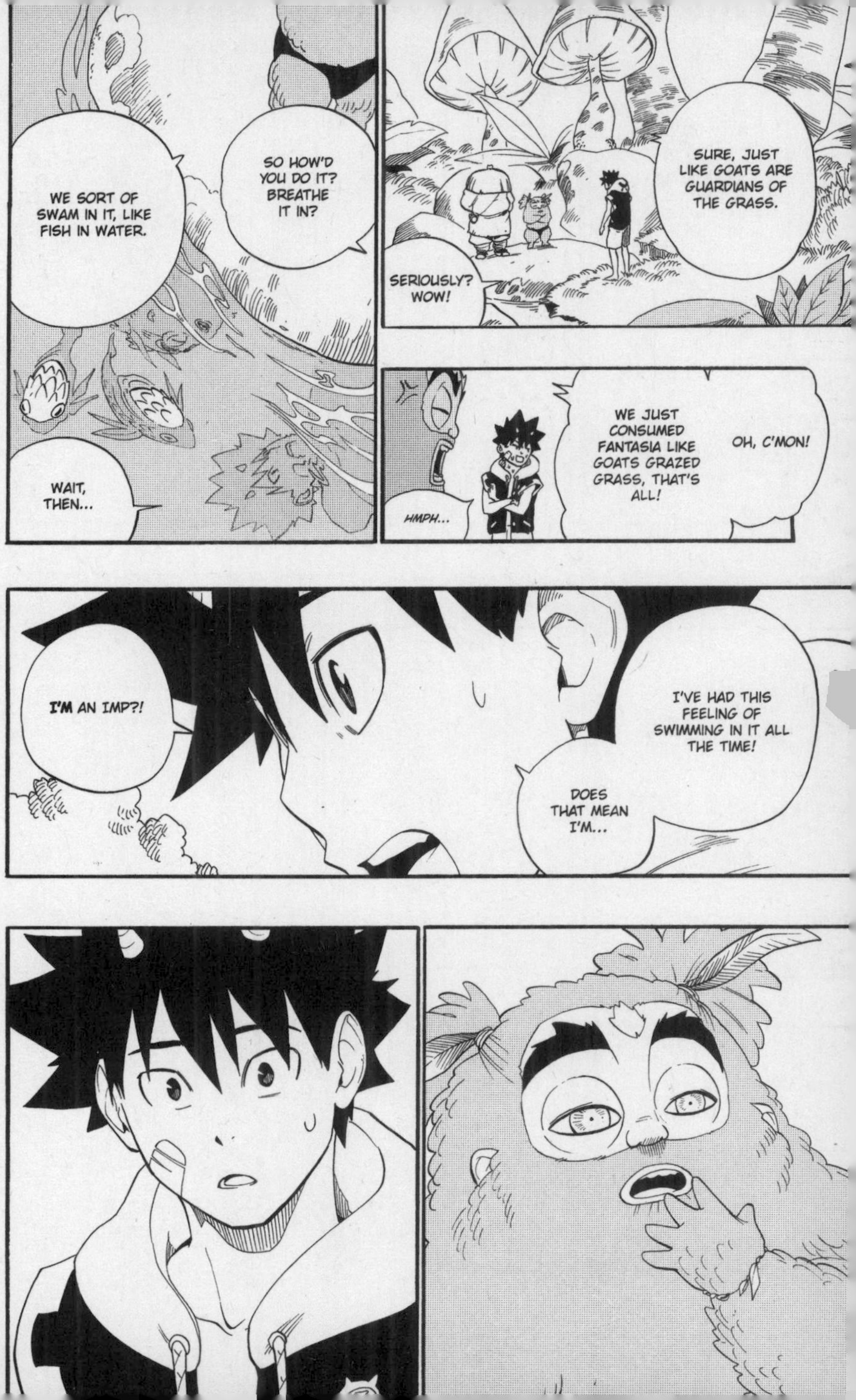
SURE, JUST LIKE GOATS ARE GUARDIANS OF THE GRASS.
SERIOUSLY? WOW!
OH, C'MON!
WE JUST CONSUMED FANTASIA LIKE GOATS GRAZED GRASS, THAT'S ALL!
HMPH...
SO HOW'D YOU DO IT? BREATHE IT IN?
WE SORT OF SWAM IN IT, LIKE FISH IN WATER.
WAIT, THEN...
I'VE HAD THIS FEELING OF SWIMMING IN IT ALL THE TIME!
DOES THAT MEAN I'M...
I'M AN IMP?!

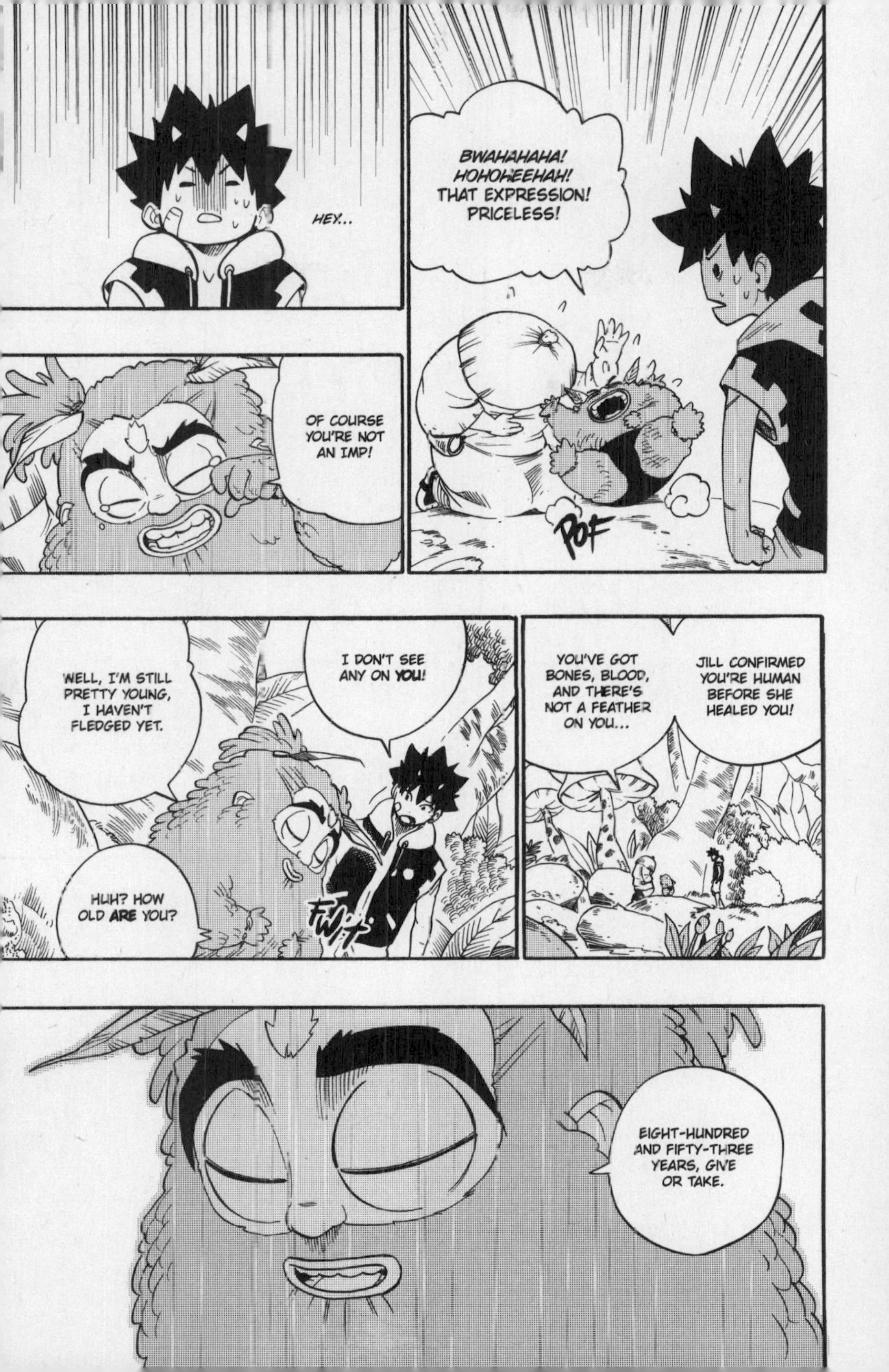
BWAHAHAHA! HOHOHEEHAH! THAT EXPRESSION! PRICELESS!
POF
HEY...
OF COURSE YOU'RE NOT AN IMP!
JILL CONFIRMED YOU'RE HUMAN BEFORE SHE HEALED YOU!
YOU'VE GOT BONES, BLOOD, AND THERE'S NOT A FEATHER ON YOU...
I DON'T SEE ANY ON **YOU**!
WELL, I'M STILL PRETTY YOUNG, I HAVEN'T FLEDGED YET.
FWIT
HUH? HOW OLD **ARE** YOU?
EIGHT-HUNDRED AND FIFTY-THREE YEARS, GIVE OR TAKE.

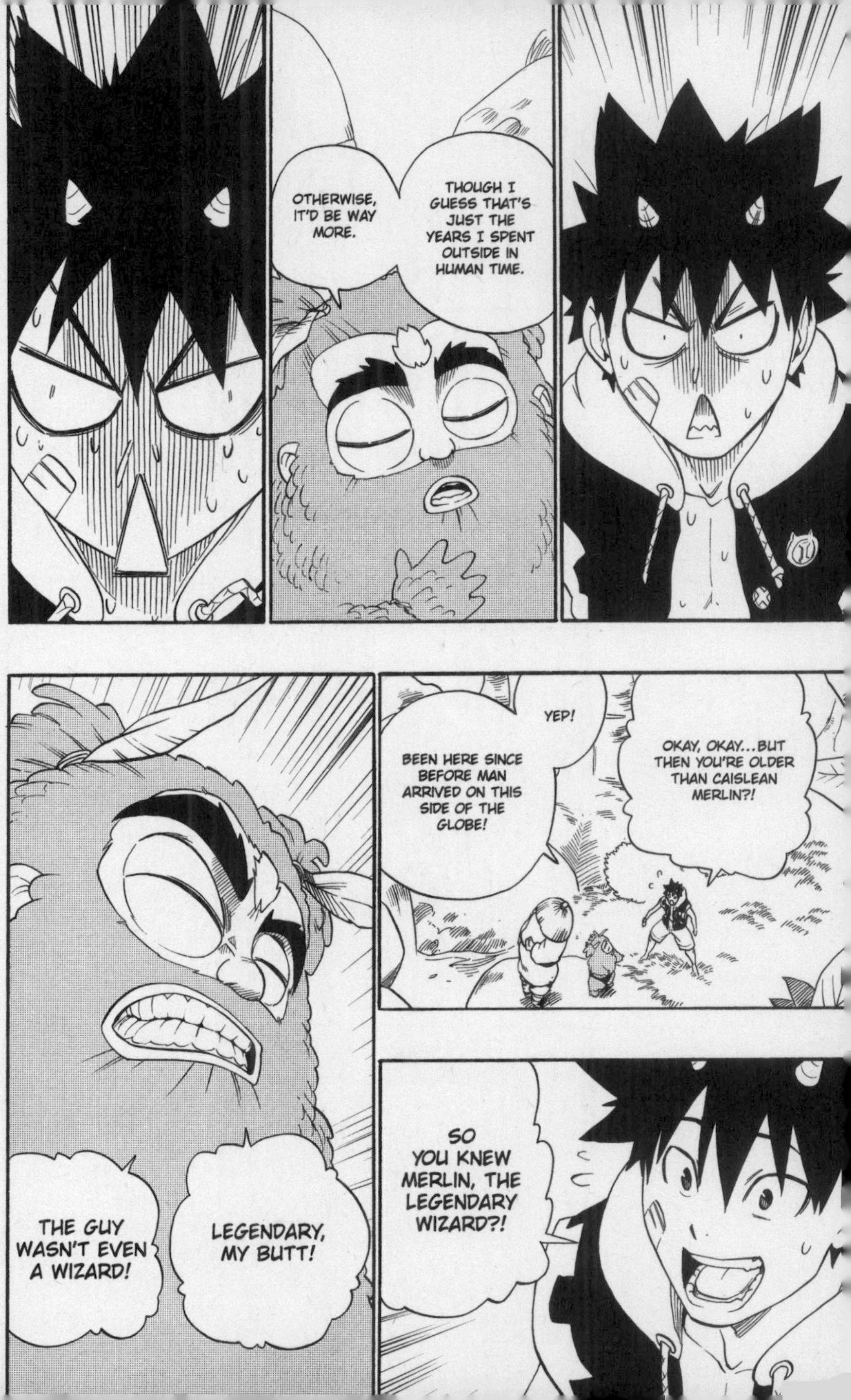
THOUGH I GUESS THAT'S JUST THE YEARS I SPENT OUTSIDE IN HUMAN TIME.
OTHERWISE, IT'D BE WAY MORE.
OKAY, OKAY...BUT THEN YOU'RE OLDER THAN CAISLEAN MERLIN?!
YEP!
BEEN HERE SINCE BEFORE MAN ARRIVED ON THIS SIDE OF THE GLOBE!
SO YOU KNEW MERLIN, THE LEGENDARY WIZARD?!
LEGENDARY, MY BUTT!
THE GUY WASN'T EVEN A WIZARD!

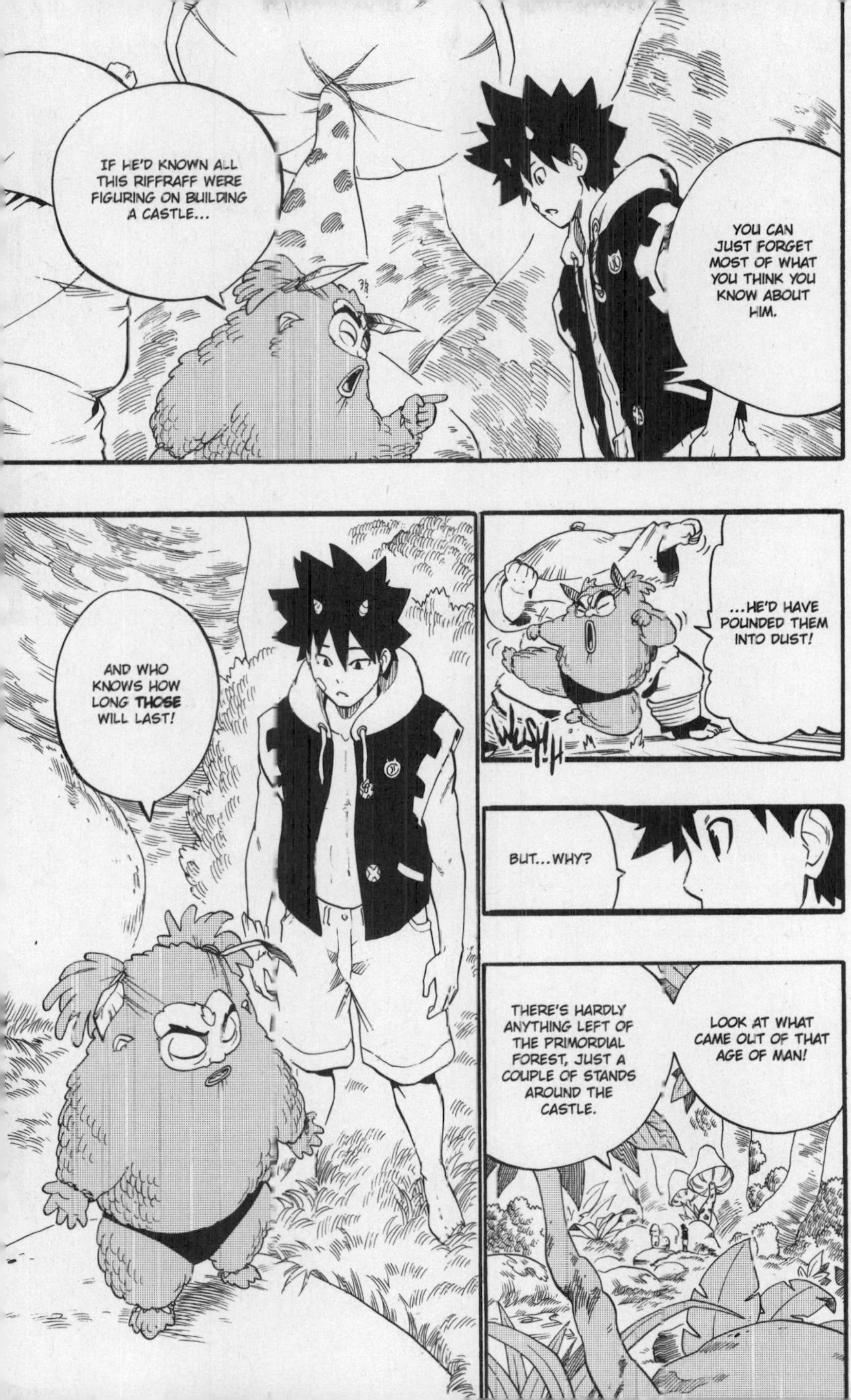
YOU CAN JUST FORGET MOST OF WHAT YOU THINK YOU KNOW ABOUT HIM.
IF HE'D KNOWN ALL THIS RIFFRAFF WERE FIGURING ON BUILDING A CASTLE...
...HE'D HAVE POUNDED THEM INTO DUST!
BUT...WHY?
LOOK AT WHAT CAME OUT OF THAT AGE OF MAN!
THERE'S HARDLY ANYTHING LEFT OF THE PRIMORDIAL FOREST, JUST A COUPLE OF STANDS AROUND THE CASTLE.
AND WHO KNOWS HOW LONG **THOSE** WILL LAST!

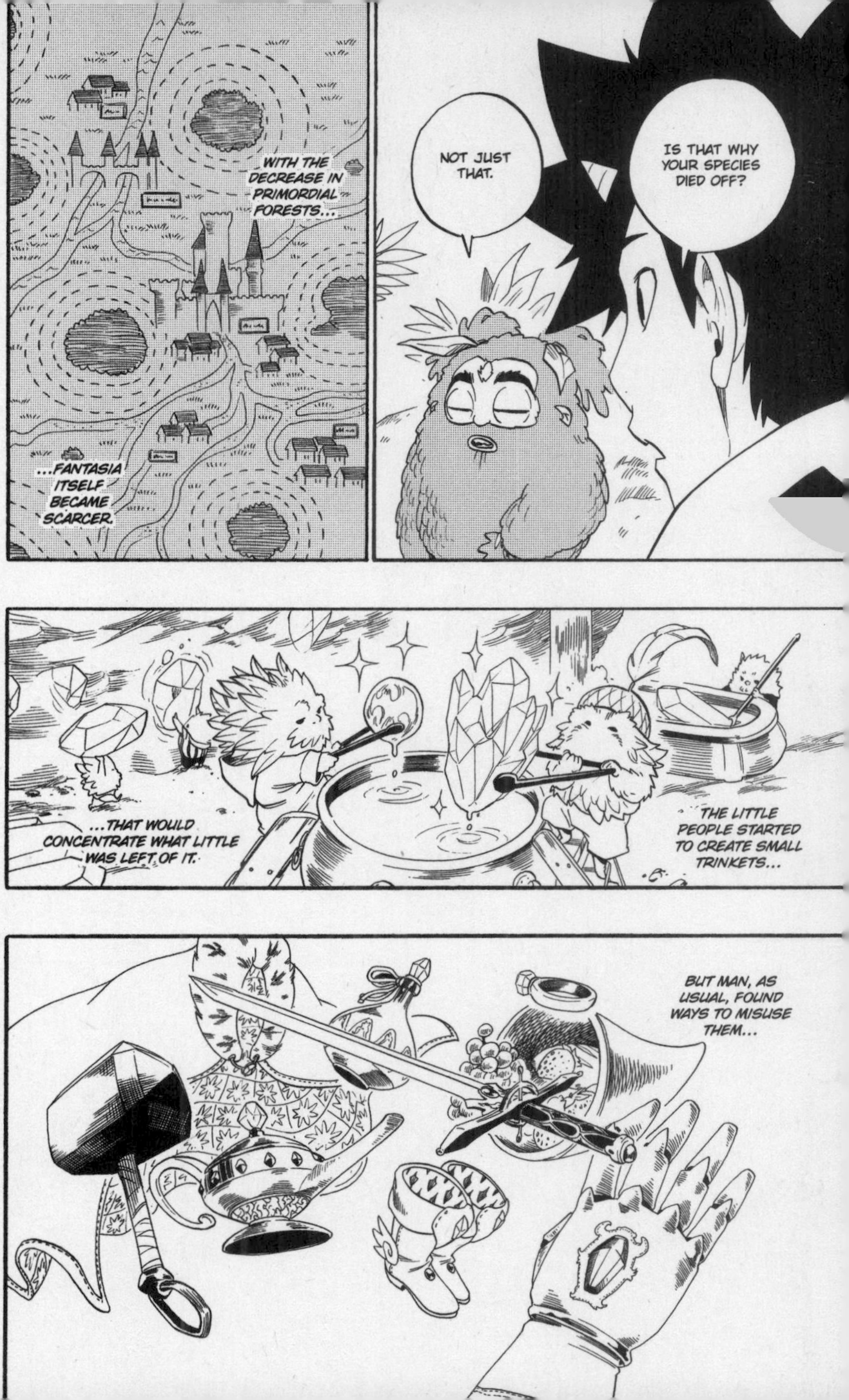
IS THAT WHY YOUR SPECIES DIED OFF?
NOT JUST THAT.
WITH THE DECREASE IN PRIMORDIAL FORESTS...
...FANTASIA ITSELF BECAME SCARCER.
THE LITTLE PEOPLE STARTED TO CREATE SMALL TRINKETS...
...THAT WOULD CONCENTRATE WHAT LITTLE WAS LEFT OF IT.
BUT MAN, AS USUAL, FOUND WAYS TO MISUSE THEM...

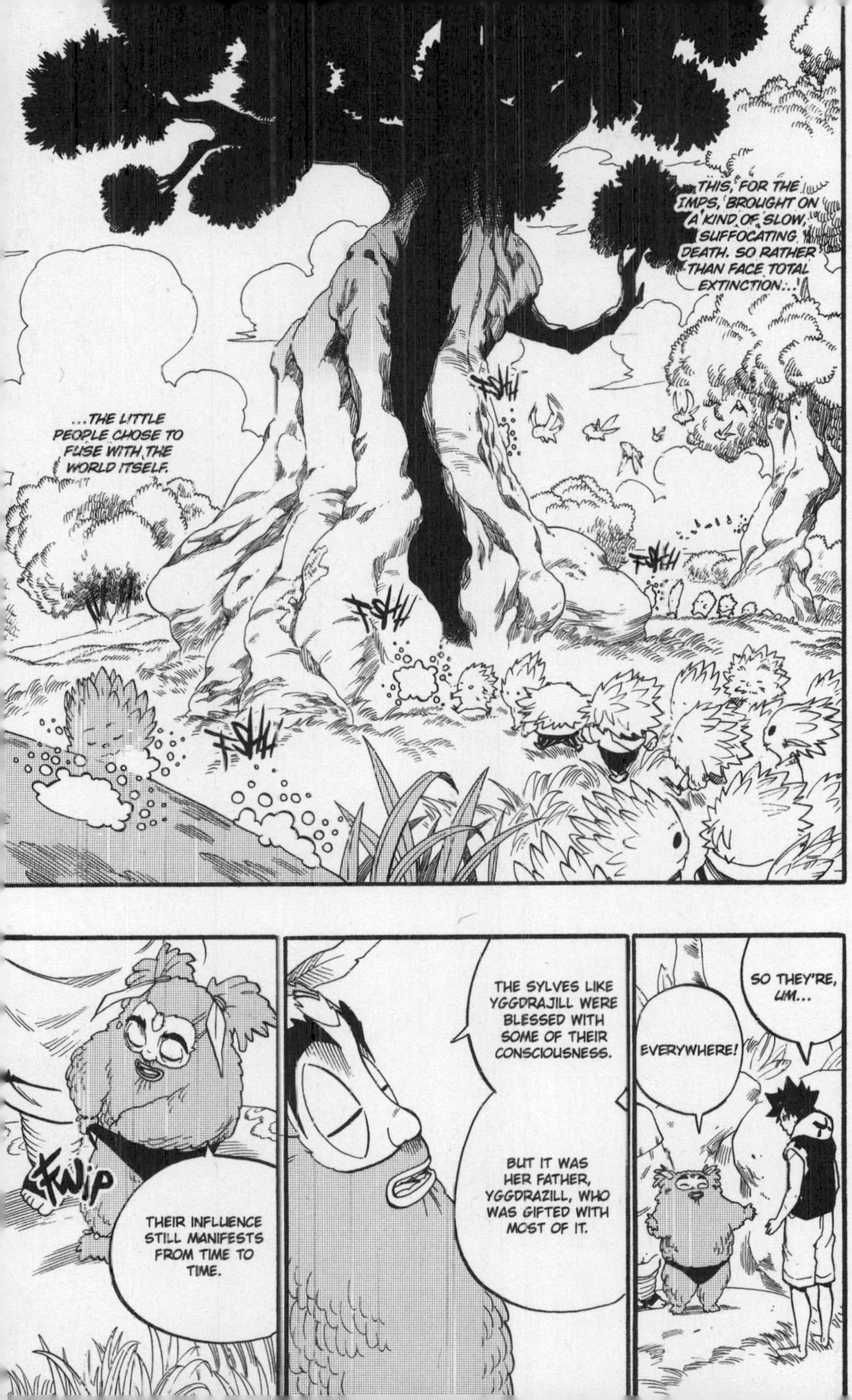
THIS, FOR THE IMPS, BROUGHT ON A KIND OF SLOW, SUFFOCATING DEATH. SO RATHER THAN FACE TOTAL EXTINCTION...!
...THE LITTLE PEOPLE CHOSE TO FUSE WITH THE WORLD ITSELF.
SO THEY'RE, UM...
EVERYWHERE!
THE SYLVES LIKE YGGDRAJILL WERE BLESSED WITH SOME OF THEIR CONSCIOUSNESS.
BUT IT WAS HER FATHER, YGGDRAZILL, WHO WAS GIFTED WITH MOST OF IT.
FWIP
THEIR INFLUENCE STILL MANIFESTS FROM TIME TO TIME.

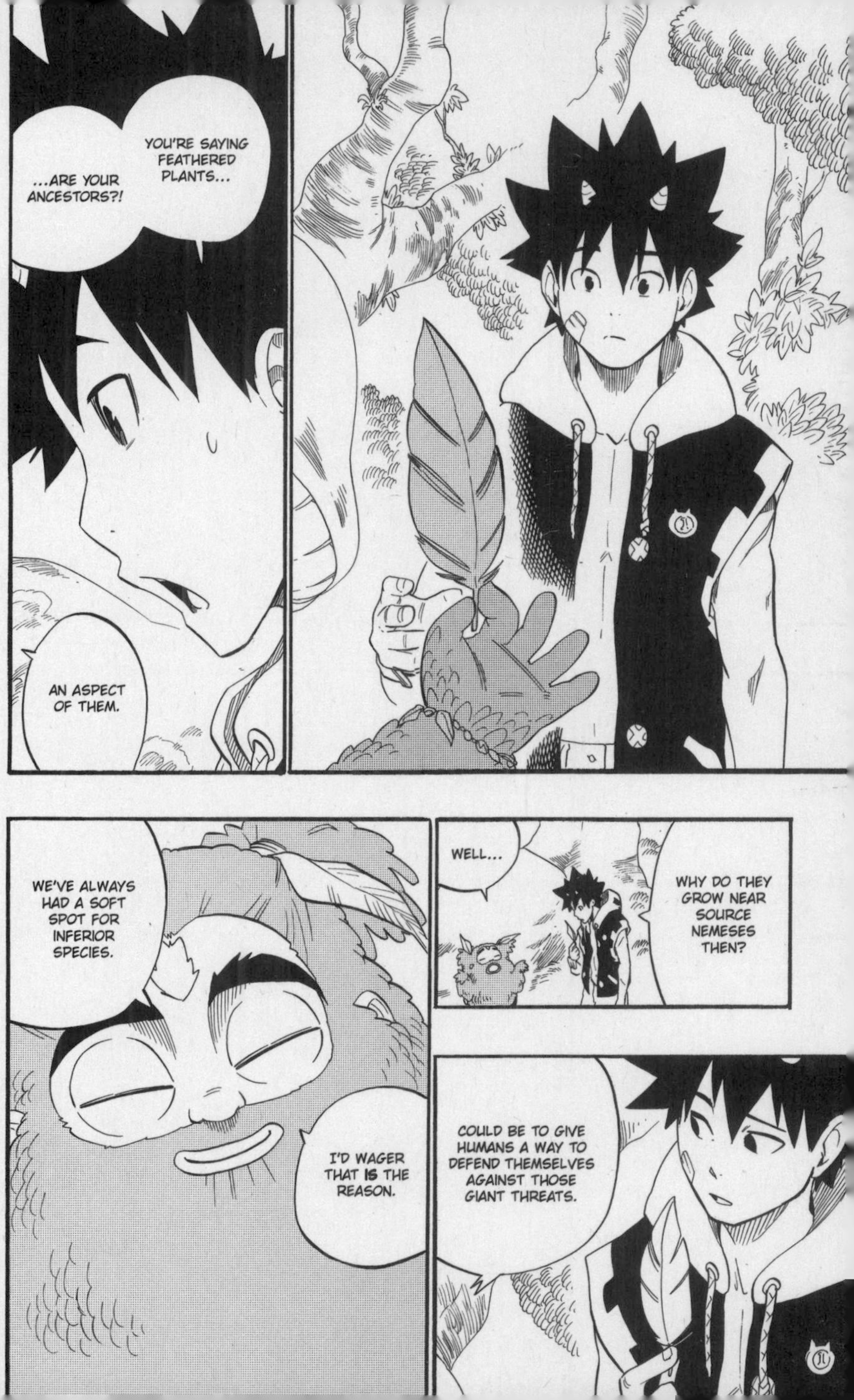
YOU'RE SAYING FEATHERED PLANTS...
...ARE YOUR ANCESTORS?!
AN ASPECT OF THEM.
WHY DO THEY GROW NEAR SOURCE NEMESES THEN?
WELL...
COULD BE TO GIVE HUMANS A WAY TO DEFEND THEMSELVES AGAINST THOSE GIANT THREATS.
I'D WAGER THAT IS THE REASON.
WE'VE ALWAYS HAD A SOFT SPOT FOR INFERIOR SPECIES.

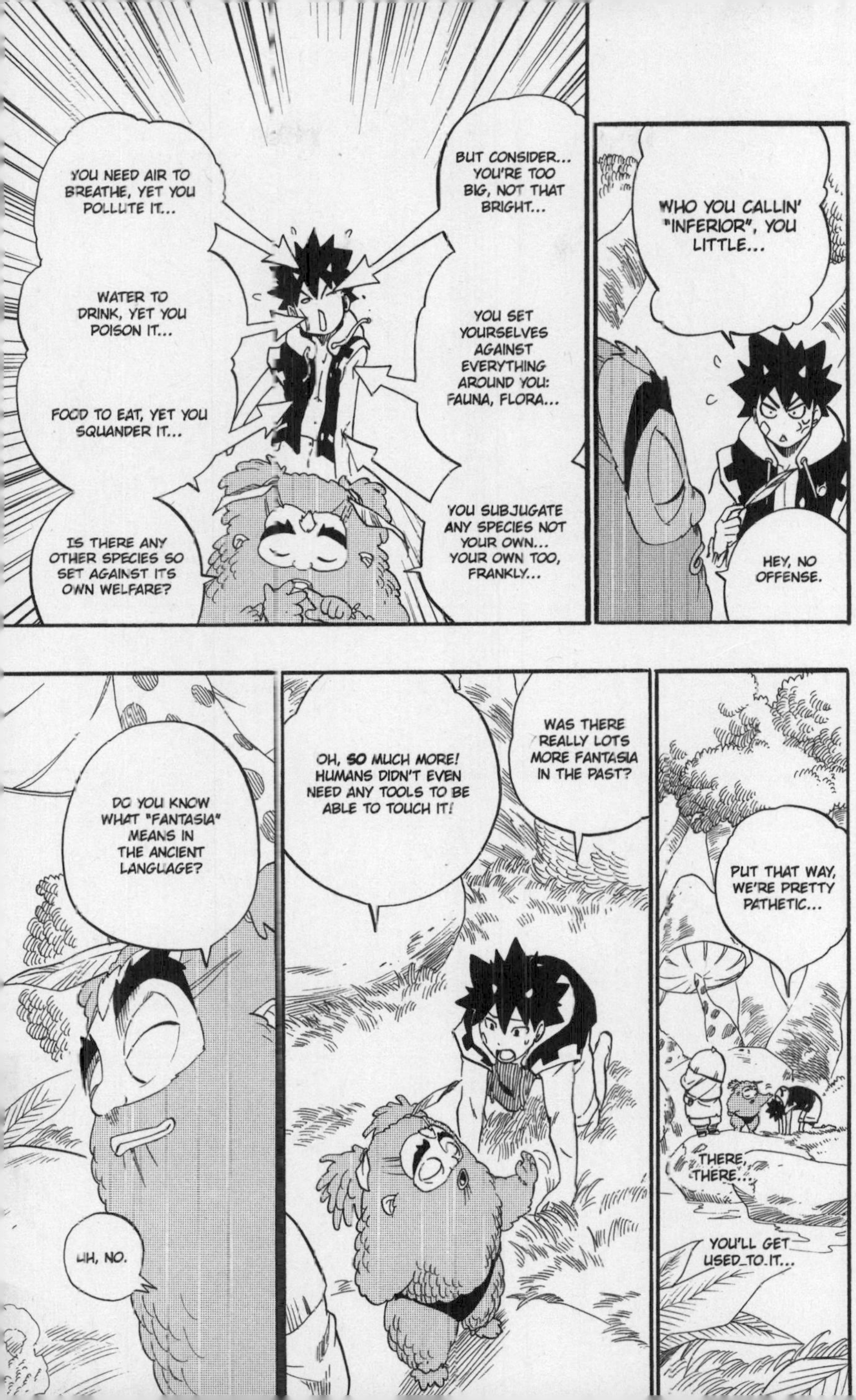
WHO YOU CALLIN' "INFERIOR", YOU LITTLE...
HEY, NO OFFENSE.
BUT CONSIDER... YOU'RE TOO BIG, NOT THAT BRIGHT...
YOU SET YOURSELVES AGAINST EVERYTHING AROUND YOU: FAUNA, FLORA...
YOU SUBJUGATE ANY SPECIES NOT YOUR OWN... YOUR OWN TOO, FRANKLY...
YOU NEED AIR TO BREATHE, YET YOU POLLUTE IT...
WATER TO DRINK, YET YOU POISON IT...
FOOD TO EAT, YET YOU SQUANDER IT...
IS THERE ANY OTHER SPECIES SO SET AGAINST ITS OWN WELFARE?
PUT THAT WAY, WE'RE PRETTY PATHETIC...
THERE, THERE...
YOU'LL GET USED TO IT...
WAS THERE REALLY LOTS MORE FANTASIA IN THE PAST?
OH, SO MUCH MORE! HUMANS DIDN'T EVEN NEED ANY TOOLS TO BE ABLE TO TOUCH IT!
DO YOU KNOW WHAT "FANTASIA" MEANS IN THE ANCIENT LANGUAGE?
UH, NO.

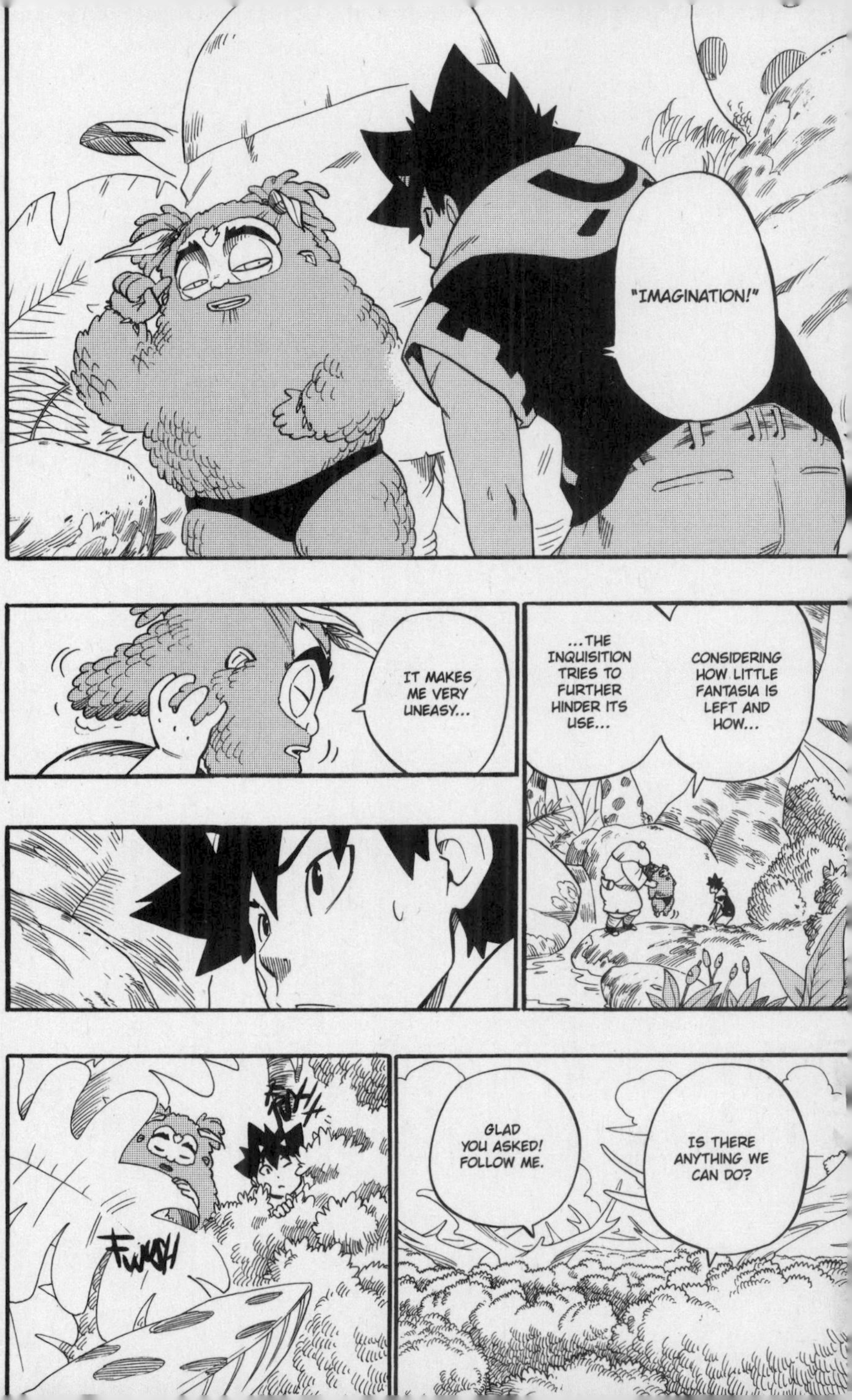
"IMAGINATION!"
CONSIDERING HOW LITTLE FANTASIA IS LEFT AND HOW...
...THE INQUISITION TRIES TO FURTHER HINDER ITS USE...
IT MAKES ME VERY UNEASY...
IS THERE ANYTHING WE CAN DO?
GLAD YOU ASKED! FOLLOW ME.
FWASH

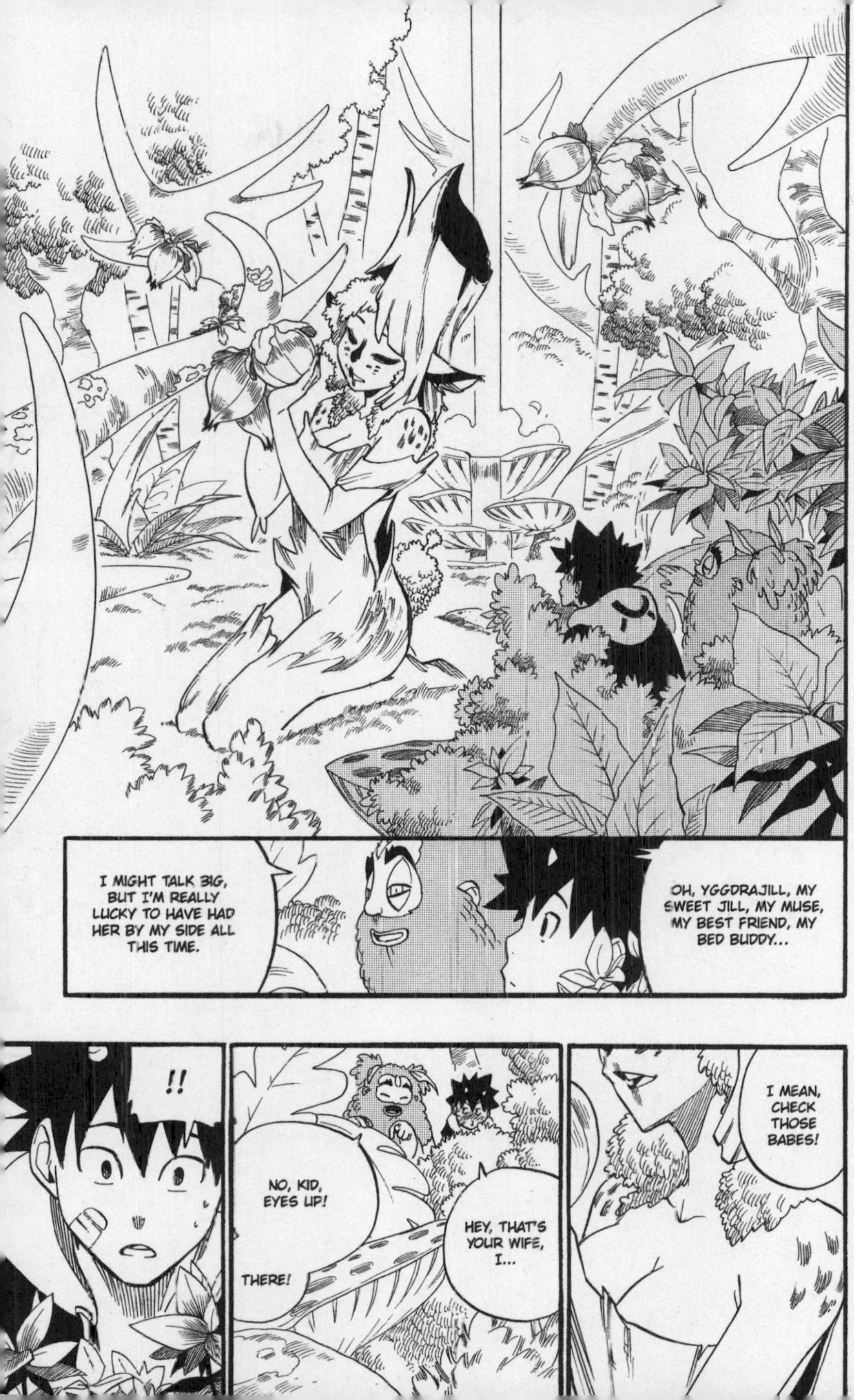
OH, YGGDRAJILL, MY SWEET JILL, MY MUSE, MY BEST FRIEND, MY BED BUDDY...
I MIGHT TALK BIG, BUT I'M REALLY LUCKY TO HAVE HAD HER BY MY SIDE ALL THIS TIME.
I MEAN, CHECK THOSE BABES!
HEY, THAT'S YOUR WIFE, I...
NO, KID, EYES UP!
THERE!
!!

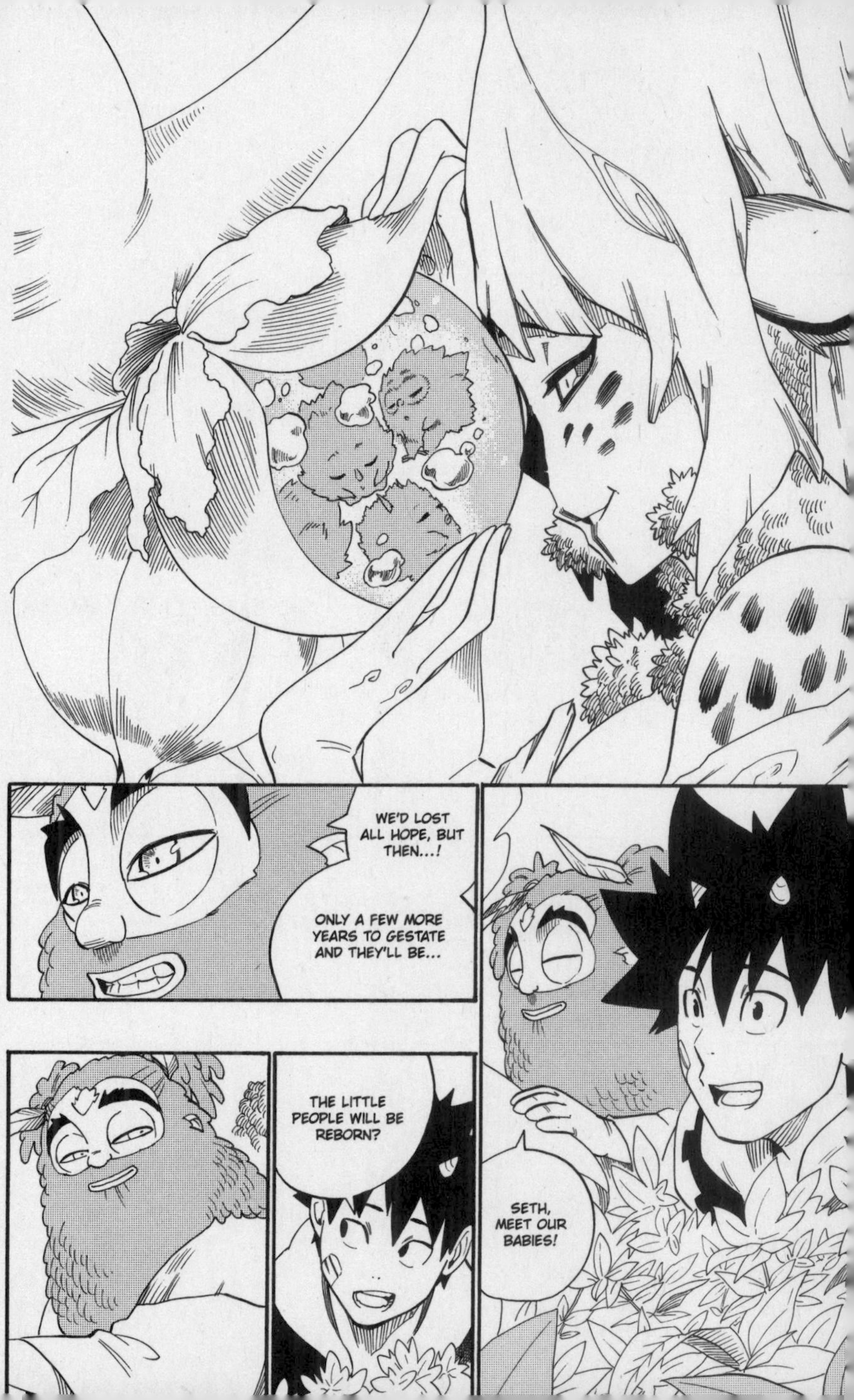
SETH, MEET OUR BABIES!
WE'D LOST ALL HOPE, BUT THEN...!
ONLY A FEW MORE YEARS TO GESTATE AND THEY'LL BE...
THE LITTLE PEOPLE WILL BE REBORN?

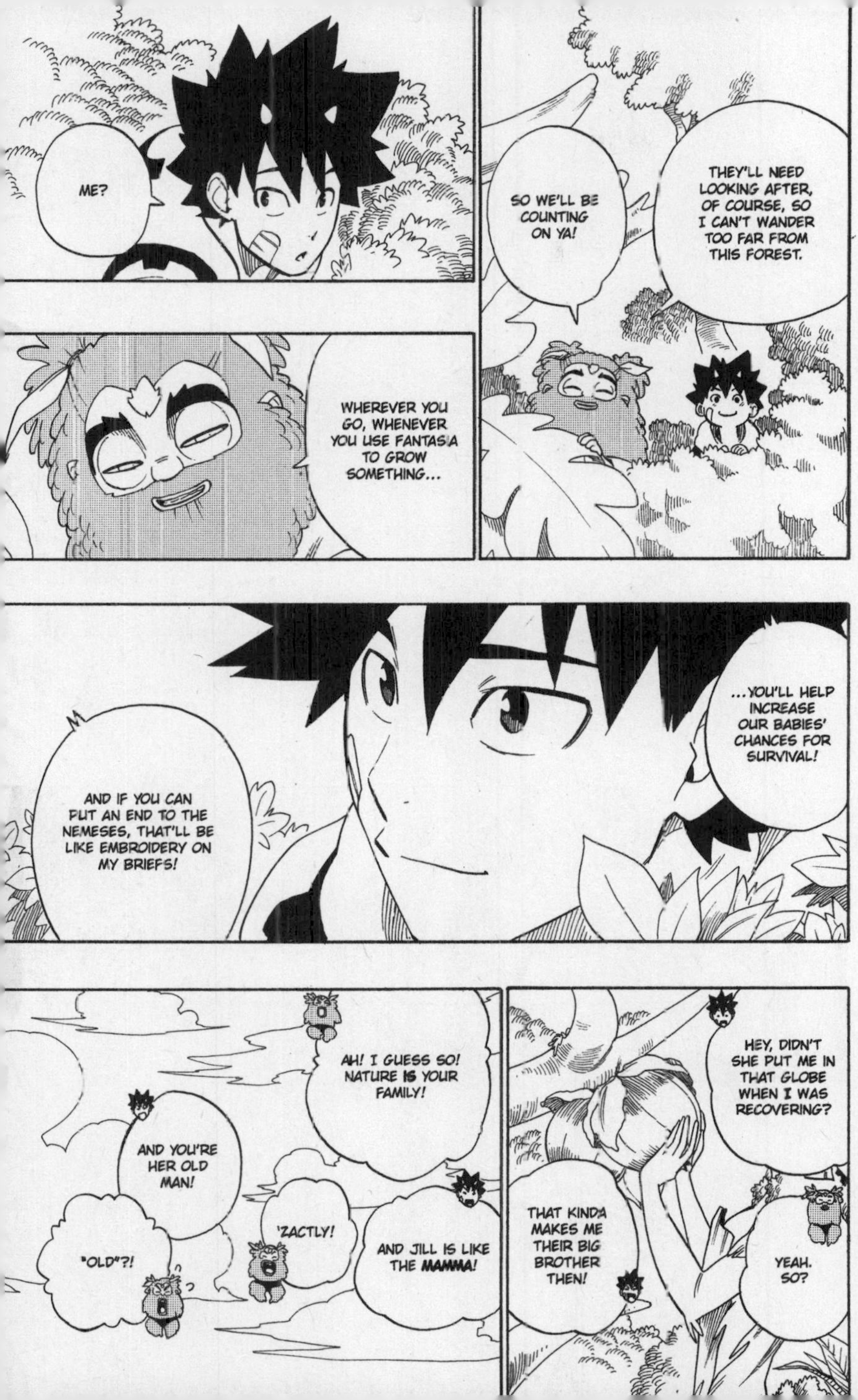
THEY'LL NEED LOOKING AFTER, OF COURSE, SO I CAN'T WANDER TOO FAR FROM THIS FOREST.
SO WE'LL BE COUNTING ON YA!
ME?
WHEREVER YOU GO, WHENEVER YOU USE FANTASIA TO GROW SOMETHING...
...YOU'LL HELP INCREASE OUR BABIES' CHANCES FOR SURVIVAL!
AND IF YOU CAN PUT AN END TO THE NEMESES, THAT'LL BE LIKE EMBROIDERY ON MY BRIEFS!
HEY, DIDN'T SHE PUT ME IN THAT GLOBE WHEN I WAS RECOVERING?
YEAH. SO?
THAT KINDA MAKES ME THEIR BIG BROTHER THEN!
AH! I GUESS SO! NATURE IS YOUR FAMILY!
AND YOU'RE HER OLD MAN!
AND JILL IS LIKE THE MAMMA!
'ZACTLY!
"OLD"?!

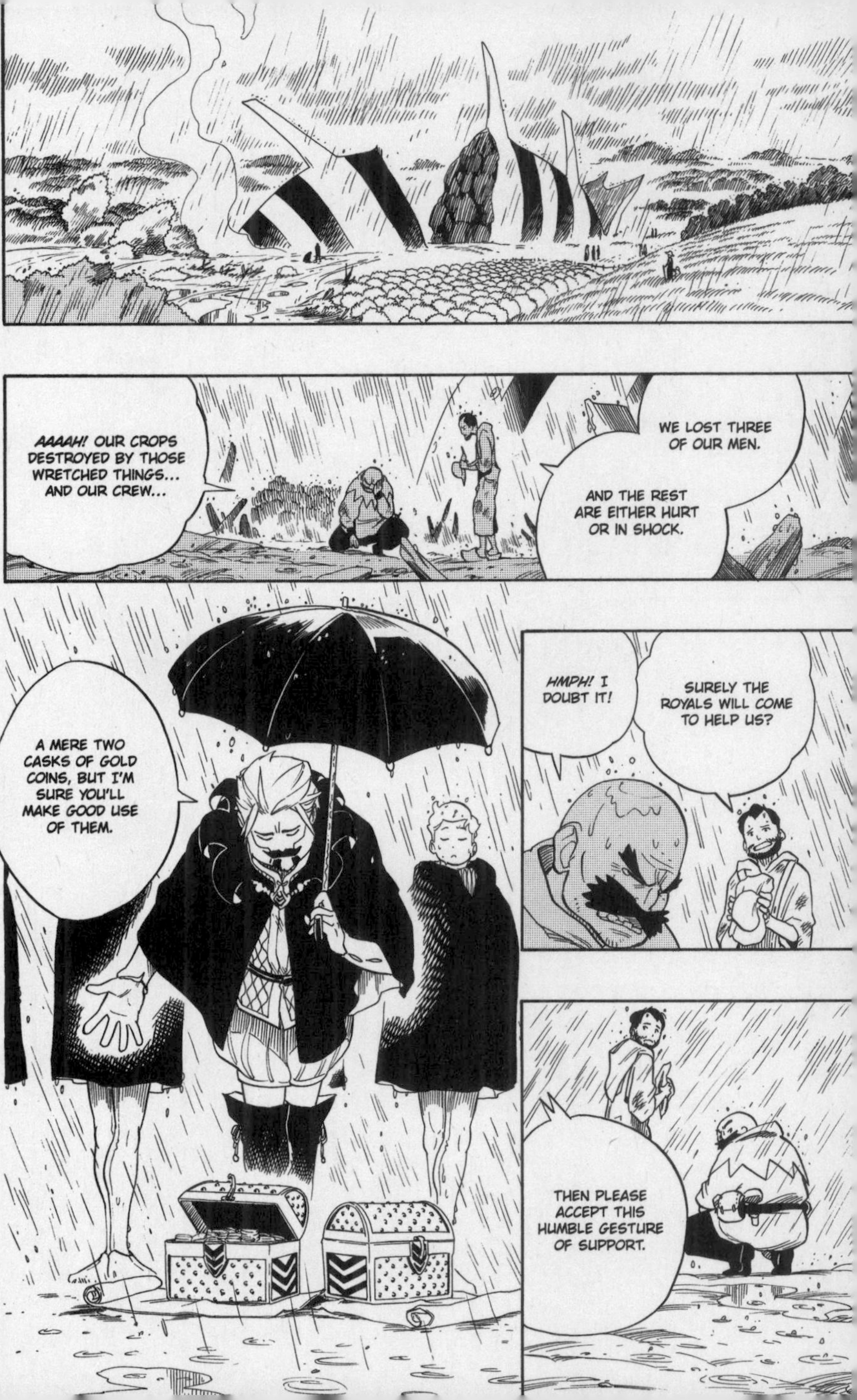
WE LOST THREE OF OUR MEN.
AND THE REST ARE EITHER HURT OR IN SHOCK.
AAAAH! OUR CROPS DESTROYED BY THOSE WRETCHED THINGS... AND OUR CREW...
SURELY THE ROYALS WILL COME TO HELP US?
HMPH! I DOUBT IT!
THEN PLEASE ACCEPT THIS HUMBLE GESTURE OF SUPPORT.
A MERE TWO CASKS OF GOLD COINS, BUT I'M SURE YOU'LL MAKE GOOD USE OF THEM.

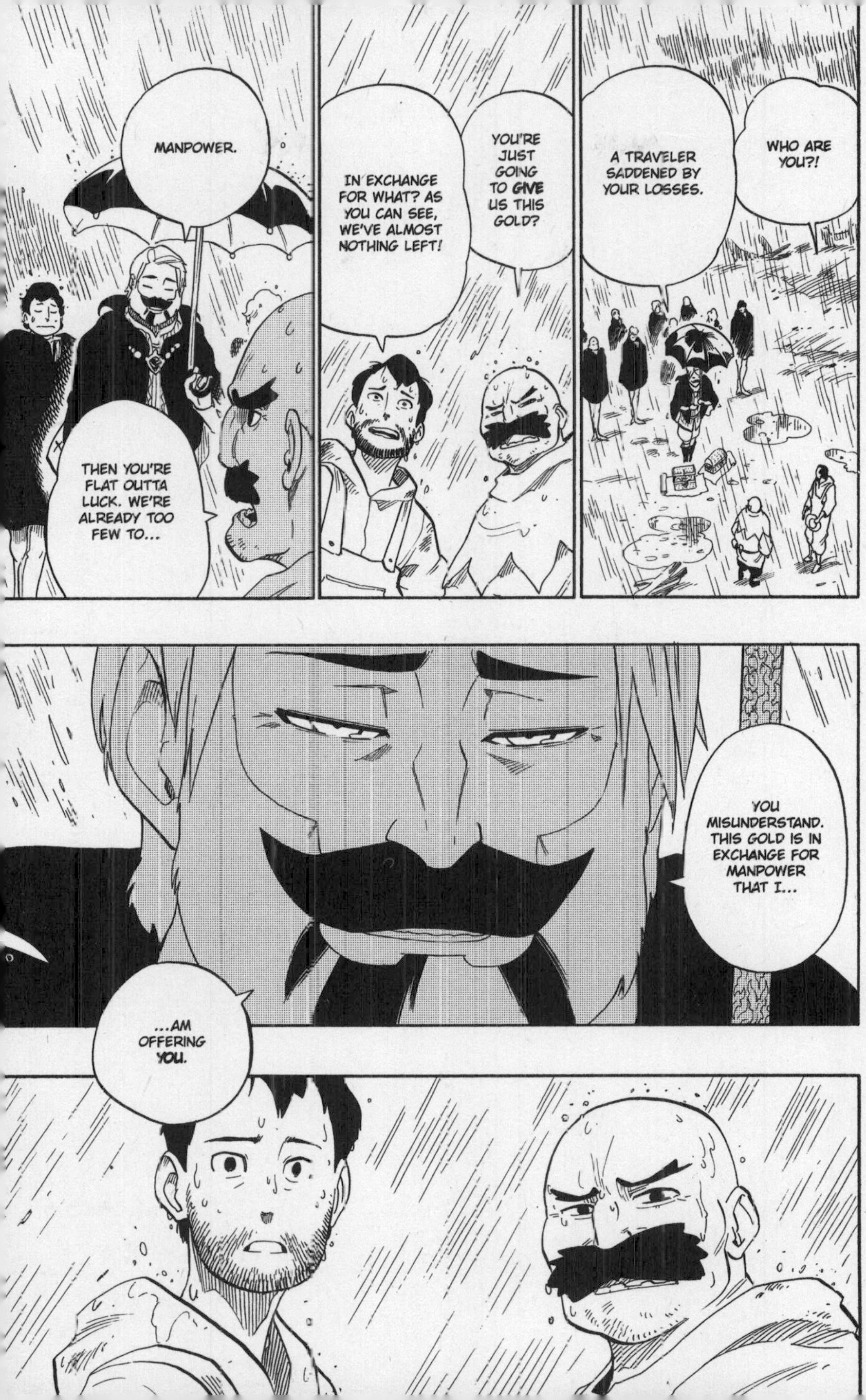
WHO ARE YOU?!
A TRAVELER SADDENED BY YOUR LOSSES.
YOU'RE JUST GOING TO GIVE US THIS GOLD?
IN EXCHANGE FOR WHAT? AS YOU CAN SEE, WE'VE ALMOST NOTHING LEFT!
MANPOWER.
THEN YOU'RE FLAT OUTTA LUCK. WE'RE ALREADY TOO FEW TO...
YOU MISUNDERSTAND. THIS GOLD IS IN EXCHANGE FOR MANPOWER THAT I...
...AM OFFERING YOU.

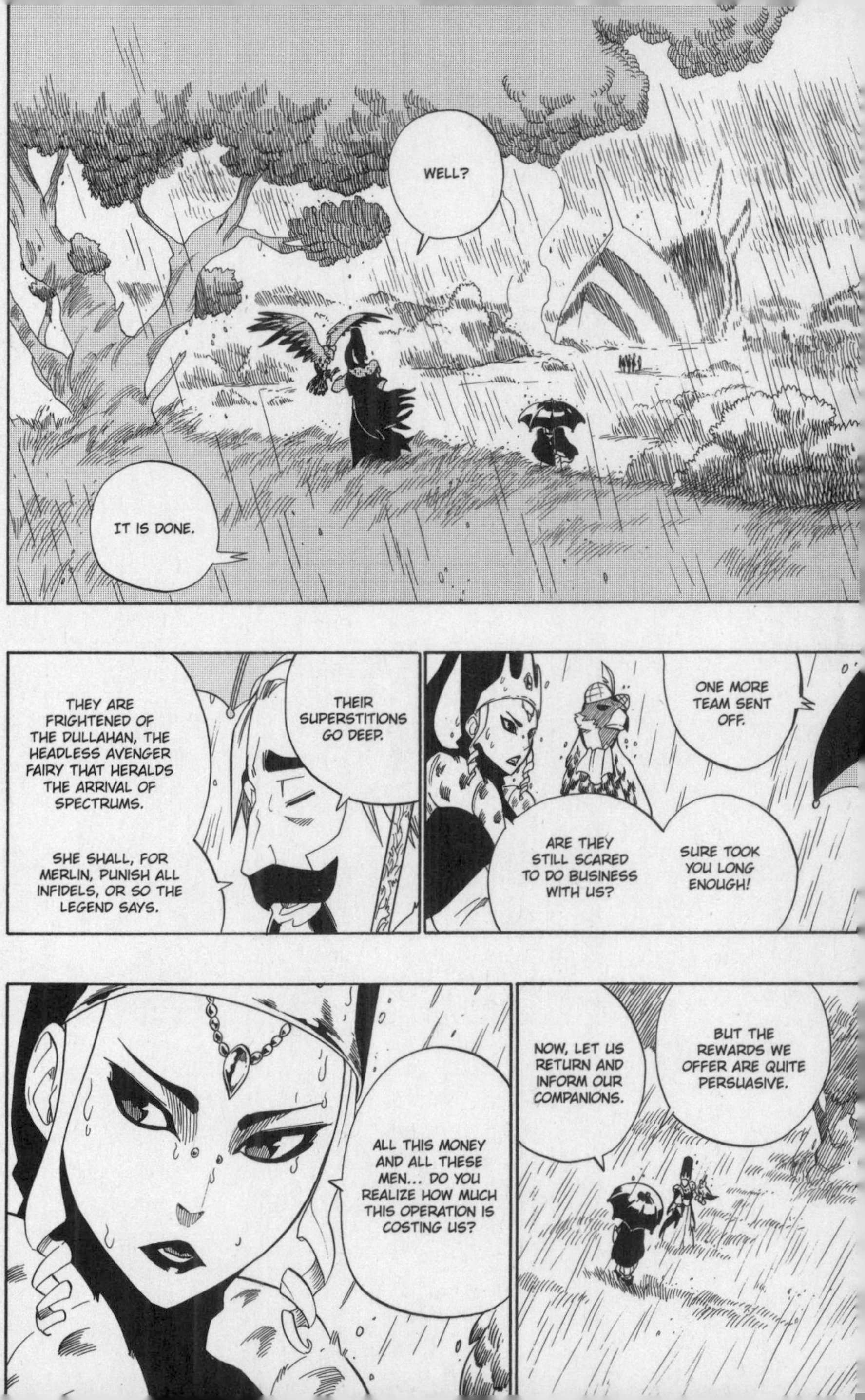
WELL?
IT IS DONE.
ONE MORE TEAM SENT OFF.
SURE TOOK YOU LONG ENOUGH!
ARE THEY STILL SCARED TO DO BUSINESS WITH US?
THEIR SUPERSTITIONS GO DEEP.
THEY ARE FRIGHTENED OF THE DULLAHAN, THE HEADLESS AVENGER FAIRY THAT HERALDS THE ARRIVAL OF SPECTRUMS.
SHE SHALL, FOR MERLIN, PUNISH ALL INFIDELS, OR SO THE LEGEND SAYS.
BUT THE REWARDS WE OFFER ARE QUITE PERSUASIVE.
NOW, LET US RETURN AND INFORM OUR COMPANIONS.
ALL THIS MONEY AND ALL THESE MEN... DO YOU REALIZE HOW MUCH THIS OPERATION IS COSTING US?

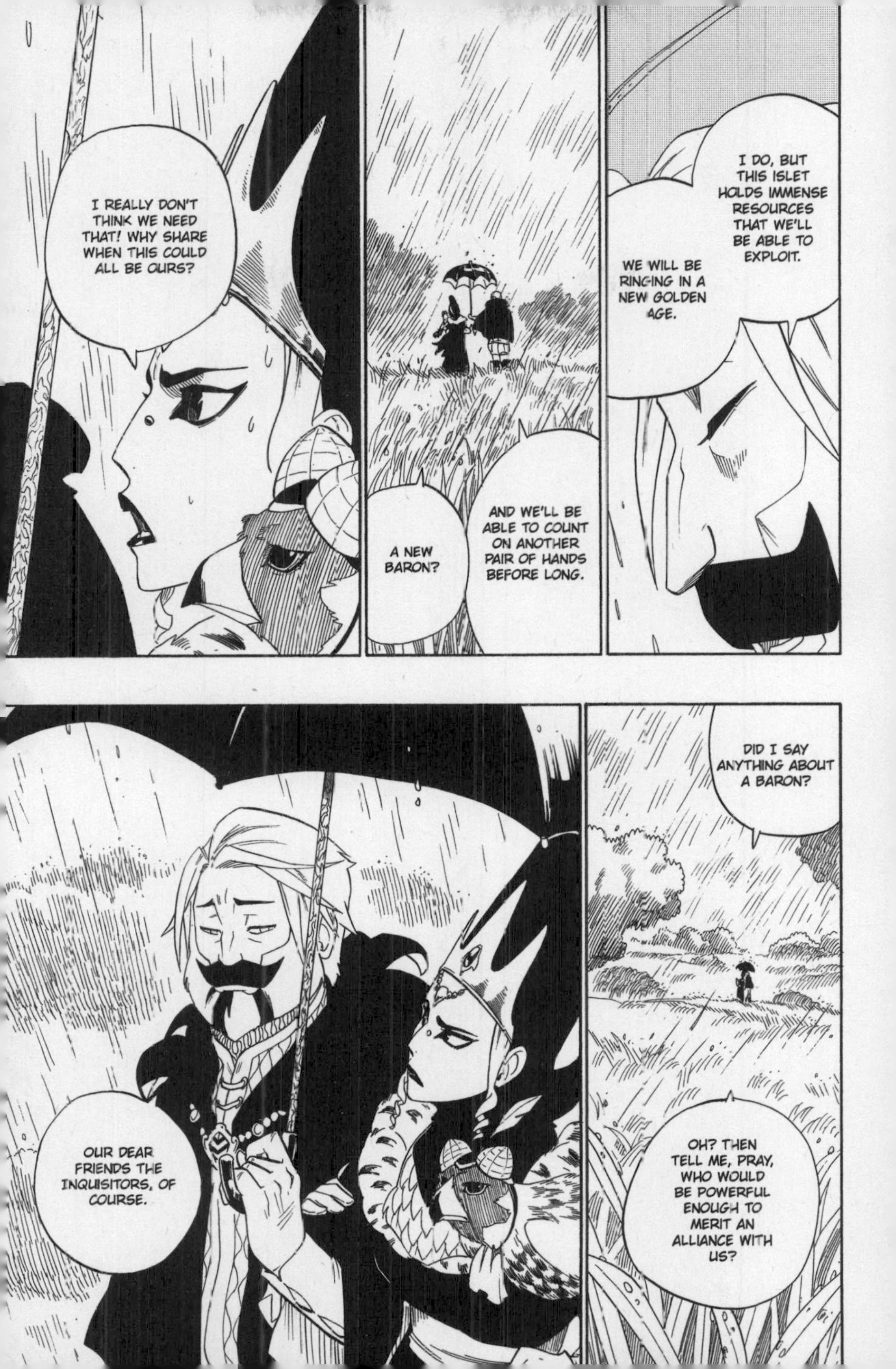
I DO, BUT THIS ISLET HOLDS IMMENSE RESOURCES THAT WE'LL BE ABLE TO EXPLOIT.
WE WILL BE RINGING IN A NEW GOLDEN AGE.
AND WE'LL BE ABLE TO COUNT ON ANOTHER PAIR OF HANDS BEFORE LONG.
A NEW BARON?
I REALLY DON'T THINK WE NEED THAT! WHY SHARE WHEN THIS COULD ALL BE OURS?
DID I SAY ANYTHING ABOUT A BARON?
OH? THEN TELL ME, PRAY, WHO WOULD BE POWERFUL ENOUGH TO MERIT AN ALLIANCE WITH US?
OUR DEAR FRIENDS THE INQUISITORS, OF COURSE.

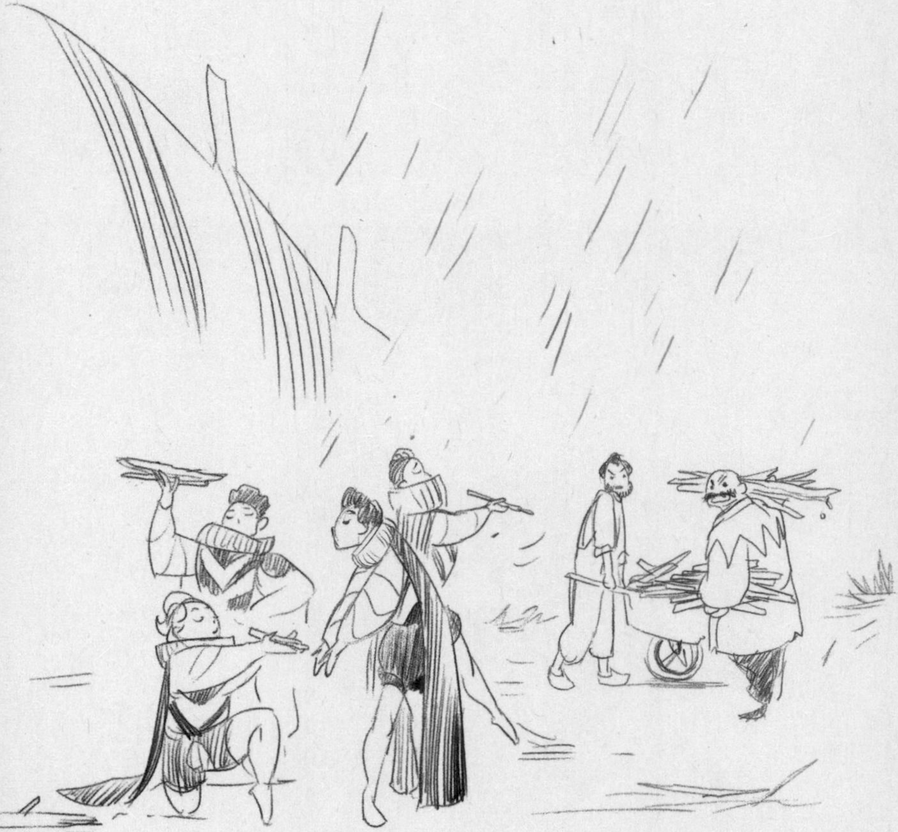

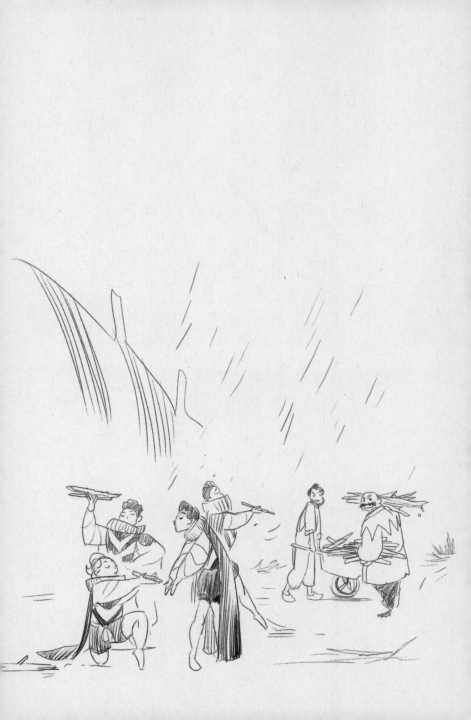

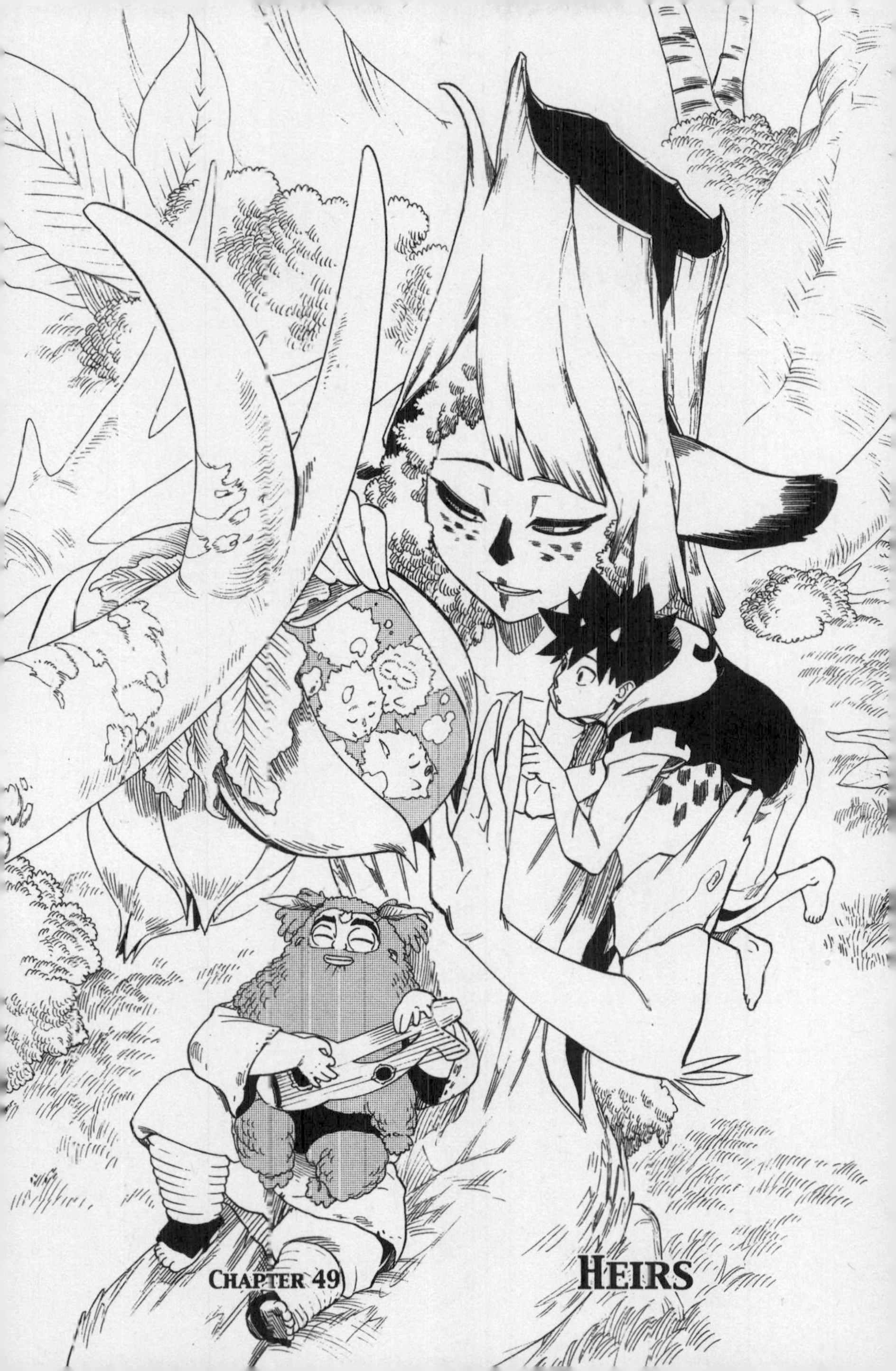
CHAPTER 49
HEIRS

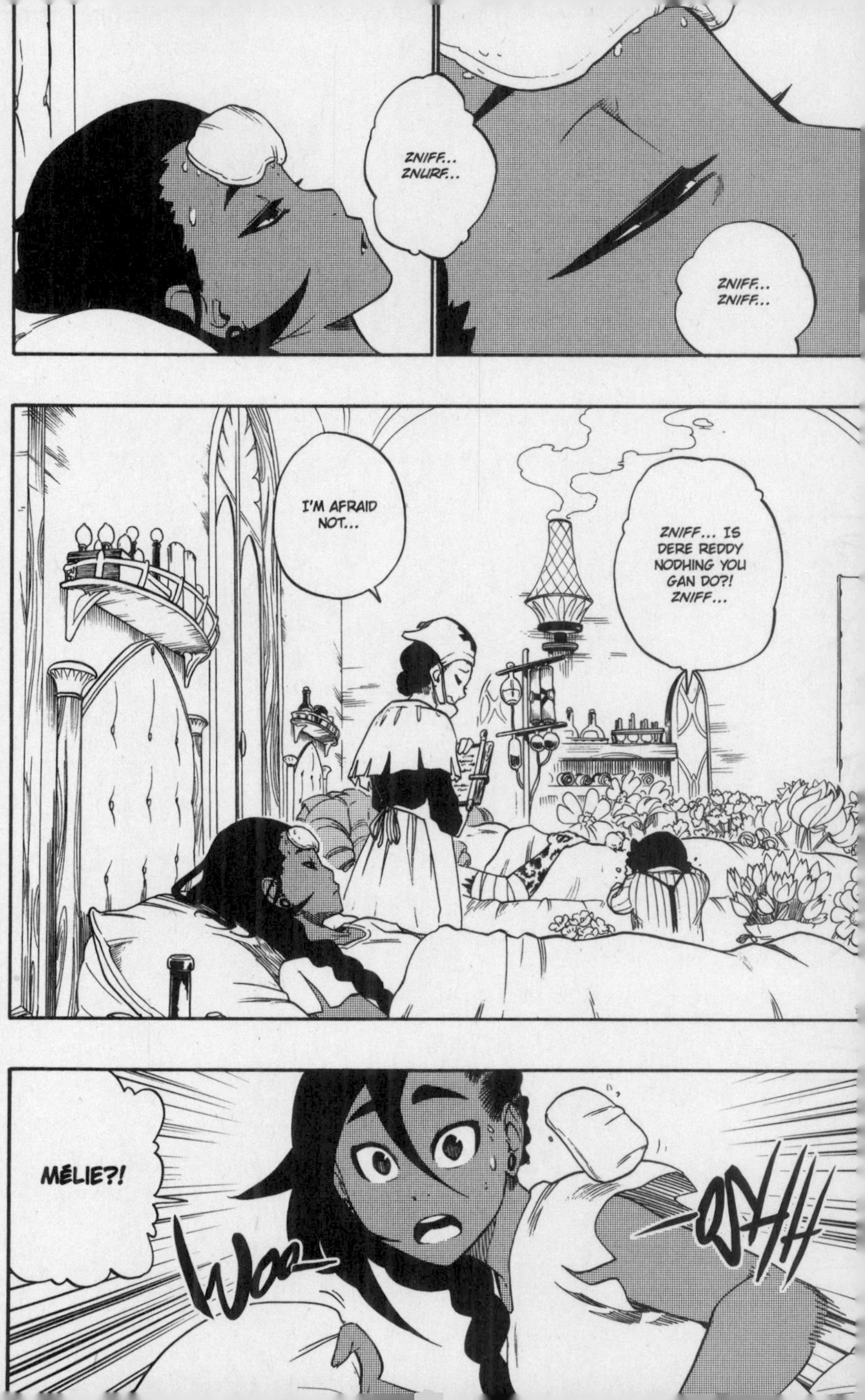
ZNIFF... ZNIFF...
ZNIFF... ZNURF...
ZNIFF... IS DERE REDDY NODHING YOU GAN DO?! ZNIFF...
I'M AFRAID NOT...
MÉLIE?!

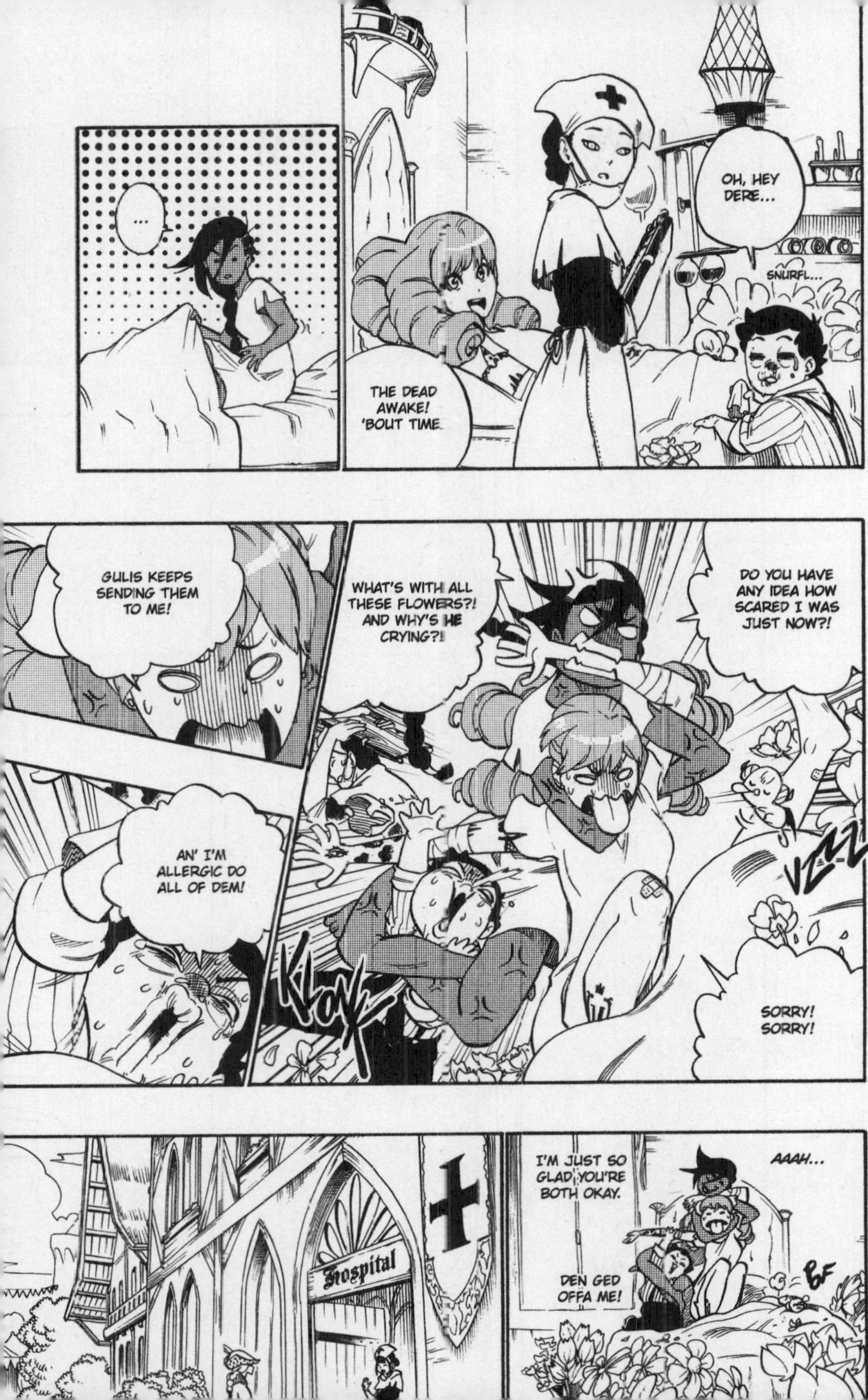
OH, HEY DERE...
SNURFL...
THE DEAD AWAKE! 'BOUT TIME.
...
DO YOU HAVE ANY IDEA HOW SCARED I WAS JUST NOW?!
WHAT'S WITH ALL THESE FLOWERS?! AND WHY'S HE CRYING?!
VZZZ
SORRY! SORRY!
KLONK
GULIS KEEPS SENDING THEM TO ME!
AN' I'M ALLERGIC DO ALL OF DEM!
AAAH...
I'M JUST SO GLAD YOU'RE BOTH OKAY.
DEN GED OFFA ME!
Hospital

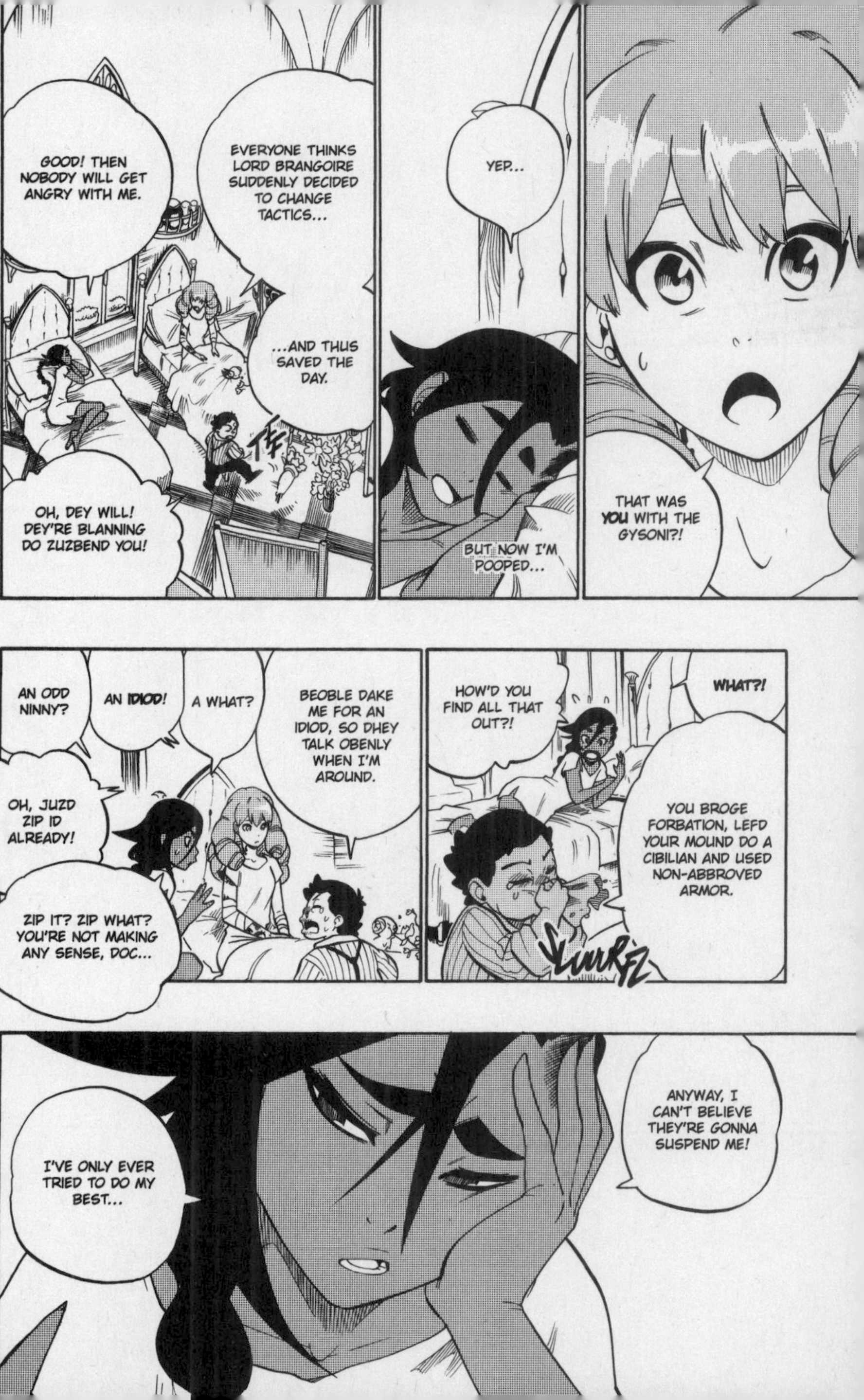
THAT WAS YOU WITH THE GYSONI?!
YEP...
BUT NOW I'M POOPED...
EVERYONE THINKS LORD BRANGOIRE SUDDENLY DECIDED TO CHANGE TACTICS...
...AND THUS SAVED THE DAY.
GOOD! THEN NOBODY WILL GET ANGRY WITH ME.
OH, DEY WILL! DEY'RE BLANNING DO ZUZBEND YOU!
WHAT?!
HOW'D YOU FIND ALL THAT OUT?!
YOU BROGE FORBATION, LEFD YOUR MOUND DO A CIBILIAN AND USED NON-ABBROVED ARMOR.
BEOBLE DAKE ME FOR AN IDIOD, SO DHEY TALK OBENLY WHEN I'M AROUND.
A WHAT?
AN IDIOD!
AN ODD NINNY?
OH, JUZD ZIP ID ALREADY!
ZIP IT? ZIP WHAT? YOU'RE NOT MAKING ANY SENSE, DOC...
ANYWAY, I CAN'T BELIEVE THEY'RE GONNA SUSPEND ME!
I'VE ONLY EVER TRIED TO DO MY BEST...

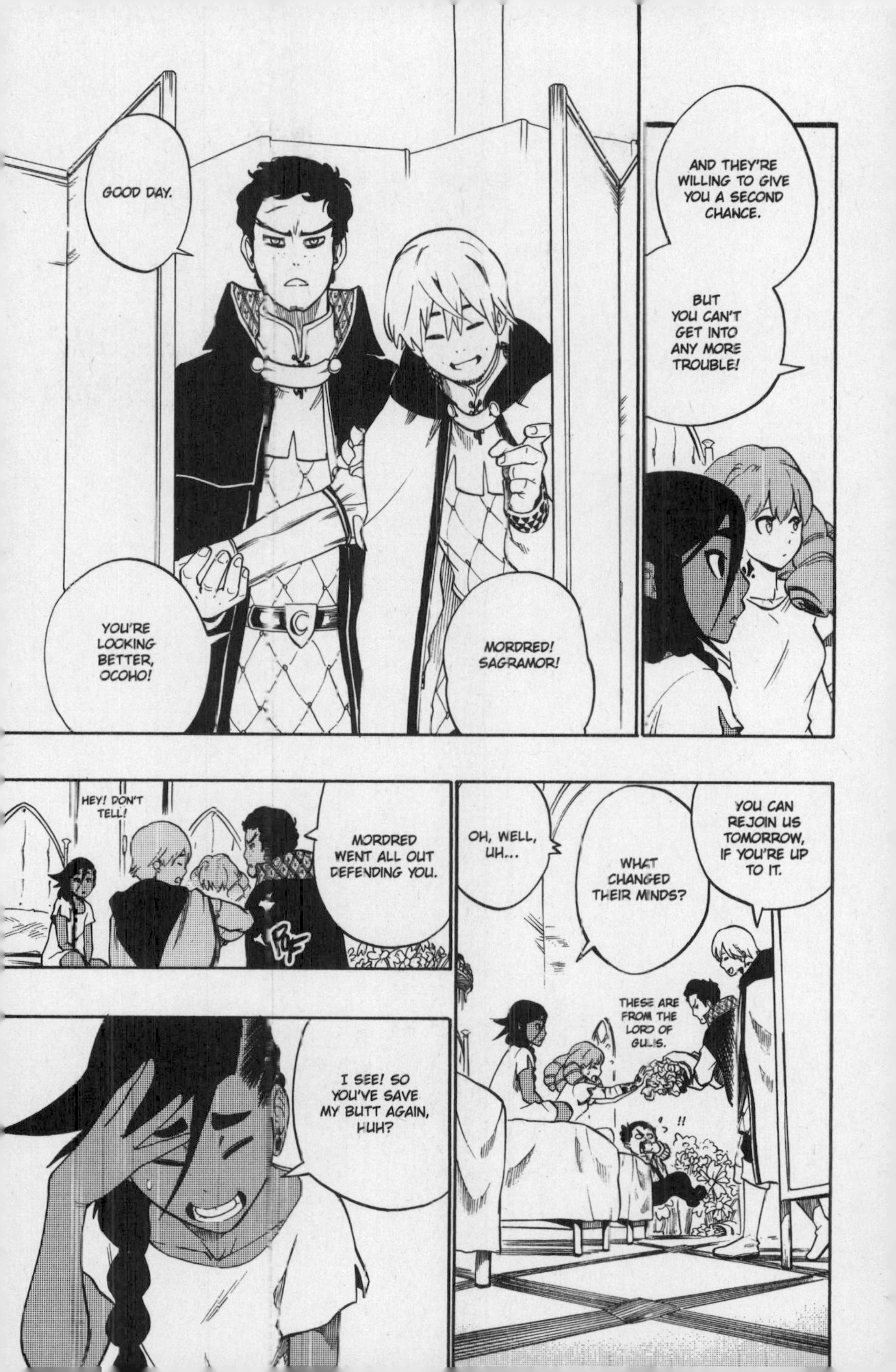
AND THEY'RE WILLING TO GIVE YOU A SECOND CHANCE.
BUT YOU CAN'T GET INTO ANY MORE TROUBLE!
MORDRED! SAGRAMOR!
GOOD DAY.
YOU'RE LOOKING BETTER, OCOHO!
YOU CAN REJOIN US TOMORROW, IF YOU'RE UP TO IT.
WHAT CHANGED THEIR MINDS?
OH, WELL, UH...
THESE ARE FROM THE LORD OF GULIS.
?! !!
MORDRED WENT ALL OUT DEFENDING YOU.
HEY! DON'T TELL!
POF
I SEE! SO YOU'VE SAVE MY BUTT AGAIN, HUH?

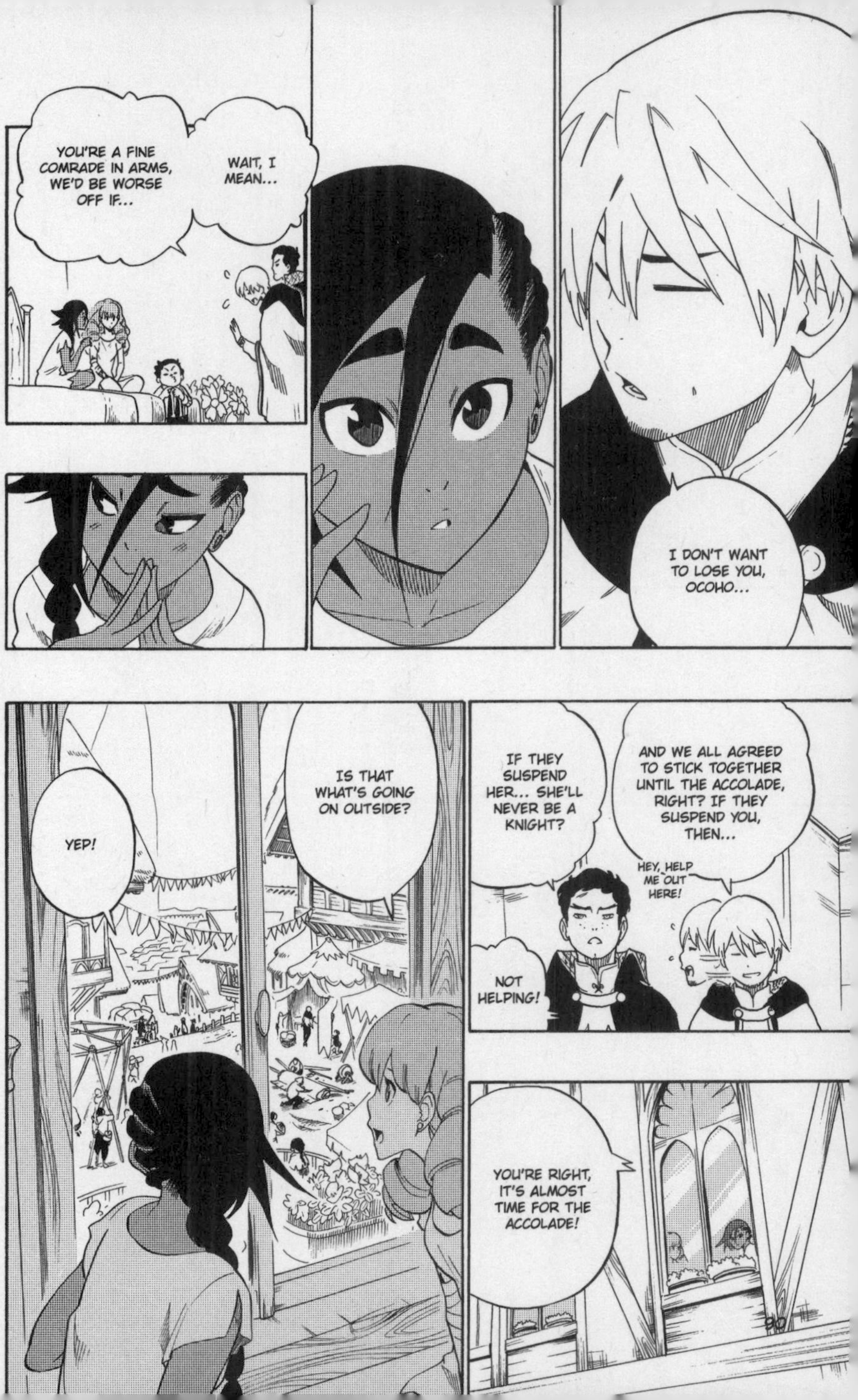
I DON'T WANT TO LOSE YOU, OCOHO...
YOU'RE A FINE COMRADE IN ARMS, WE'D BE WORSE OFF IF...
WAIT, I MEAN...
AND WE ALL AGREED TO STICK TOGETHER UNTIL THE ACCOLADE, RIGHT? IF THEY SUSPEND YOU, THEN...
IF THEY SUSPEND HER... SHE'LL NEVER BE A KNIGHT?
HEY, HELP ME OUT HERE!
NOT HELPING!
YOU'RE RIGHT, IT'S ALMOST TIME FOR THE ACCOLADE!
IS THAT WHAT'S GOING ON OUTSIDE?
YEP!

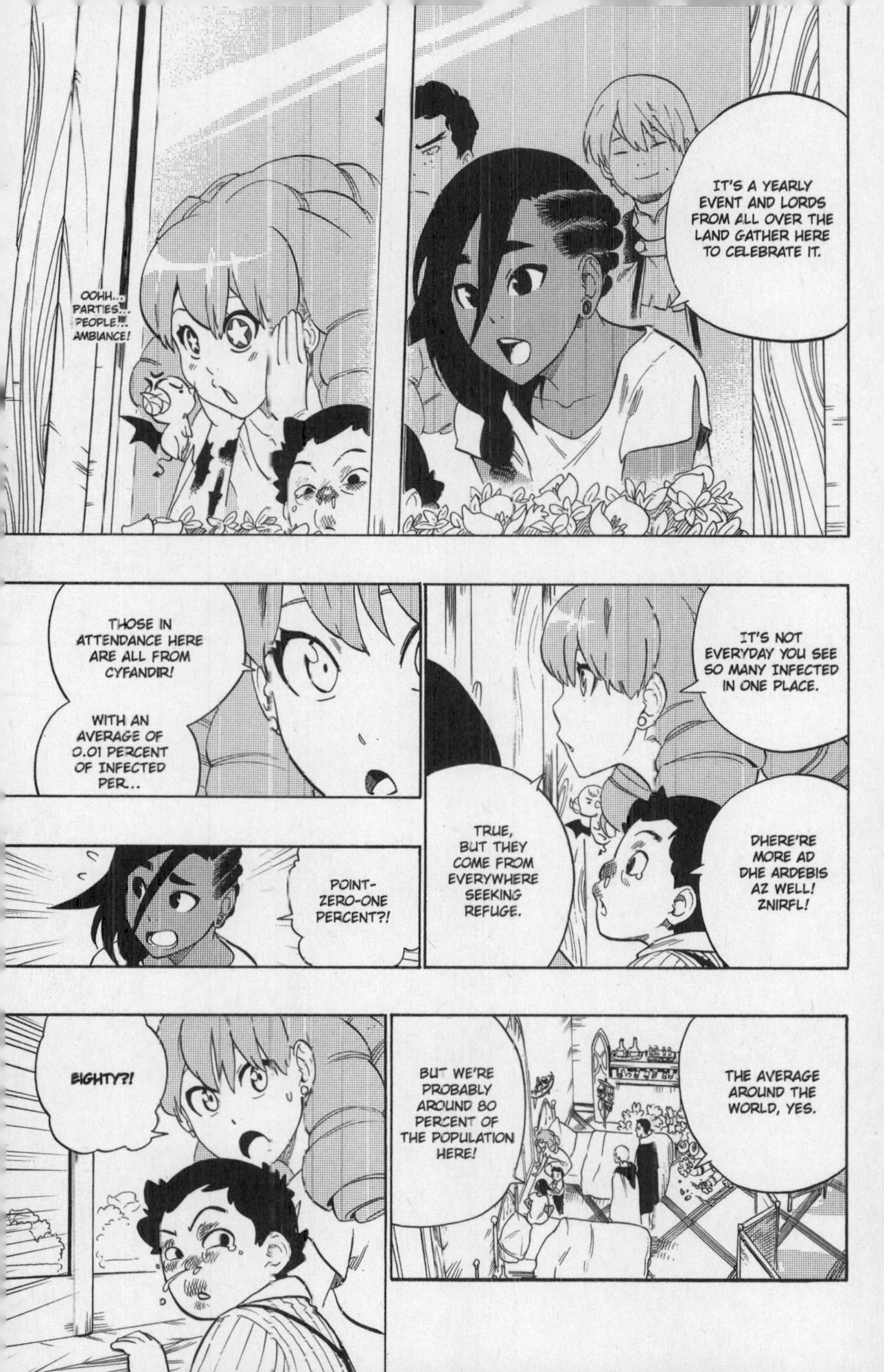
IT'S A YEARLY EVENT AND LORDS FROM ALL OVER THE LAND GATHER HERE TO CELEBRATE IT.
OOHH... PARTIES!... PEOPLE!... AMBIANCE!
IT'S NOT EVERYDAY YOU SEE SO MANY INFECTED IN ONE PLACE.
DHERE'RE MORE AD DHE ARDEBIS AZ WELL! ZNIRFL!
TRUE, BUT THEY COME FROM EVERYWHERE SEEKING REFUGE.
THOSE IN ATTENDANCE HERE ARE ALL FROM CYFANDIR!
WITH AN AVERAGE OF 0.01 PERCENT OF INFECTED PER...
POINT-ZERO-ONE PERCENT?!
THE AVERAGE AROUND THE WORLD, YES.
BUT WE'RE PROBABLY AROUND 80 PERCENT OF THE POPULATION HERE!
EIGHTY?!

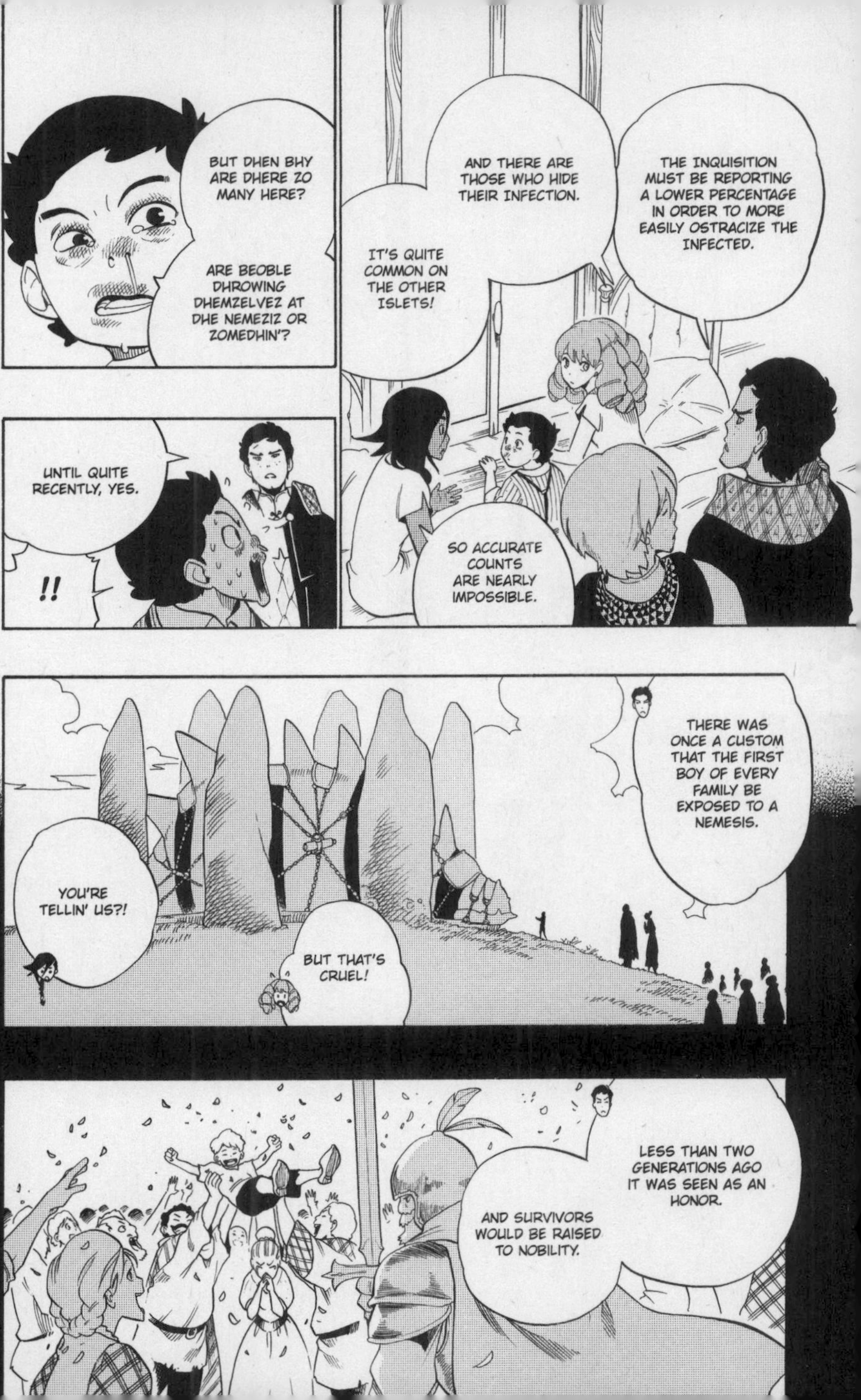
THE INQUISITION MUST BE REPORTING A LOWER PERCENTAGE IN ORDER TO MORE EASILY OSTRACIZE THE INFECTED.
AND THERE ARE THOSE WHO HIDE THEIR INFECTION.
IT'S QUITE COMMON ON THE OTHER ISLETS!
SO ACCURATE COUNTS ARE NEARLY IMPOSSIBLE.
BUT DHEN BHY ARE DHERE ZO MANY HERE?
ARE BEOBLE DHROWING DHEMZELVEZ AT DHE NEMEZIZ OR ZOMEDHIN'?
UNTIL QUITE RECENTLY, YES.
!!
THERE WAS ONCE A CUSTOM THAT THE FIRST BOY OF EVERY FAMILY BE EXPOSED TO A NEMESIS.
BUT THAT'S CRUEL!
YOU'RE TELLIN' US?!
LESS THAN TWO GENERATIONS AGO IT WAS SEEN AS AN HONOR.
AND SURVIVORS WOULD BE RAISED TO NOBILITY.

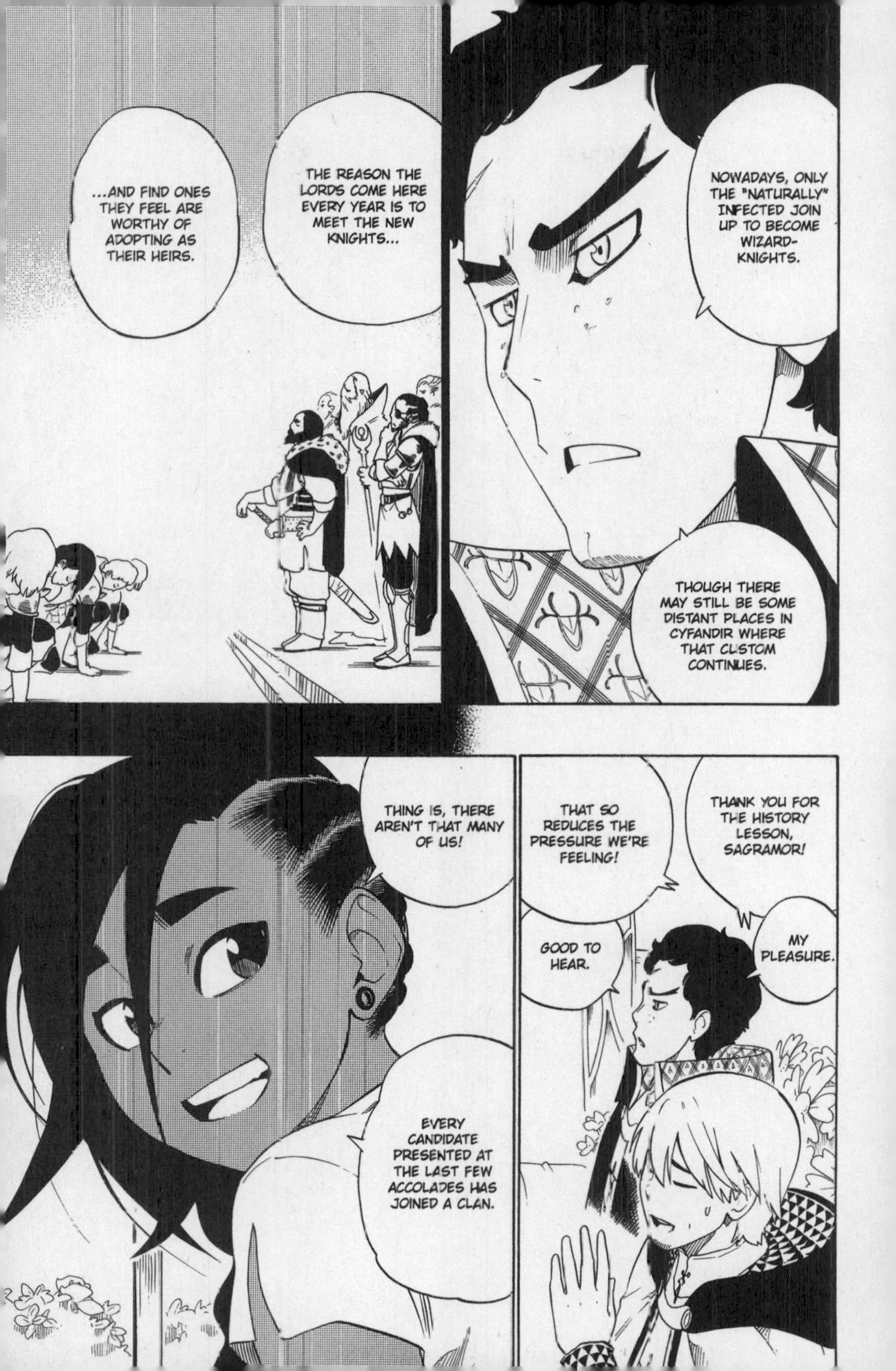
NOWADAYS, ONLY THE "NATURALLY" INFECTED JOIN UP TO BECOME WIZARD-KNIGHTS.
THOUGH THERE MAY STILL BE SOME DISTANT PLACES IN CYFANDIR WHERE THAT CUSTOM CONTINUES.
THE REASON THE LORDS COME HERE EVERY YEAR IS TO MEET THE NEW KNIGHTS...
...AND FIND ONES THEY FEEL ARE WORTHY OF ADOPTING AS THEIR HEIRS.
THANK YOU FOR THE HISTORY LESSON, SAGRAMOR!
THAT SO REDUCES THE PRESSURE WE'RE FEELING!
MY PLEASURE.
GOOD TO HEAR.
THING IS, THERE AREN'T THAT MANY OF US!
EVERY CANDIDATE PRESENTED AT THE LAST FEW ACCOLADES HAS JOINED A CLAN.

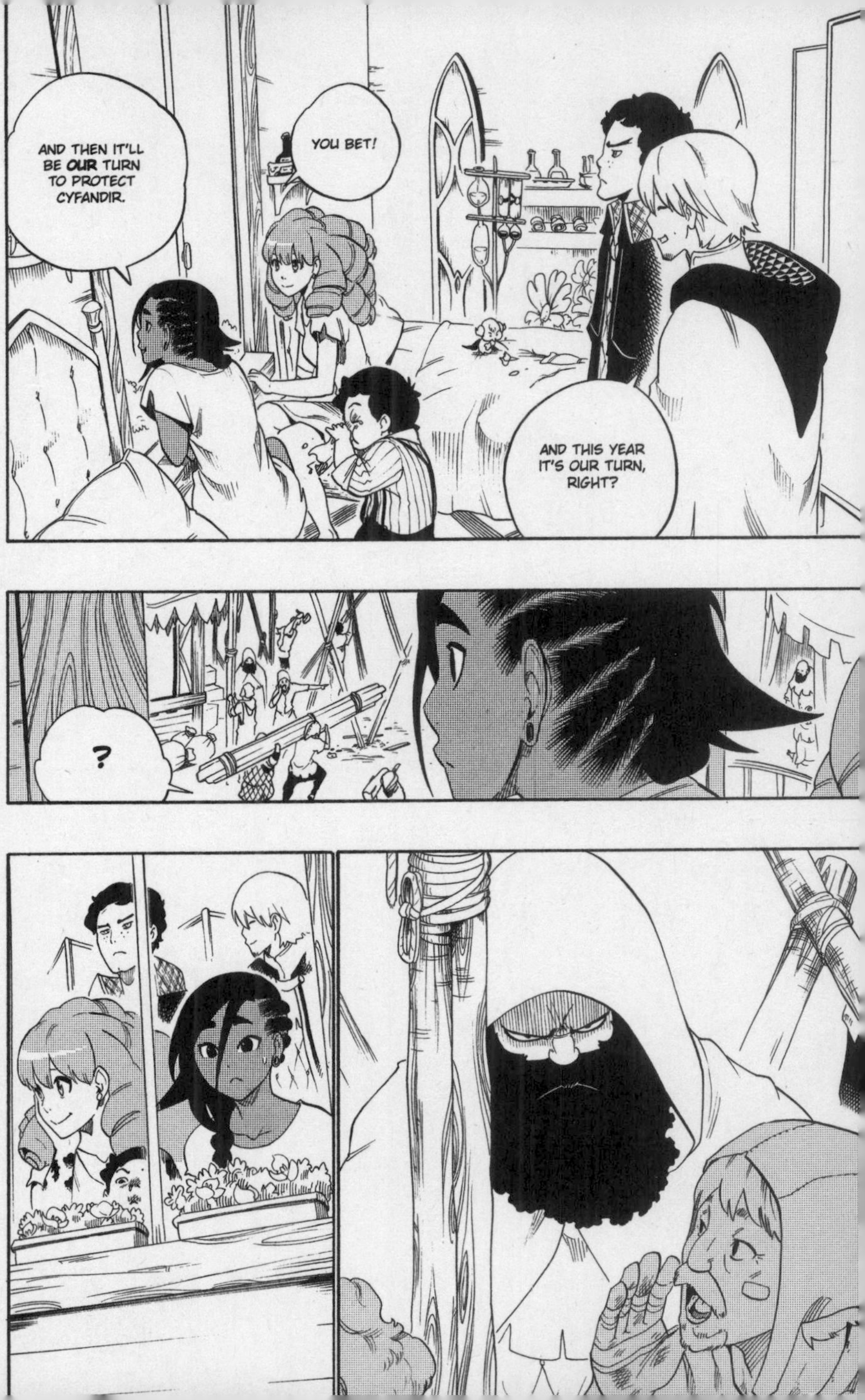
AND THIS YEAR IT'S OUR TURN, RIGHT?
YOU BET!
AND THEN IT'LL BE OUR TURN TO PROTECT CYFANDIR.
?

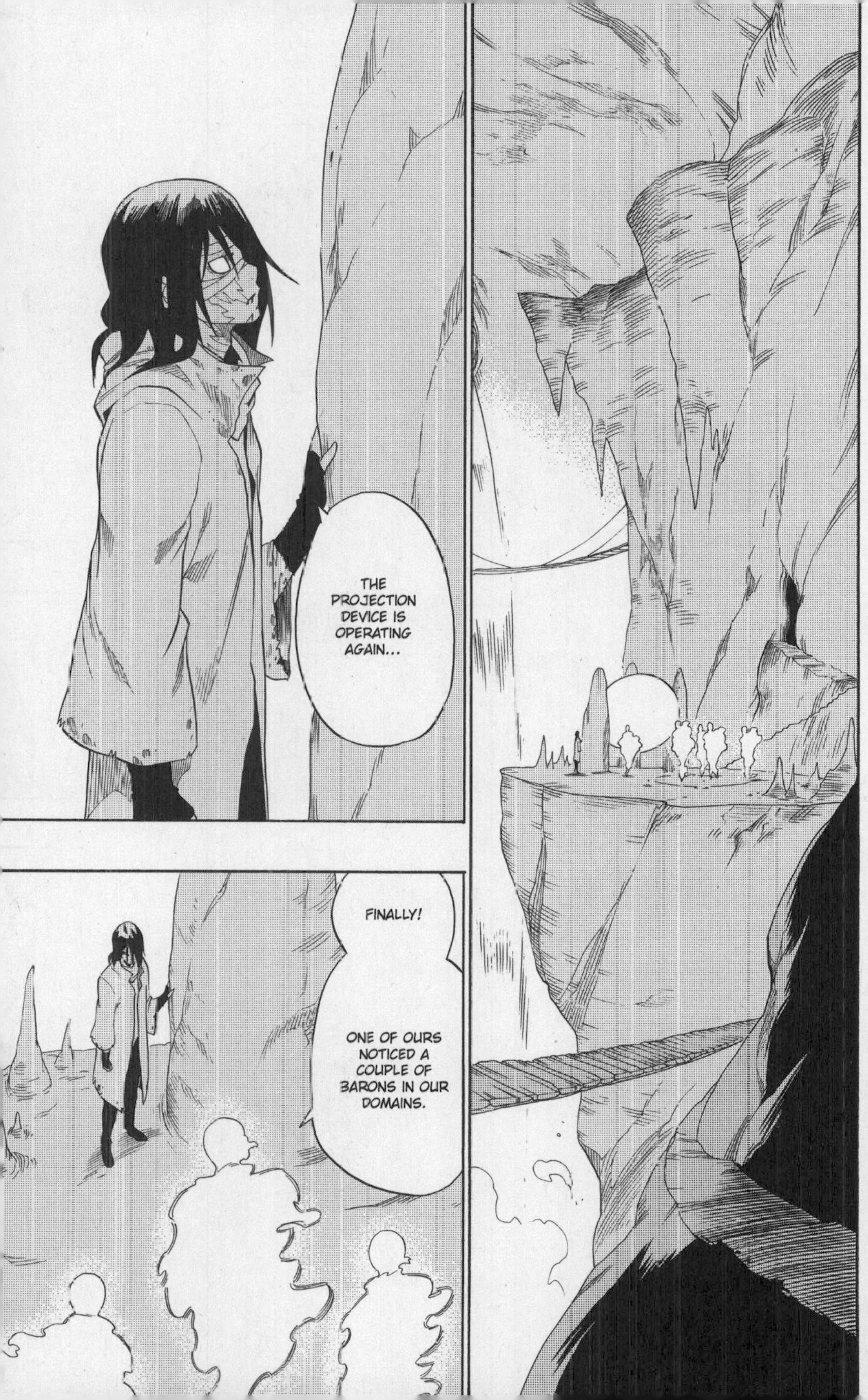
THE PROJECTION DEVICE IS OPERATING AGAIN...
FINALLY!
ONE OF OURS NOTICED A COUPLE OF BARONS IN OUR DOMAINS.

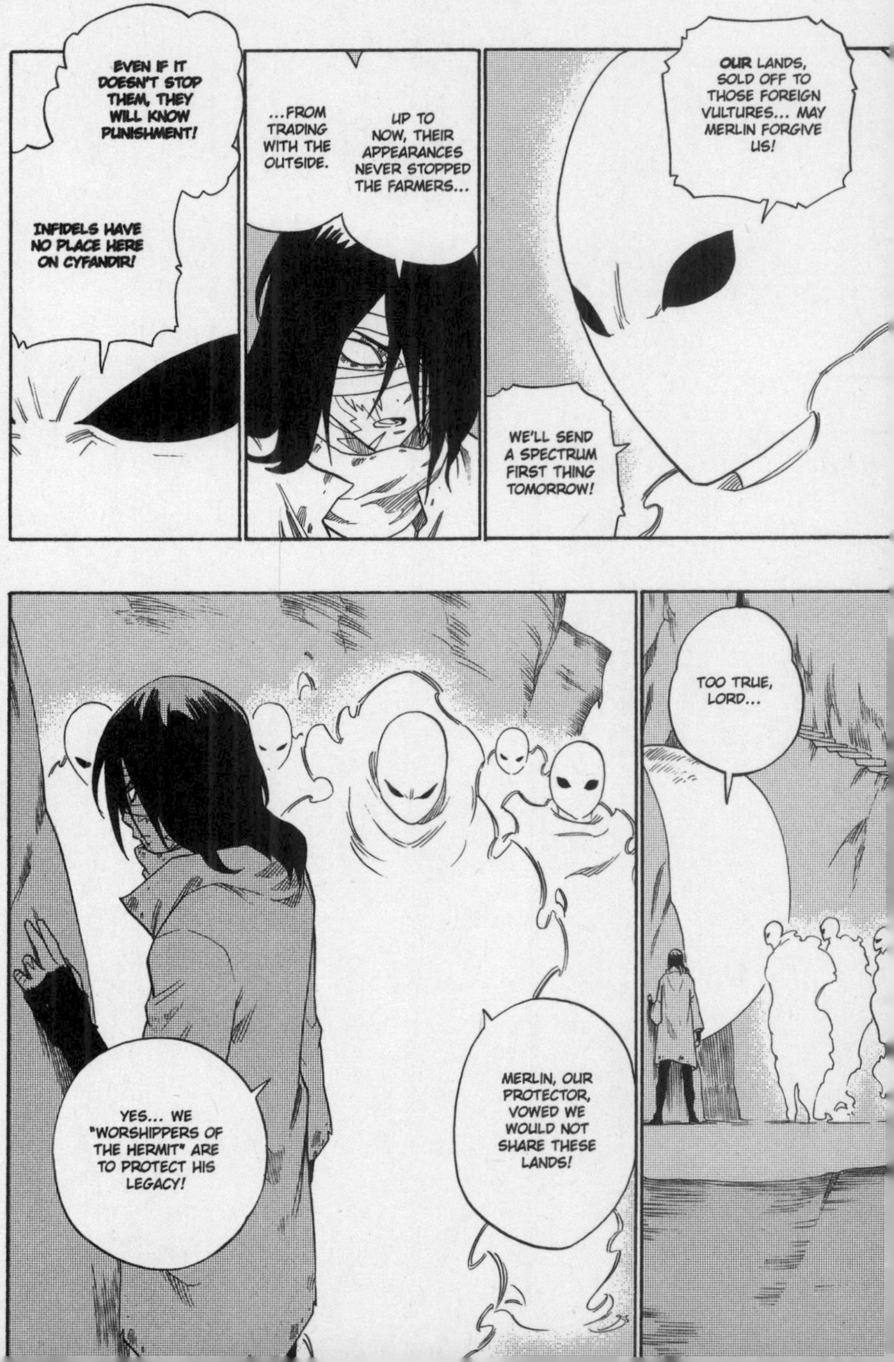
OUR LANDS, SOLD OFF TO THOSE FOREIGN VULTURES... MAY MERLIN FORGIVE US!
WE'LL SEND A SPECTRUM FIRST THING TOMORROW!
UP TO NOW, THEIR APPEARANCES NEVER STOPPED THE FARMERS...
...FROM TRADING WITH THE OUTSIDE.
EVEN IF IT DOESN'T STOP THEM, THEY WILL KNOW PUNISHMENT!
INFIDELS HAVE NO PLACE HERE ON CYFANDIR!
TOO TRUE, LORD...
MERLIN, OUR PROTECTOR, VOWED WE WOULD NOT SHARE THESE LANDS!
YES... WE "WORSHIPPERS OF THE HERMIT" ARE TO PROTECT HIS LEGACY!

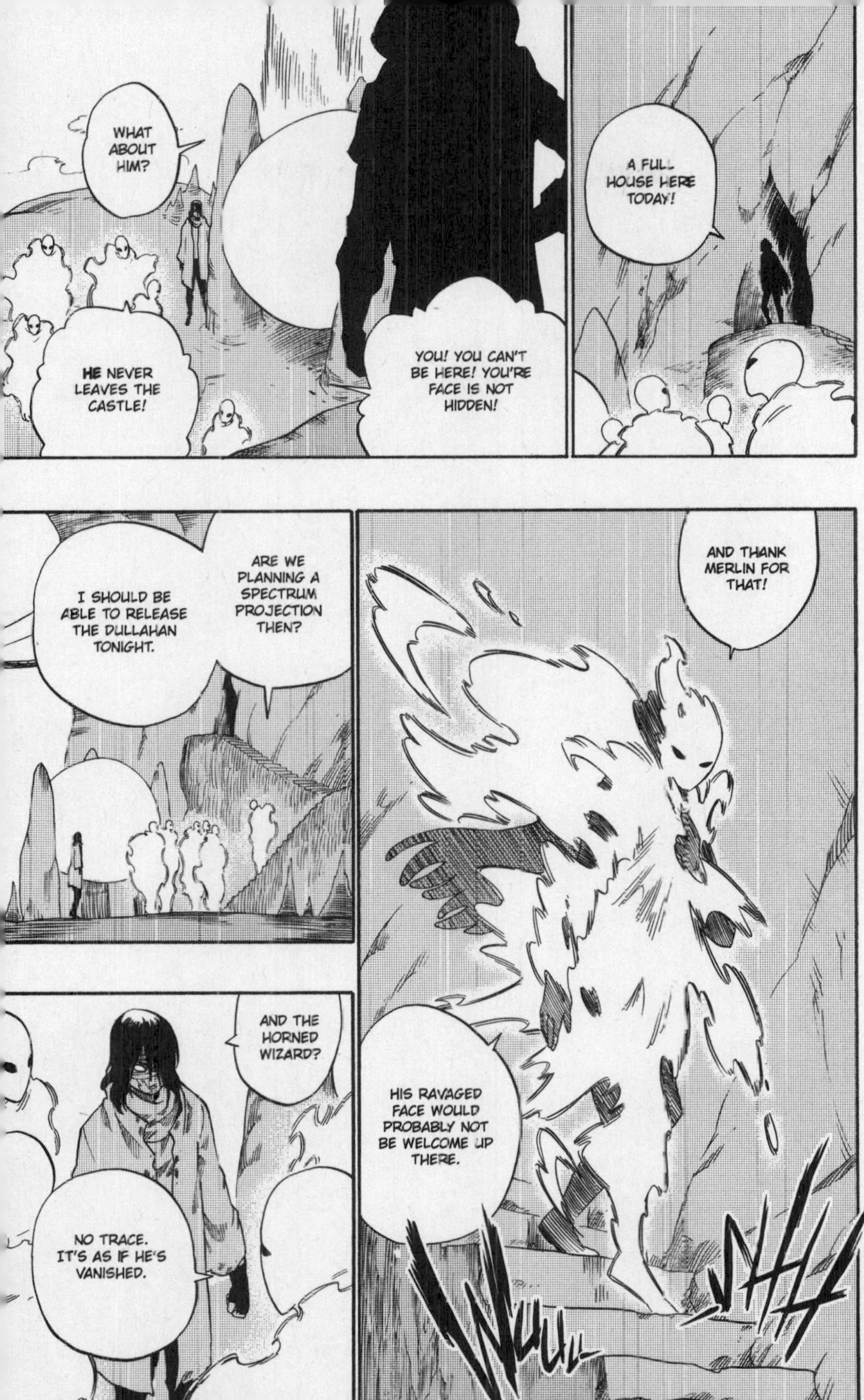
A FULL HOUSE HERE TODAY!
YOU! YOU CAN'T BE HERE! YOU'RE FACE IS NOT HIDDEN!
WHAT ABOUT HIM?
HE NEVER LEAVES THE CASTLE!
AND THANK MERLIN FOR THAT!
HIS RAVAGED FACE WOULD PROBABLY NOT BE WELCOME UP THERE.
ARE WE PLANNING A SPECTRUM PROJECTION THEN?
I SHOULD BE ABLE TO RELEASE THE DULLAHAN TONIGHT.
AND THE HORNED WIZARD?
NO TRACE. IT'S AS IF HE'S VANISHED.

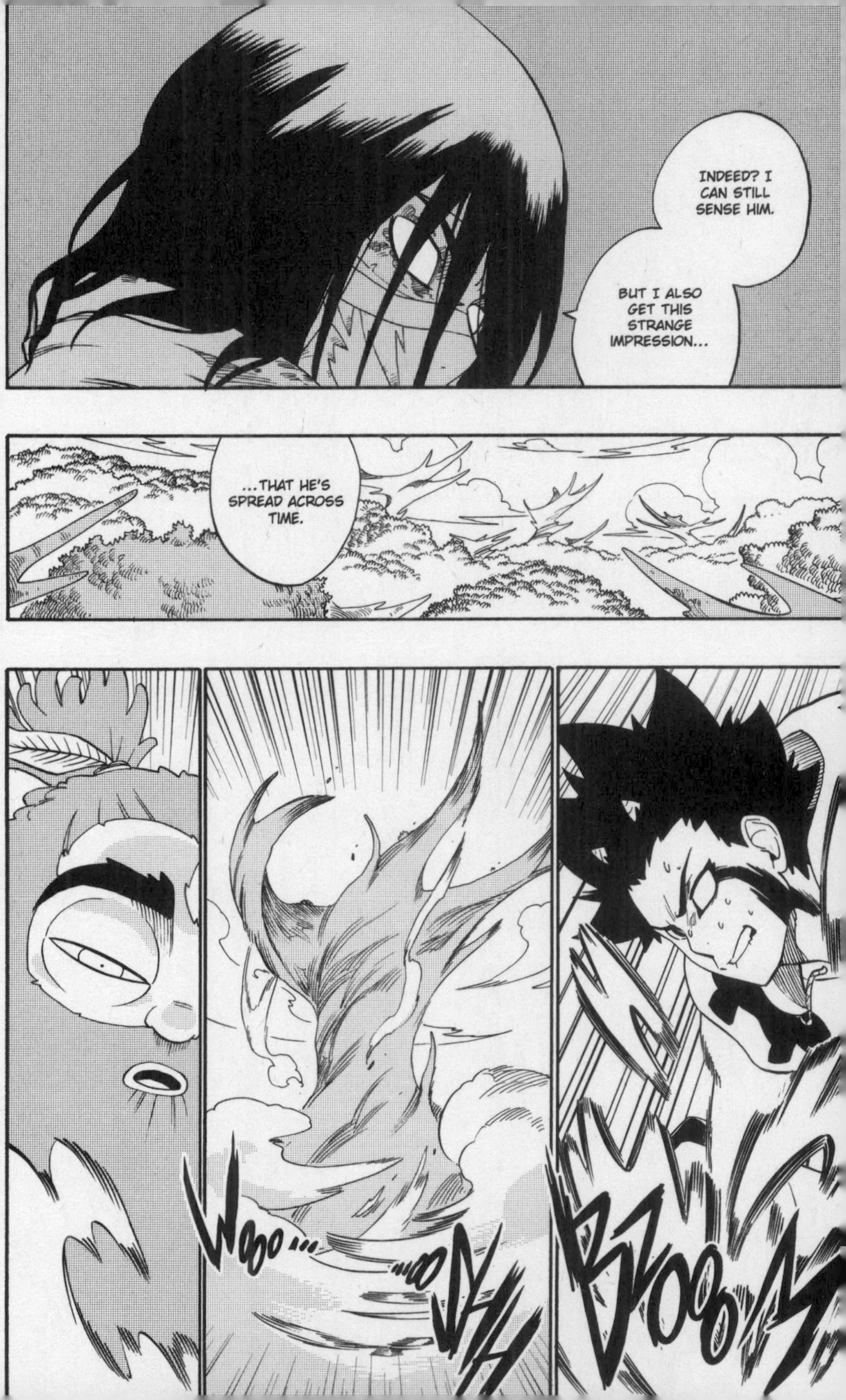
INDEED? I CAN STILL SENSE HIM.
BUT I ALSO GET THIS STRANGE IMPRESSION...
...THAT HE'S SPREAD ACROSS TIME.
BZOOOM
WOOO...
...OOSH

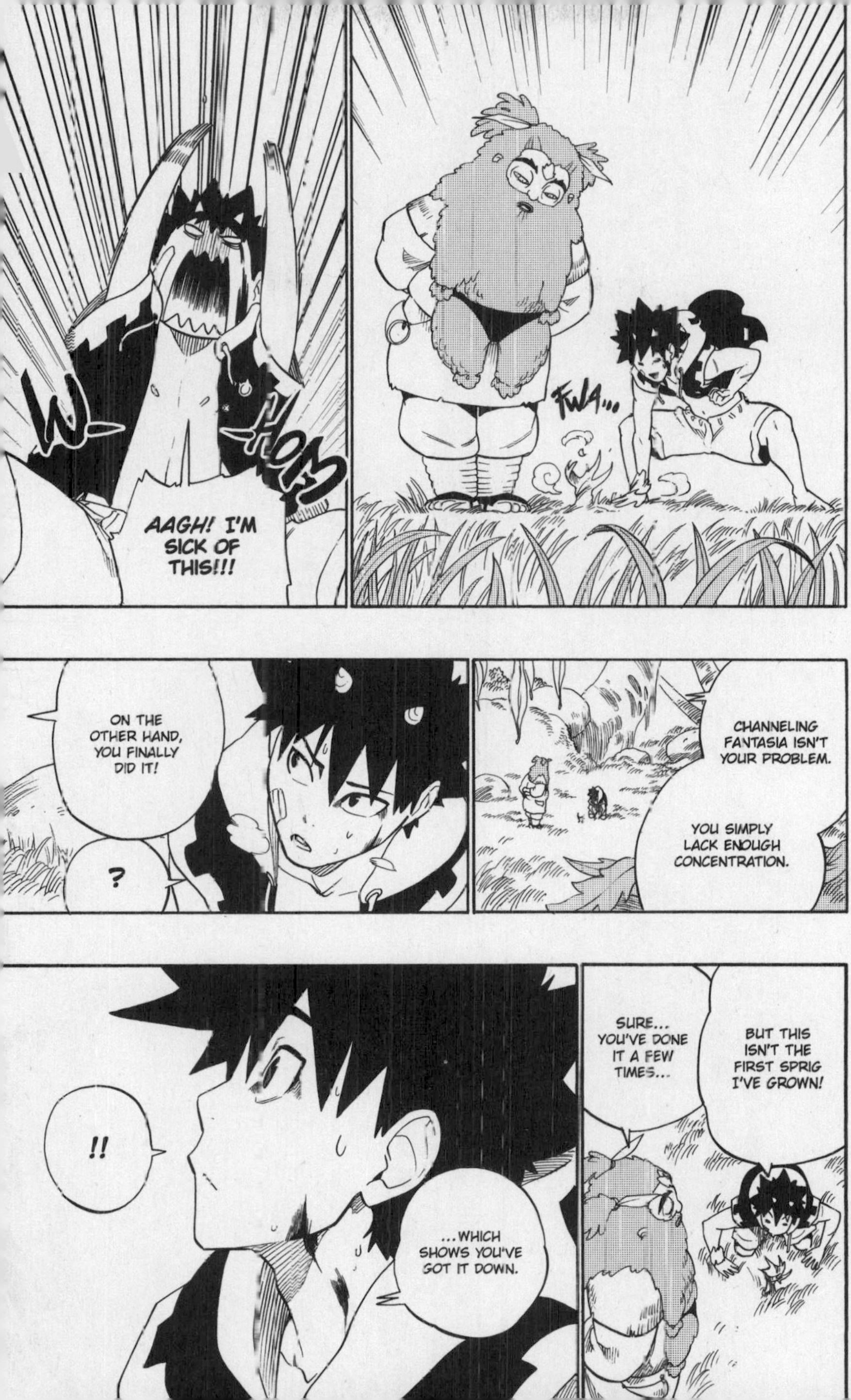
FWA...
WHOOM
AAGH! I'M SICK OF THIS!!!
CHANNELING FANTASIA ISN'T YOUR PROBLEM.
YOU SIMPLY LACK ENOUGH CONCENTRATION.
ON THE OTHER HAND, YOU FINALLY DID IT!
?
BUT THIS ISN'T THE FIRST SPRIG I'VE GROWN!
SURE... YOU'VE DONE IT A FEW TIMES...
...WHICH SHOWS YOU'VE GOT IT DOWN.
!!

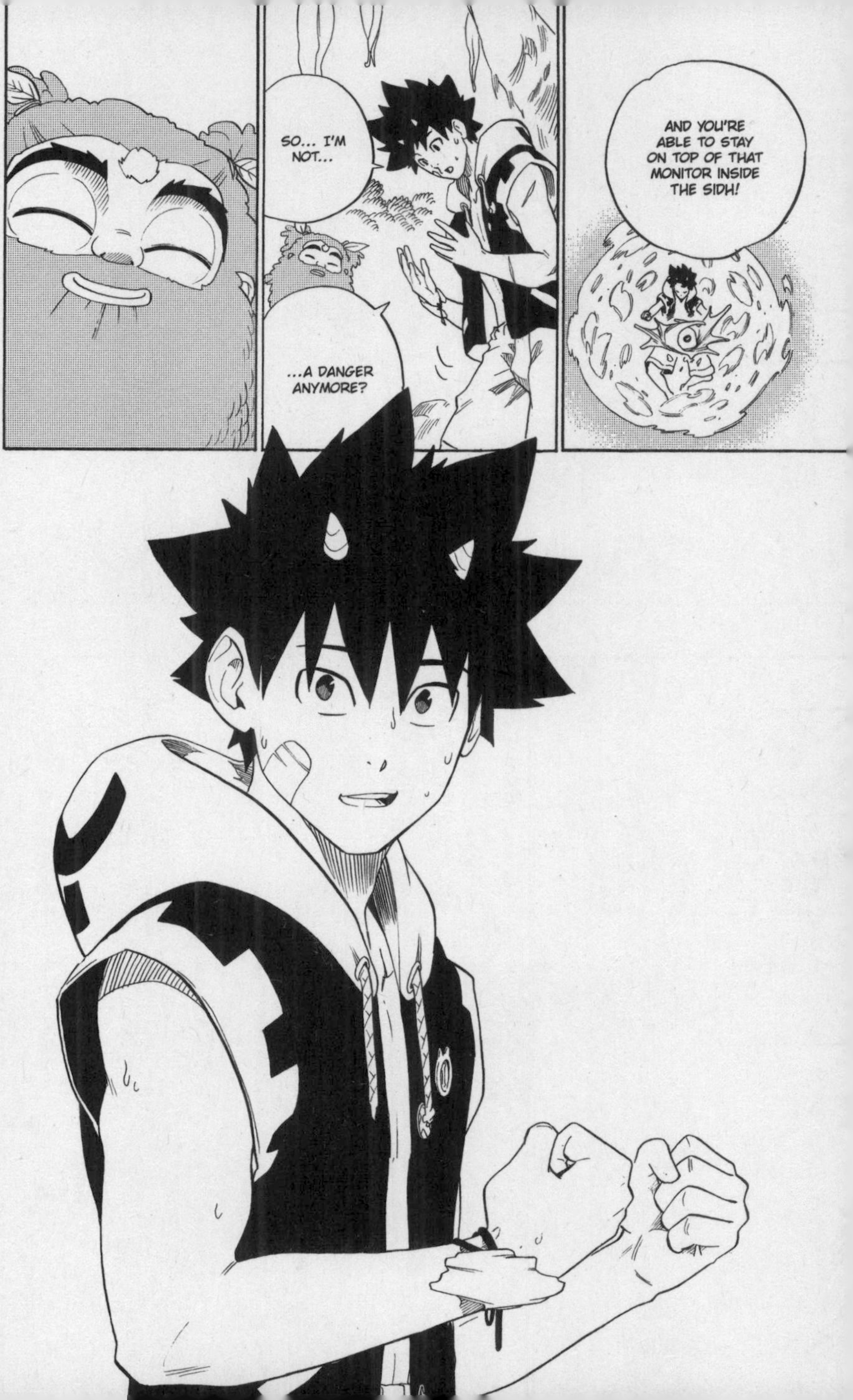
AND YOU'RE ABLE TO STAY ON TOP OF THAT MONITOR INSIDE THE SIDH!
SO... I'M NOT...
...A DANGER ANYMORE?

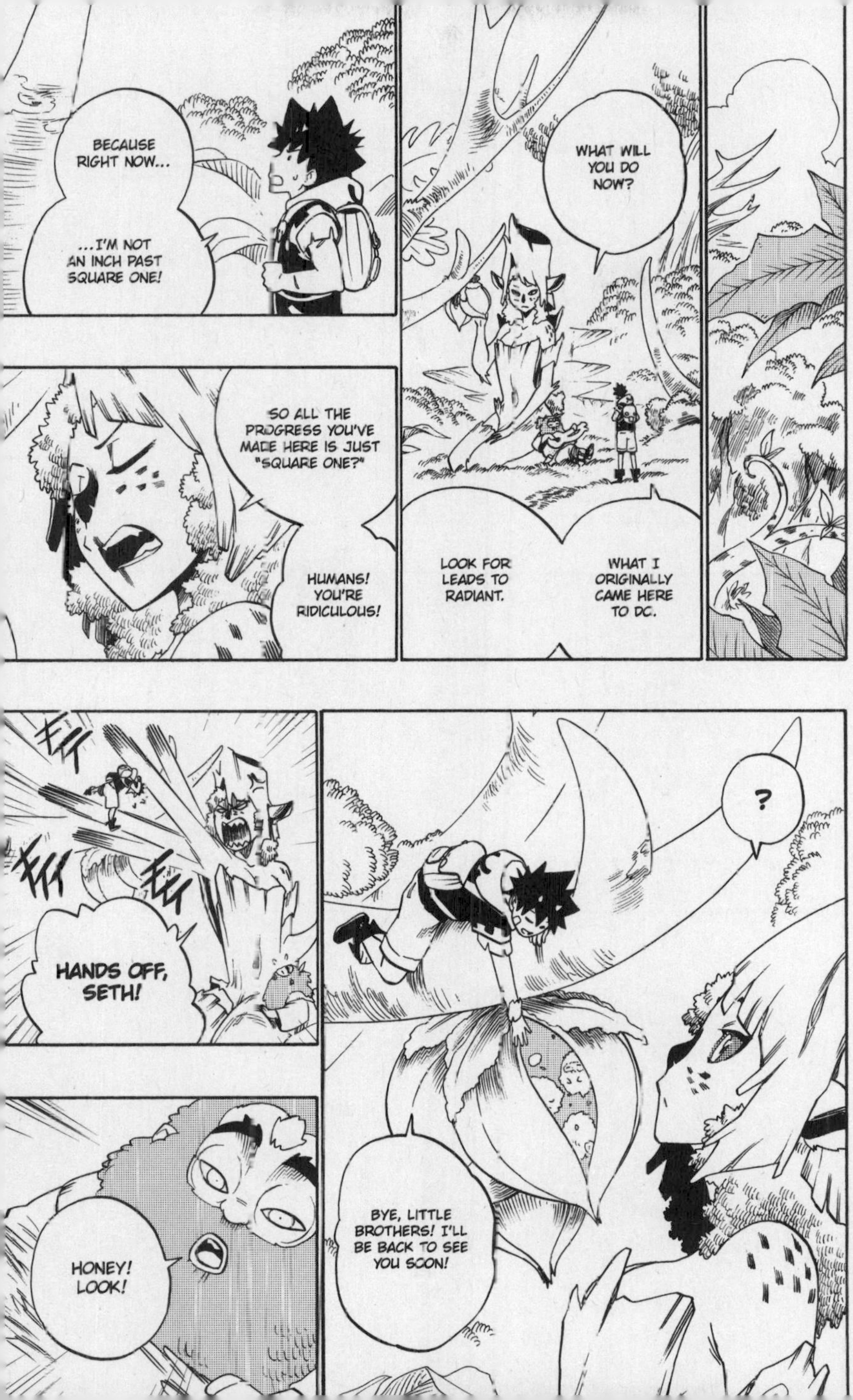
WHAT WILL YOU DO NOW?
WHAT I ORIGINALLY CAME HERE TO DC.
LOOK FOR LEADS TO RADIANT.
BECAUSE RIGHT NOW...
...I'M NOT AN INCH PAST SQUARE ONE!
SO ALL THE PROGRESS YOU'VE MADE HERE IS JUST "SQUARE ONE?"
HUMANS! YOU'RE RIDICULOUS!
?
BYE, LITTLE BROTHERS! I'LL BE BACK TO SEE YOU SOON!
HANDS OFF, SETH!
HONEY! LOOK!

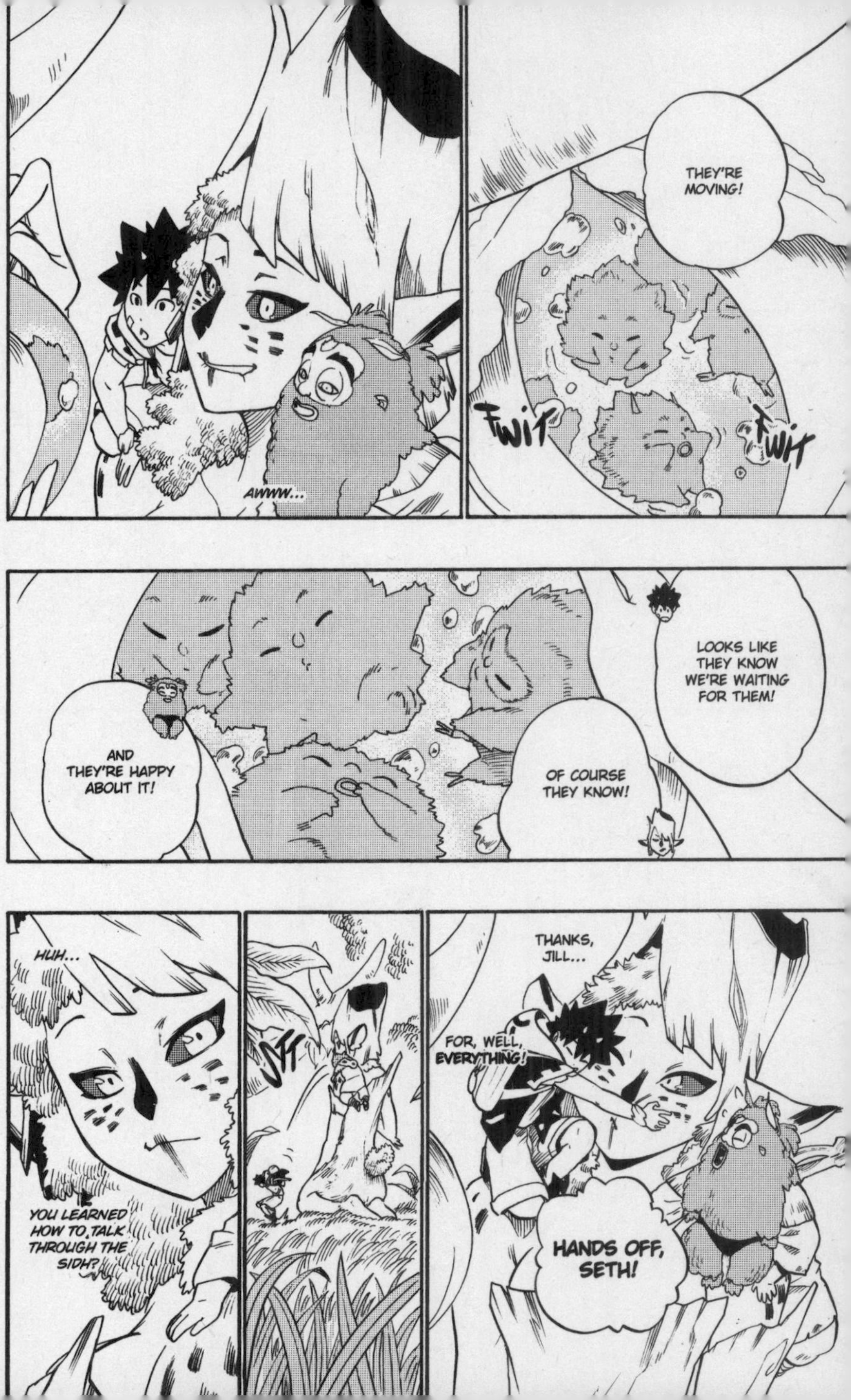
THEY'RE MOVING!
FWIT
FWIT
AWWW...
LOOKS LIKE THEY KNOW WE'RE WAITING FOR THEM!
OF COURSE THEY KNOW!
AND THEY'RE HAPPY ABOUT IT!
THANKS, JILL...
FOR, WELL, EVERYTHING!
HANDS OFF, SETH!
HUH...
YOU LEARNED HOW TO TALK THROUGH THE SIDH?

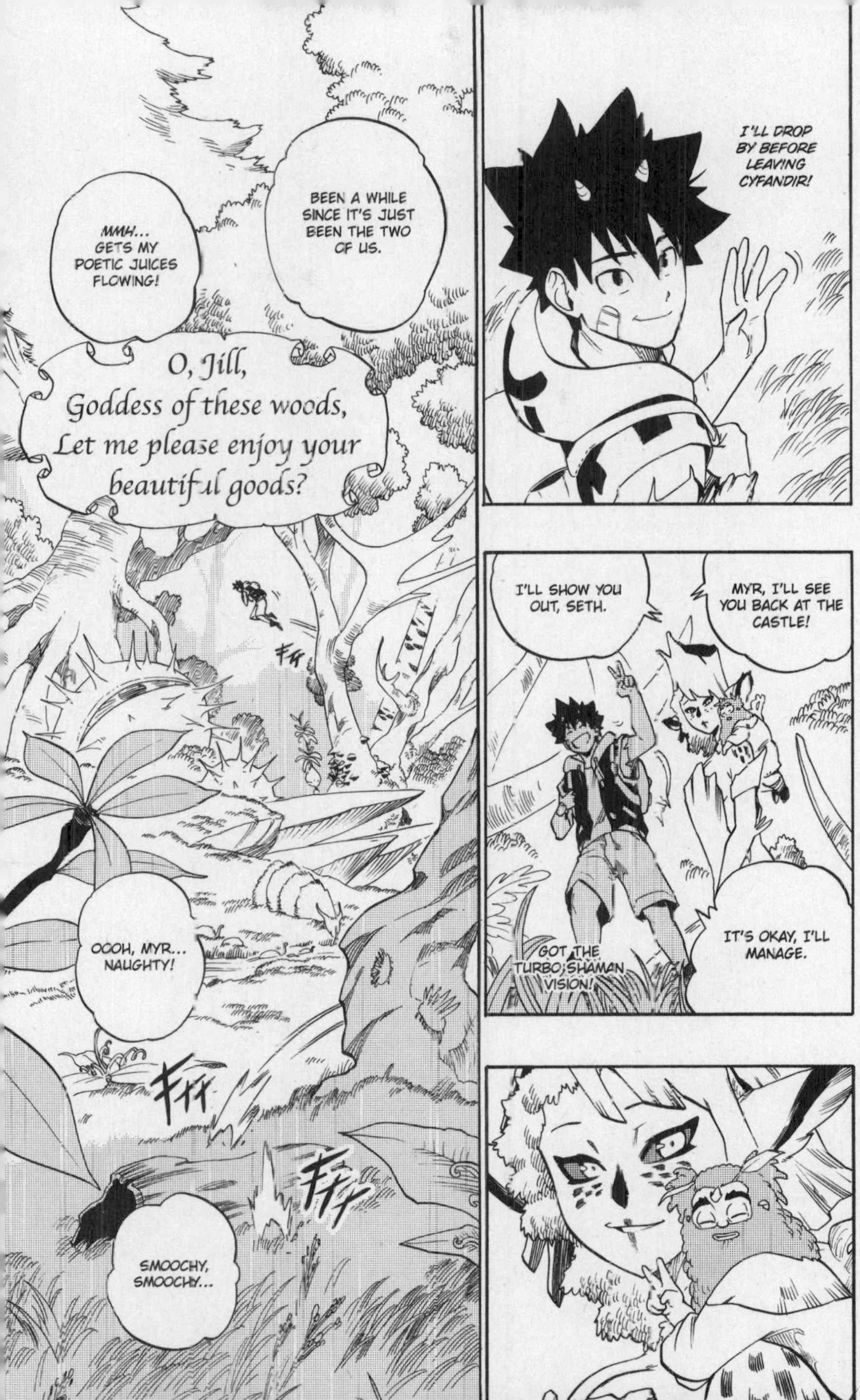

I'LL DROP BY BEFORE LEAVING CYFANDIR!
MYR, I'LL SEE YOU BACK AT THE CASTLE!
I'LL SHOW YOU OUT, SETH.
IT'S OKAY, I'LL MANAGE.
GOT THE TURBO SHAMAN VISION!
BEEN A WHILE SINCE IT'S JUST BEEN THE TWO OF US.
MMH... GETS MY POETIC JUICES FLOWING!
O, Jill, Goddess of these woods, Let me please enjoy your beautiful goods?
OOOH, MYR... NAUGHTY!
SMOOCHY, SMOOCHY...

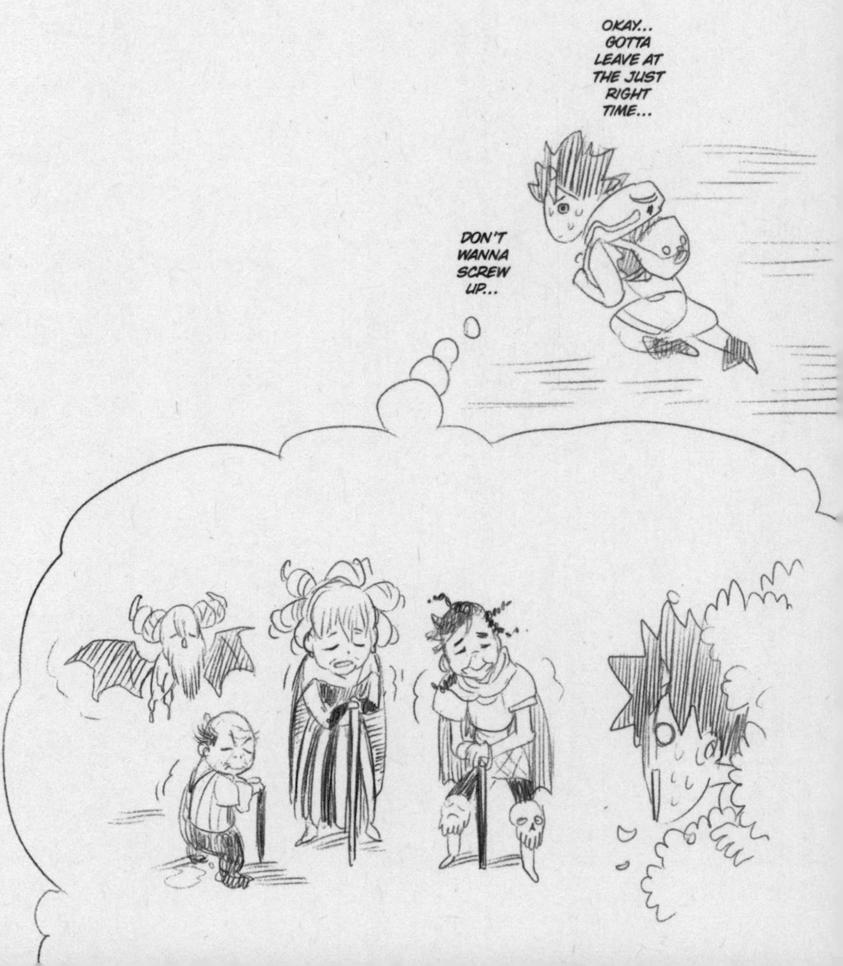
OKAY... GOTTA LEAVE AT THE JUST RIGHT TIME...
DON'T WANNA SCREW UP...

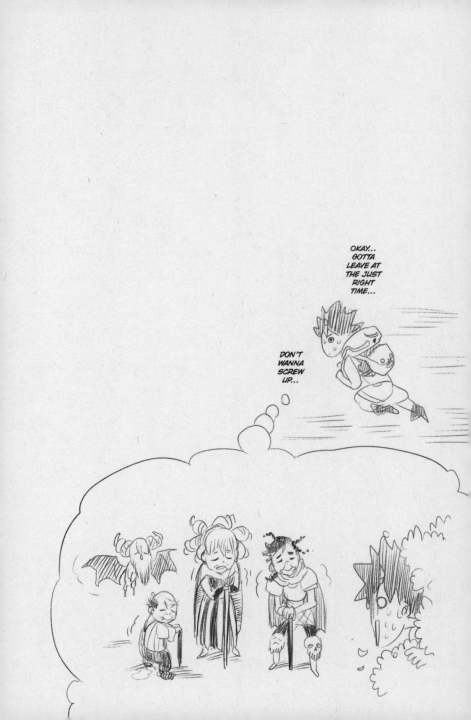

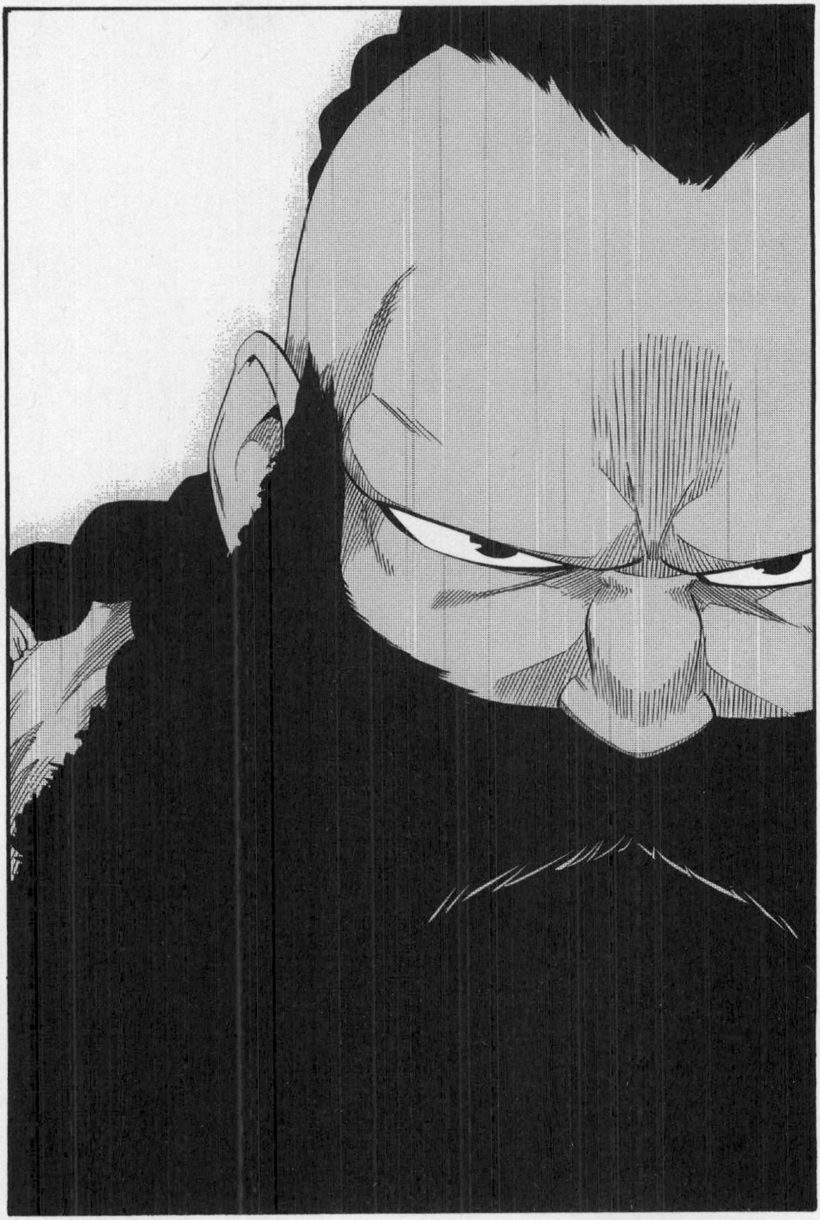

Chapter 50

The Tail

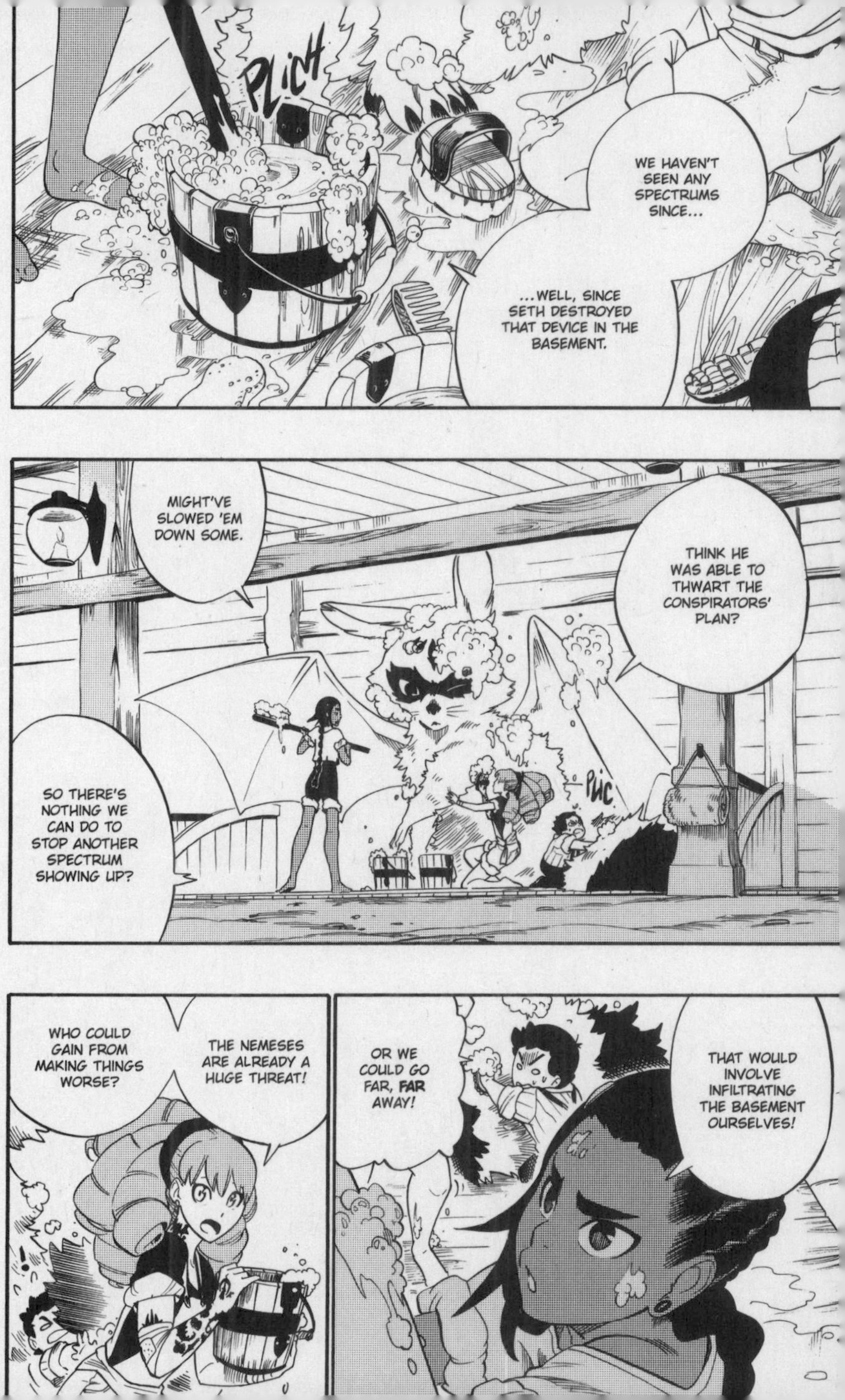
PLICH
WE HAVEN'T SEEN ANY SPECTRUMS SINCE...
...WELL, SINCE SETH DESTROYED THAT DEVICE IN THE BASEMENT.
THINK HE WAS ABLE TO THWART THE CONSPIRATORS' PLAN?
MIGHT'VE SLOWED 'EM DOWN SOME.
PLIC
SO THERE'S NOTHING WE CAN DO TO STOP ANOTHER SPECTRUM SHOWING UP?
THAT WOULD INVOLVE INFILTRATING THE BASEMENT OURSELVES!
OR WE COULD GO FAR, **FAR** AWAY!
THE NEMESES ARE ALREADY A HUGE THREAT!
WHO COULD GAIN FROM MAKING THINGS WORSE?

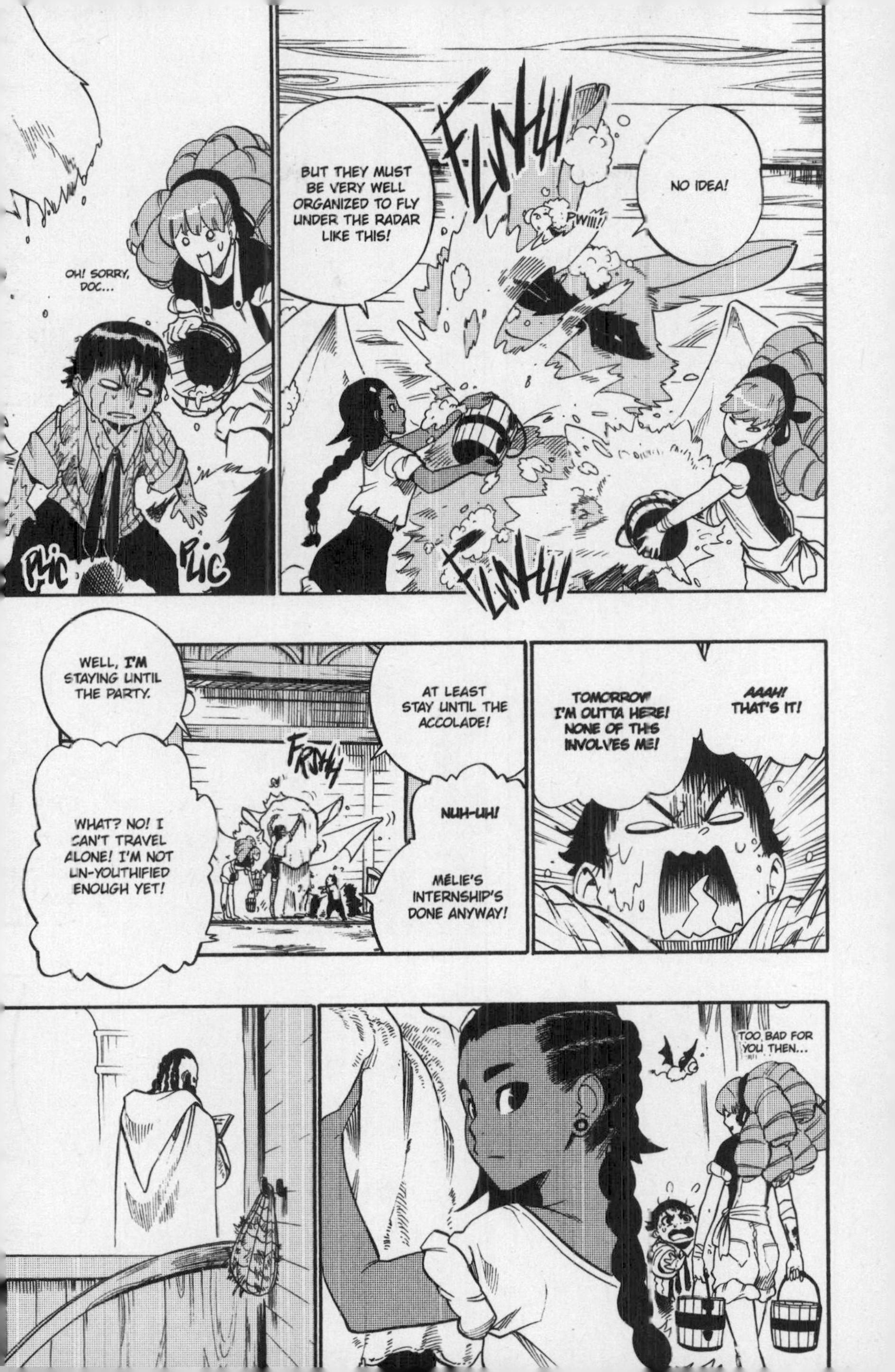
FLNHH
NO IDEA!
BUT THEY MUST BE VERY WELL ORGANIZED TO FLY UNDER THE RADAR LIKE THIS!
PWIII!!
FLNHH
OH! SORRY, DOC...
PLIC
PLIC
AAAH! THAT'S IT!
TOMORROW I'M OUTTA HERE! NONE OF THIS INVOLVES ME!
AT LEAST STAY UNTIL THE ACCOLADE!
WELL, I'M STAYING UNTIL THE PARTY.
FRSHH
NUH-UH!
MÉLIE'S INTERNSHIP'S DONE ANYWAY!
WHAT? NO! I CAN'T TRAVEL ALONE! I'M NOT UN-YOUTHIFIED ENOUGH YET!
TOO BAD FOR YOU THEN...

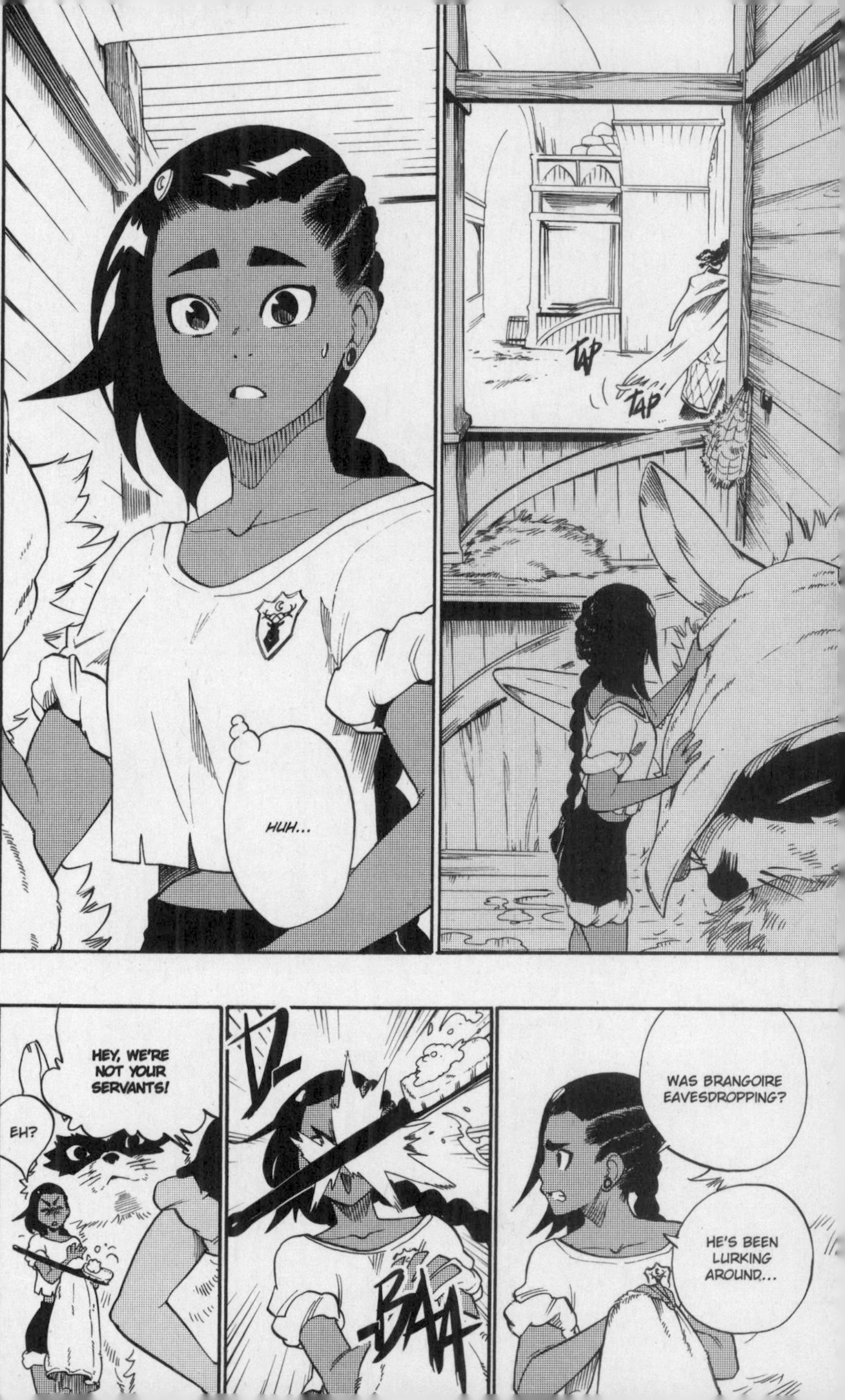
TAP
TAP
HUH...
WAS BRANGOIRE EAVESDROPPING?
HE'S BEEN LURKING AROUND...
-BAA
HEY, WE'RE NOT YOUR SERVANTS!
EH?

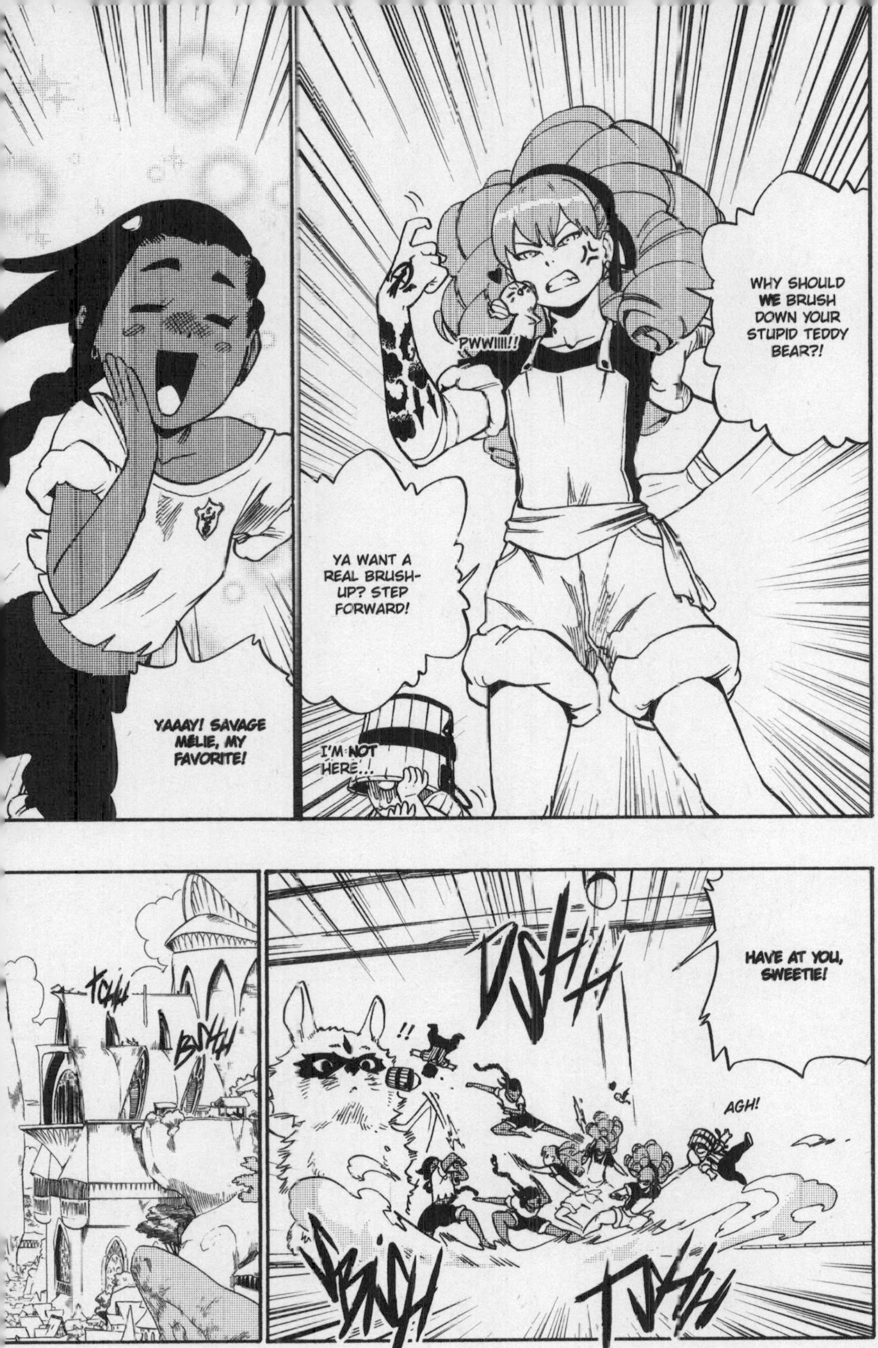
WHY SHOULD WE BRUSH DOWN YOUR STUPID TEDDY BEAR?!
PWWIIII!!
YA WANT A REAL BRUSH-UP? STEP FORWARD!
I'M NOT HERE...
YAAAY! SAVAGE MÉLIE, MY FAVORITE!
HAVE AT YOU, SWEETIE!
AGH!

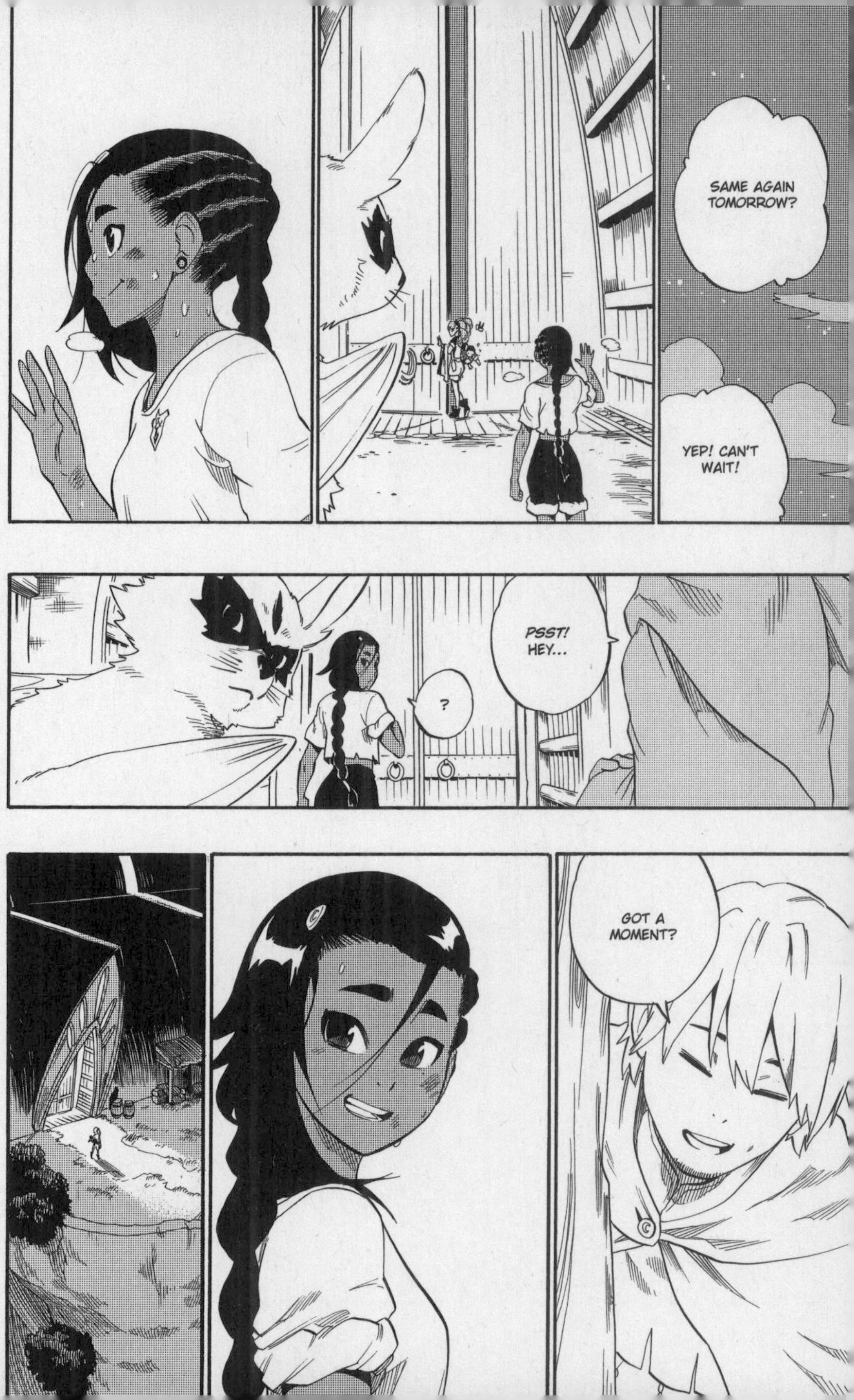
SAME AGAIN TOMORROW?
YEP! CAN'T WAIT!
PSST! HEY...
?
GOT A MOMENT?

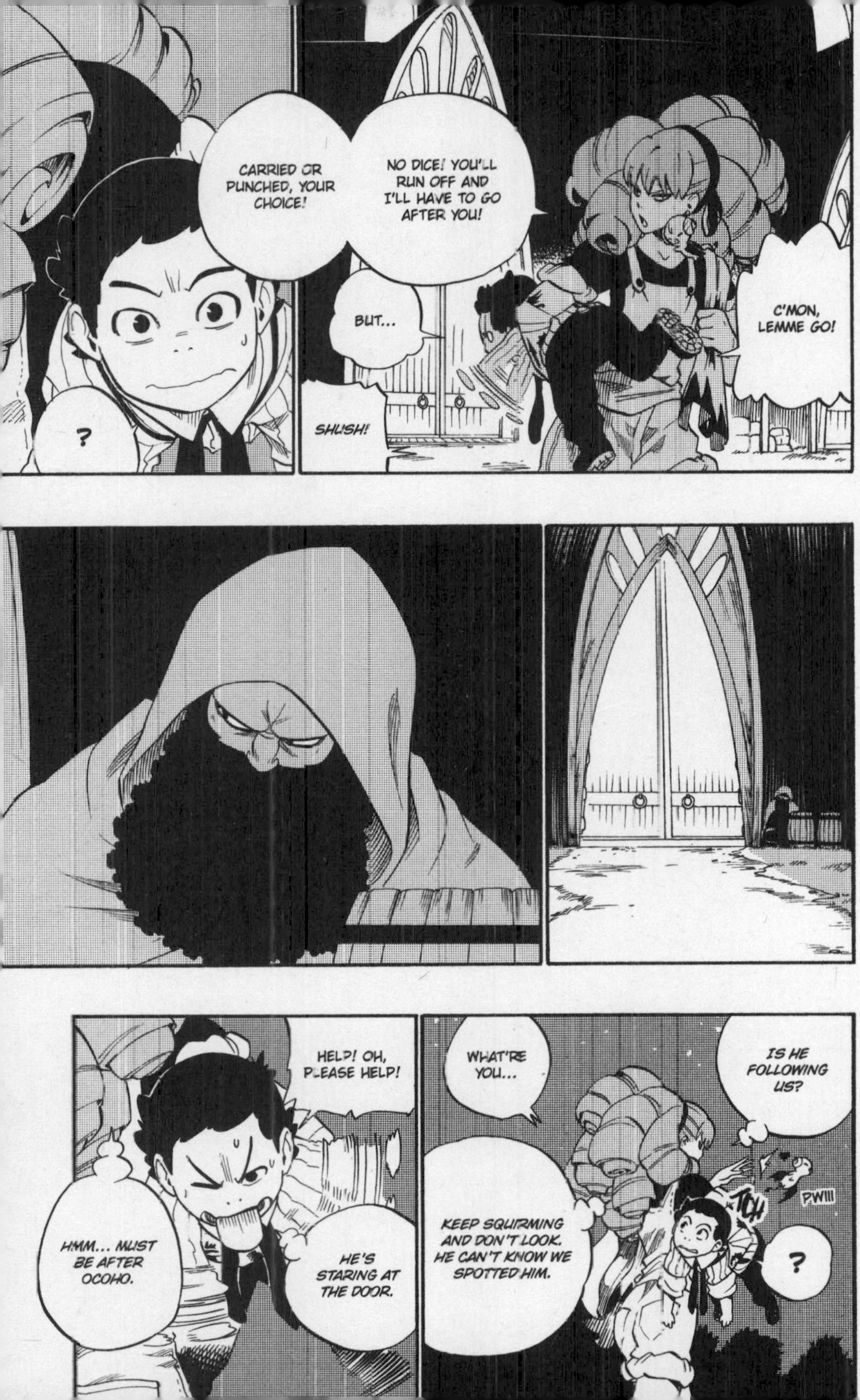
C'MON, LEMME GO!
NO DICE! YOU'LL RUN OFF AND I'LL HAVE TO GO AFTER YOU!
CARRIED OR PUNCHED, YOUR CHOICE!
BUT...
SHUSH!
?
IS HE FOLLOWING US?
WHAT'RE YOU...
TCH
PWIII
KEEP SQUIRMING AND DON'T LOOK. HE CAN'T KNOW WE SPOTTED HIM.
?
HELP! OH, PLEASE HELP!
HE'S STARING AT THE DOOR.
HMM... MUST BE AFTER OCOHO.

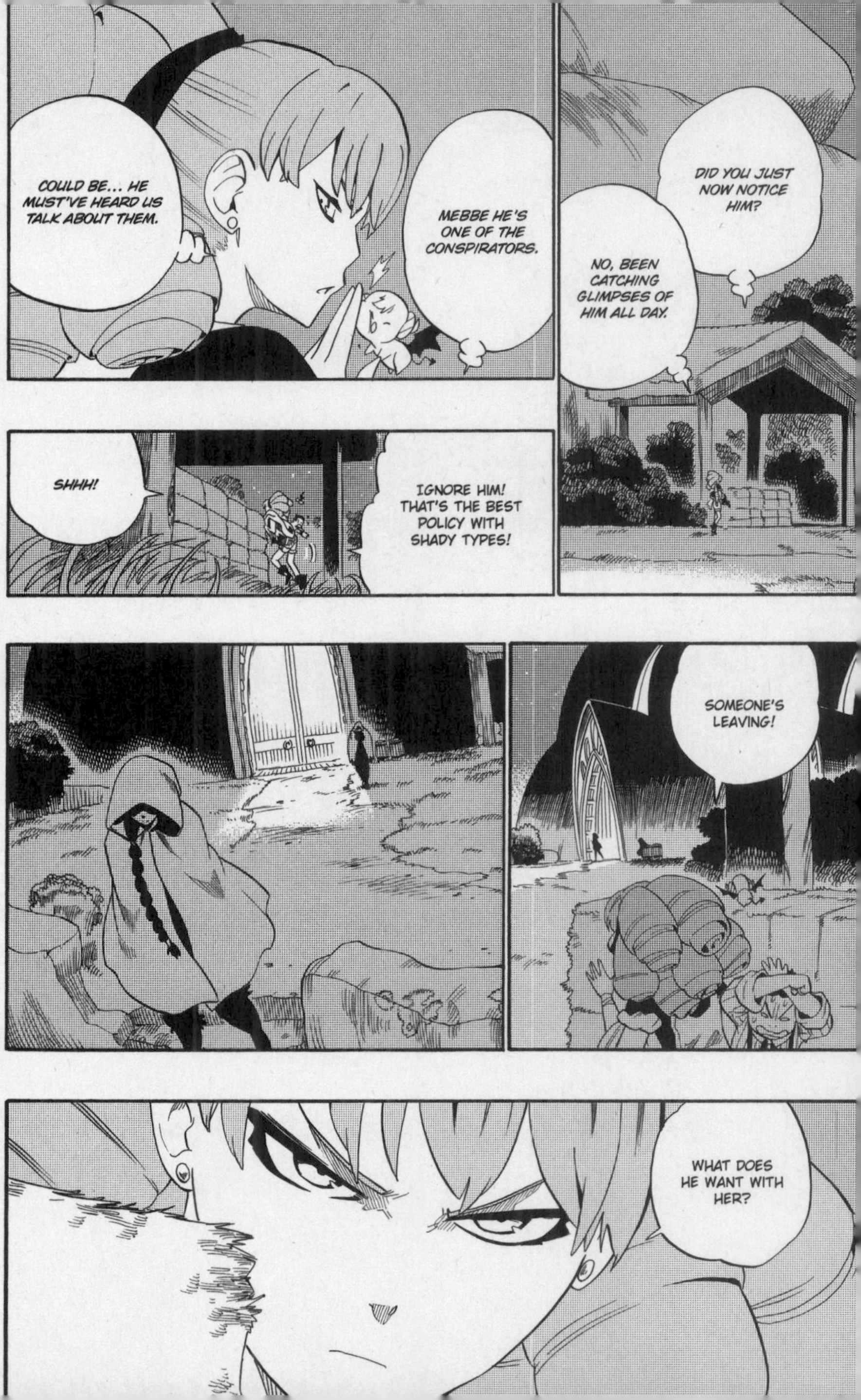
DID YOU JUST NOW NOTICE HIM?
NO, BEEN CATCHING GLIMPSES OF HIM ALL DAY.
MEBBE HE'S ONE OF THE CONSPIRATORS.
COULD BE... HE MUST'VE HEARD US TALK ABOUT THEM.
IGNORE HIM! THAT'S THE BEST POLICY WITH SHADY TYPES!
SHHH!
SOMEONE'S LEAVING!
WHAT DOES HE WANT WITH HER?

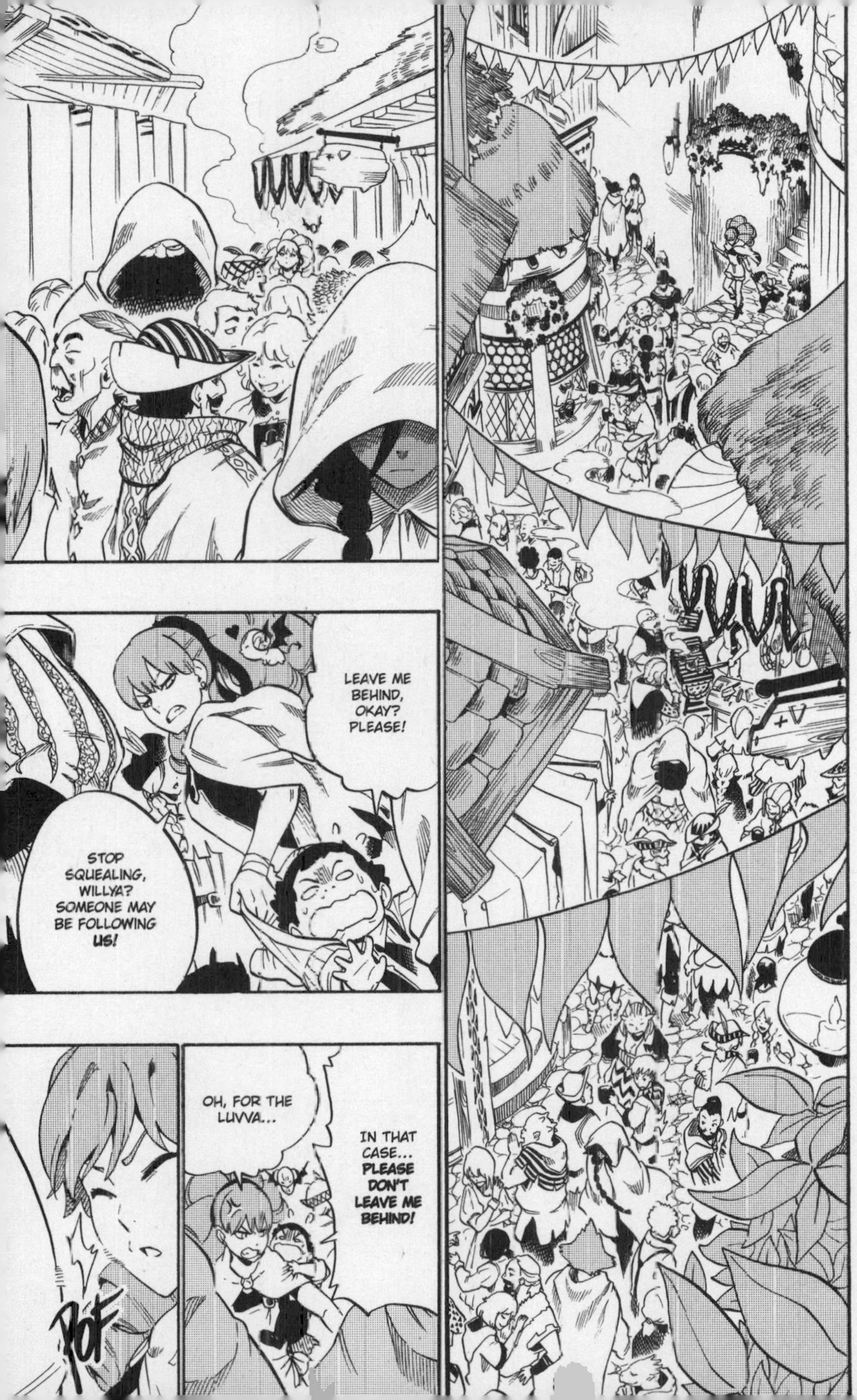
+V
LEAVE ME BEHIND, OKAY? PLEASE!
STOP SQUEALING, WILLYA? SOMEONE MAY BE FOLLOWING **US!**
OH, FOR THE LUVVA...
IN THAT CASE... **PLEASE DON'T LEAVE ME BEHIND!**
POF

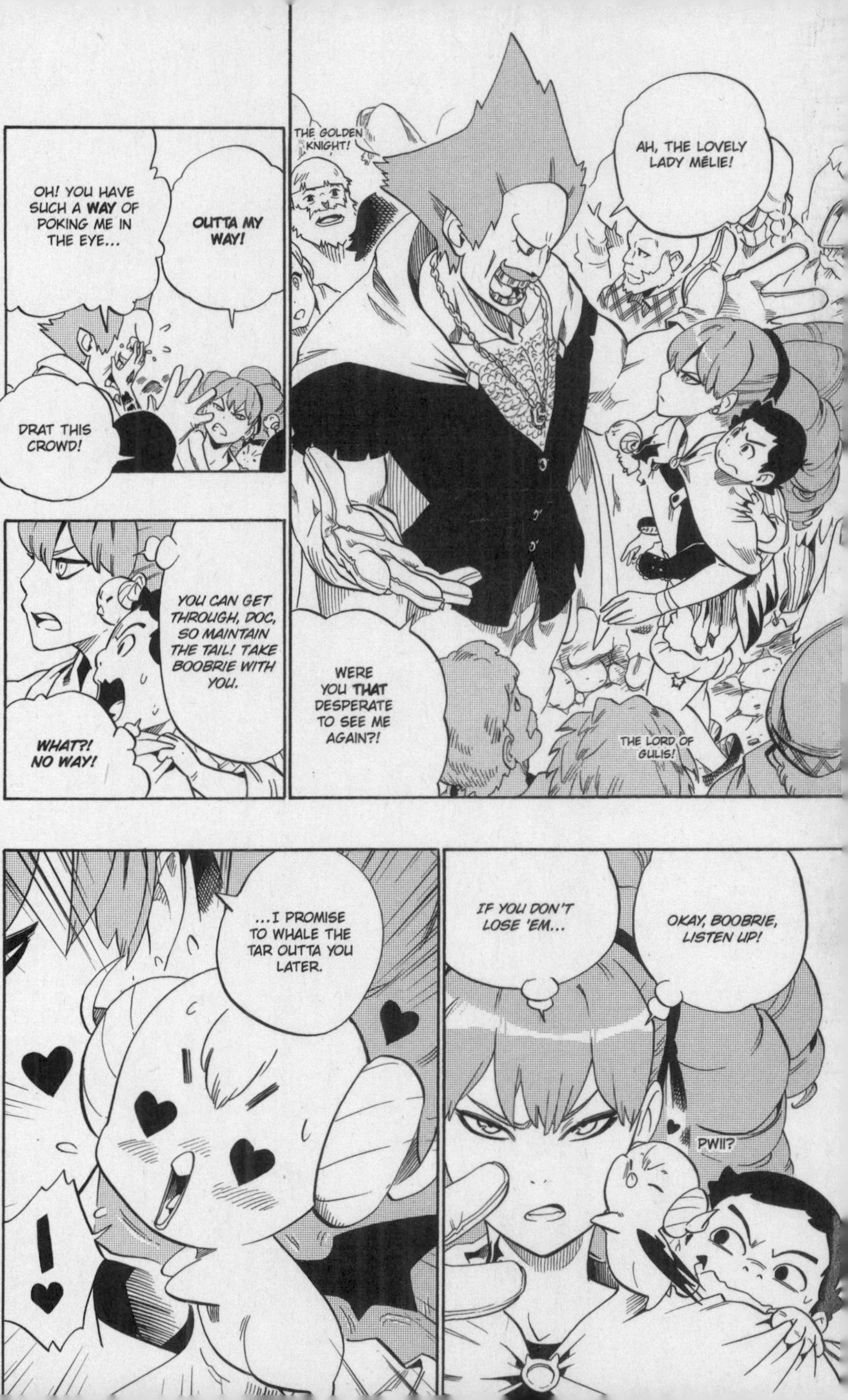
AH, THE LOVELY LADY MÉLIE!
THE GOLDEN KNIGHT!
THE LORD OF GULIS!
WERE YOU **THAT** DESPERATE TO SEE ME AGAIN?!
OUTTA MY WAY!
OH! YOU HAVE SUCH A **WAY** OF POKING ME IN THE EYE...
DRAT THIS CROWD!
YOU CAN GET THROUGH, DOC, SO MAINTAIN THE TAIL! TAKE BOOBRIE WITH YOU.
WHAT?! NO WAY!
OKAY, BOOBRIE, LISTEN UP!
IF YOU DON'T LOSE 'EM...
PWII?
...I PROMISE TO WHALE THE TAR OUTTA YOU LATER.

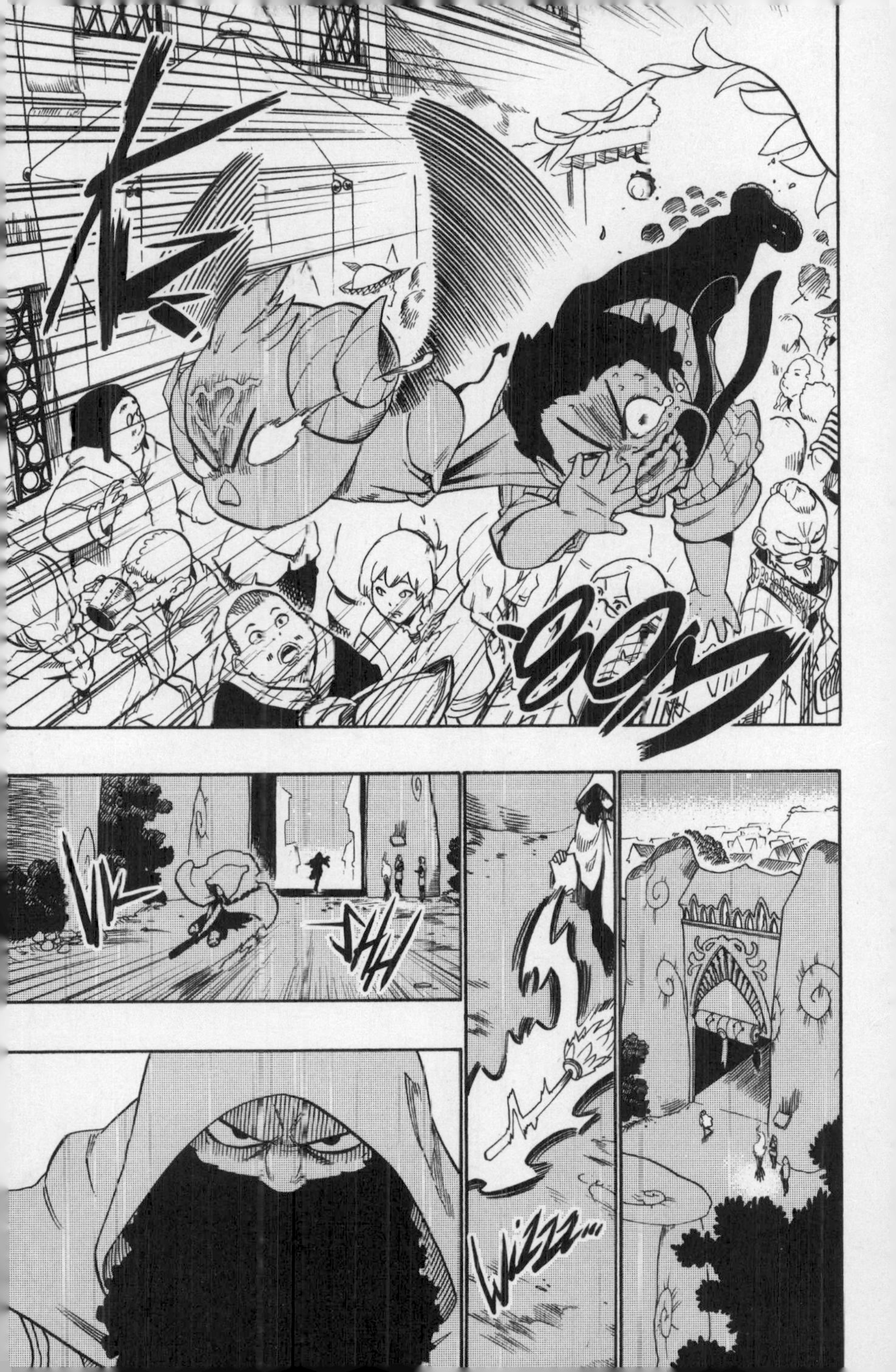
SHH
WIZZZ...

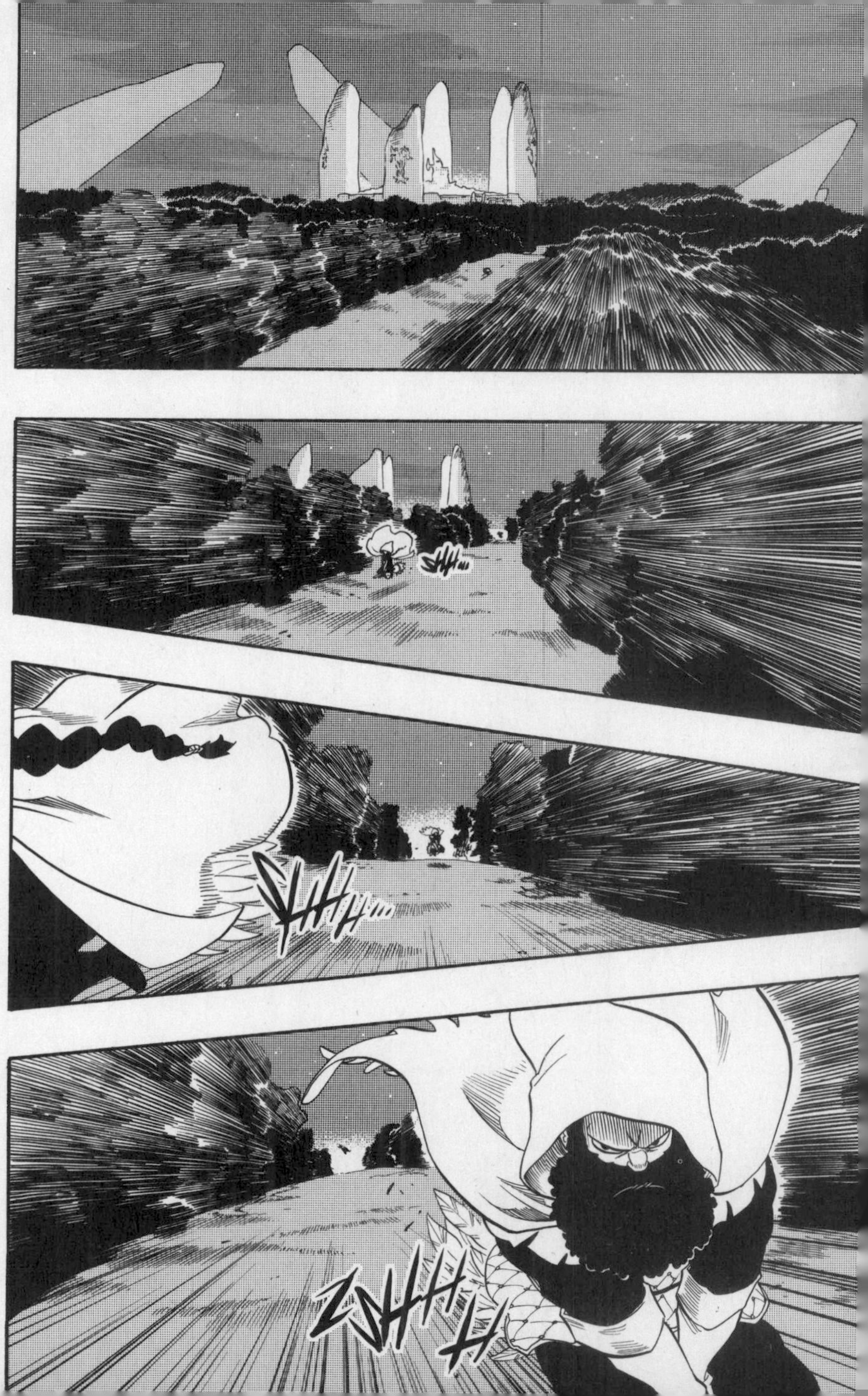
SHH...
SHHH...
ZSHHH

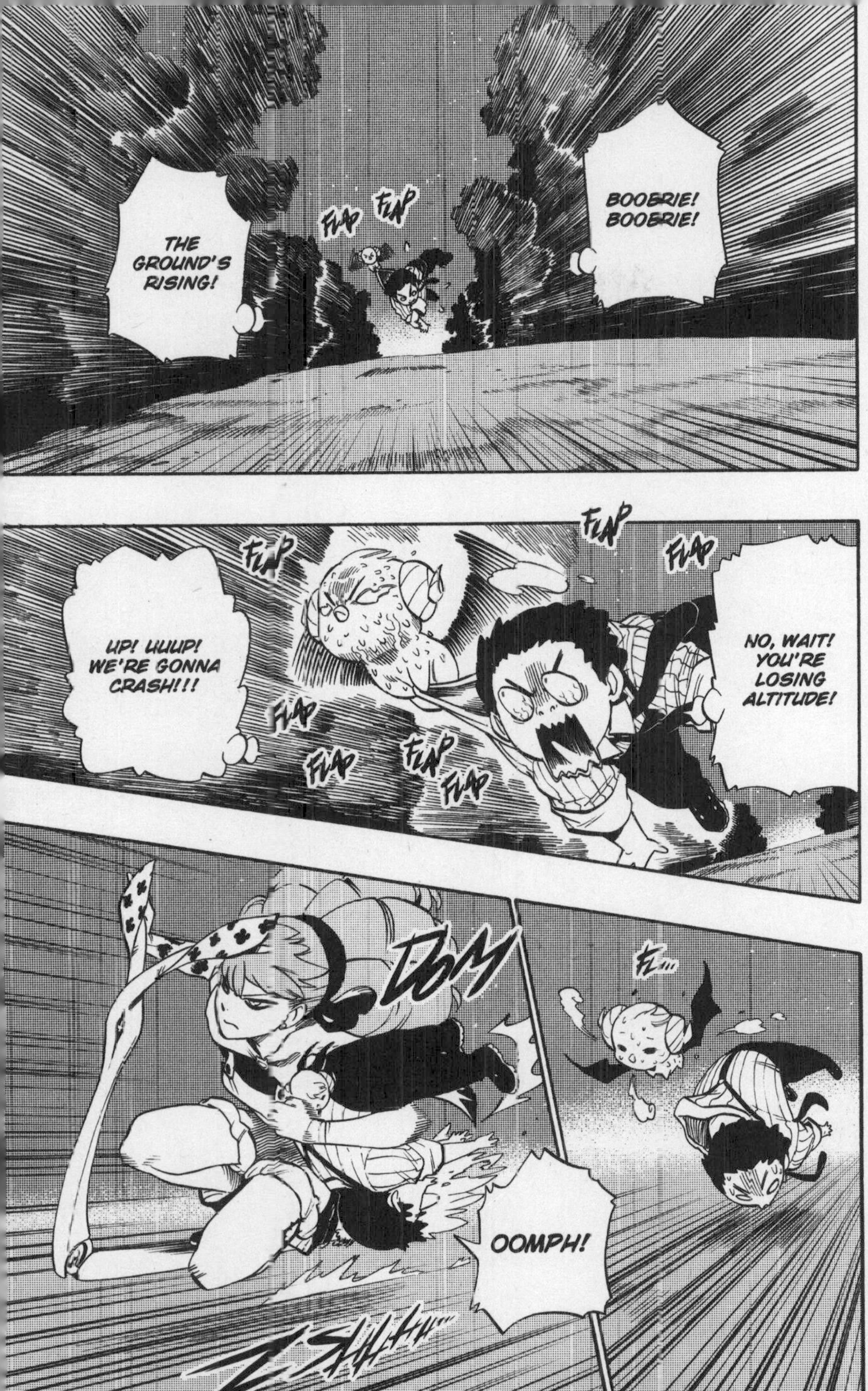
BOOBRIE! BOOBRIE!
FLAP FLAP
THE GROUND'S RISING!
NO, WAIT! YOU'RE LOSING ALTITUDE!
FLAP FLAP FLAP
UP! UUUP! WE'RE GONNA CRASH!!!
FLAP FLAP FLAP FLAP
FL...
DOM
OOMPH!

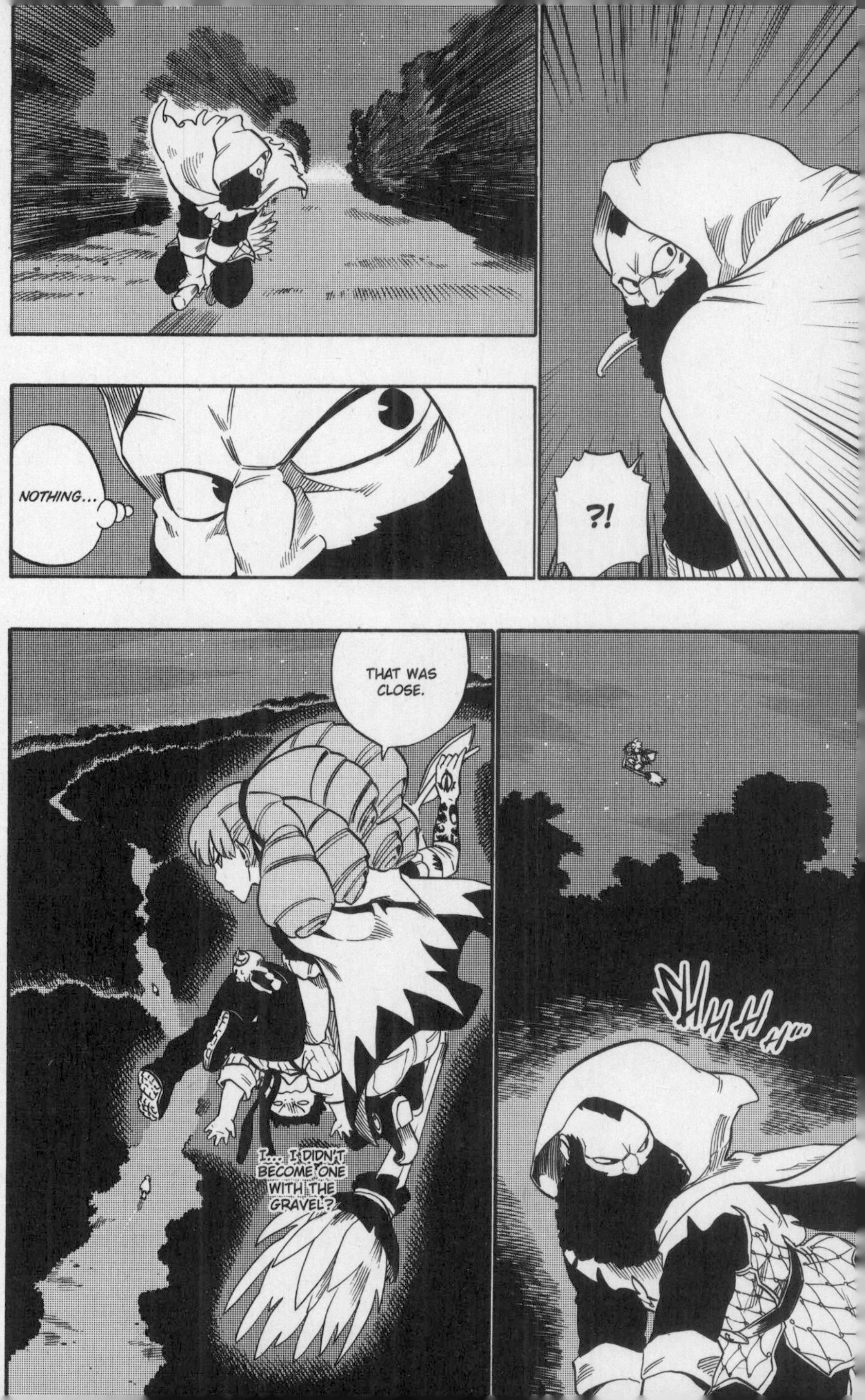
?!
NOTHING...
SHHHH...
THAT WAS CLOSE.
I... I DIDN'T BECOME ONE WITH THE GRAVEL?

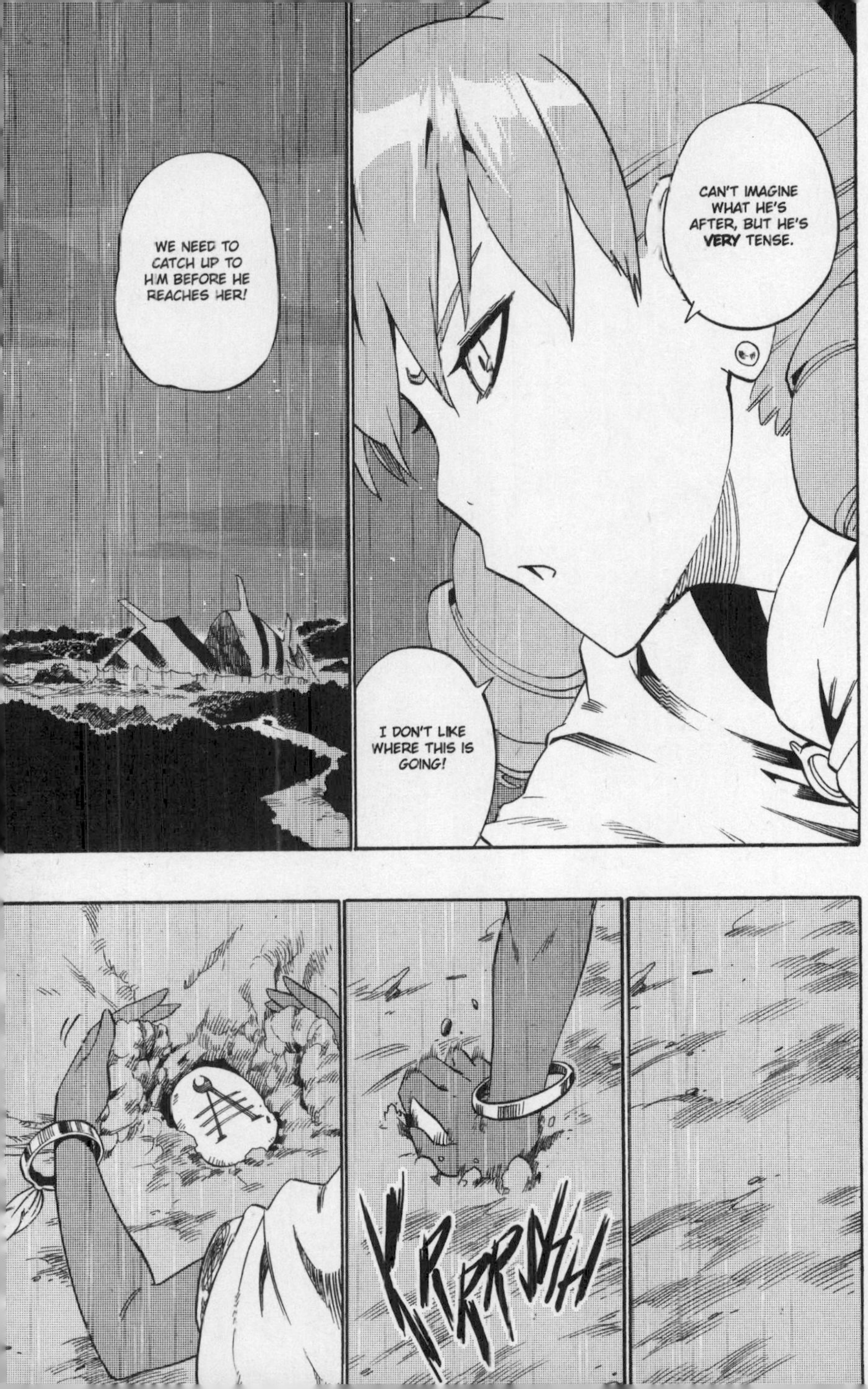
CAN'T IMAGINE WHAT HE'S AFTER, BUT HE'S **VERY** TENSE.
I DON'T LIKE WHERE THIS IS GOING!
WE NEED TO CATCH UP TO HIM BEFORE HE REACHES HER!
KRRRSH

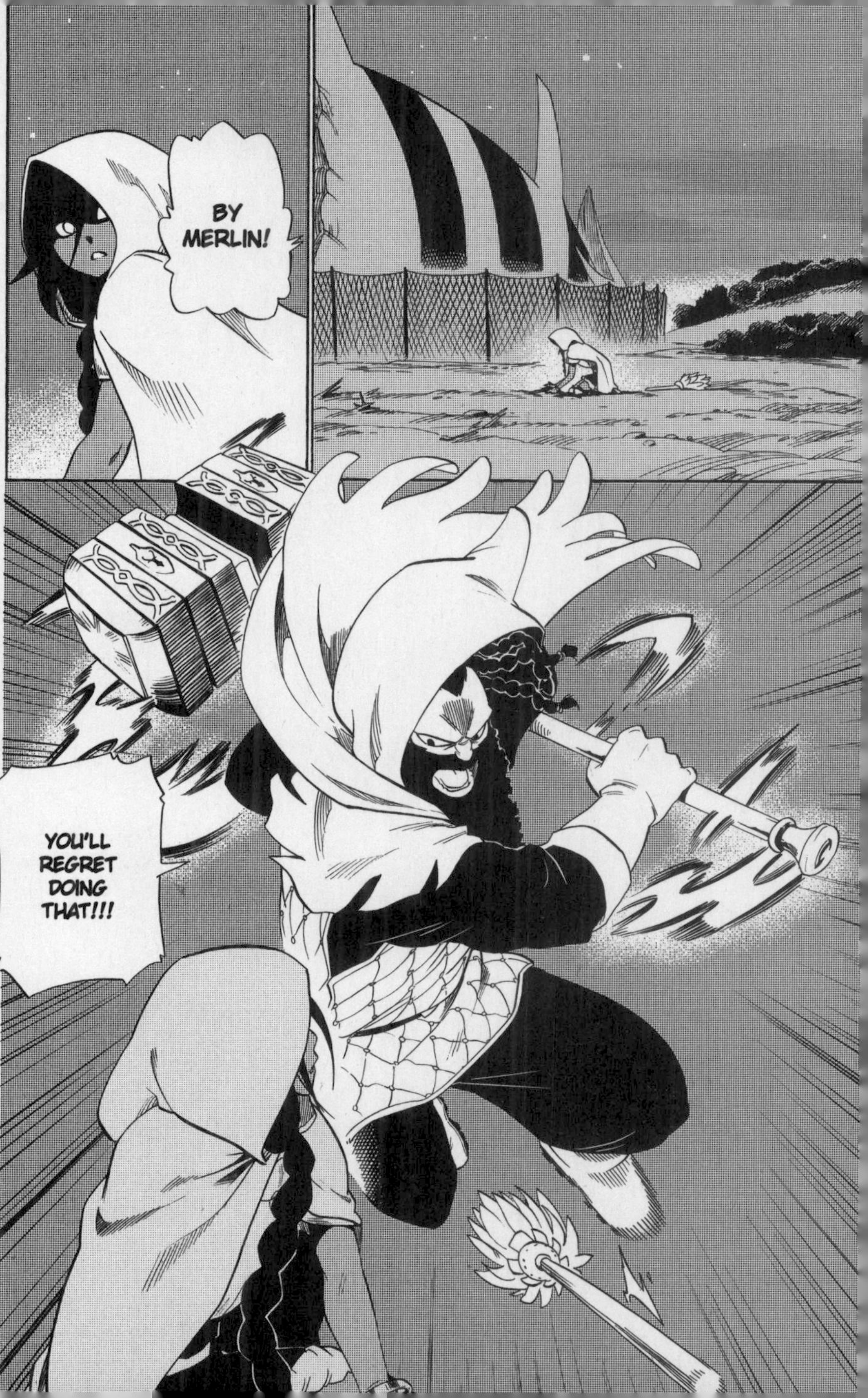
BY MERLIN!
YOU'LL REGRET DOING THAT!!!

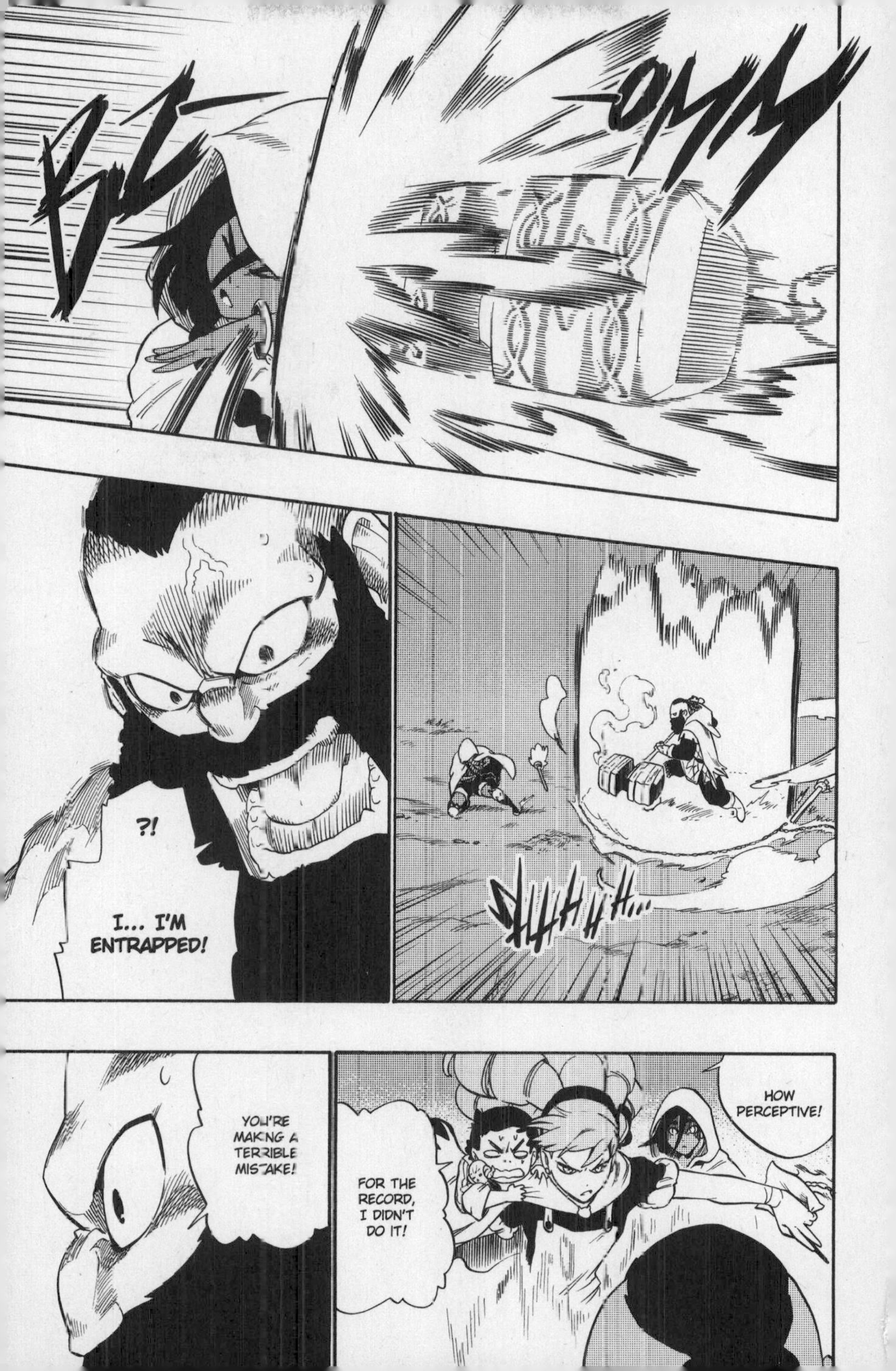
?!
I... I'M ENTRAPPED!
HOW PERCEPTIVE!
FOR THE RECORD, I DIDN'T DO IT!
YOU'RE MAKING A TERRIBLE MISTAKE!

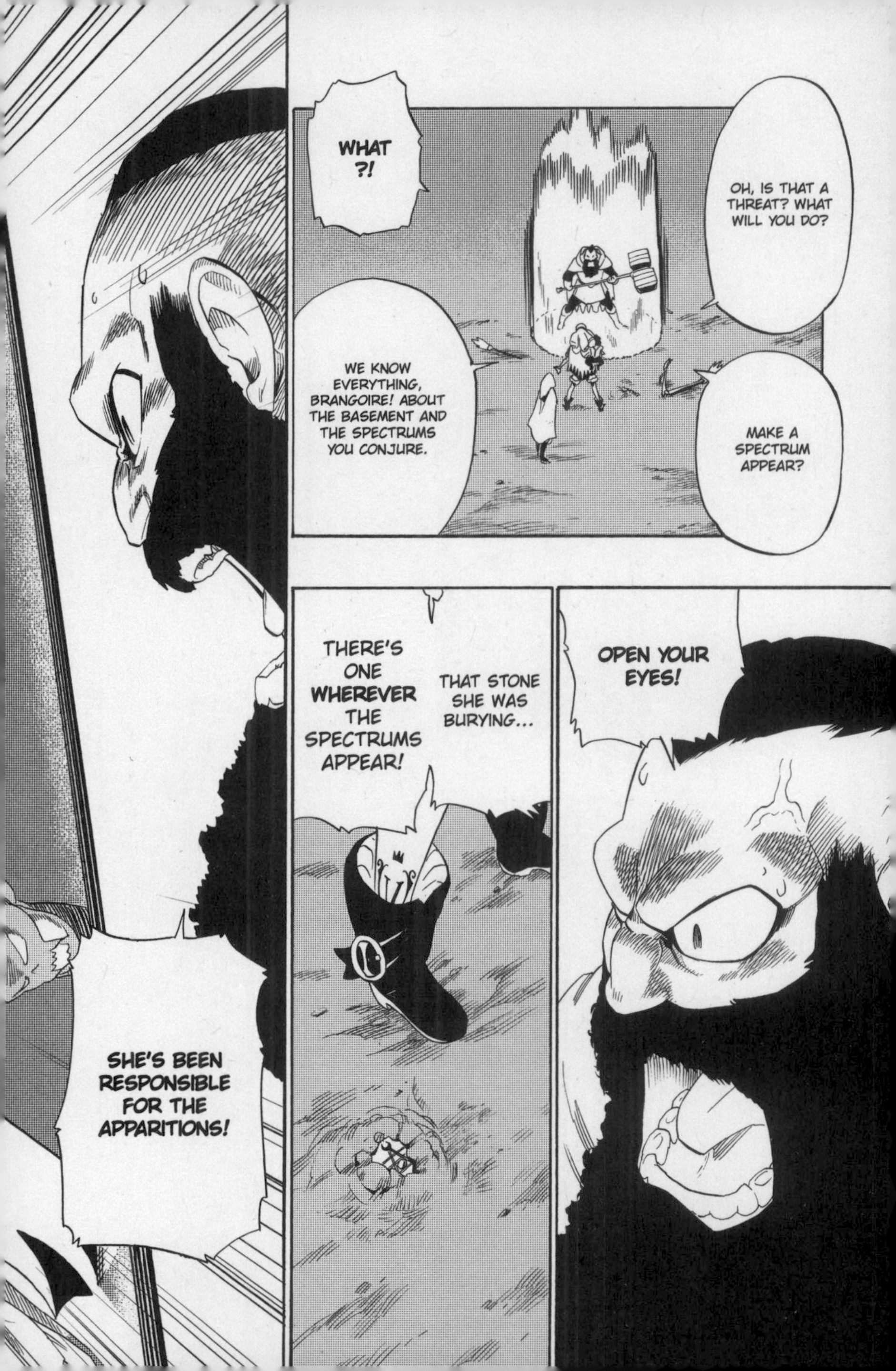
OH, IS THAT A THREAT? WHAT WILL YOU DO?
MAKE A SPECTRUM APPEAR?
WHAT ?!
WE KNOW EVERYTHING, BRANGOIRE! ABOUT THE BASEMENT AND THE SPECTRUMS YOU CONJURE.
OPEN YOUR EYES!
THAT STONE SHE WAS BURYING...
THERE'S ONE WHEREVER THE SPECTRUMS APPEAR!
SHE'S BEEN RESPONSIBLE FOR THE APPARITIONS!

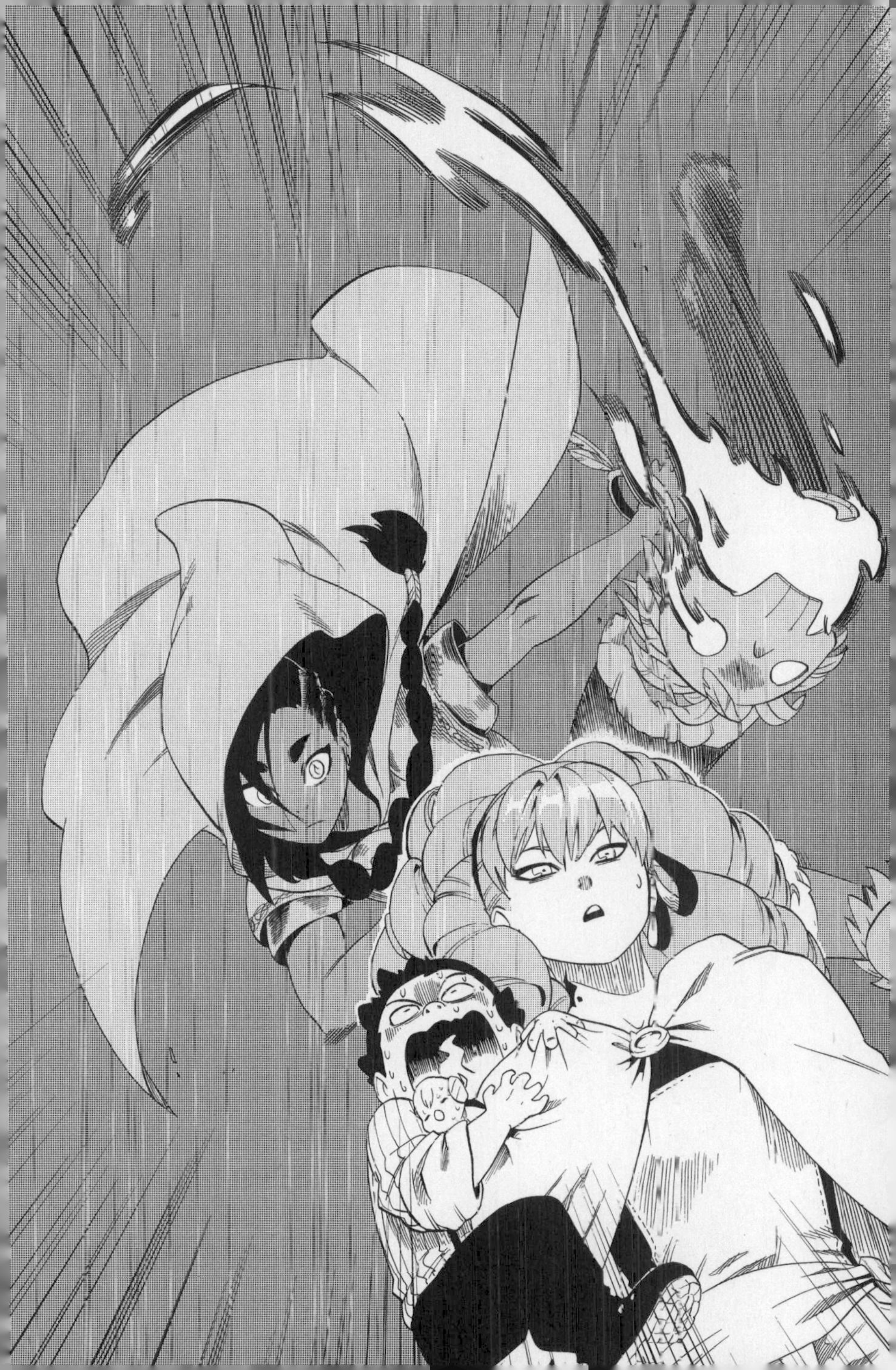

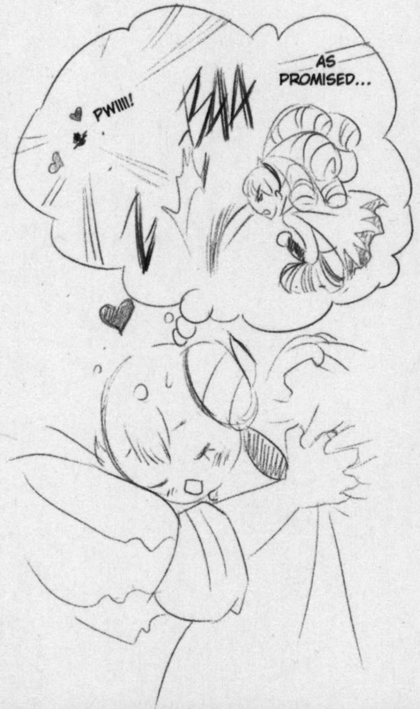
AS PROMISED...
PWIIII!

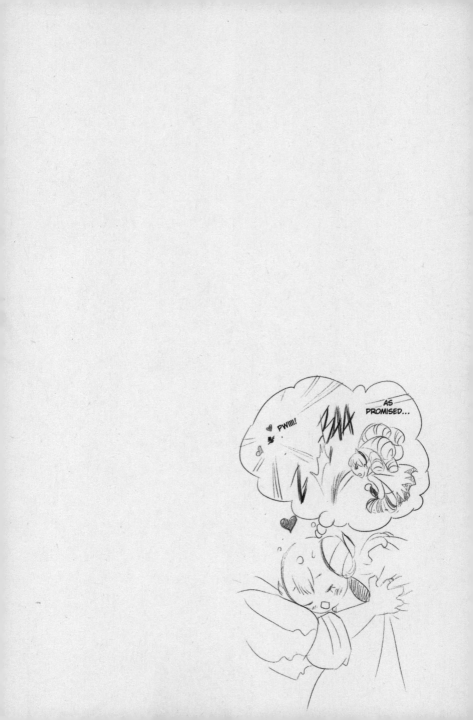

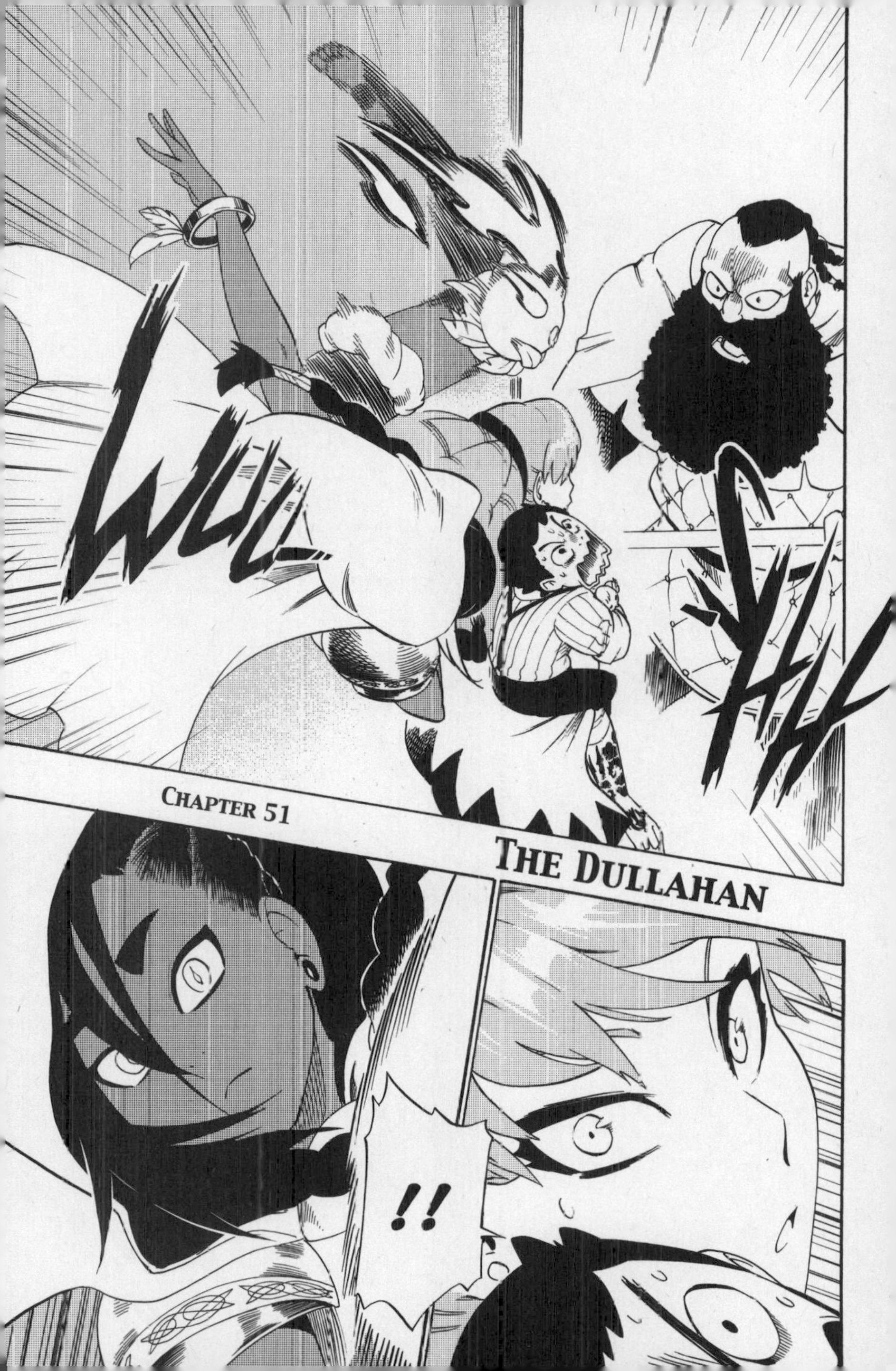
WUU
THK
WAM
Chapter 51
The Dullahan
!!

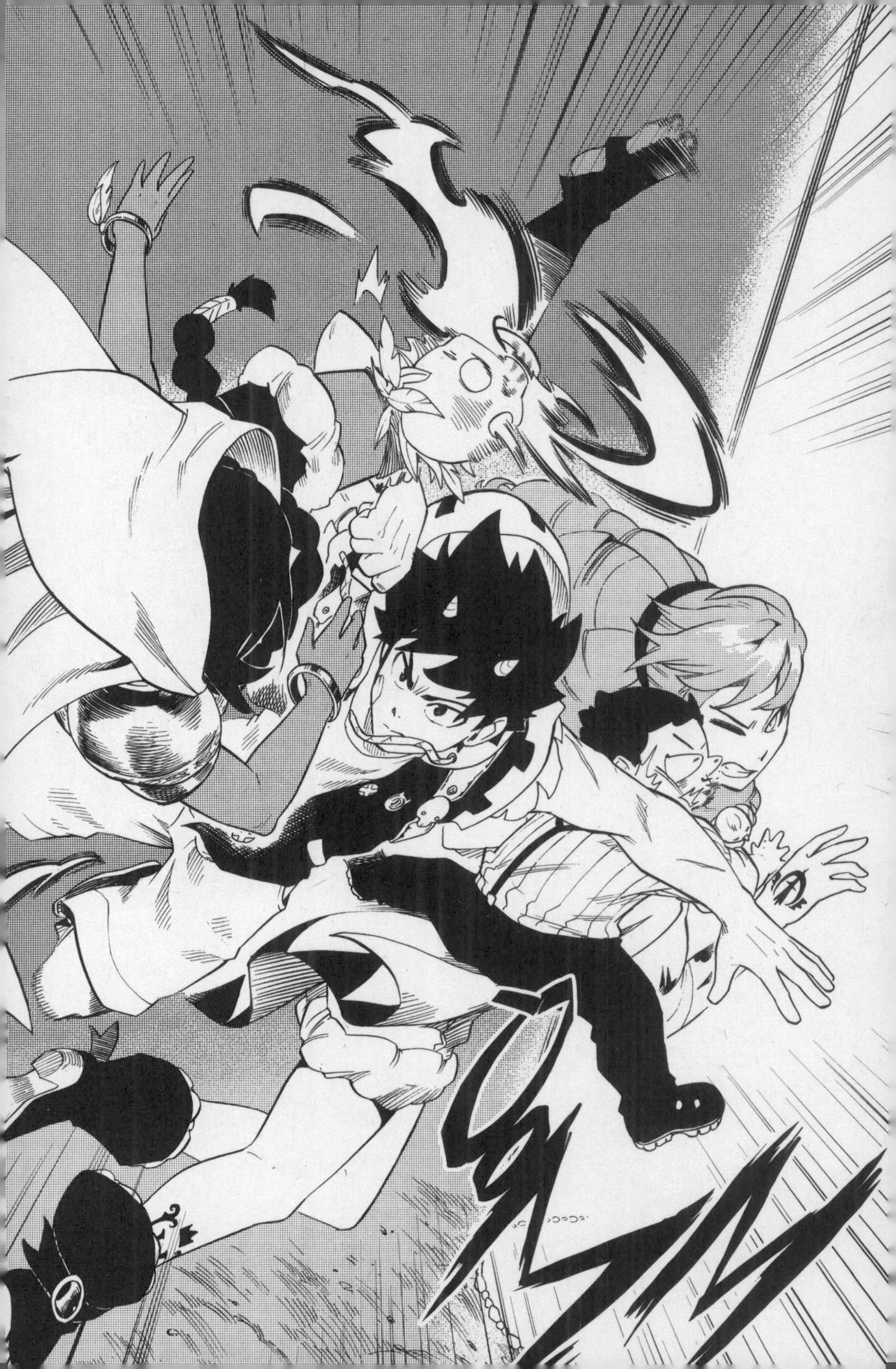

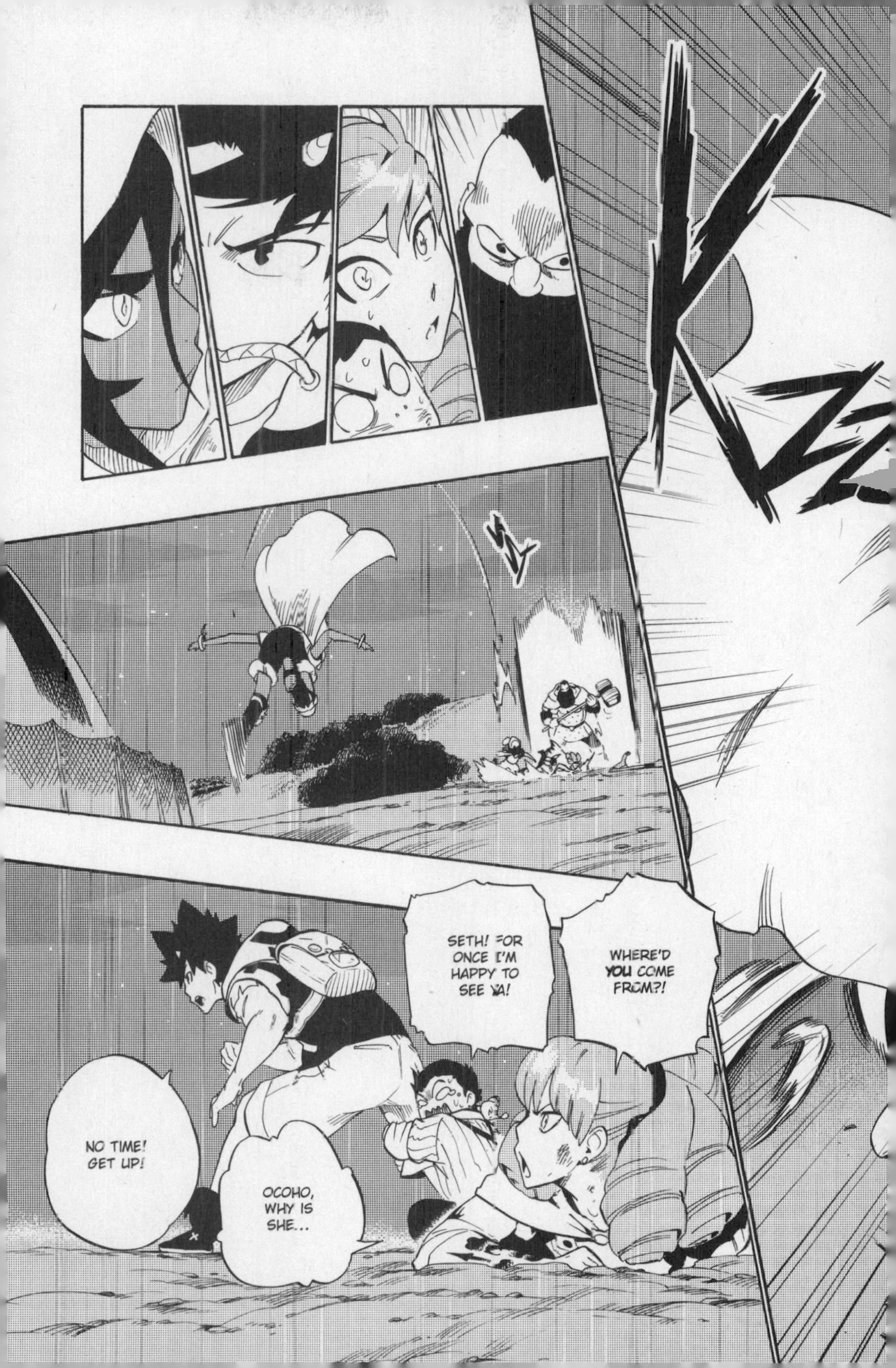

WHERE'D YOU COME FROM?!
SETH! FOR ONCE I'M HAPPY TO SEE YA!
OCOHO, WHY IS SHE...
NO TIME! GET UP!

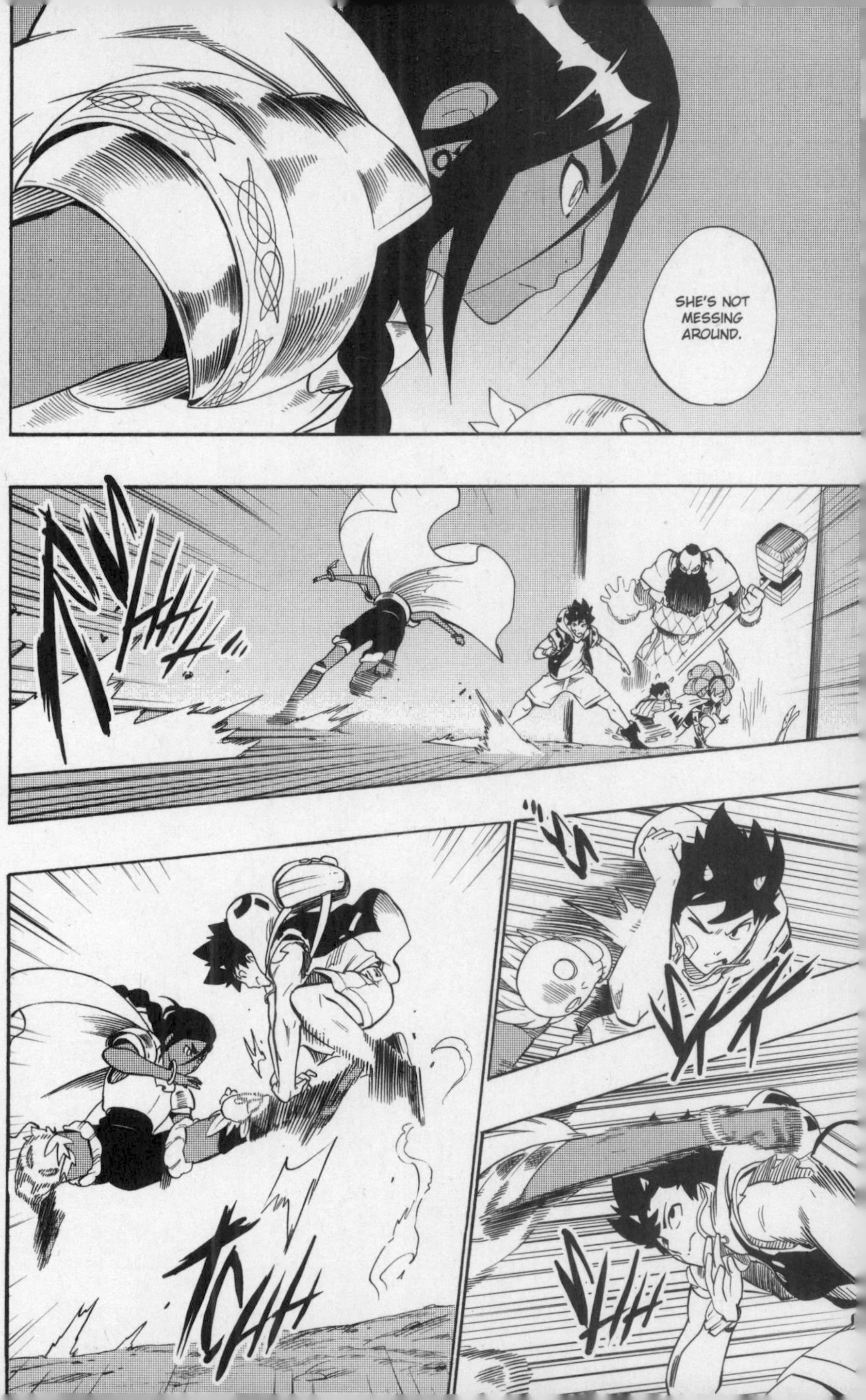
SHE'S NOT MESSING AROUND.
FSSHHH
SWK
TCHH
SHHH

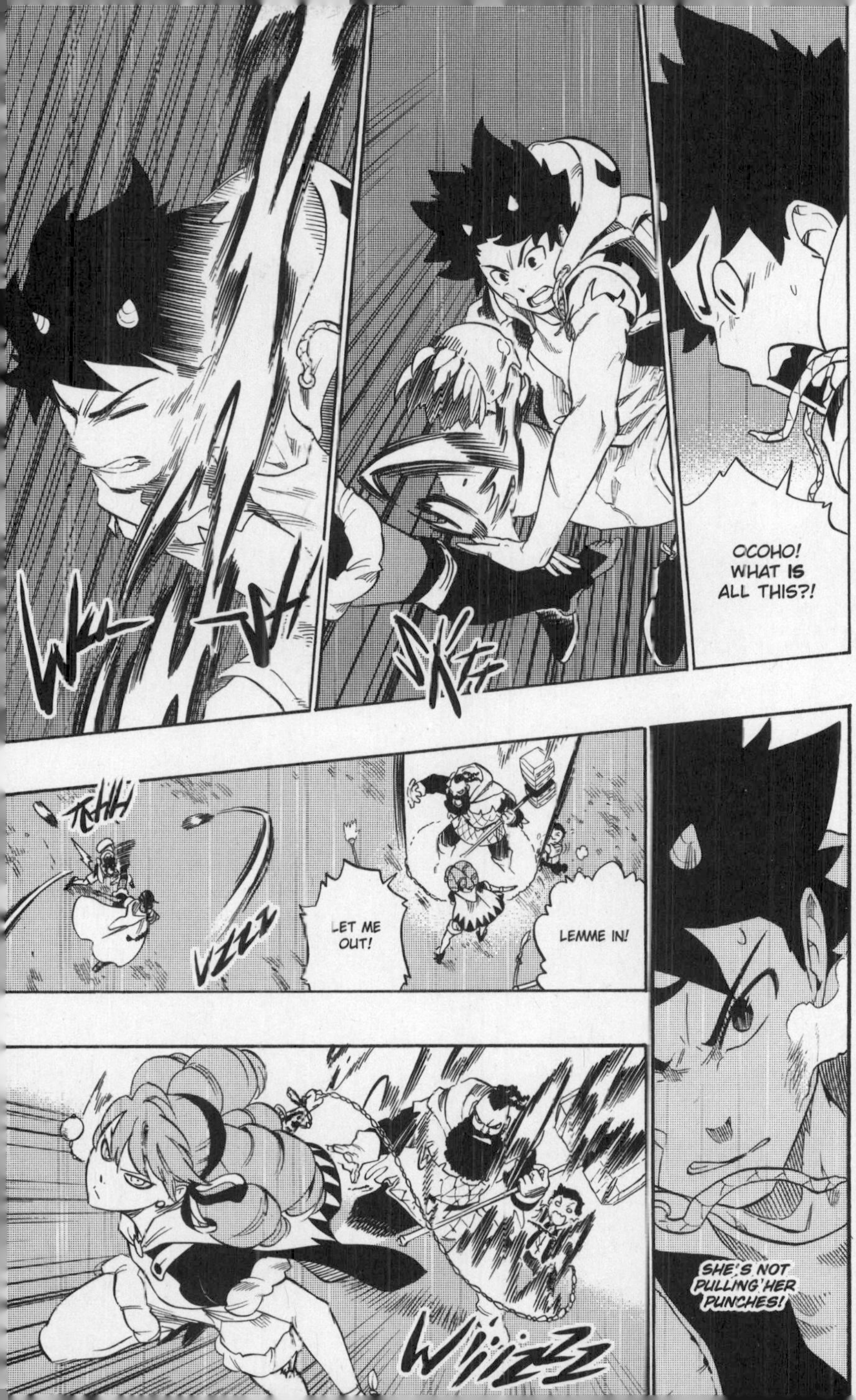
OCOHO! WHAT IS ALL THIS?!
SHE'S NOT PULLING HER PUNCHES!
LEMME IN!
LET ME OUT!
TCHH
VZZZ

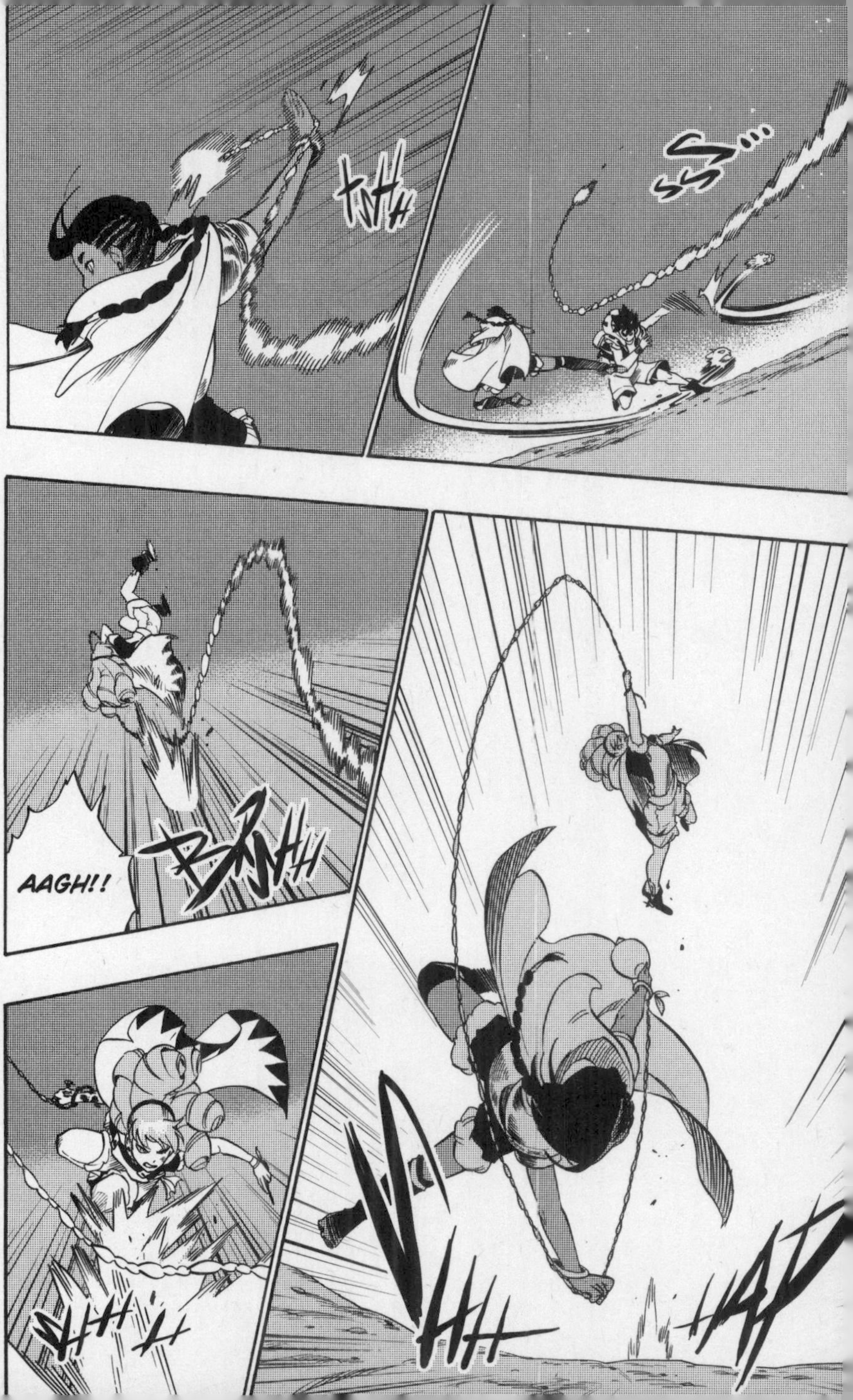
SSS...
TSHH
WHHH
HAP
BASHH
AAGH!!
SHHHH

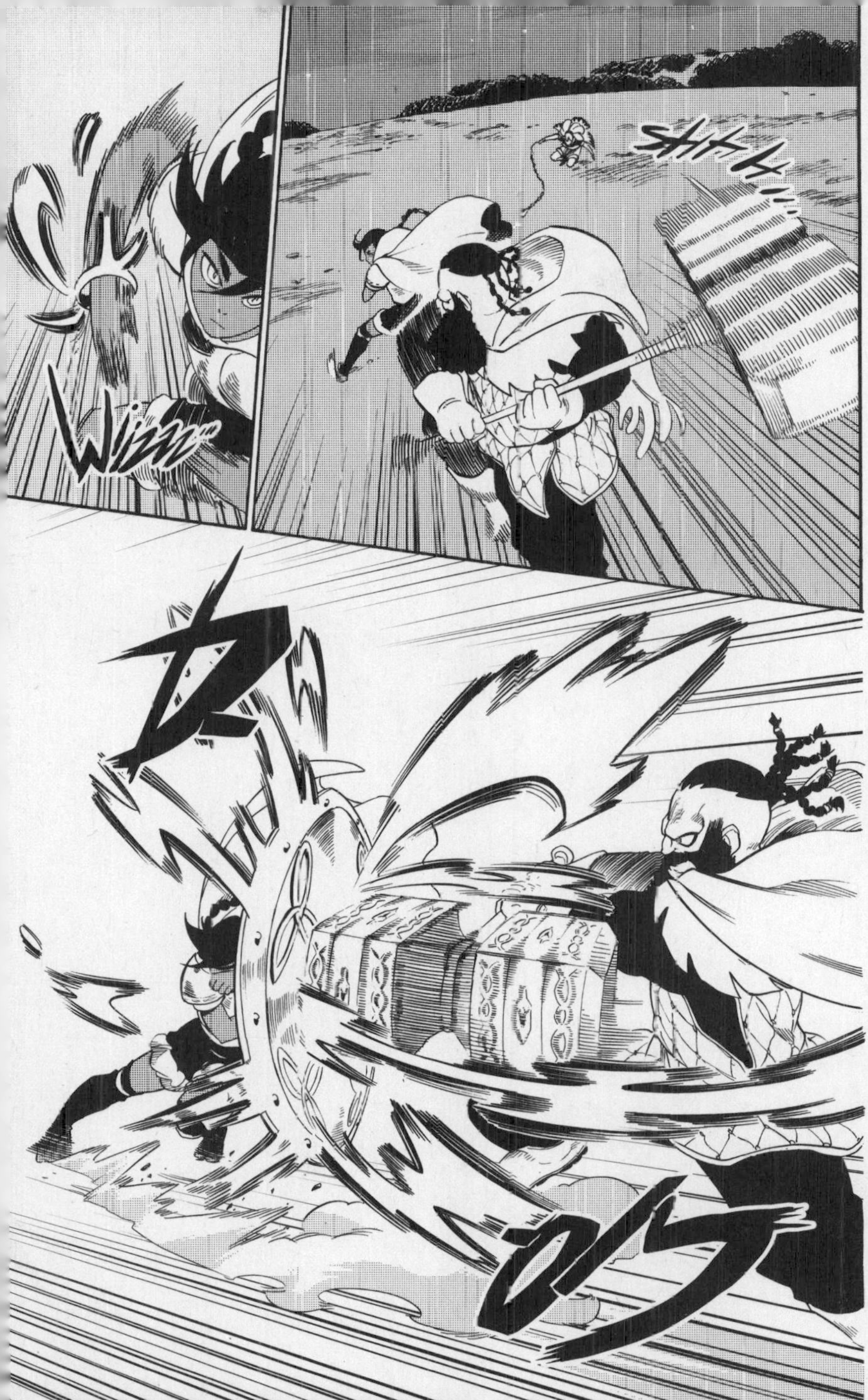
SHFF F...
WIZZZ...

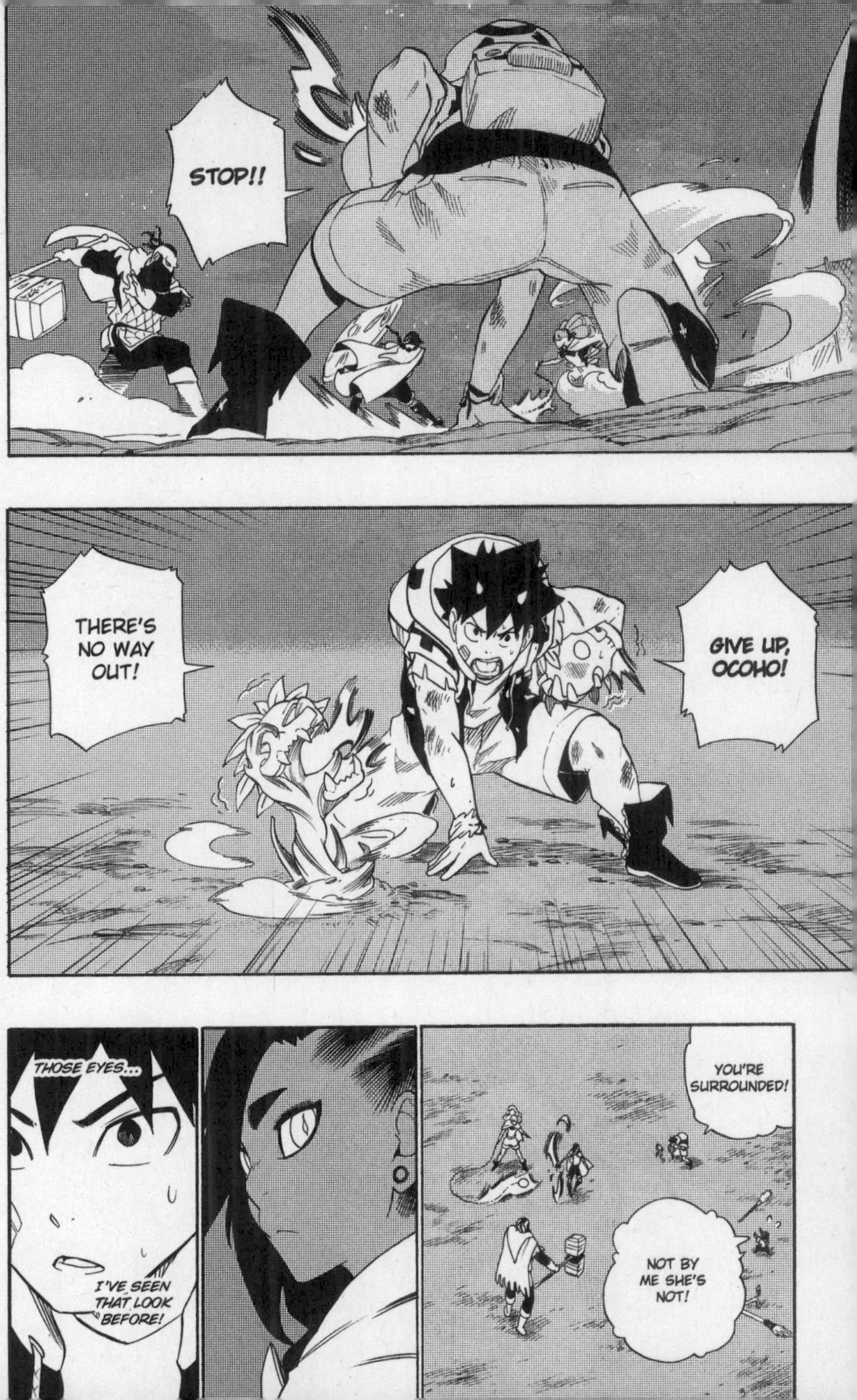
STOP!!
GIVE UP, OCOHO!
THERE'S NO WAY OUT!
YOU'RE SURROUNDED!
NOT BY ME SHE'S NOT!
THOSE EYES...
I'VE SEEN THAT LOOK BEFORE!

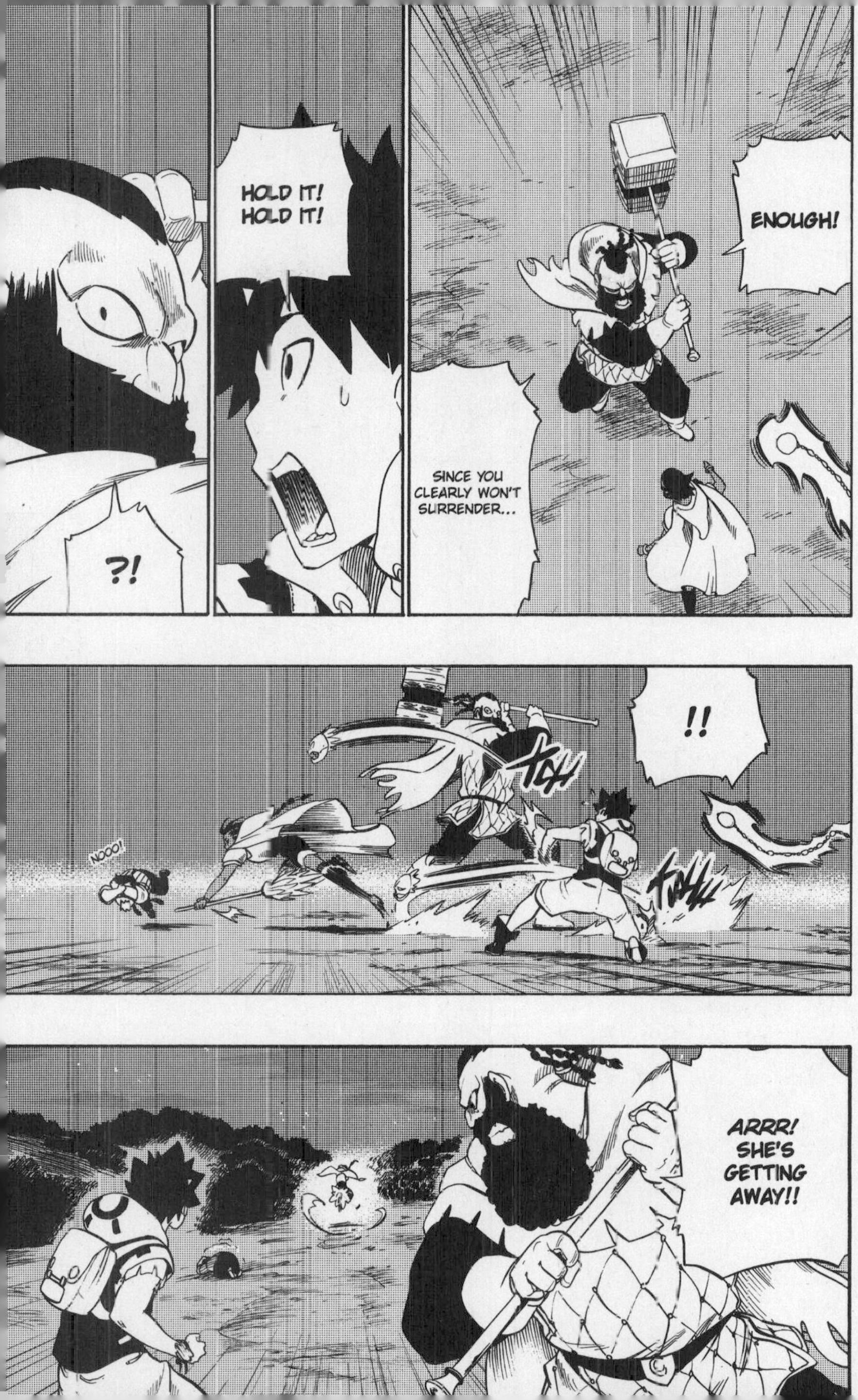
ENOUGH!
SINCE YOU CLEARLY WON'T SURRENDER...
HOLD IT! HOLD IT!
?!
!!
TCH
NOOO!
ARRR! SHE'S GETTING AWAY!!

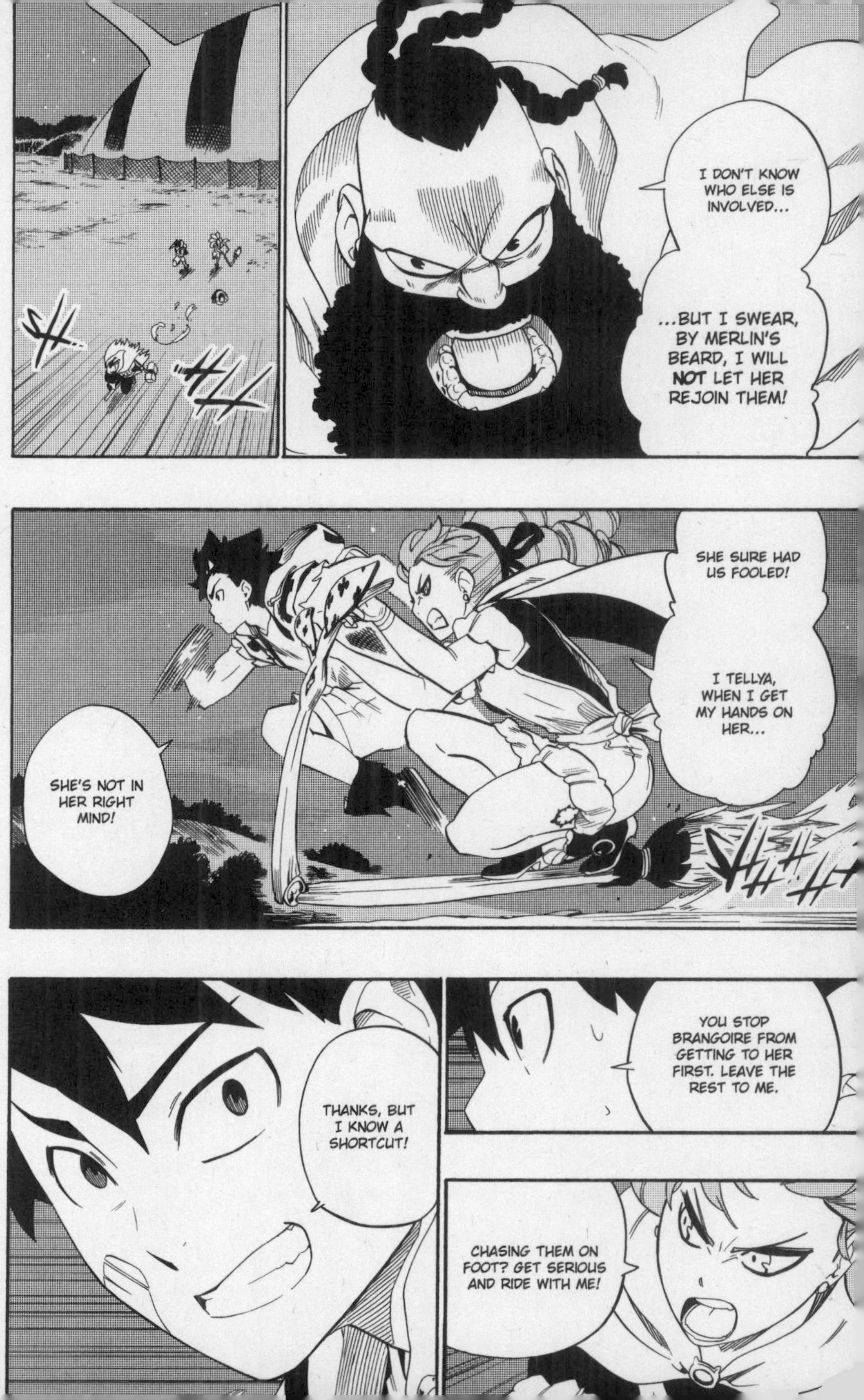
I DON'T KNOW WHO ELSE IS INVOLVED...
...BUT I SWEAR, BY MERLIN'S BEARD, I WILL **NOT** LET HER REJOIN THEM!
SHE SURE HAD US FOOLED!
I TELLYA, WHEN I GET MY HANDS ON HER...
SHE'S NOT IN HER RIGHT MIND!
YOU STOP BRANGOIRE FROM GETTING TO HER FIRST. LEAVE THE REST TO ME.
CHASING THEM ON FOOT? GET SERIOUS AND RIDE WITH ME!
THANKS, BUT I KNOW A SHORTCUT!

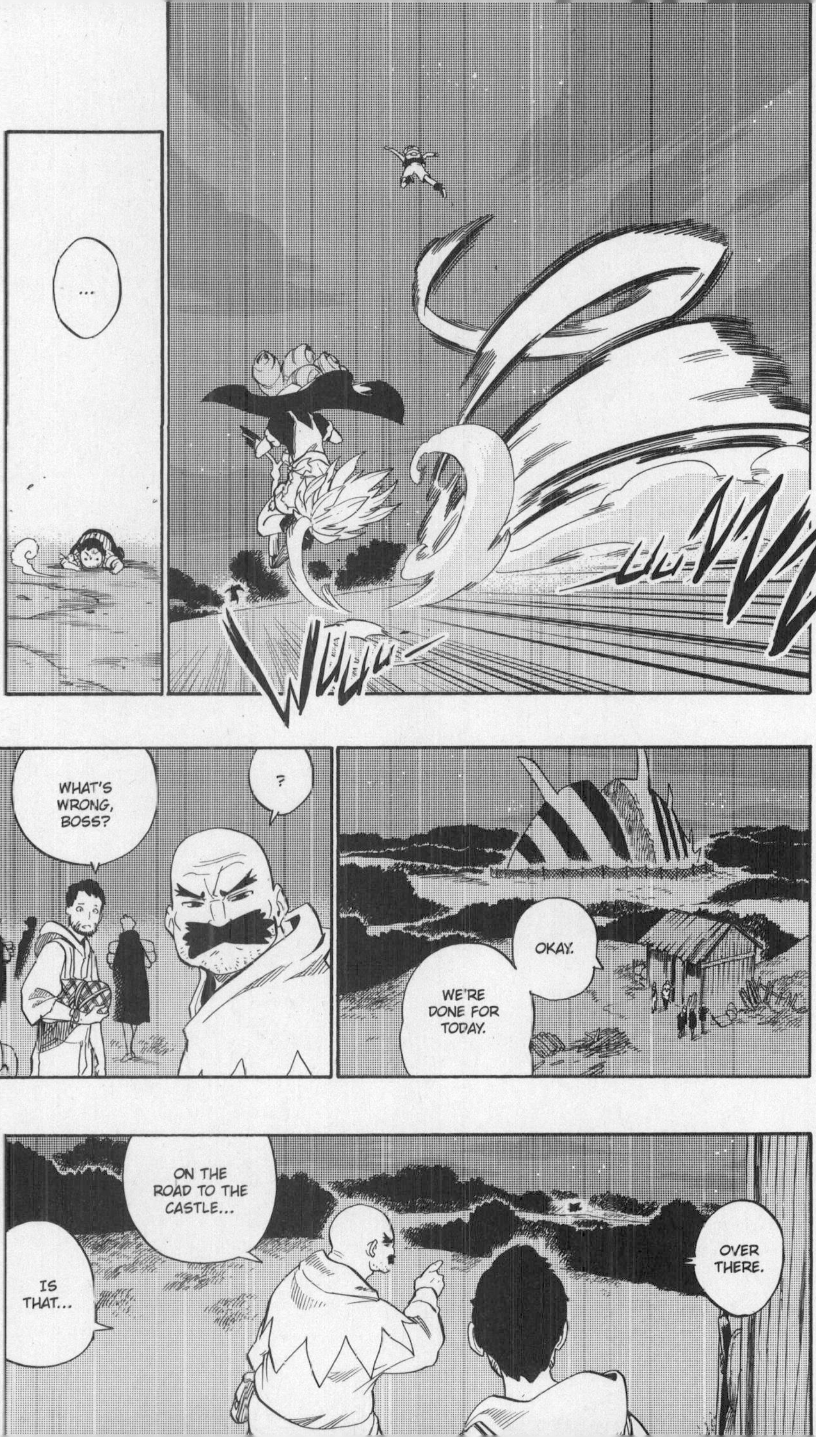
...
OKAY.
WE'RE DONE FOR TODAY.
?
WHAT'S WRONG, BOSS?
OVER THERE.
ON THE ROAD TO THE CASTLE...
IS THAT...

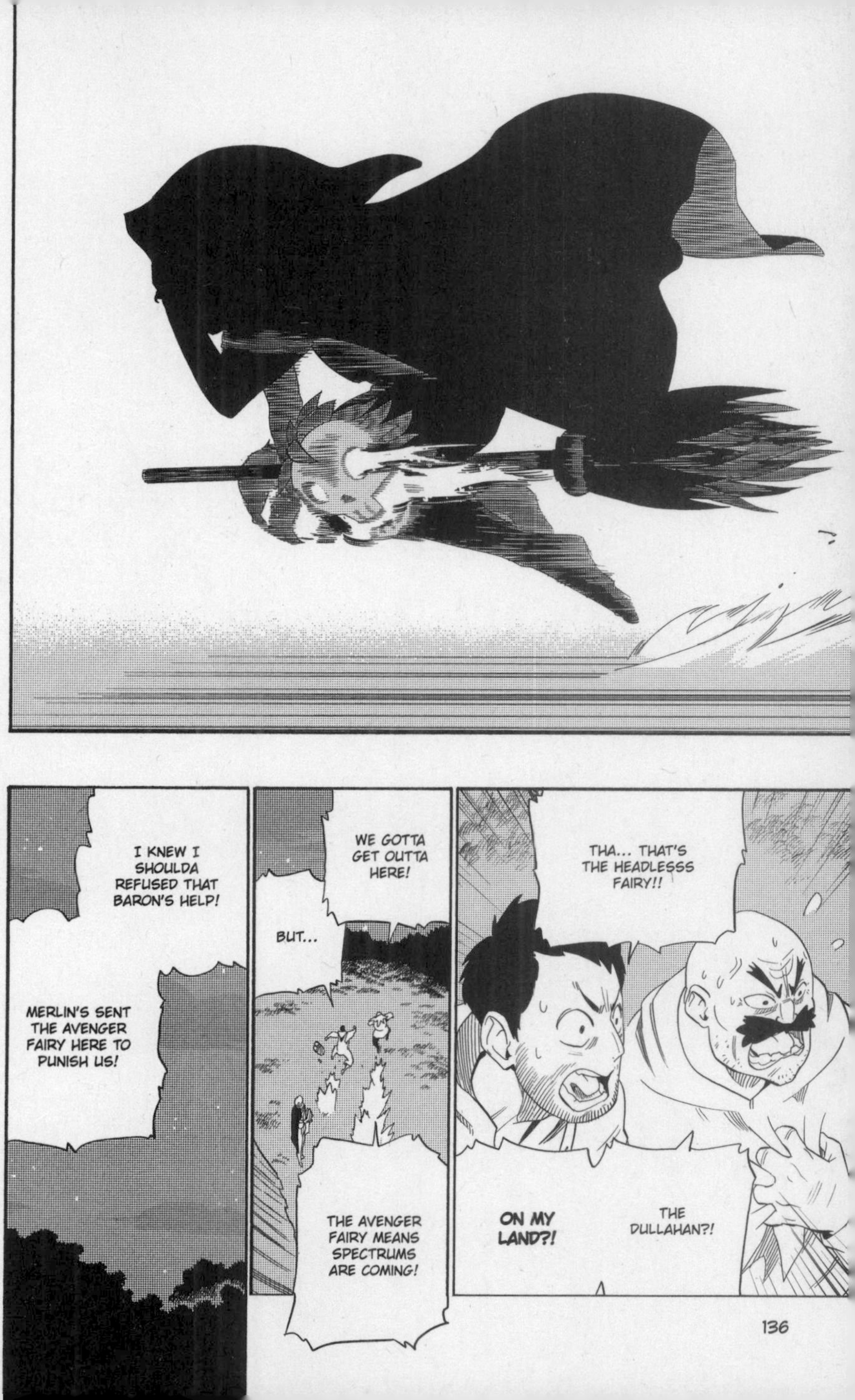
THA... THAT'S THE HEADLESSS FAIRY!!
THE DULLAHAN?!
ON MY LAND?!
WE GOTTA GET OUTTA HERE!
BUT...
THE AVENGER FAIRY MEANS SPECTRUMS ARE COMING!
I KNEW I SHOULDA REFUSED THAT BARON'S HELP!
MERLIN'S SENT THE AVENGER FAIRY HERE TO PUNISH US!

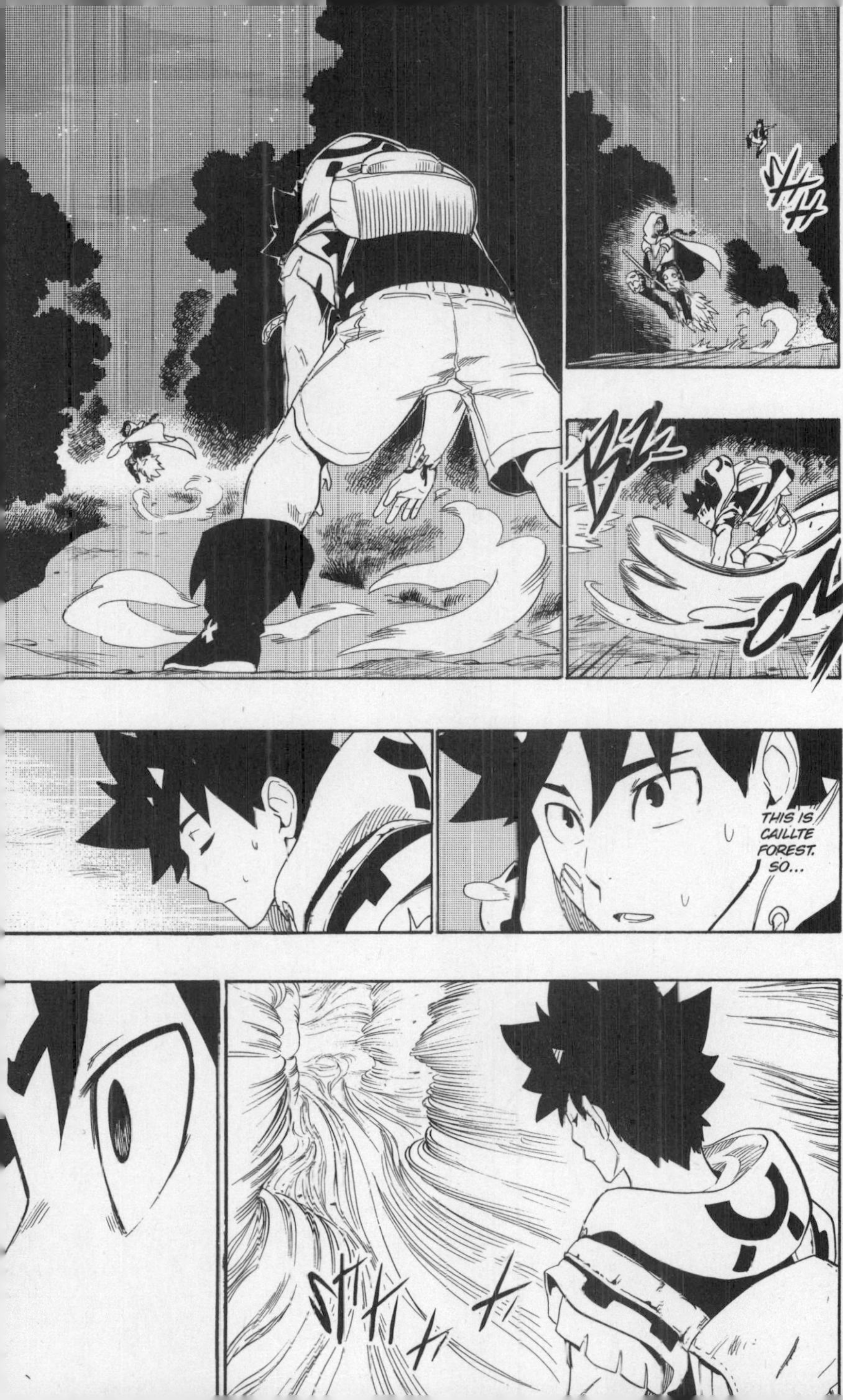
THIS IS CAILLTE FOREST. SO...

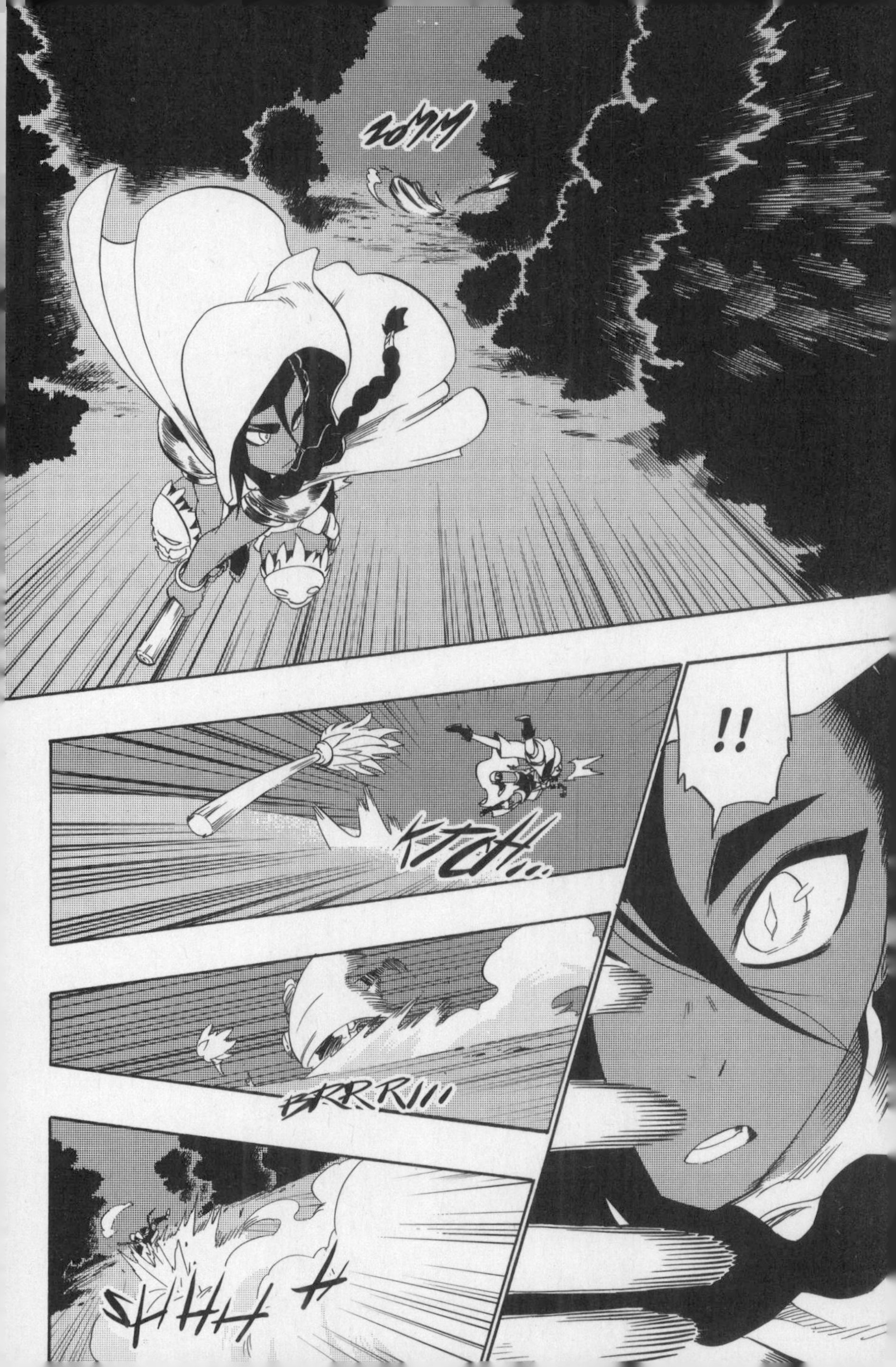
ZOOM
!!
KTCH...
BRRRIII
SHHHH

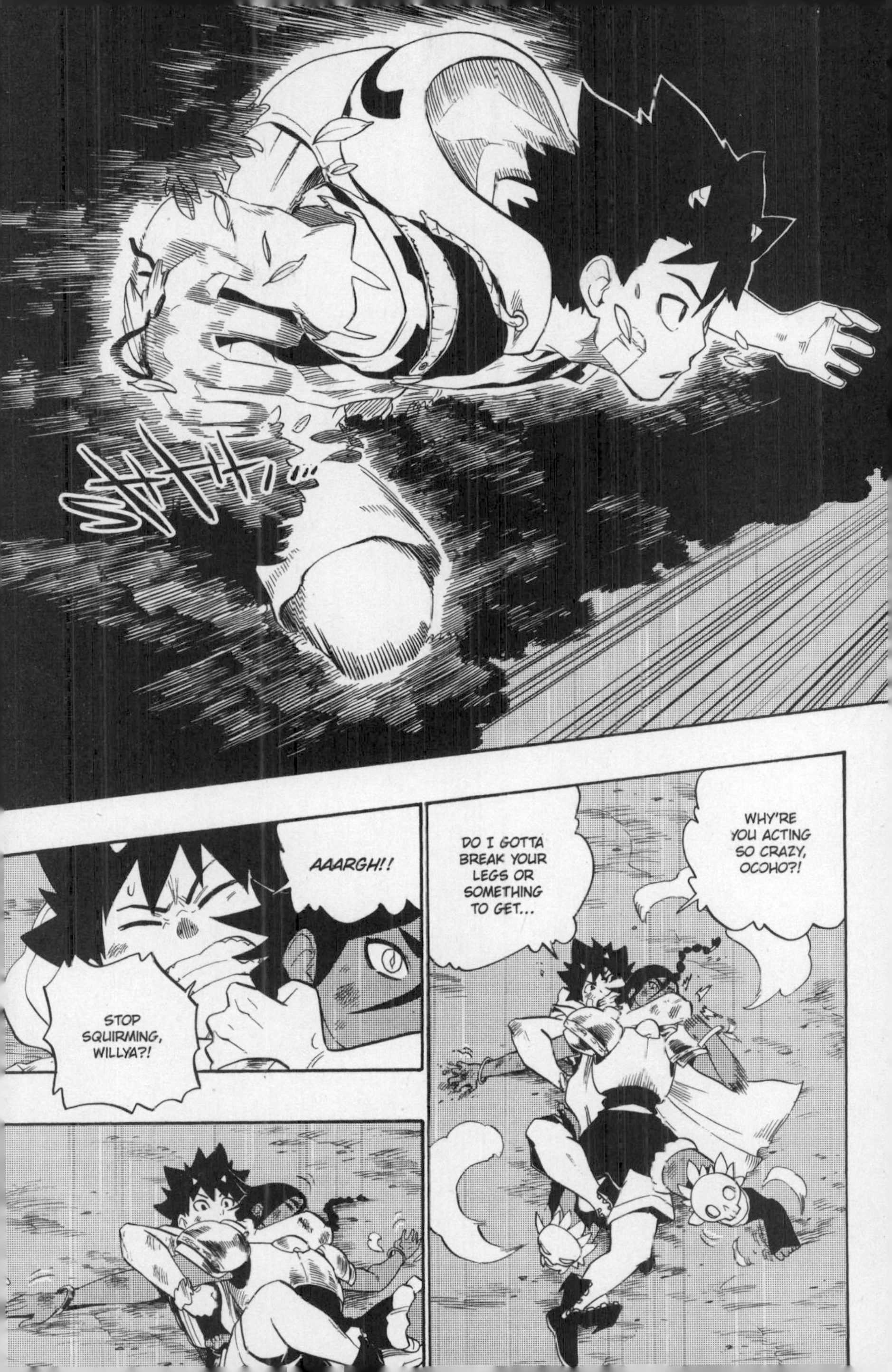
WHY'RE YOU ACTING SO CRAZY, OCOHO?!
DO I GOTTA BREAK YOUR LEGS OR SOMETHING TO GET...
AAARGH!!
STOP SQUIRMING, WILLYA?!

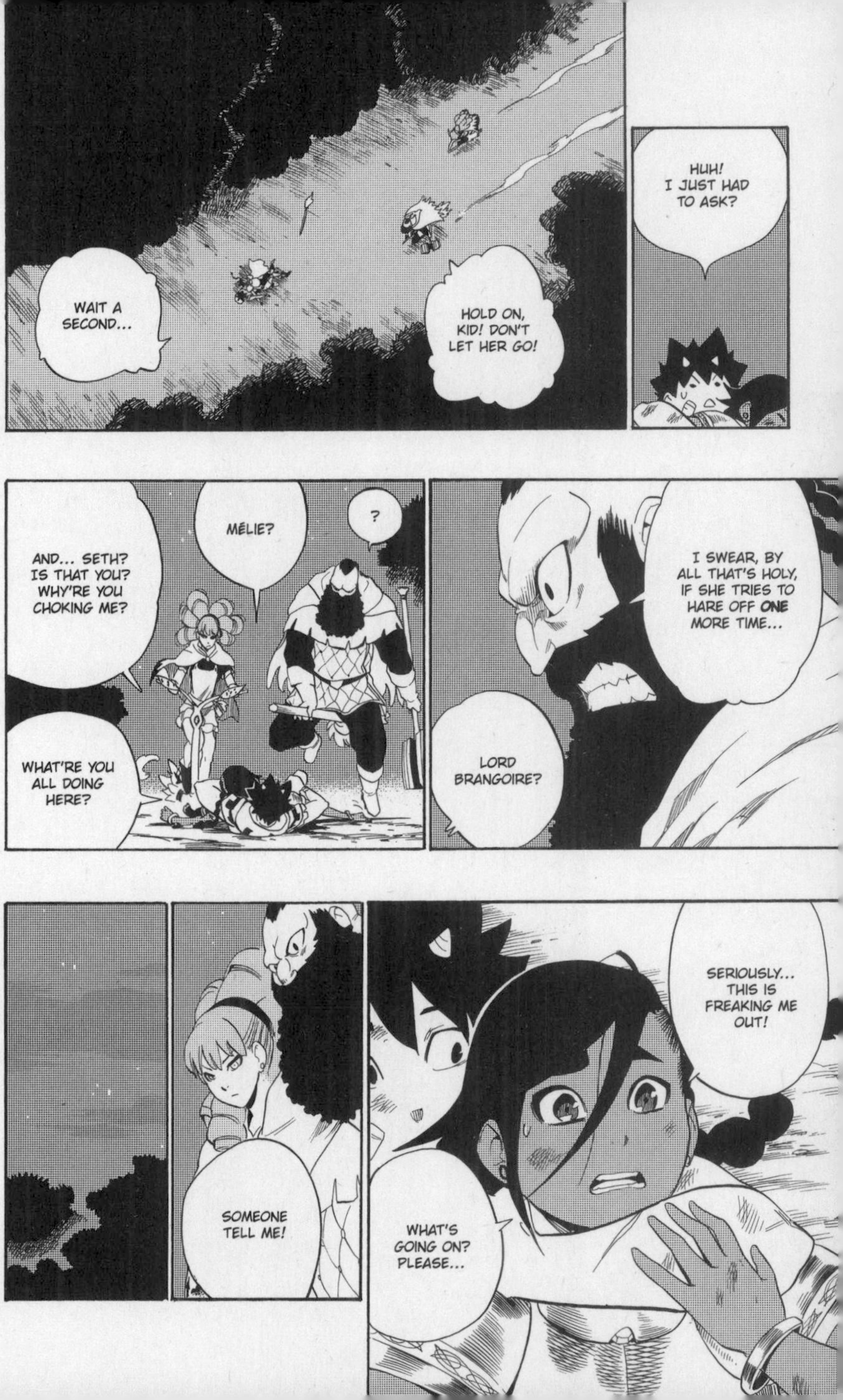
HUH! I JUST HAD TO ASK?
HOLD ON, KID! DON'T LET HER GO!
WAIT A SECOND...
I SWEAR, BY ALL THAT'S HOLY, IF SHE TRIES TO HARE OFF **ONE** MORE TIME...
LORD BRANGOIRE?
?
MÉLIE?
AND... SETH? IS THAT YOU? WHY'RE YOU CHOKING ME?
WHAT'RE YOU ALL DOING HERE?
SERIOUSLY... THIS IS FREAKING ME OUT!
WHAT'S GOING ON? PLEASE...
SOMEONE TELL ME!

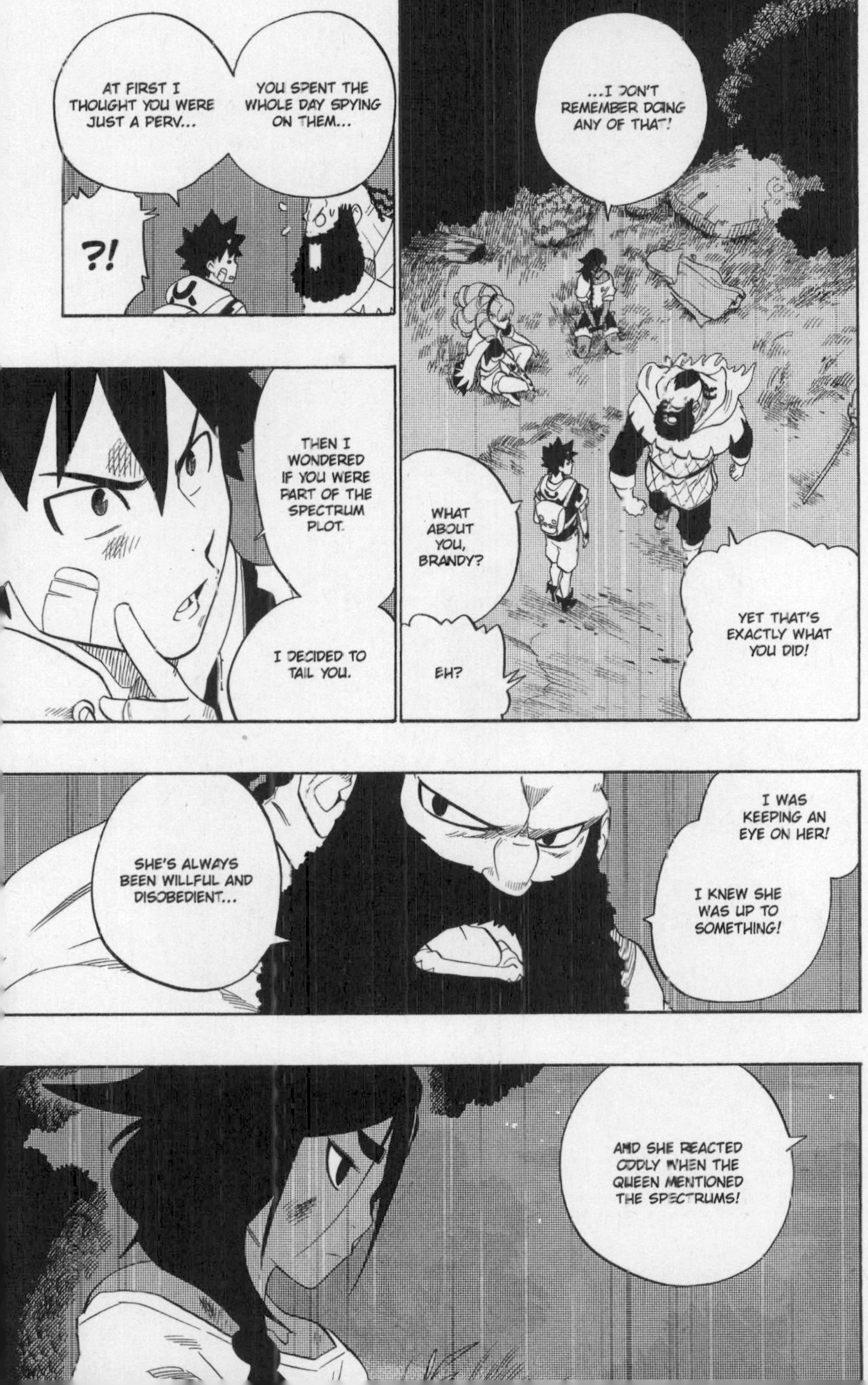
...I DON'T REMEMBER DOING ANY OF THAT!
YET THAT'S EXACTLY WHAT YOU DID!
WHAT ABOUT YOU, BRANDY?
EH?
YOU SPENT THE WHOLE DAY SPYING ON THEM...
AT FIRST I THOUGHT YOU WERE JUST A PERV...
?!
THEN I WONDERED IF YOU WERE PART OF THE SPECTRUM PLOT.
I DECIDED TO TAIL YOU.
I WAS KEEPING AN EYE ON HER!
I KNEW SHE WAS UP TO SOMETHING!
SHE'S ALWAYS BEEN WILLFUL AND DISOBEDIENT...
AND SHE REACTED ODDLY WHEN THE QUEEN MENTIONED THE SPECTRUMS!

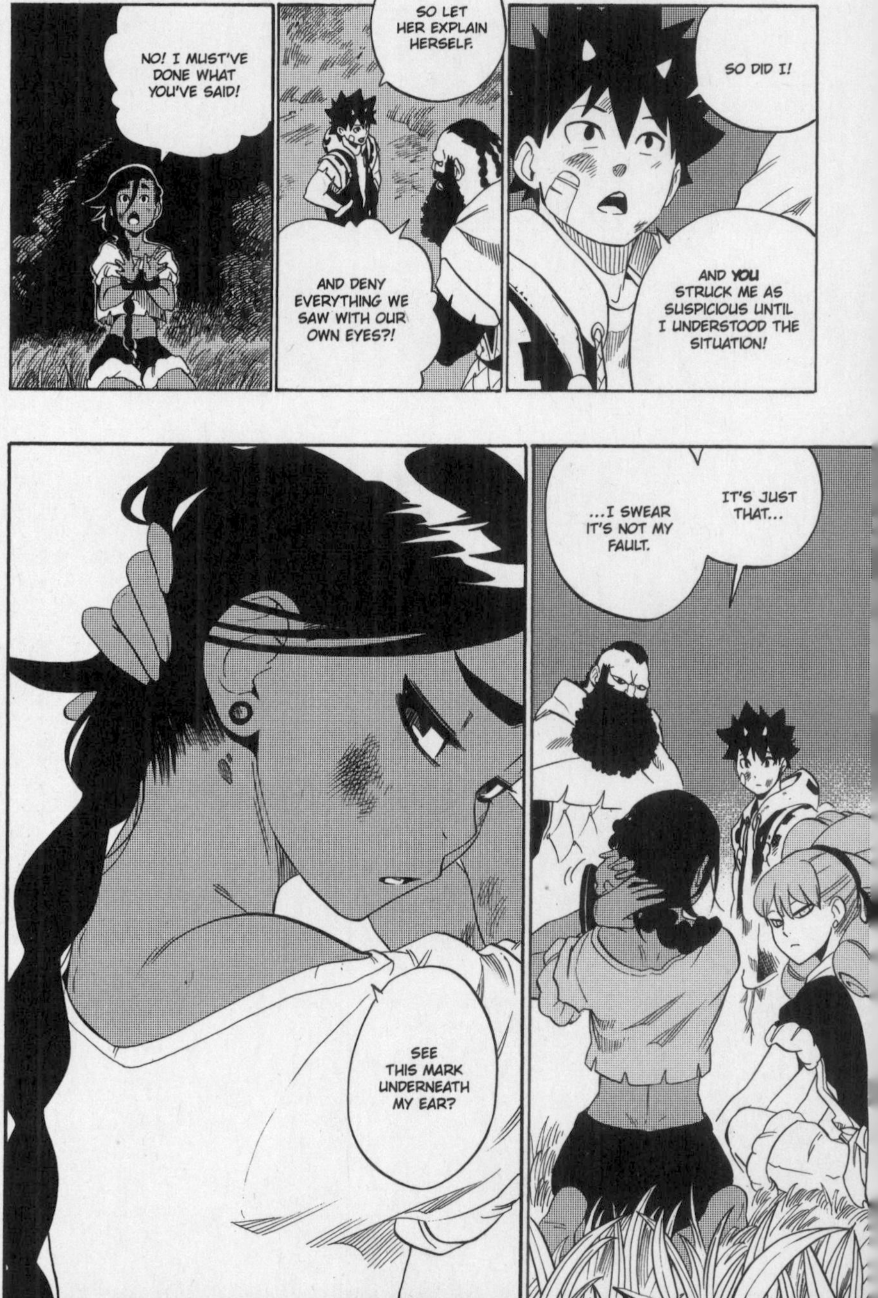
SO DID I!
AND YOU STRUCK ME AS SUSPICIOUS UNTIL I UNDERSTOOD THE SITUATION!
SO LET HER EXPLAIN HERSELF.
AND DENY EVERYTHING WE SAW WITH OUR OWN EYES?!
NO! I MUST'VE DONE WHAT YOU'VE SAID!
IT'S JUST THAT...
...I SWEAR IT'S NOT MY FAULT.
SEE THIS MARK UNDERNEATH MY EAR?

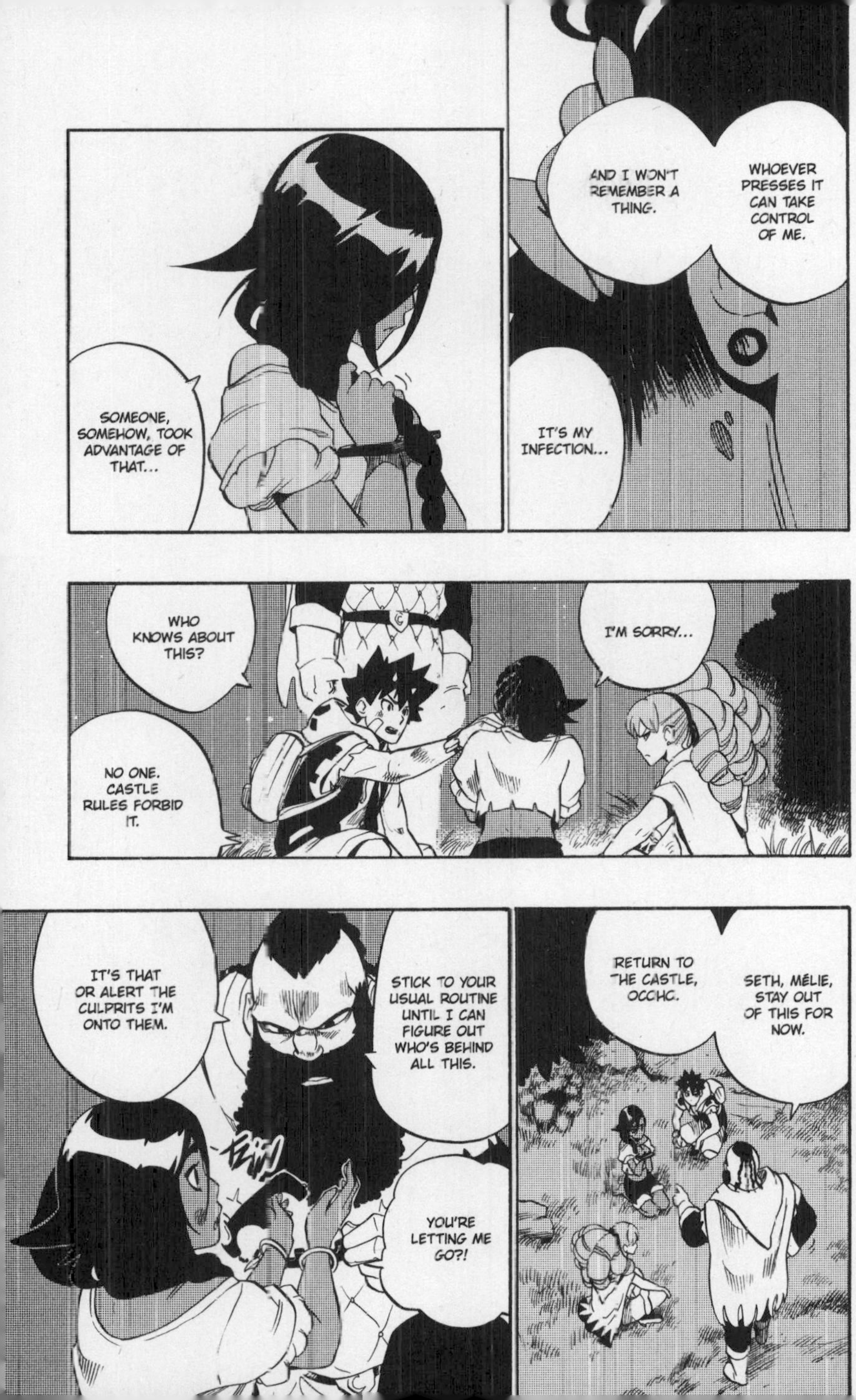
WHOEVER PRESSES IT CAN TAKE CONTROL OF ME.
AND I WON'T REMEMBER A THING.
IT'S MY INFECTION...
SOMEONE, SOMEHOW, TOOK ADVANTAGE OF THAT...
I'M SORRY...
WHO KNOWS ABOUT THIS?
NO ONE. CASTLE RULES FORBID IT.
SETH, MÉLIE, STAY OUT OF THIS FOR NOW.
RETURN TO THE CASTLE, OCCHO.
STICK TO YOUR USUAL ROUTINE UNTIL I CAN FIGURE OUT WHO'S BEHIND ALL THIS.
IT'S THAT OR ALERT THE CULPRITS I'M ONTO THEM.
YOU'RE LETTING ME GO?!

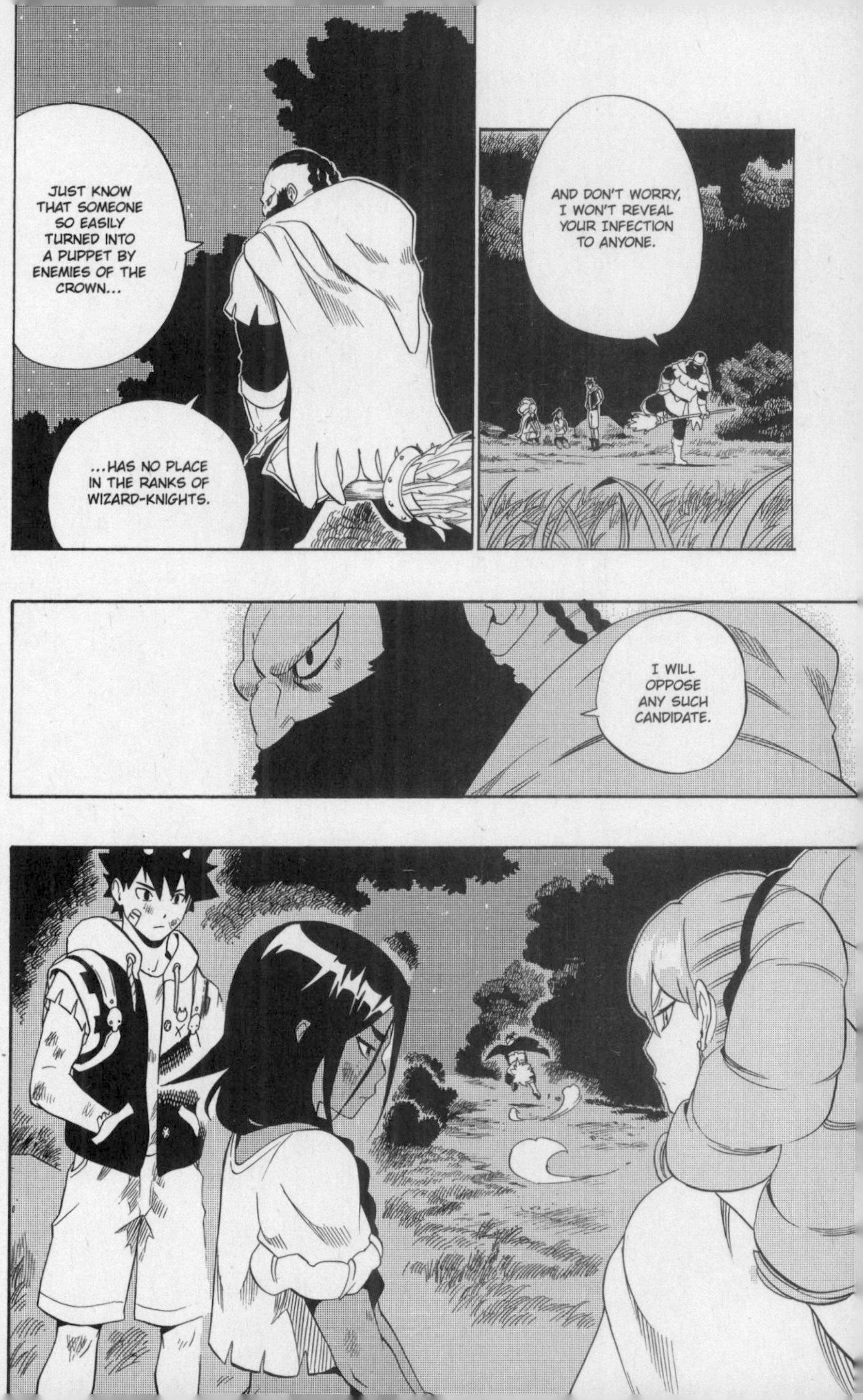
AND DON'T WORRY, I WON'T REVEAL YOUR INFECTION TO ANYONE.
JUST KNOW THAT SOMEONE SO EASILY TURNED INTO A PUPPET BY ENEMIES OF THE CROWN...
...HAS NO PLACE IN THE RANKS OF WIZARD-KNIGHTS.
I WILL OPPOSE ANY SUCH CANDIDATE.

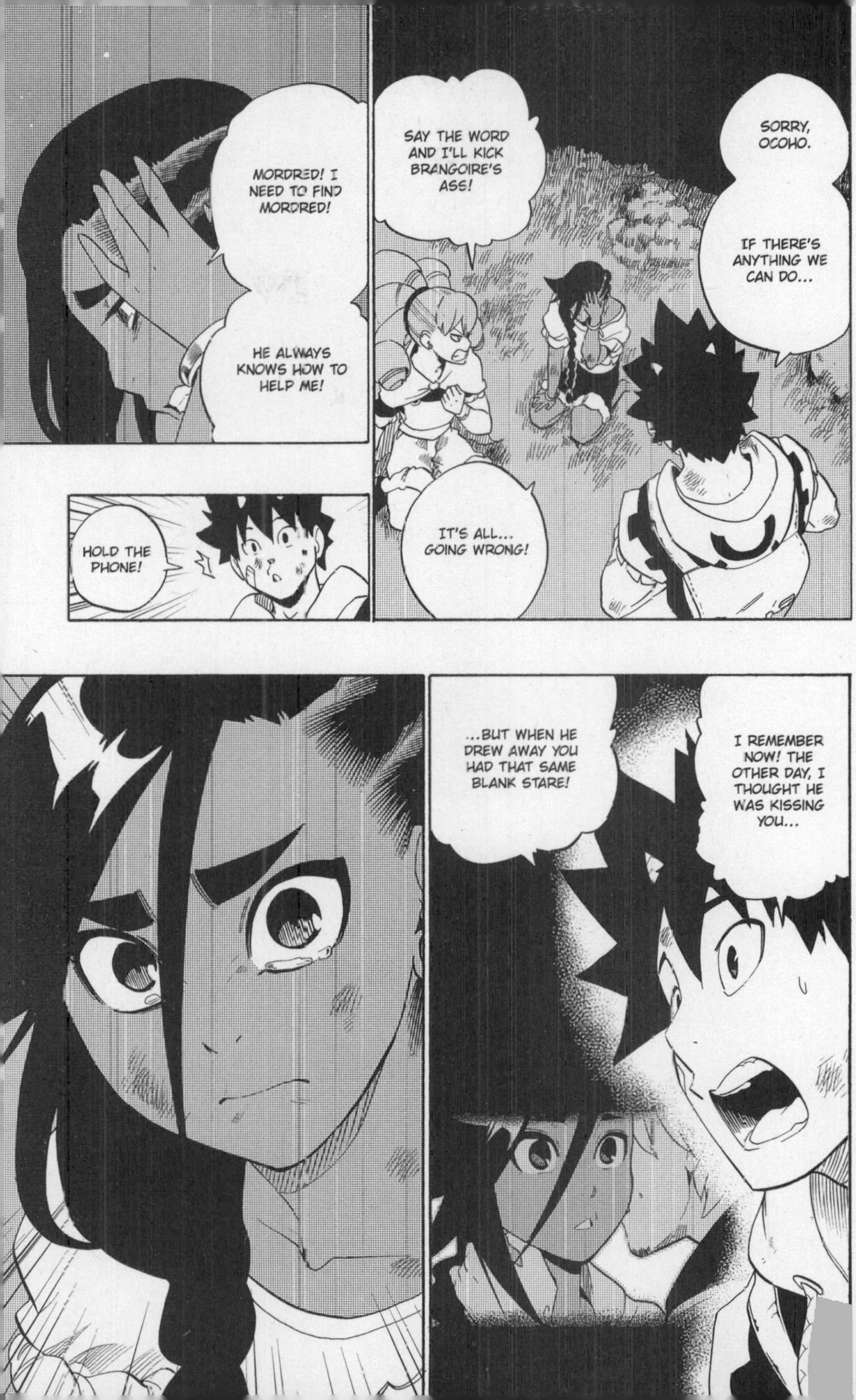
SORRY, OCOHO.
IF THERE'S ANYTHING WE CAN DO...
SAY THE WORD AND I'LL KICK BRANGOIRE'S ASS!
IT'S ALL... GOING WRONG!
MORDRED! I NEED TO FIND MORDRED!
HE ALWAYS KNOWS HOW TO HELP ME!
HOLD THE PHONE!
I REMEMBER NOW! THE OTHER DAY, I THOUGHT HE WAS KISSING YOU...
...BUT WHEN HE DREW AWAY YOU HAD THAT SAME BLANK STARE!

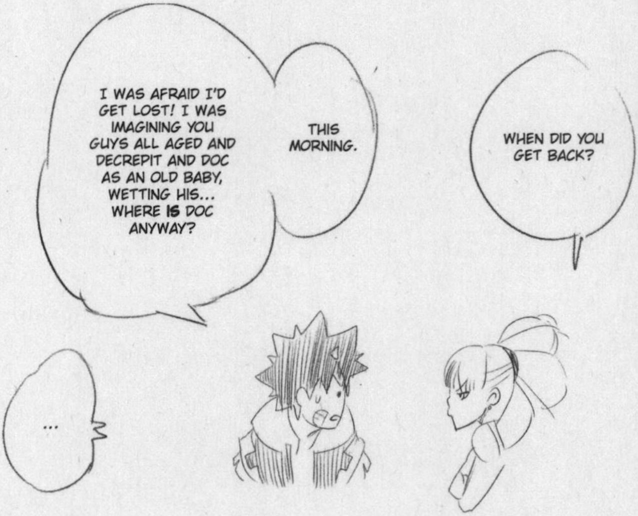
WHEN DID YOU GET BACK?
THIS MORNING.
I WAS AFRAID I'D GET LOST! I WAS IMAGINING YOU GUYS ALL AGED AND DECREPIT AND DOC AS AN OLD BABY, WETTING HIS... WHERE IS DOC ANYWAY?
...

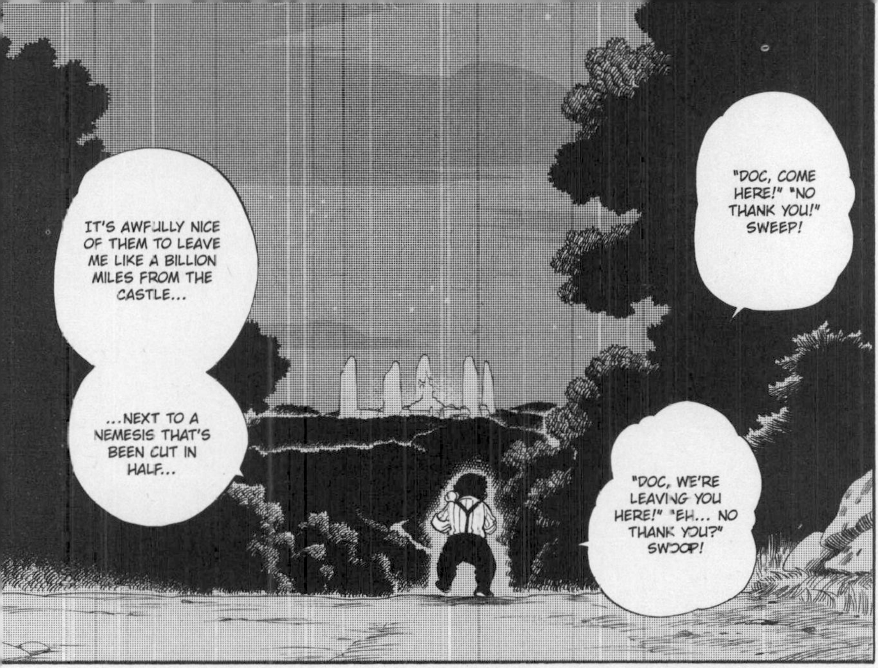
"DOC, COME HERE!" "NO THANK YOU!" SWEEP!
IT'S AWFULLY NICE OF THEM TO LEAVE ME LIKE A BILLION MILES FROM THE CASTLE...
...NEXT TO A NEMESIS THAT'S BEEN CUT IN HALF...
"DOC, WE'RE LEAVING YOU HERE!" "EH... NO THANK YOU?" SWOOP!

Chapter 52 The Strength of Rocks

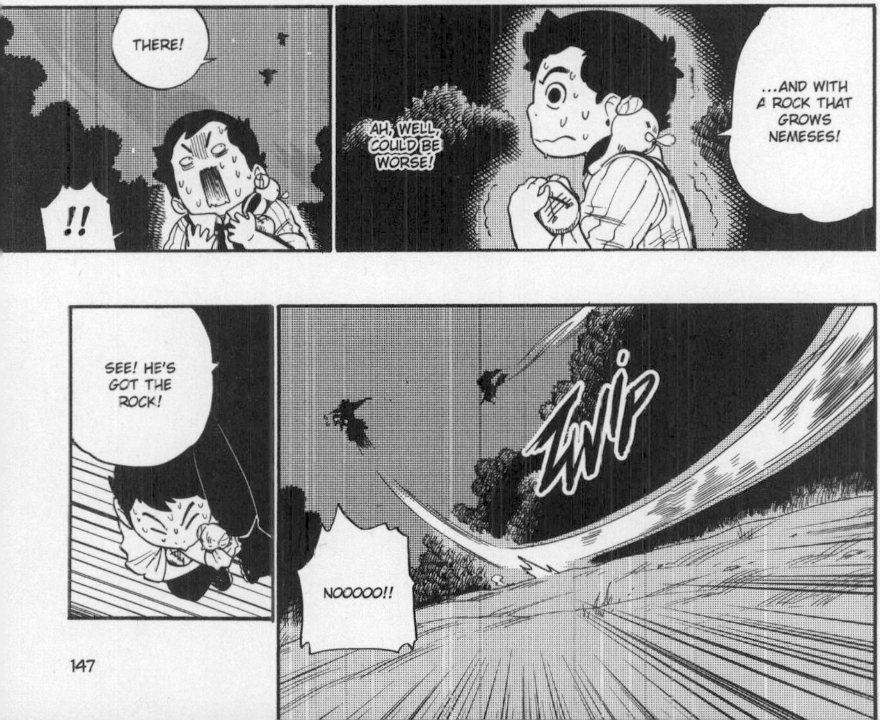
...AND WITH A ROCK THAT GROWS NEMESES!
AH, WELL, COULD BE WORSE!
THERE!
!!
ZWIP
NOOOOO!!
SEE! HE'S GOT THE ROCK!

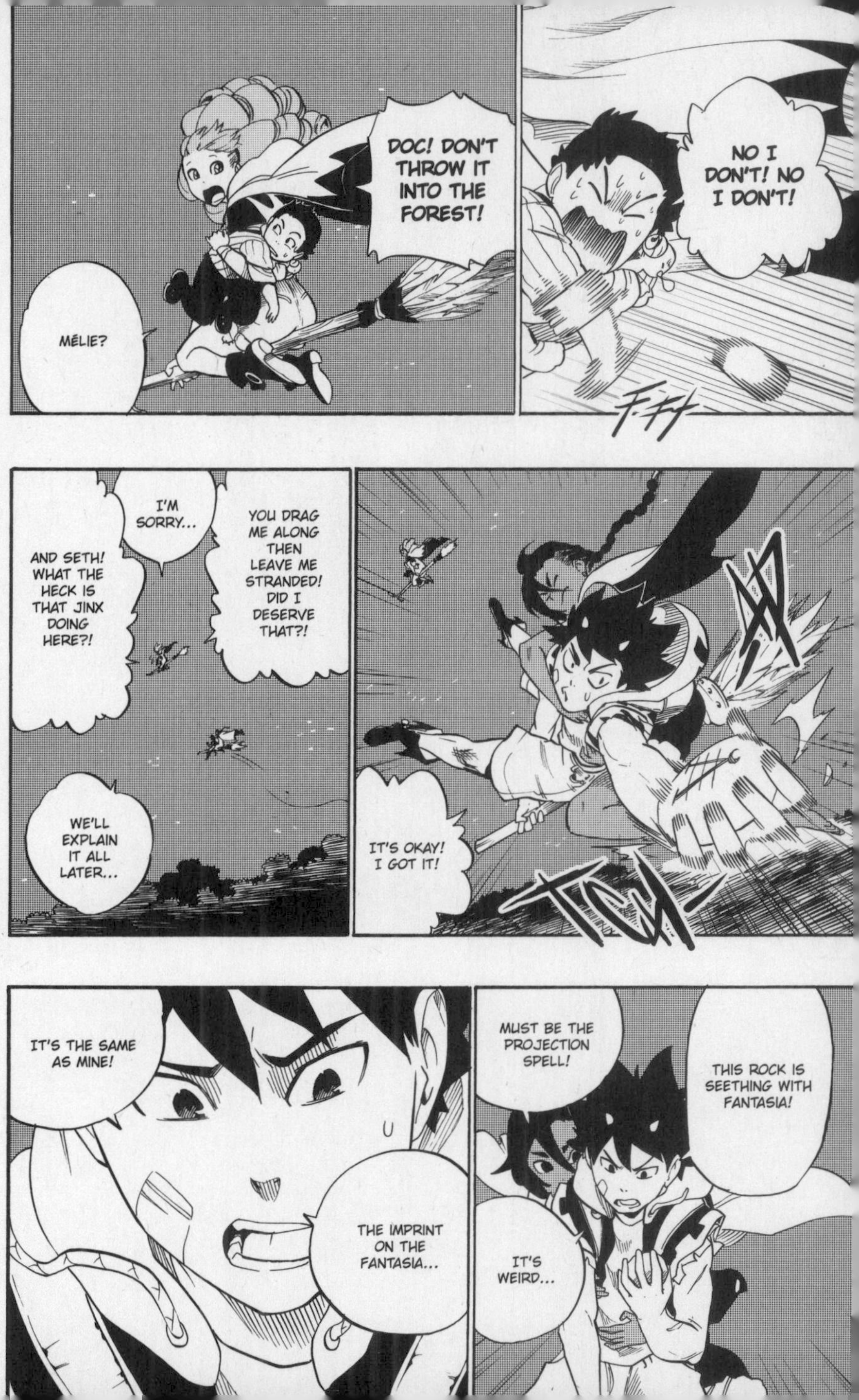
NO I DON'T! NO I DON'T!
DOC! DON'T THROW IT INTO THE FOREST!
MÉLIE?
IT'S OKAY! I GOT IT!
YOU DRAG ME ALONG THEN LEAVE ME STRANDED! DID I DESERVE THAT?!
I'M SORRY...
AND SETH! WHAT THE HECK IS THAT JINX DOING HERE?!
WE'LL EXPLAIN IT ALL LATER...
THIS ROCK IS SEETHING WITH FANTASIA!
MUST BE THE PROJECTION SPELL!
IT'S WEIRD...
THE IMPRINT ON THE FANTASIA...
IT'S THE SAME AS MINE!

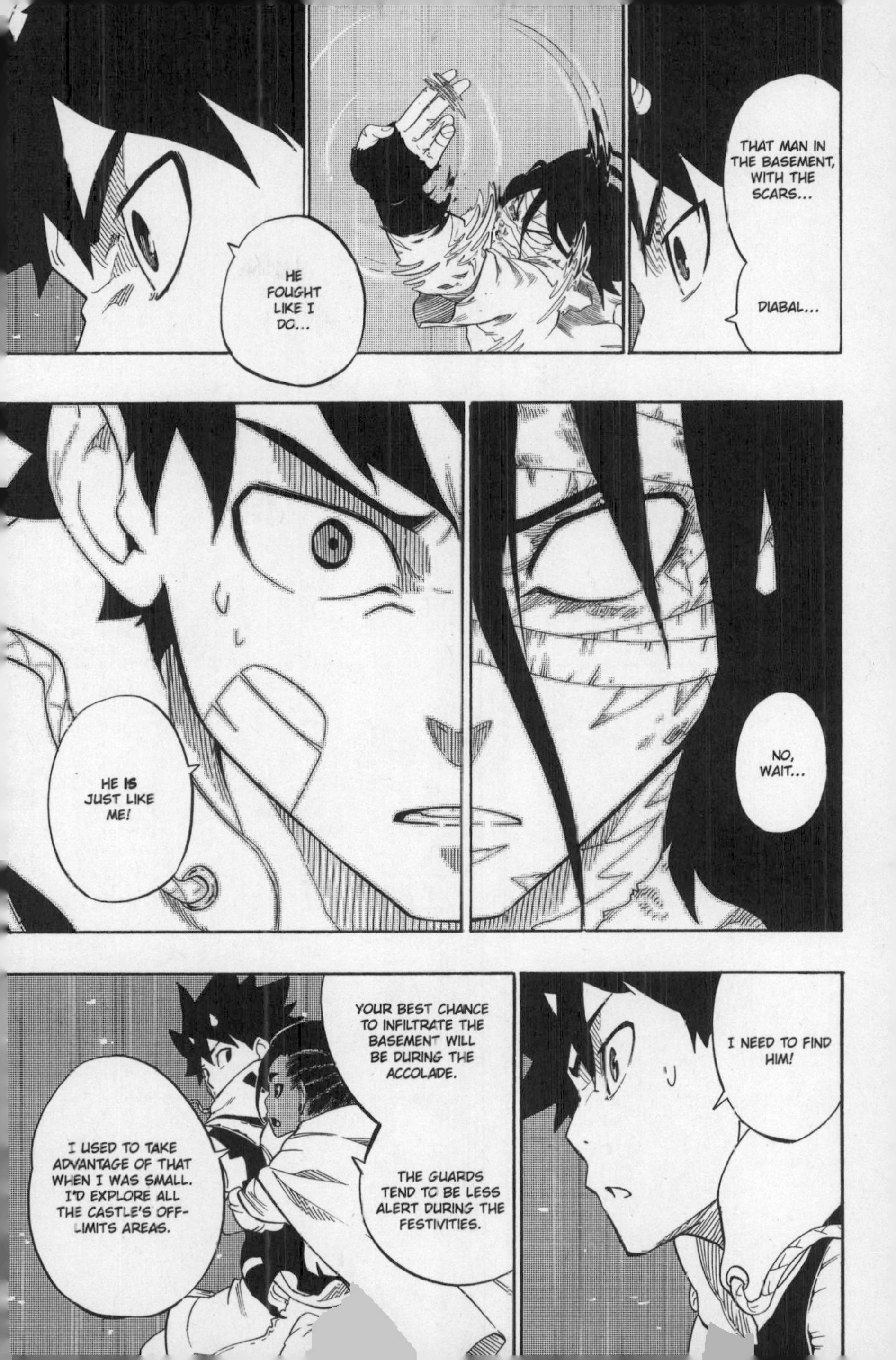
THAT MAN IN THE BASEMENT, WITH THE SCARS...
DIABAL...
HE FOUGHT LIKE I DO...
NO, WAIT...
HE IS JUST LIKE ME!
I NEED TO FIND HIM!
YOUR BEST CHANCE TO INFILTRATE THE BASEMENT WILL BE DURING THE ACCOLADE.
THE GUARDS TEND TO BE LESS ALERT DURING THE FESTIVITIES.
I USED TO TAKE ADVANTAGE OF THAT WHEN I WAS SMALL. I'D EXPLORE ALL THE CASTLE'S OFF-LIMITS AREAS.

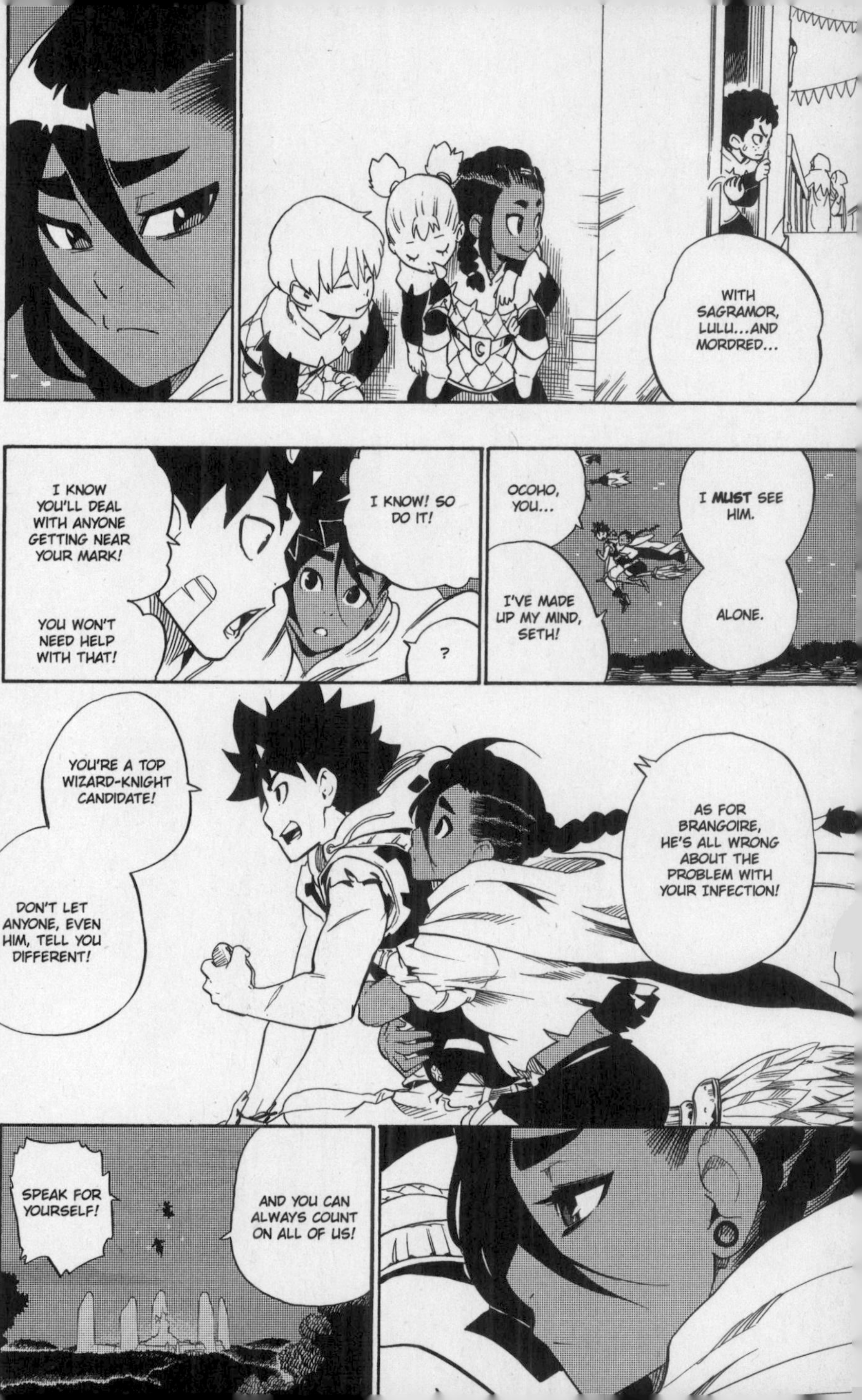
WITH SAGRAMOR, LULU...AND MORDRED...
I **MUST** SEE HIM.
ALONE.
OCOHO, YOU...
I'VE MADE UP MY MIND, SETH!
I KNOW! SO DO IT!
?
I KNOW YOU'LL DEAL WITH ANYONE GETTING NEAR YOUR MARK!
YOU WON'T NEED HELP WITH THAT!
AS FOR BRANGOIRE, HE'S ALL WRONG ABOUT THE PROBLEM WITH YOUR INFECTION!
YOU'RE A TOP WIZARD-KNIGHT CANDIDATE!
DON'T LET ANYONE, EVEN HIM, TELL YOU DIFFERENT!
AND YOU CAN ALWAYS COUNT ON ALL OF US!
SPEAK FOR YOURSELF!

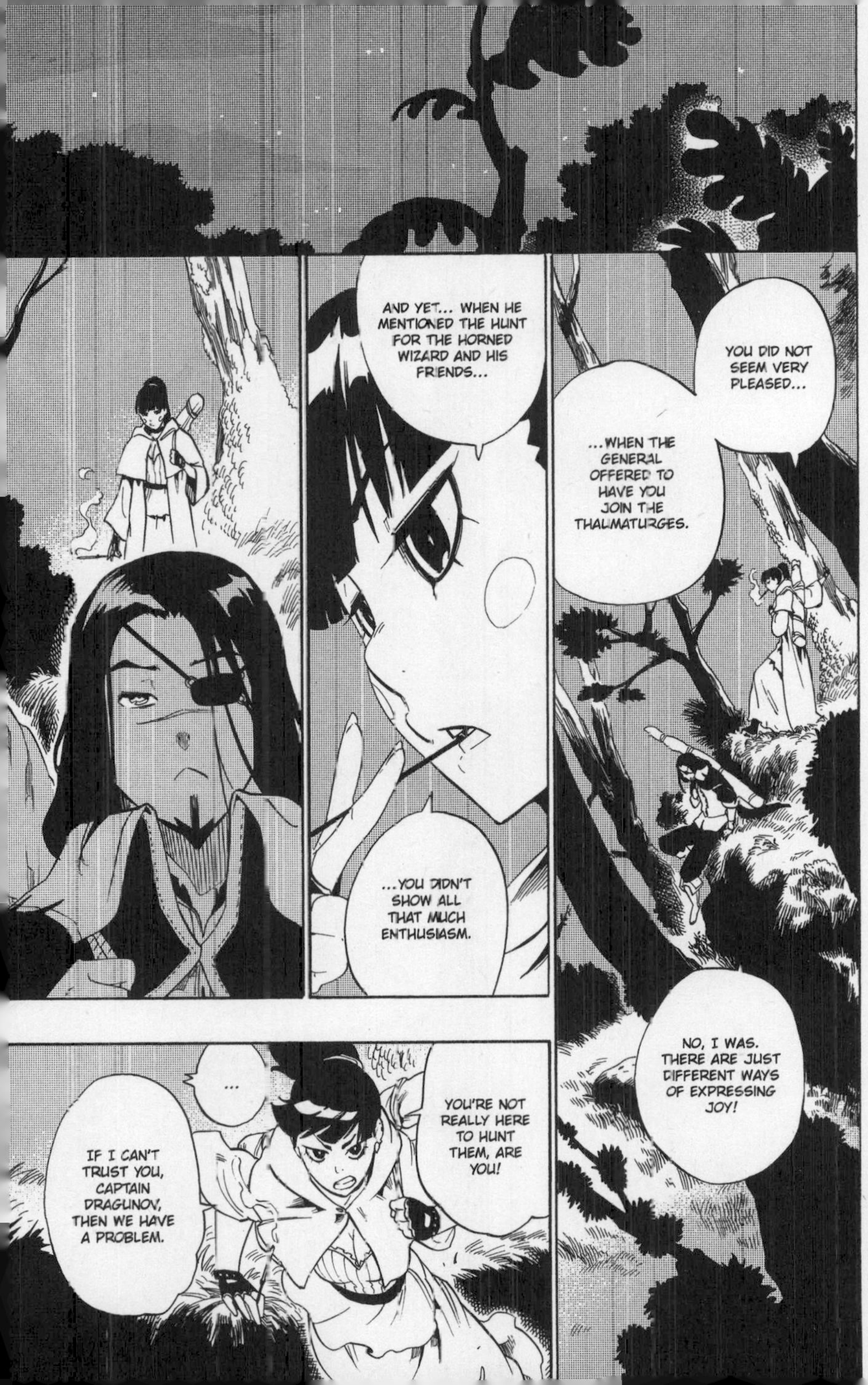
YOU DID NOT SEEM VERY PLEASED...
...WHEN THE GENERAL OFFERED TO HAVE YOU JOIN THE THAUMATURGES.
NO, I WAS. THERE ARE JUST DIFFERENT WAYS OF EXPRESSING JOY!
AND YET... WHEN HE MENTIONED THE HUNT FOR THE HORNED WIZARD AND HIS FRIENDS...
...YOU DIDN'T SHOW ALL THAT MUCH ENTHUSIASM.
YOU'RE NOT REALLY HERE TO HUNT THEM, ARE YOU!
...
IF I CAN'T TRUST YOU, CAPTAIN DRAGUNOV, THEN WE HAVE A PROBLEM.

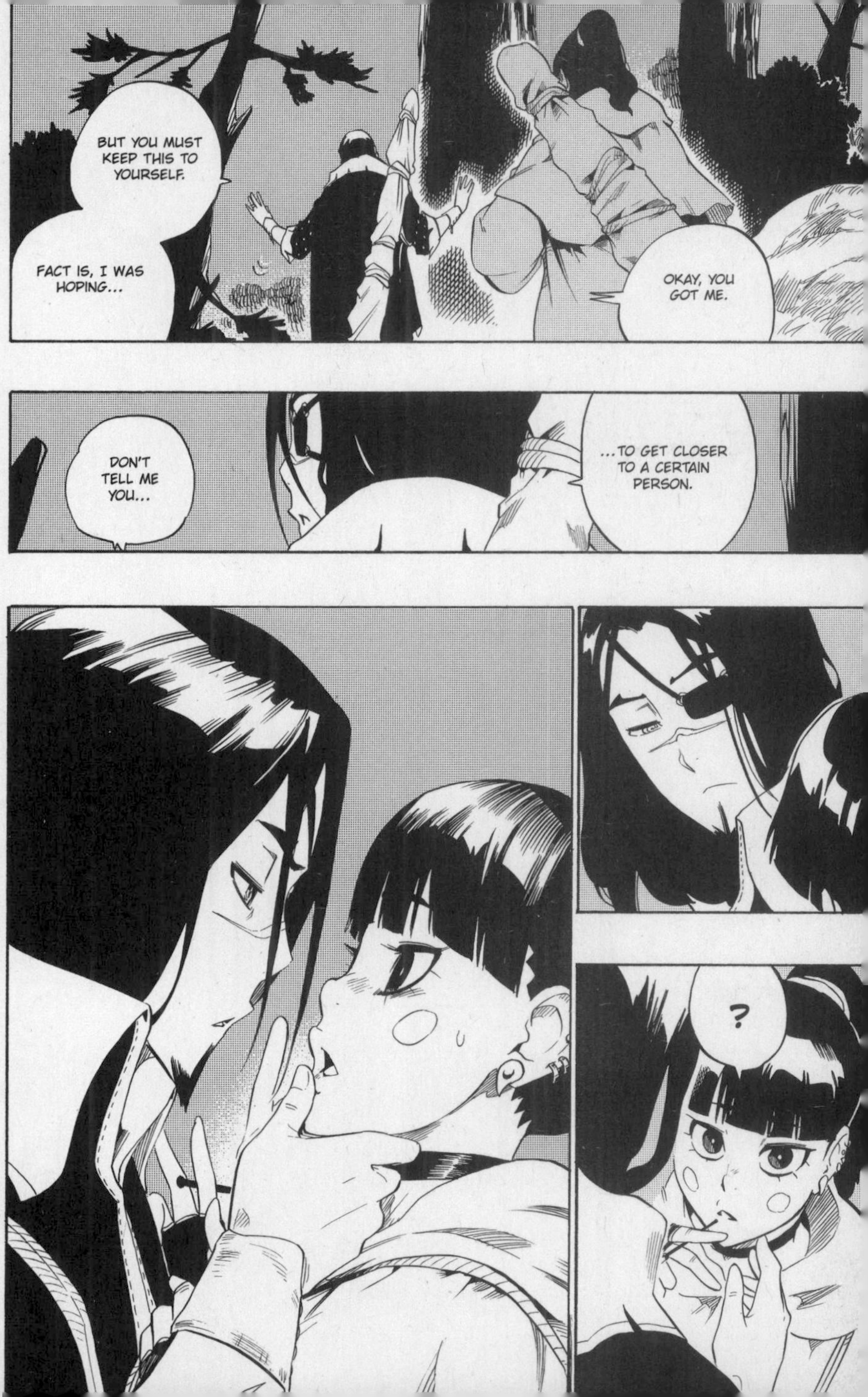
OKAY, YOU GOT ME.
BUT YOU MUST KEEP THIS TO YOURSELF.
FACT IS, I WAS HOPING...
...TO GET CLOSER TO A CERTAIN PERSON.
DON'T TELL ME YOU...
?

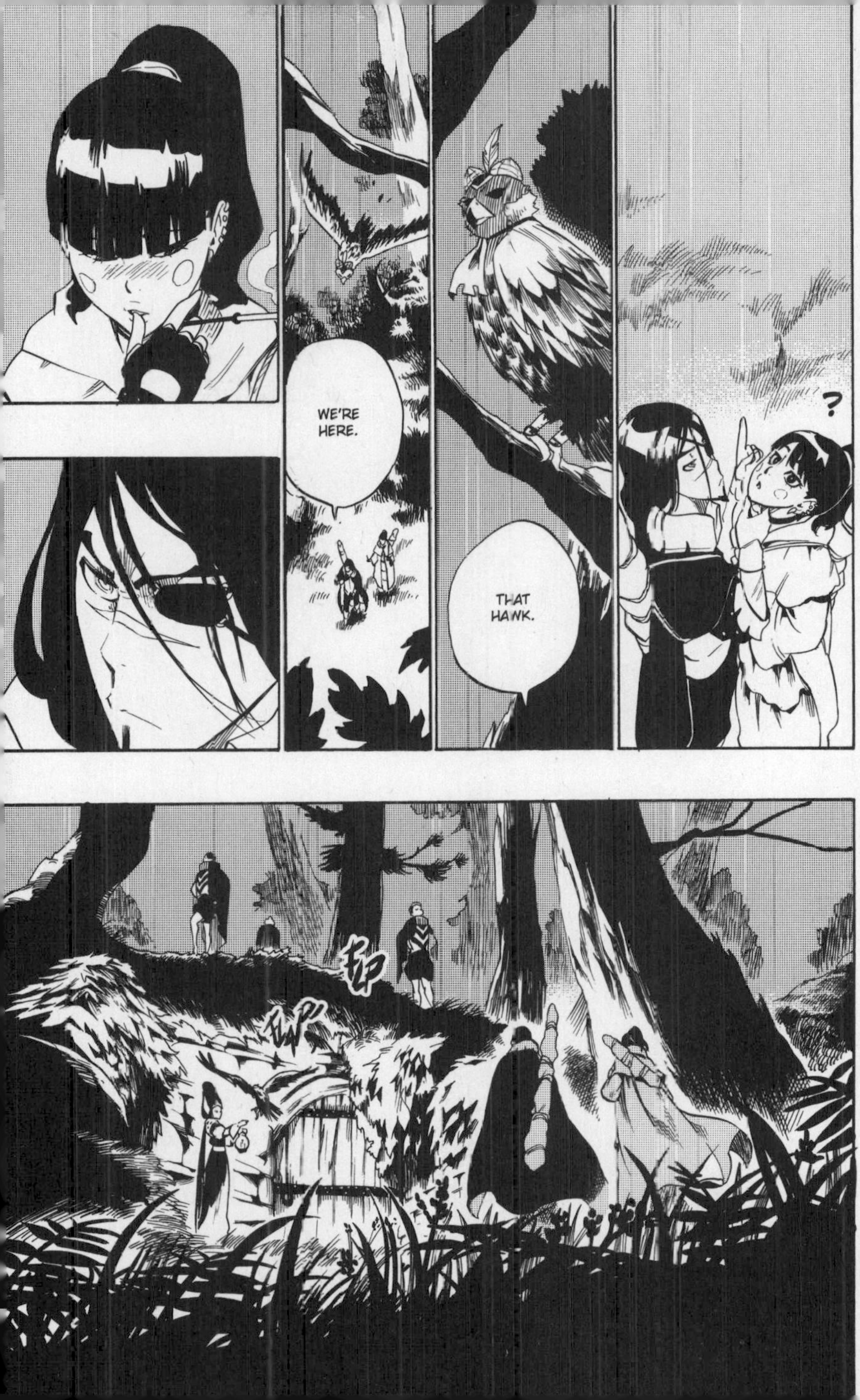
?
THAT HAWK.
WE'RE HERE.

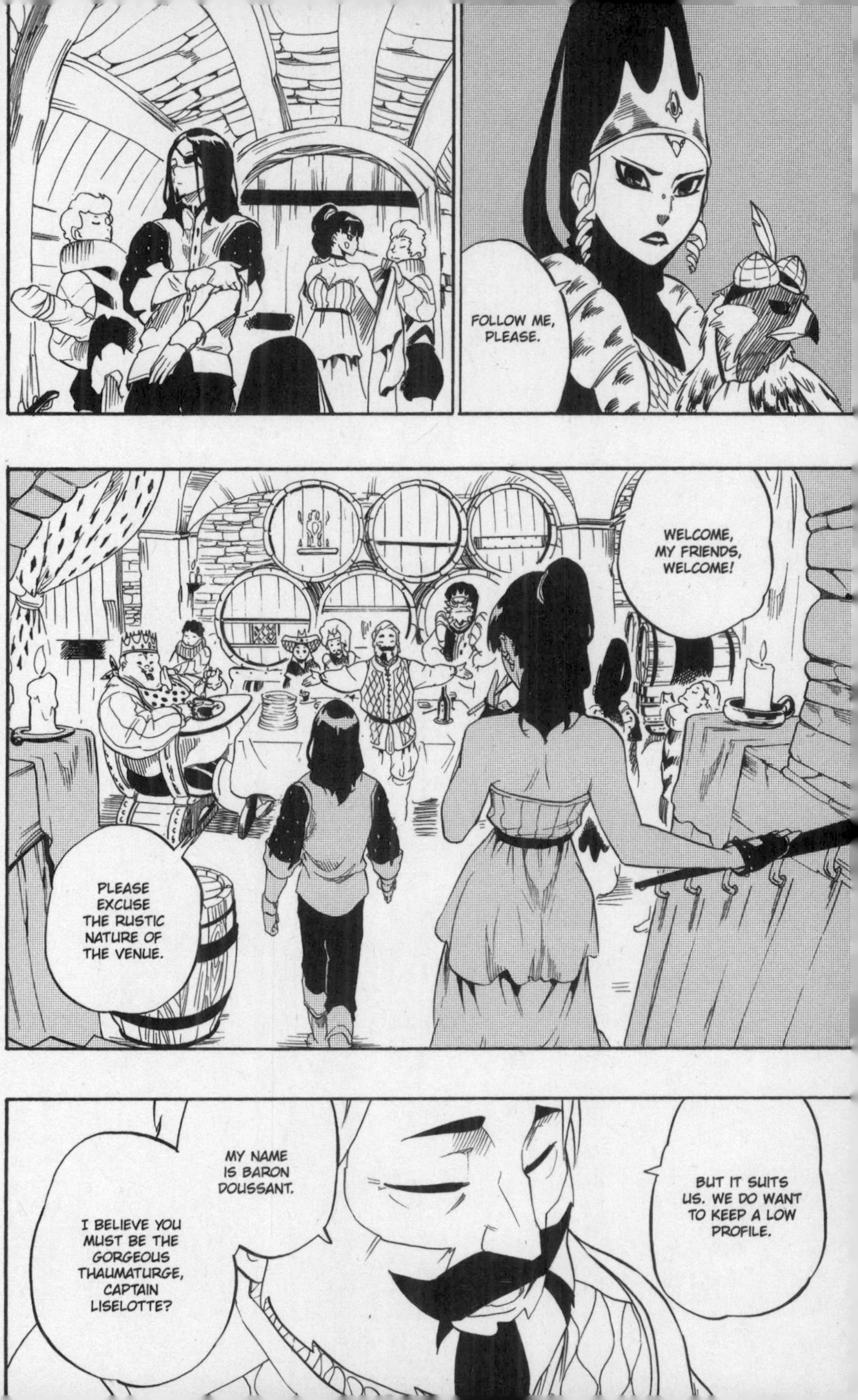
FOLLOW ME, PLEASE.
WELCOME, MY FRIENDS, WELCOME!
PLEASE EXCUSE THE RUSTIC NATURE OF THE VENUE.
BUT IT SUITS US. WE DO WANT TO KEEP A LOW PROFILE.
MY NAME IS BARON DOUSSANT.
I BELIEVE YOU MUST BE THE GORGEOUS THAUMATURGE, CAPTAIN LISELOTTE?

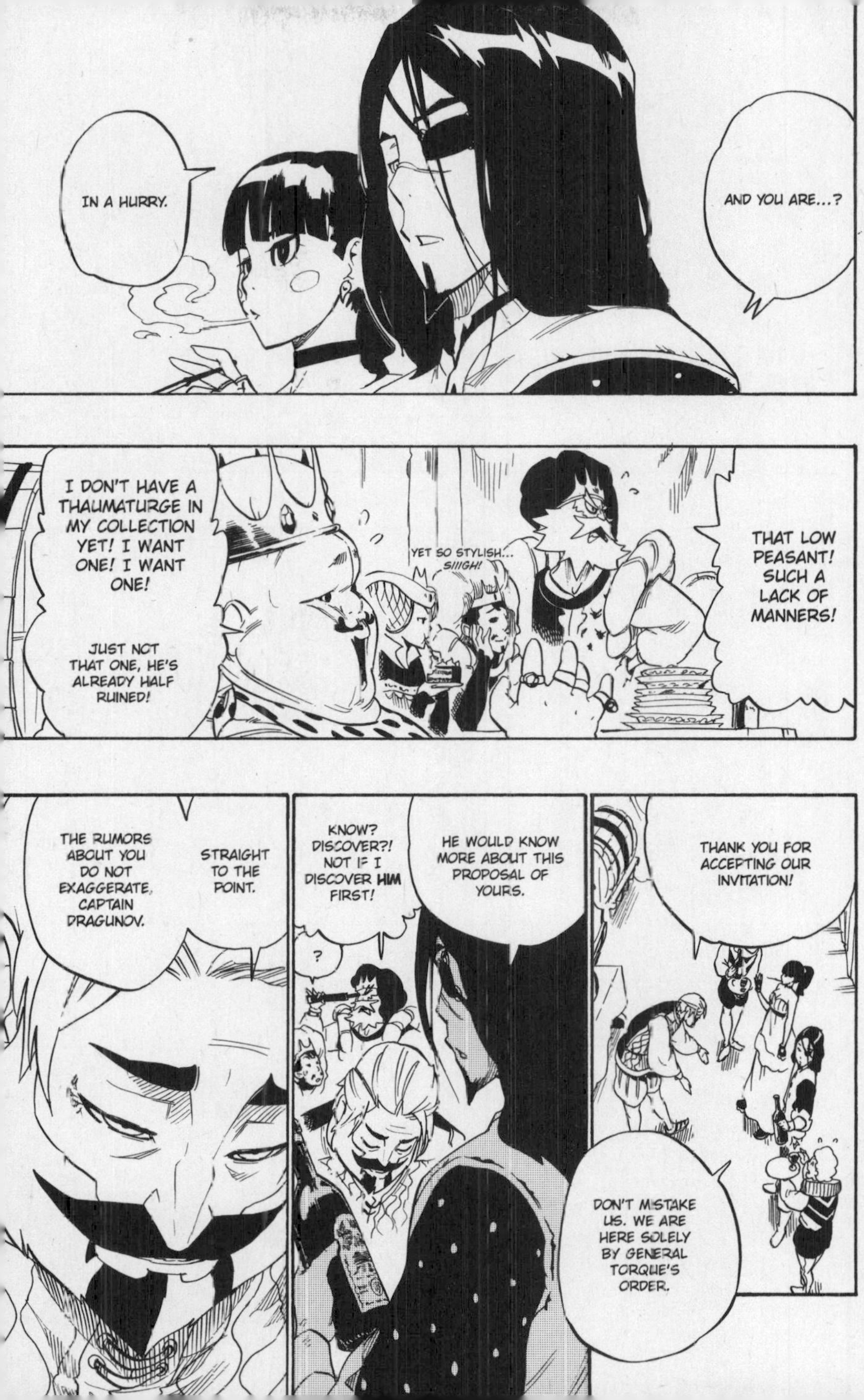
AND YOU ARE...?
IN A HURRY.
THAT LOW PEASANT! SUCH A LACK OF MANNERS!
YET SO STYLISH... SIIIGH!
I DON'T HAVE A THAUMATURGE IN MY COLLECTION YET! I WANT ONE! I WANT ONE!
JUST NOT THAT ONE, HE'S ALREADY HALF RUINED!
THANK YOU FOR ACCEPTING OUR INVITATION!
DON'T MISTAKE US. WE ARE HERE SOLELY BY GENERAL TORQUE'S ORDER.
HE WOULD KNOW MORE ABOUT THIS PROPOSAL OF YOURS.
KNOW? DISCOVER?! NOT IF I DISCOVER HIM FIRST!
?
STRAIGHT TO THE POINT.
THE RUMORS ABOUT YOU DO NOT EXAGGERATE, CAPTAIN DRAGUNOV.

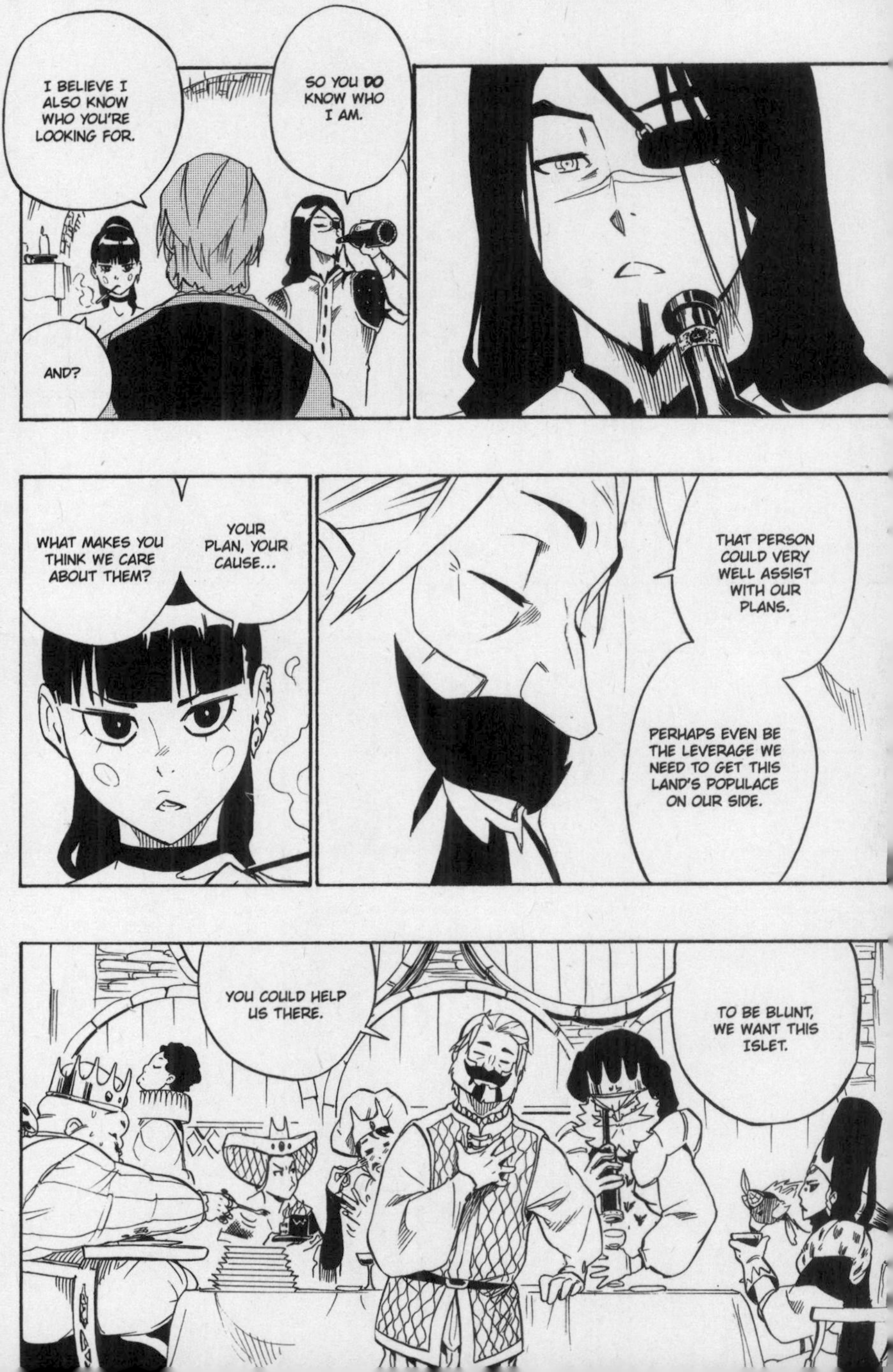
SO YOU DO KNOW WHO I AM.
I BELIEVE I ALSO KNOW WHO YOU'RE LOOKING FOR.
AND?
THAT PERSON COULD VERY WELL ASSIST WITH OUR PLANS.
PERHAPS EVEN BE THE LEVERAGE WE NEED TO GET THIS LAND'S POPULACE ON OUR SIDE.
YOUR PLAN, YOUR CAUSE...
WHAT MAKES YOU THINK WE CARE ABOUT THEM?
TO BE BLUNT, WE WANT THIS ISLET.
YOU COULD HELP US THERE.

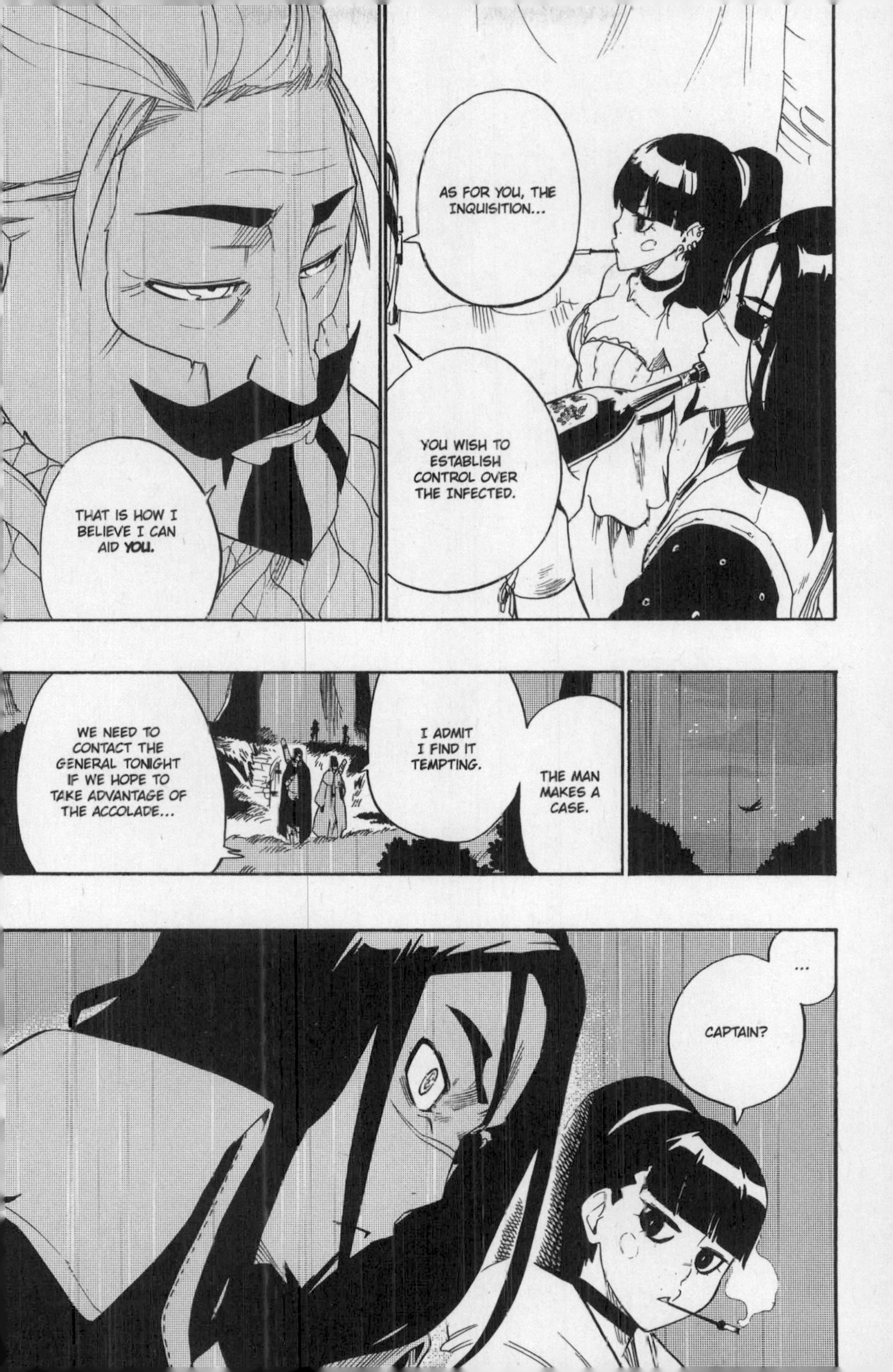
AS FOR YOU, THE INQUISITION...
YOU WISH TO ESTABLISH CONTROL OVER THE INFECTED.
THAT IS HOW I BELIEVE I CAN AID **YOU.**
I ADMIT I FIND IT TEMPTING.
THE MAN MAKES A CASE.
WE NEED TO CONTACT THE GENERAL TONIGHT IF WE HOPE TO TAKE ADVANTAGE OF THE ACCOLADE...
...
CAPTAIN?

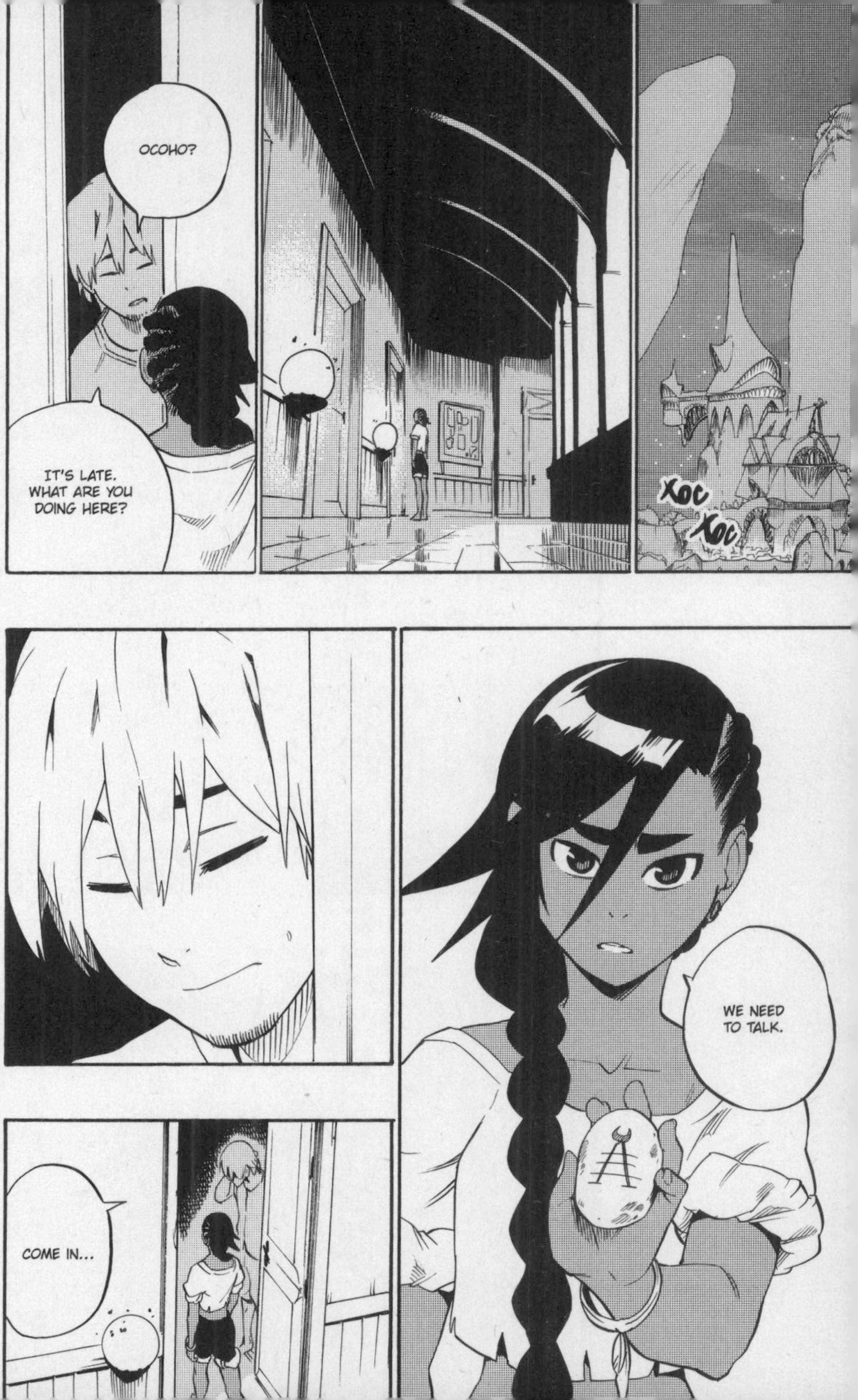
XOC
XOC
OCOHO?
IT'S LATE. WHAT ARE YOU DOING HERE?
WE NEED TO TALK.
COME IN...

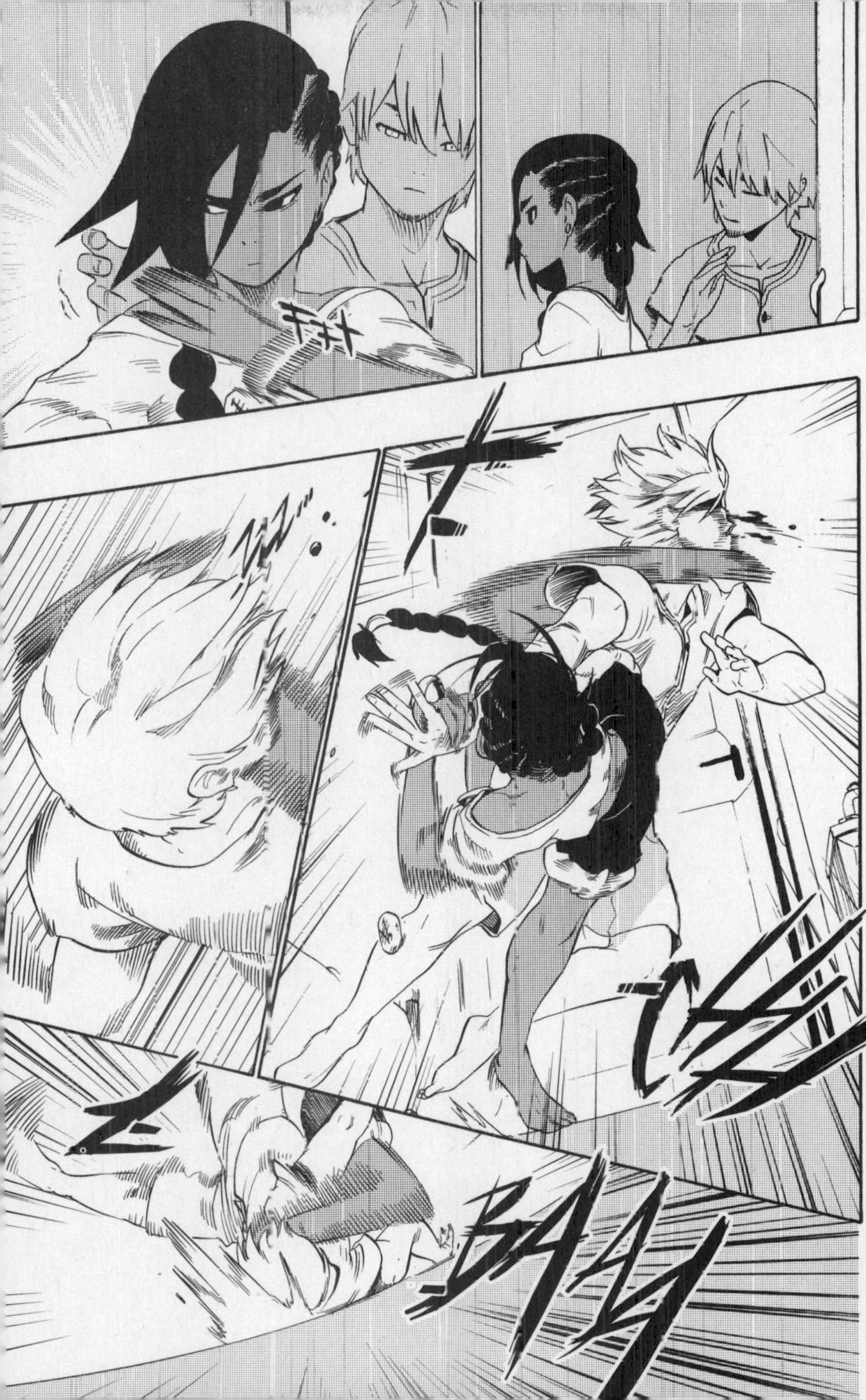
BAM

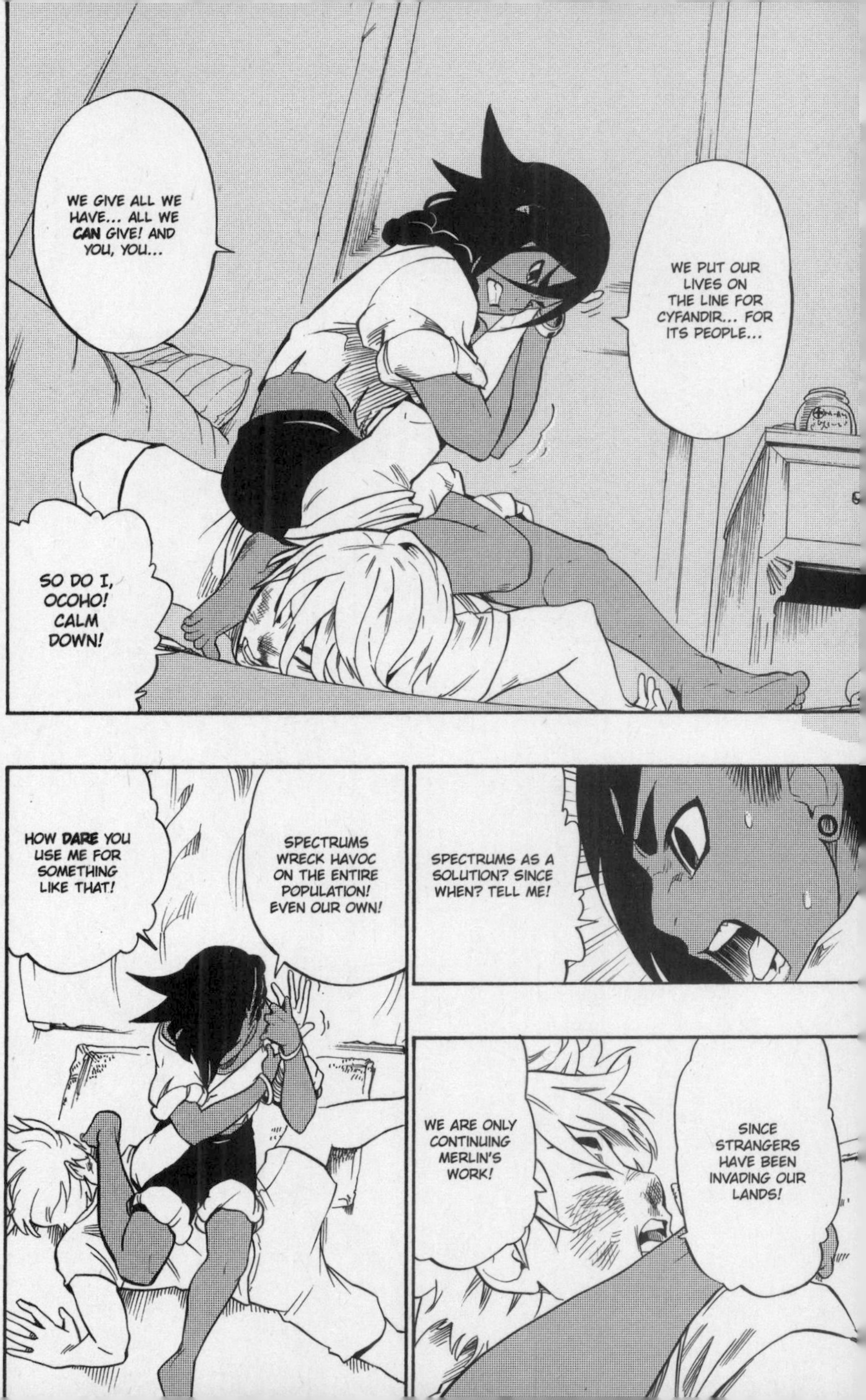
WE PUT OUR LIVES ON THE LINE FOR CYFANDIR... FOR ITS PEOPLE...
WE GIVE ALL WE HAVE... ALL WE **CAN** GIVE! AND YOU, YOU...
SO DO I, OCOHO! CALM DOWN!
SPECTRUMS AS A SOLUTION? SINCE WHEN? TELL ME!
SINCE STRANGERS HAVE BEEN INVADING OUR LANDS!
WE ARE ONLY CONTINUING MERLIN'S WORK!
SPECTRUMS WRECK HAVOC ON THE ENTIRE POPULATION! EVEN OUR OWN!
HOW **DARE** YOU USE ME FOR SOMETHING LIKE THAT!

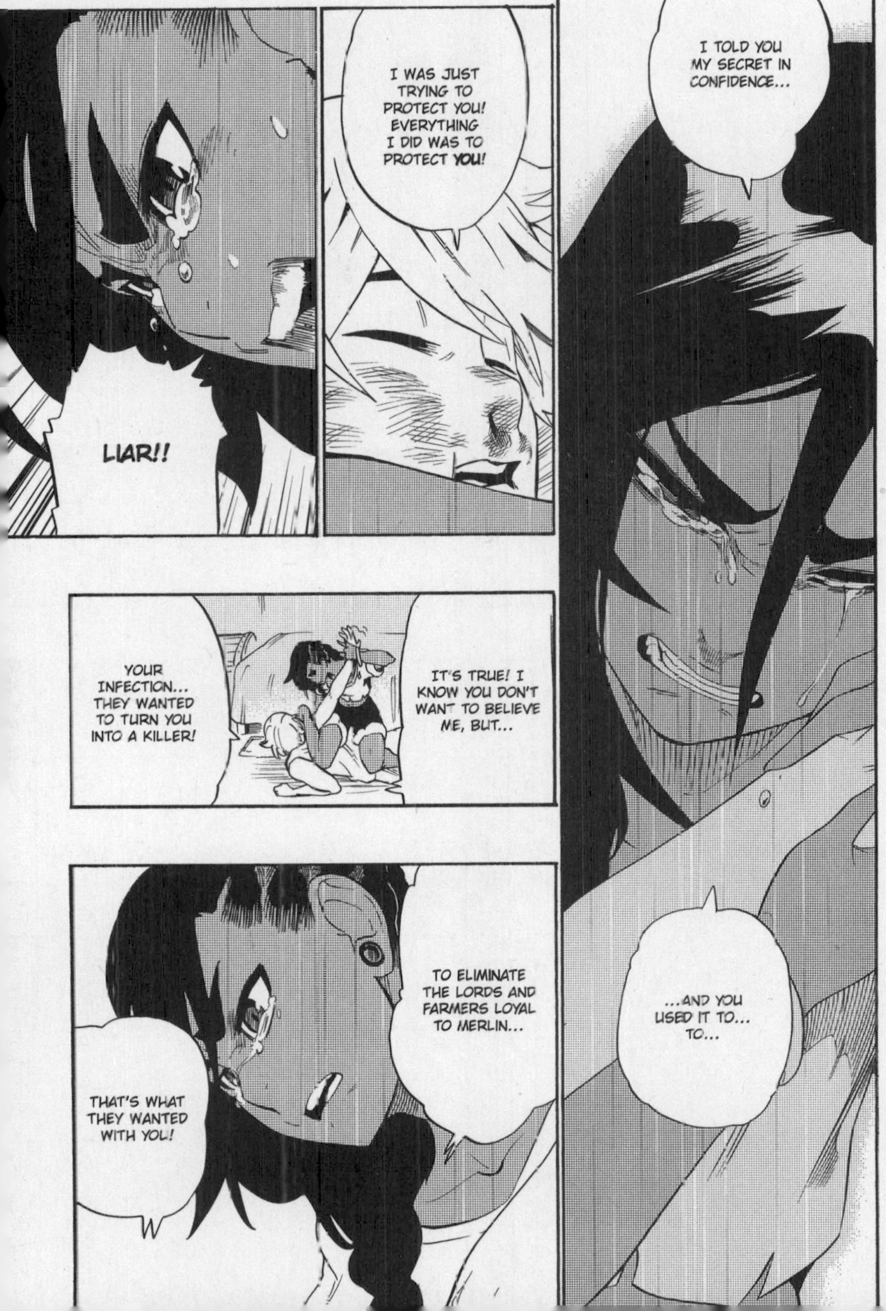
I TOLD YOU MY SECRET IN CONFIDENCE...
...AND YOU USED IT TO... TO...
I WAS JUST TRYING TO PROTECT YOU! EVERYTHING I DID WAS TO PROTECT **YOU**!
LIAR!!
IT'S TRUE! I KNOW YOU DON'T WANT TO BELIEVE ME, BUT...
YOUR INFECTION... THEY WANTED TO TURN YOU INTO A KILLER!
TO ELIMINATE THE LORDS AND FARMERS LOYAL TO MERLIN...
THAT'S WHAT THEY WANTED WITH YOU!

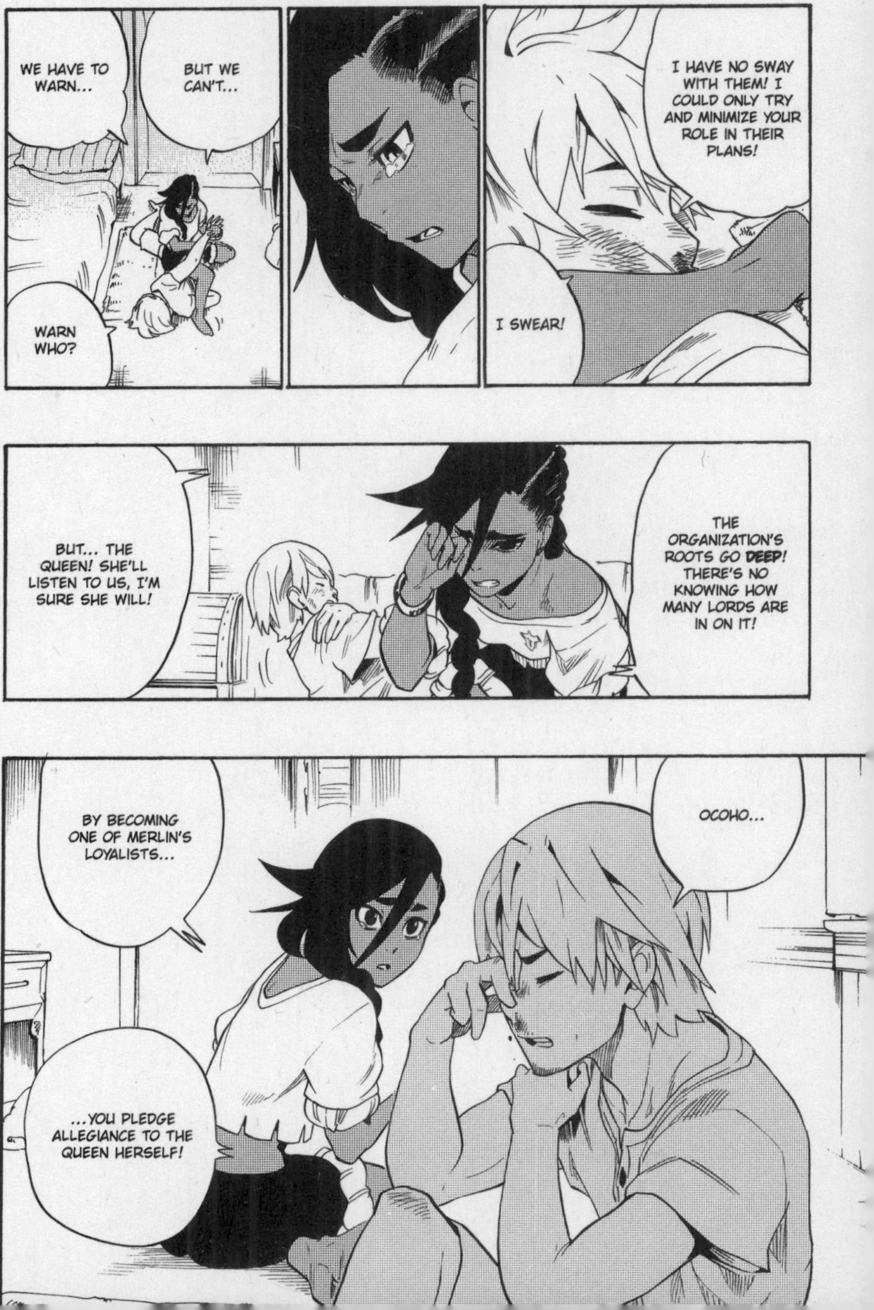
I HAVE NO SWAY WITH THEM! I COULD ONLY TRY AND MINIMIZE YOUR ROLE IN THEIR PLANS!
I SWEAR!
BUT WE CAN'T...
WE HAVE TO WARN...
WARN WHO?
THE ORGANIZATION'S ROOTS GO DEEP! THERE'S NO KNOWING HOW MANY LORDS ARE IN ON IT!
BUT... THE QUEEN! SHE'LL LISTEN TO US, I'M SURE SHE WILL!
OCOHO...
BY BECOMING ONE OF MERLIN'S LOYALISTS...
...YOU PLEDGE ALLEGIANCE TO THE QUEEN HERSELF!

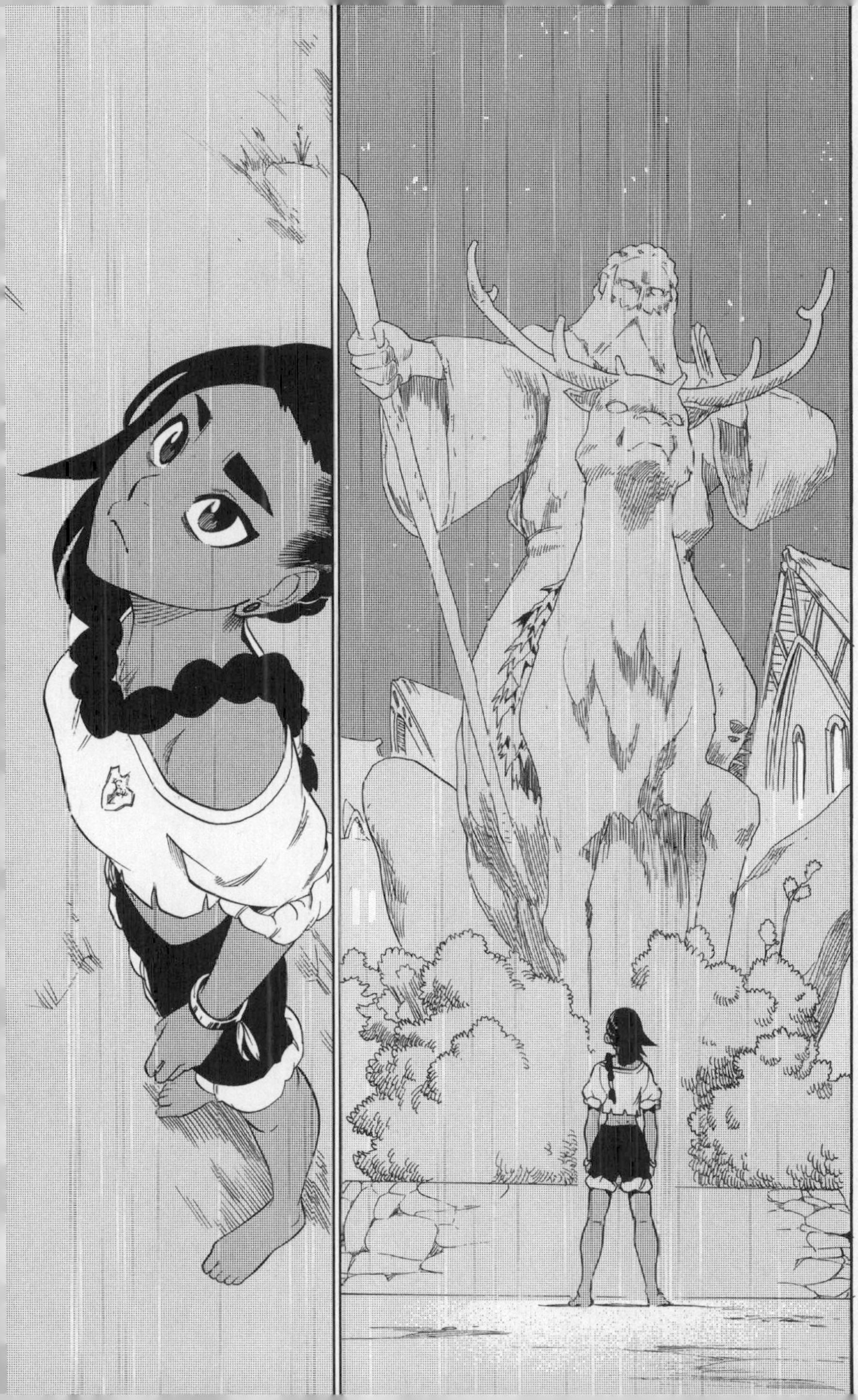

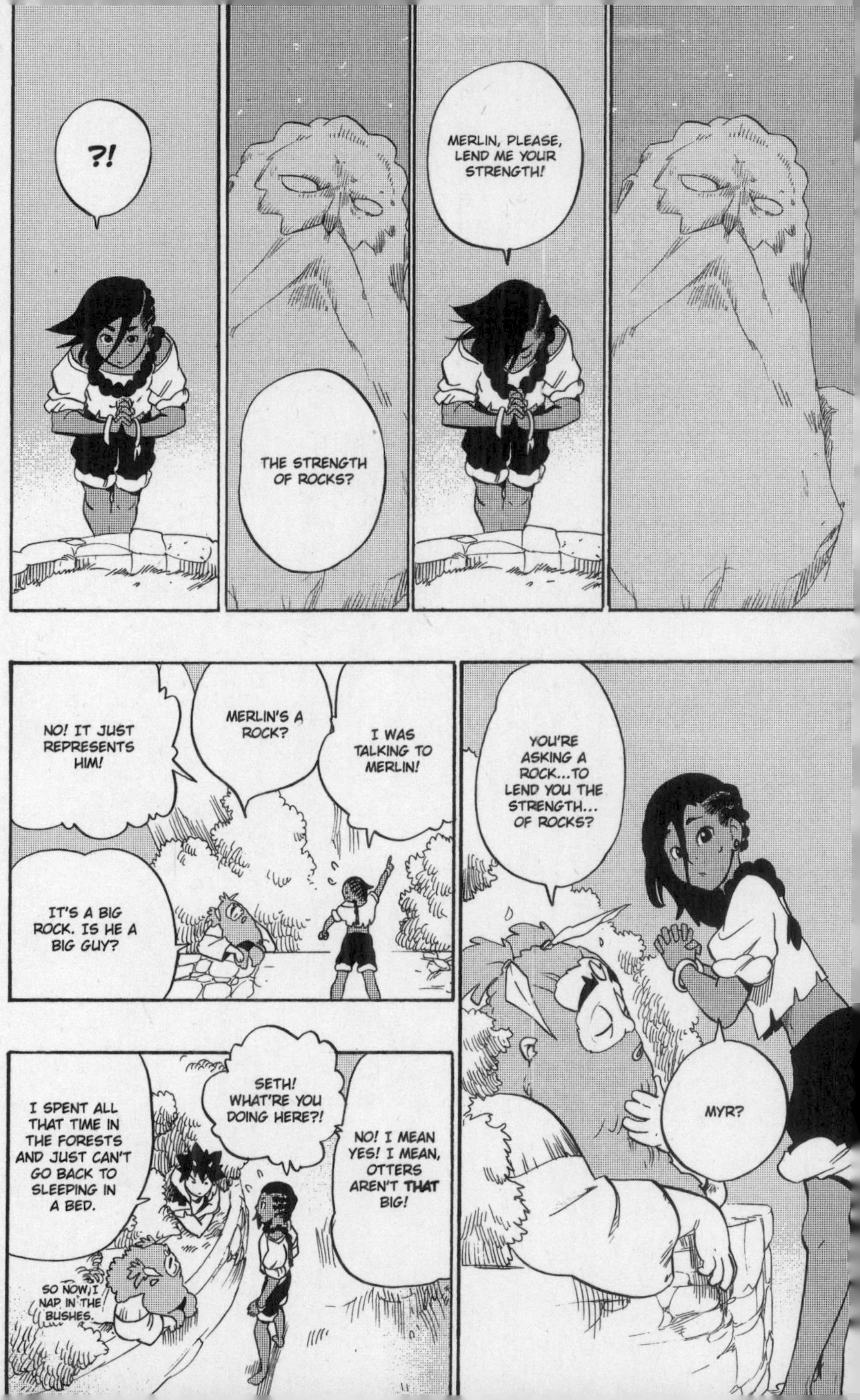
MERLIN, PLEASE, LEND ME YOUR STRENGTH!
THE STRENGTH OF ROCKS?
?!
YOU'RE ASKING A ROCK...TO LEND YOU THE STRENGTH... OF ROCKS?
MYR?
I WAS TALKING TO MERLIN!
MERLIN'S A ROCK?
NO! IT JUST REPRESENTS HIM!
IT'S A BIG ROCK. IS HE A BIG GUY?
NO! I MEAN YES! I MEAN, OTTERS AREN'T **THAT** BIG!
SETH! WHAT'RE YOU DOING HERE?!
I SPENT ALL THAT TIME IN THE FORESTS AND JUST CAN'T GO BACK TO SLEEPING IN A BED.
SO NOW, I NAP IN THE BUSHES.

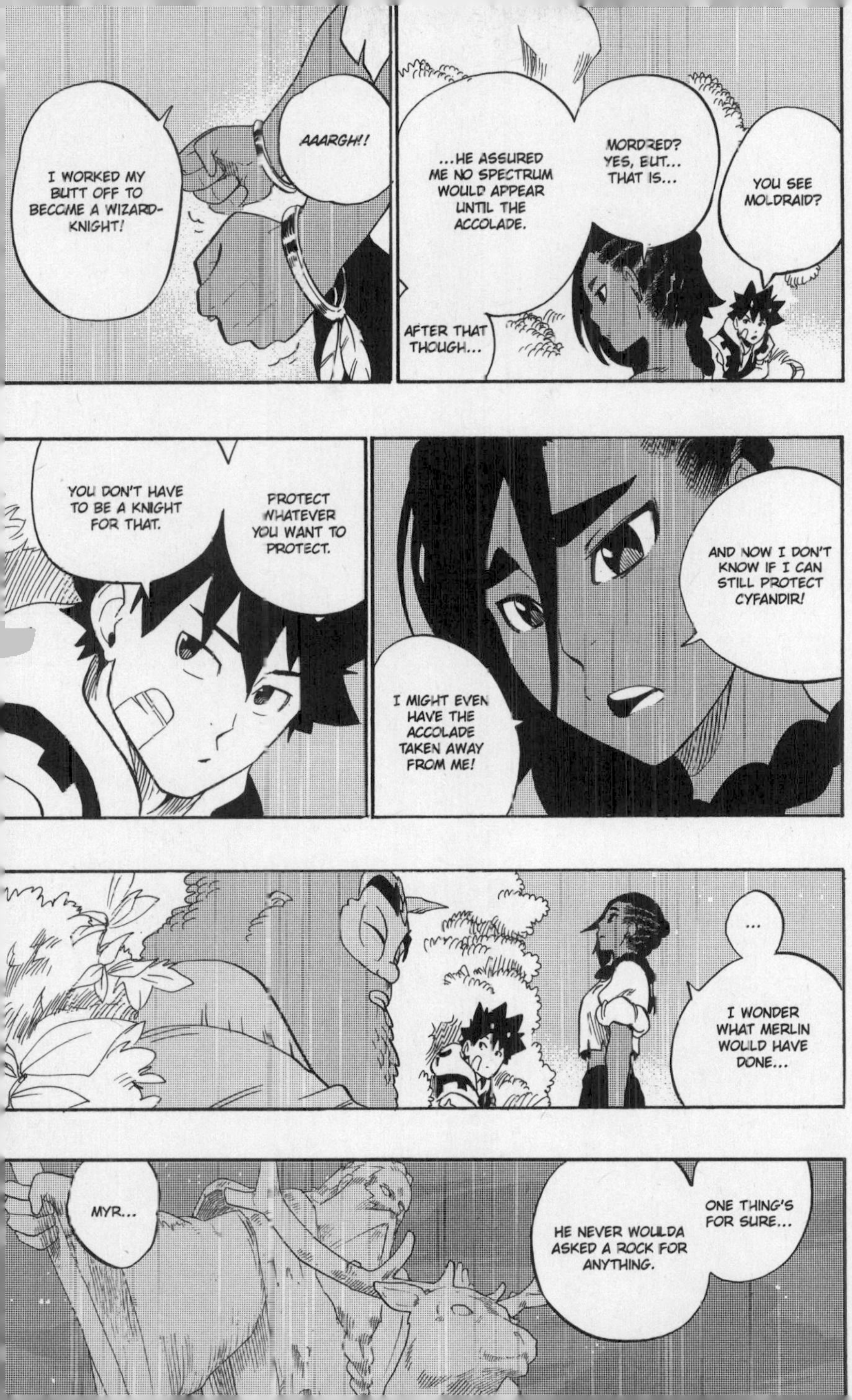
YOU SEE MOLDRAID?
MORDRED? YES, BUT... THAT IS...
...HE ASSURED ME NO SPECTRUM WOULD APPEAR UNTIL THE ACCOLADE.
AFTER THAT THOUGH...
AAARGH!!
I WORKED MY BUTT OFF TO BECOME A WIZARD-KNIGHT!
AND NOW I DON'T KNOW IF I CAN STILL PROTECT CYFANDIR!
I MIGHT EVEN HAVE THE ACCOLADE TAKEN AWAY FROM ME!
PROTECT WHATEVER YOU WANT TO PROTECT.
YOU DON'T HAVE TO BE A KNIGHT FOR THAT.
...
I WONDER WHAT MERLIN WOULD HAVE DONE...
ONE THING'S FOR SURE...
HE NEVER WOULDA ASKED A ROCK FOR ANYTHING.
MYR...

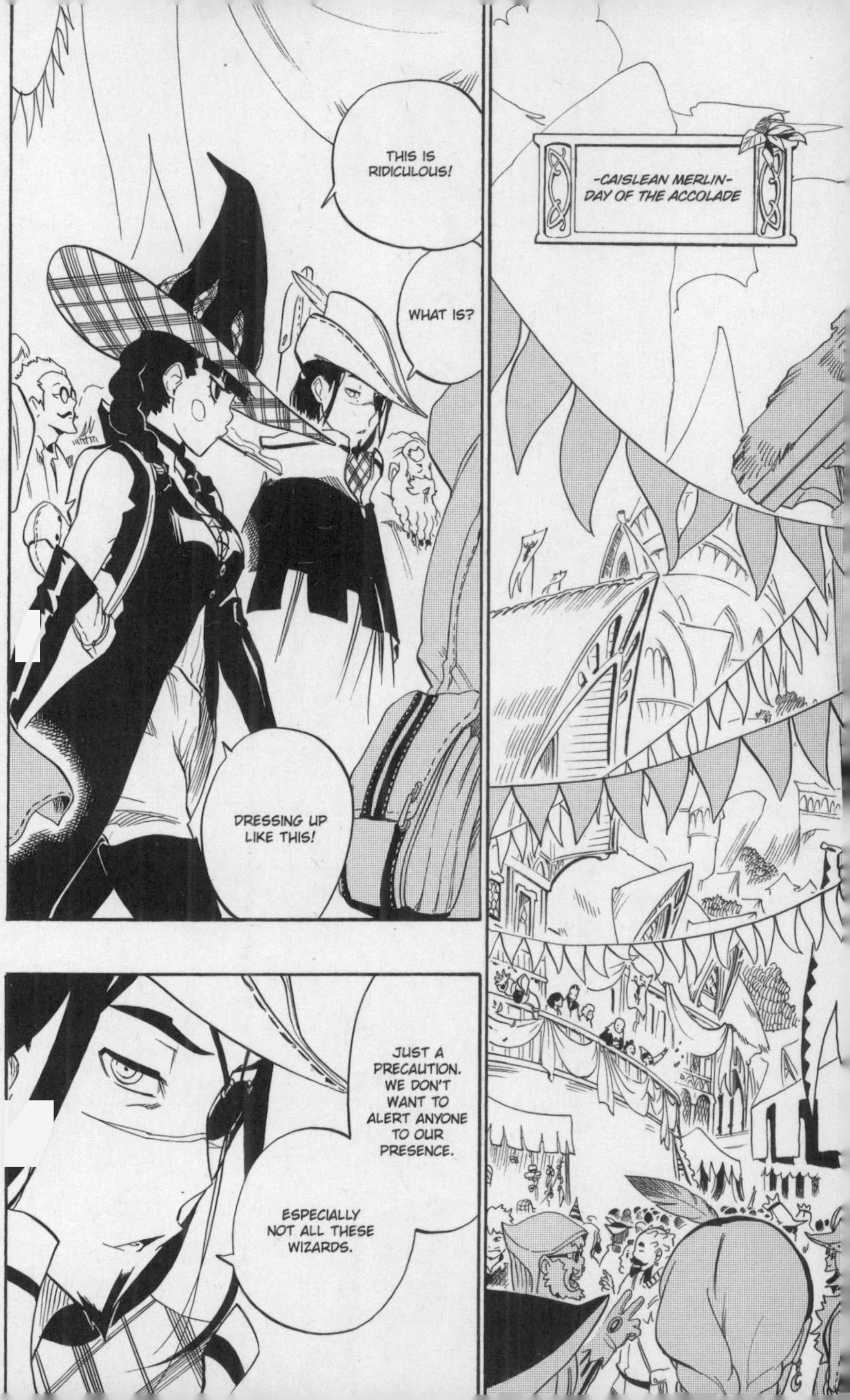
-CAISLEAN MERLIN-
DAY OF THE ACCOLADE
THIS IS RIDICULOUS!
WHAT IS?
DRESSING UP LIKE THIS!
JUST A PRECAUTION. WE DON'T WANT TO ALERT ANYONE TO OUR PRESENCE.
ESPECIALLY NOT ALL THESE WIZARDS.

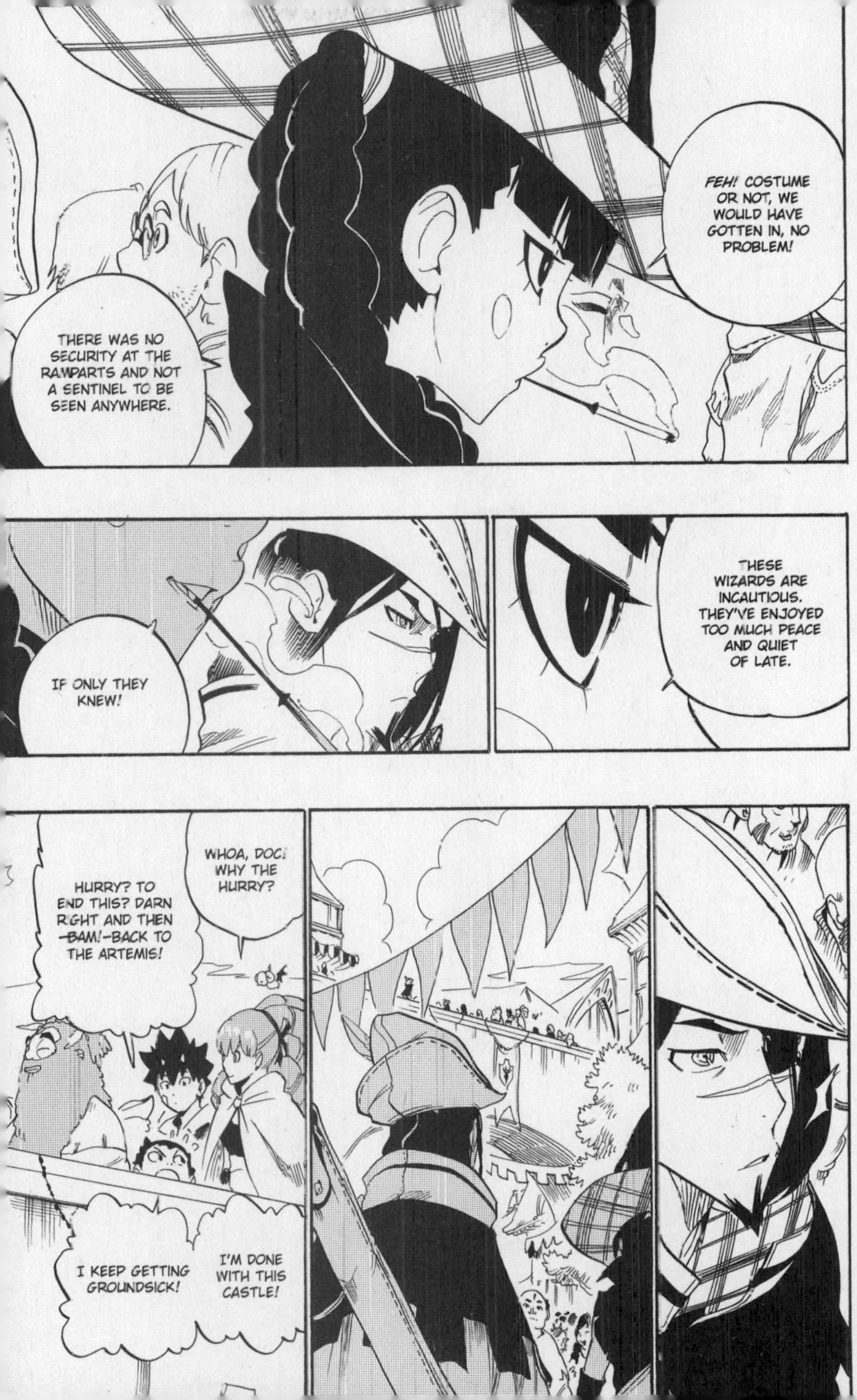
FEH! COSTUME OR NOT, WE WOULD HAVE GOTTEN IN, NO PROBLEM!
THERE WAS NO SECURITY AT THE RAMPARTS AND NOT A SENTINEL TO BE SEEN ANYWHERE.
THESE WIZARDS ARE INCAUTIOUS. THEY'VE ENJOYED TOO MUCH PEACE AND QUIET OF LATE.
IF ONLY THEY KNEW!
WHOA, DOC! WHY THE HURRY?
HURRY? TO END THIS? DARN RIGHT AND THEN —BAM!—BACK TO THE ARTEMIS!
I'M DONE WITH THIS CASTLE!
I KEEP GETTING GROUNDSICK!

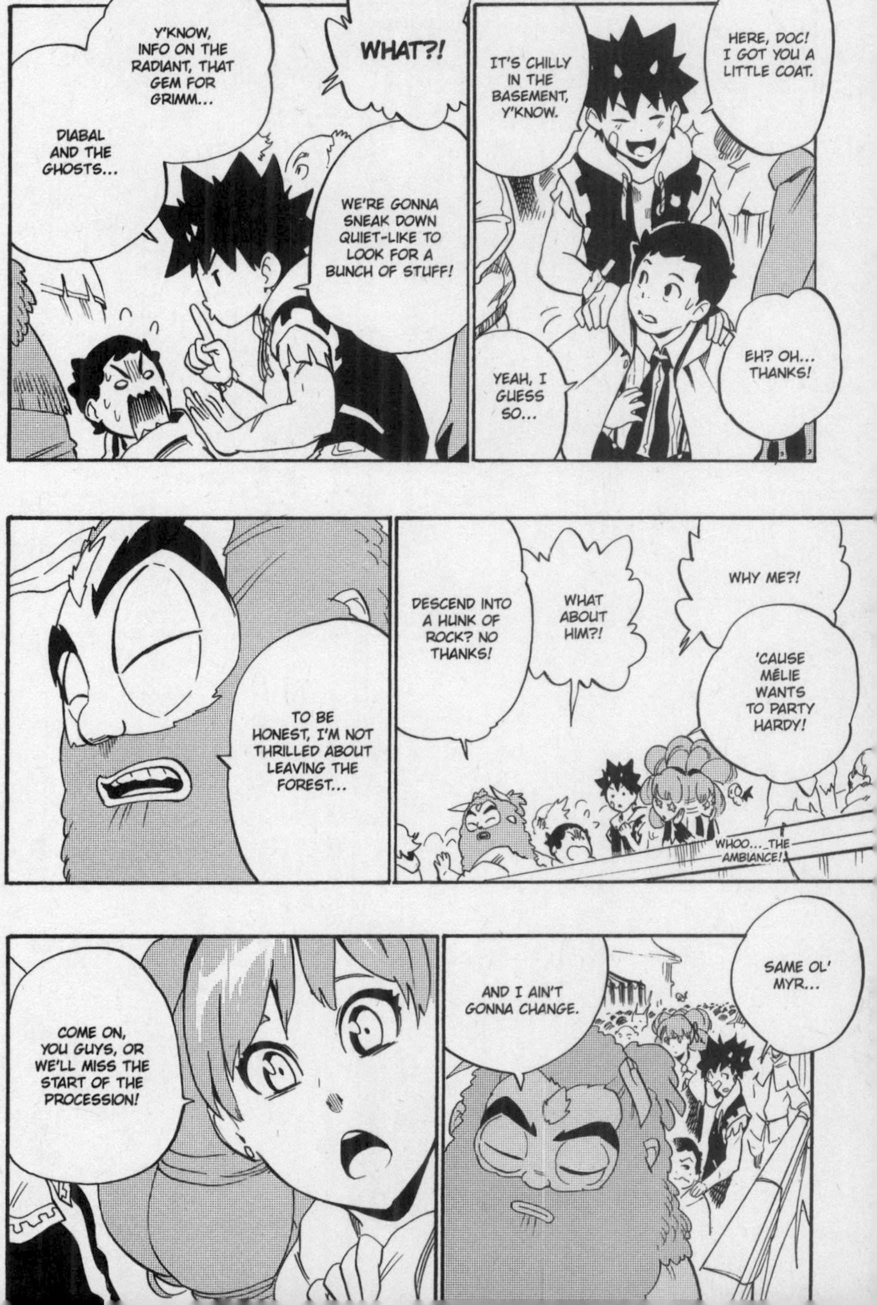
HERE, DOC! I GOT YOU A LITTLE COAT.
IT'S CHILLY IN THE BASEMENT, Y'KNOW.
EH? OH... THANKS!
YEAH, I GUESS SO...
WHAT?!
WE'RE GONNA SNEAK DOWN QUIET-LIKE TO LOOK FOR A BUNCH OF STUFF!
Y'KNOW, INFO ON THE RADIANT, THAT GEM FOR GRIMM...
DIABAL AND THE GHOSTS...
WHY ME?!
'CAUSE MÉLIE WANTS TO PARTY HARDY!
WHAT ABOUT HIM?!
DESCEND INTO A HUNK OF ROCK? NO THANKS!
WHOO... THE AMBIANCE!
TO BE HONEST, I'M NOT THRILLED ABOUT LEAVING THE FOREST...
SAME OL' MYR...
AND I AIN'T GONNA CHANGE.
COME ON, YOU GUYS, OR WE'LL MISS THE START OF THE PROCESSION!

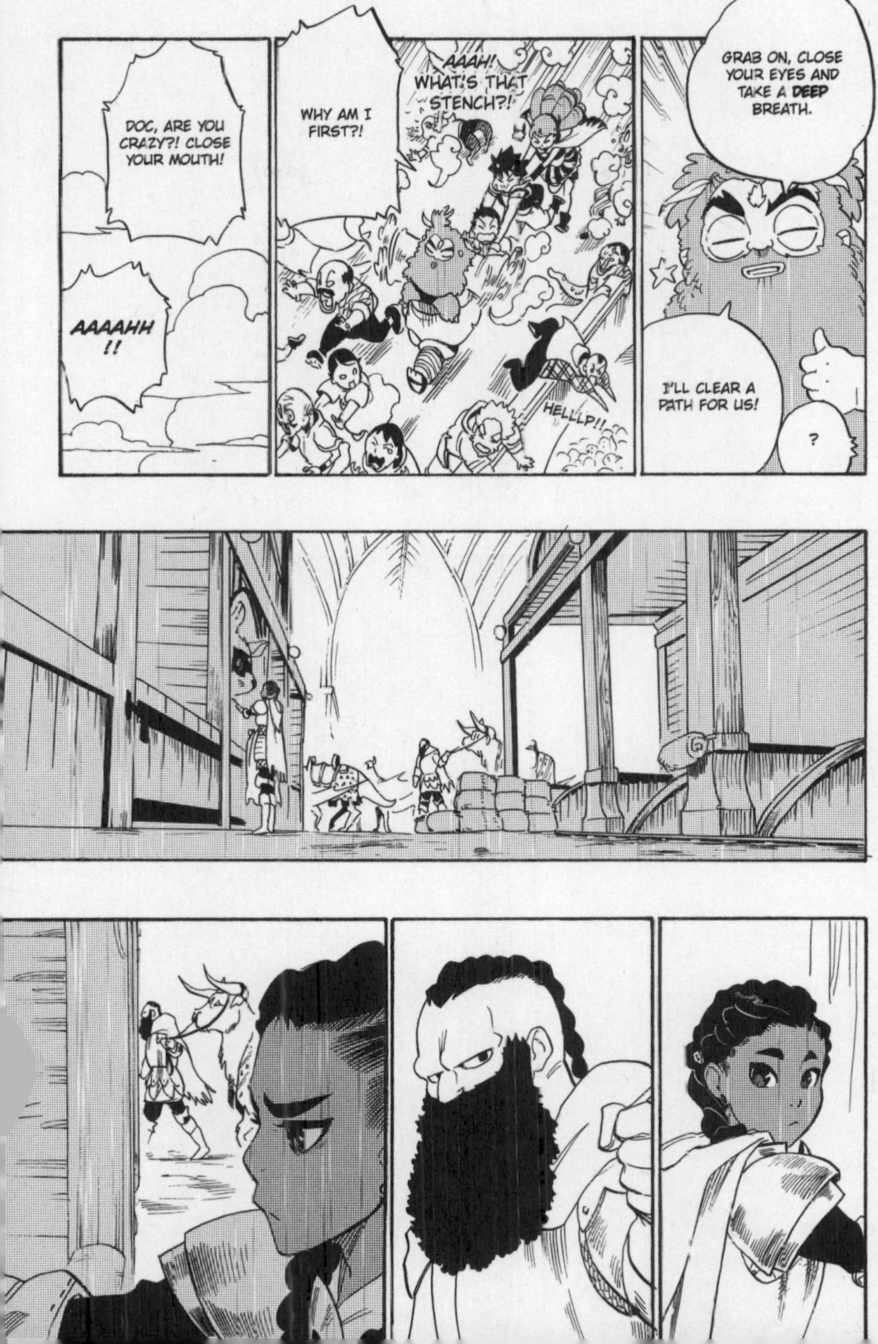
GRAB ON, CLOSE YOUR EYES AND TAKE A **DEEP** BREATH.
I'LL CLEAR A PATH FOR US!
?
AAAH! WHAT'S THAT STENCH?!
WHY AM I FIRST?!
HELLLP!!
DOC, ARE YOU CRAZY?! CLOSE YOUR MOUTH!
AAAAHH !!

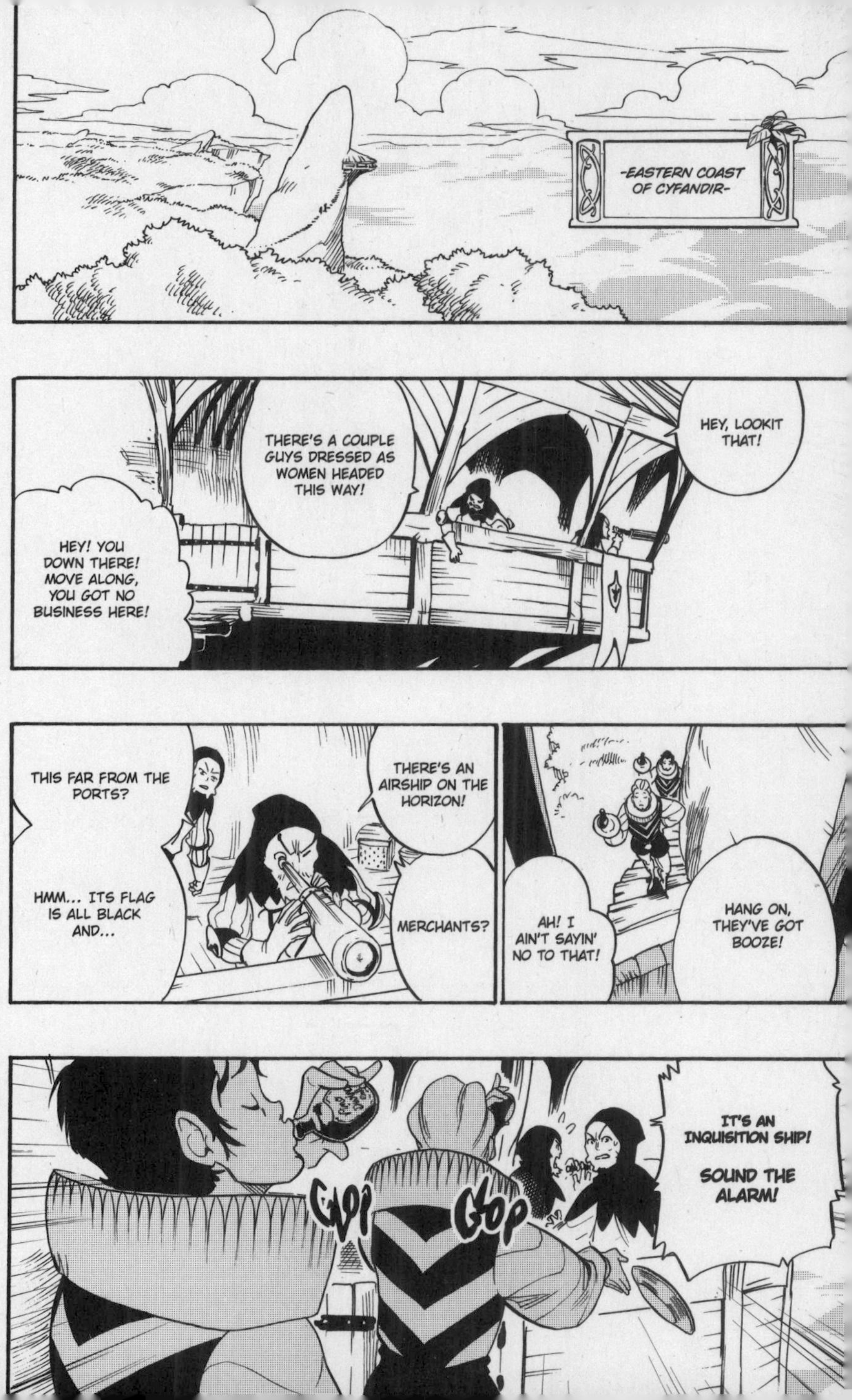
-EASTERN COAST OF CYFANDIR-
HEY, LOOKIT THAT!
THERE'S A COUPLE GUYS DRESSED AS WOMEN HEADED THIS WAY!
HEY! YOU DOWN THERE! MOVE ALONG, YOU GOT NO BUSINESS HERE!
HANG ON, THEY'VE GOT BOOZE!
AH! I AIN'T SAYIN' NO TO THAT!
THERE'S AN AIRSHIP ON THE HORIZON!
THIS FAR FROM THE PORTS?
MERCHANTS?
HMM... ITS FLAG IS ALL BLACK AND...
IT'S AN INQUISITION SHIP!
SOUND THE ALARM!
GLOP

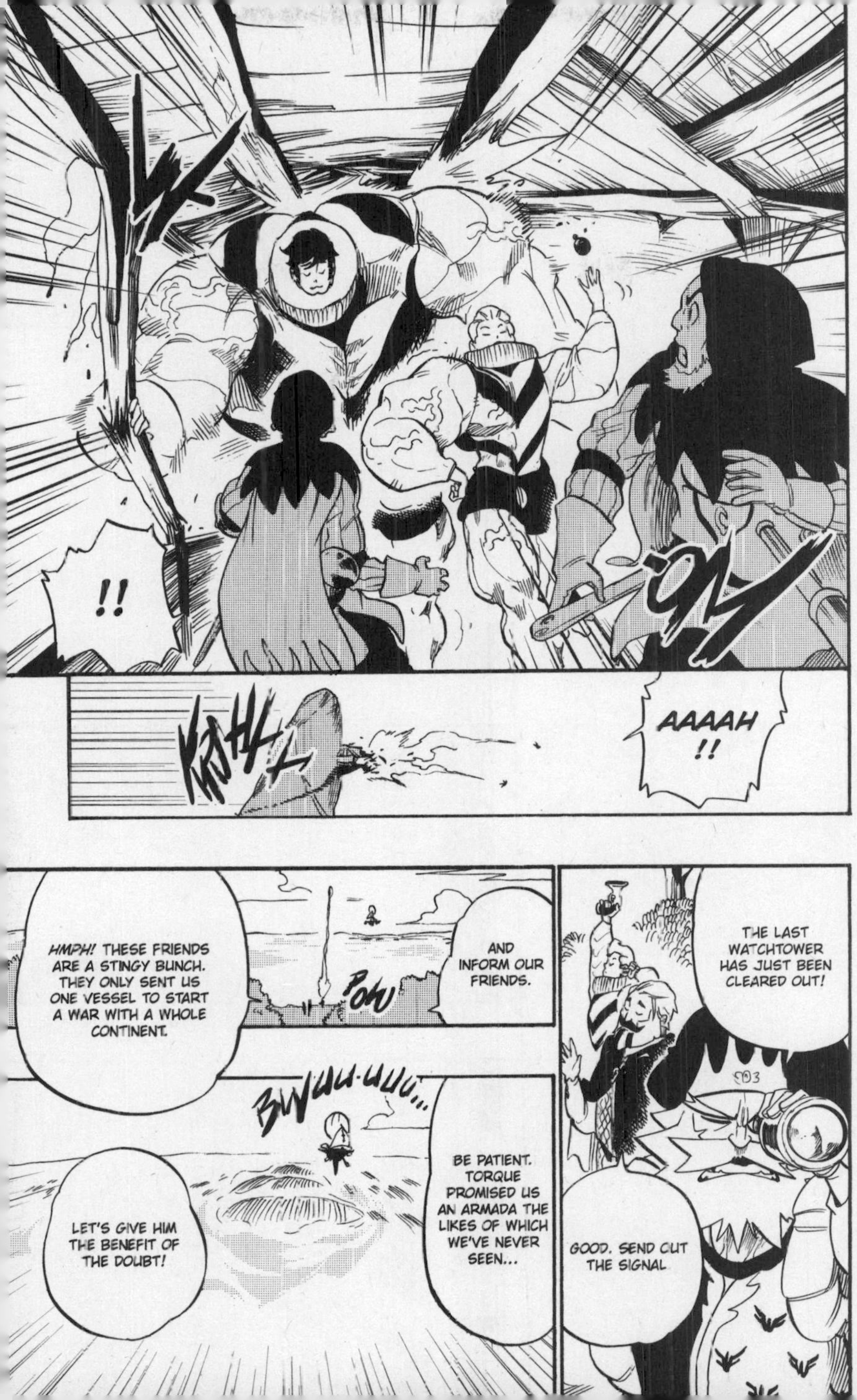
!!
AAAAH !!
THE LAST WATCHTOWER HAS JUST BEEN CLEARED OUT!
GOOD. SEND OUT THE SIGNAL
AND INFORM OUR FRIENDS.
POW
HMPH! THESE FRIENDS ARE A STINGY BUNCH. THEY ONLY SENT US ONE VESSEL TO START A WAR WITH A WHOLE CONTINENT.
BE PATIENT. TORQUE PROMISED US AN ARMADA THE LIKES OF WHICH WE'VE NEVER SEEN...
LET'S GIVE HIM THE BENEFIT OF THE DOUBT!

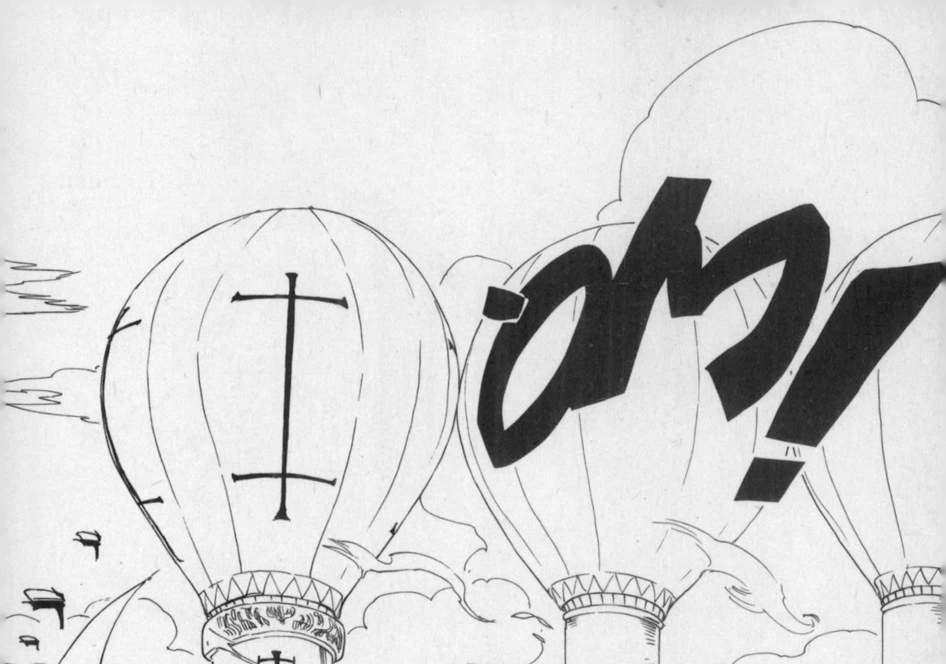

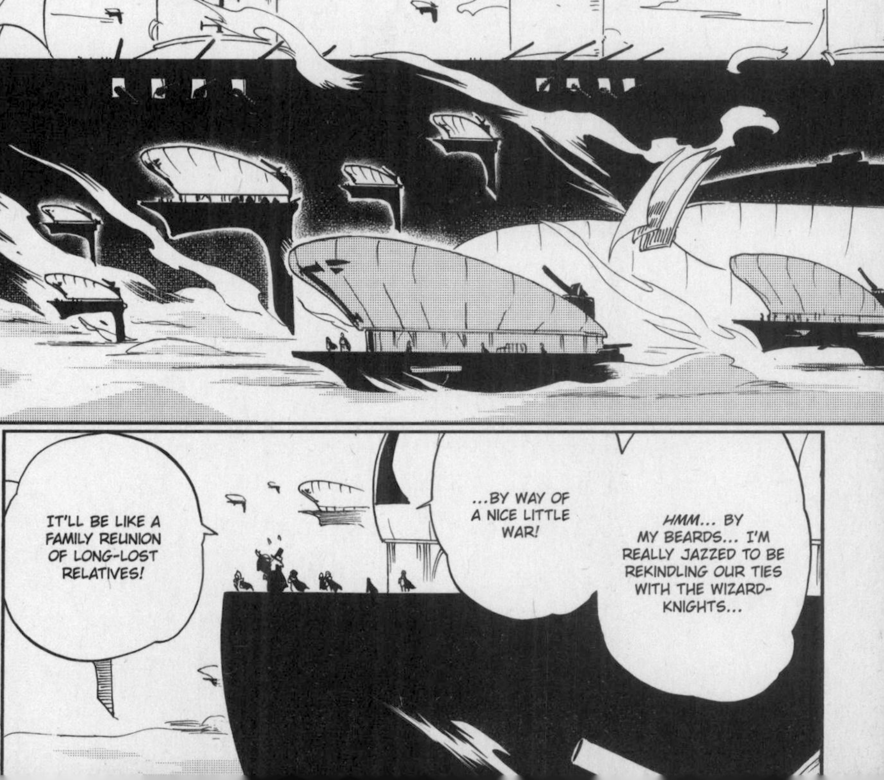
HMM... BY MY BEARDS... I'M REALLY JAZZED TO BE REKINDLING OUR TIES WITH THE WIZARD-KNIGHTS...
...BY WAY OF A NICE LITTLE WAR!
IT'LL BE LIKE A FAMILY REUNION OF LONG-LOST RELATIVES!

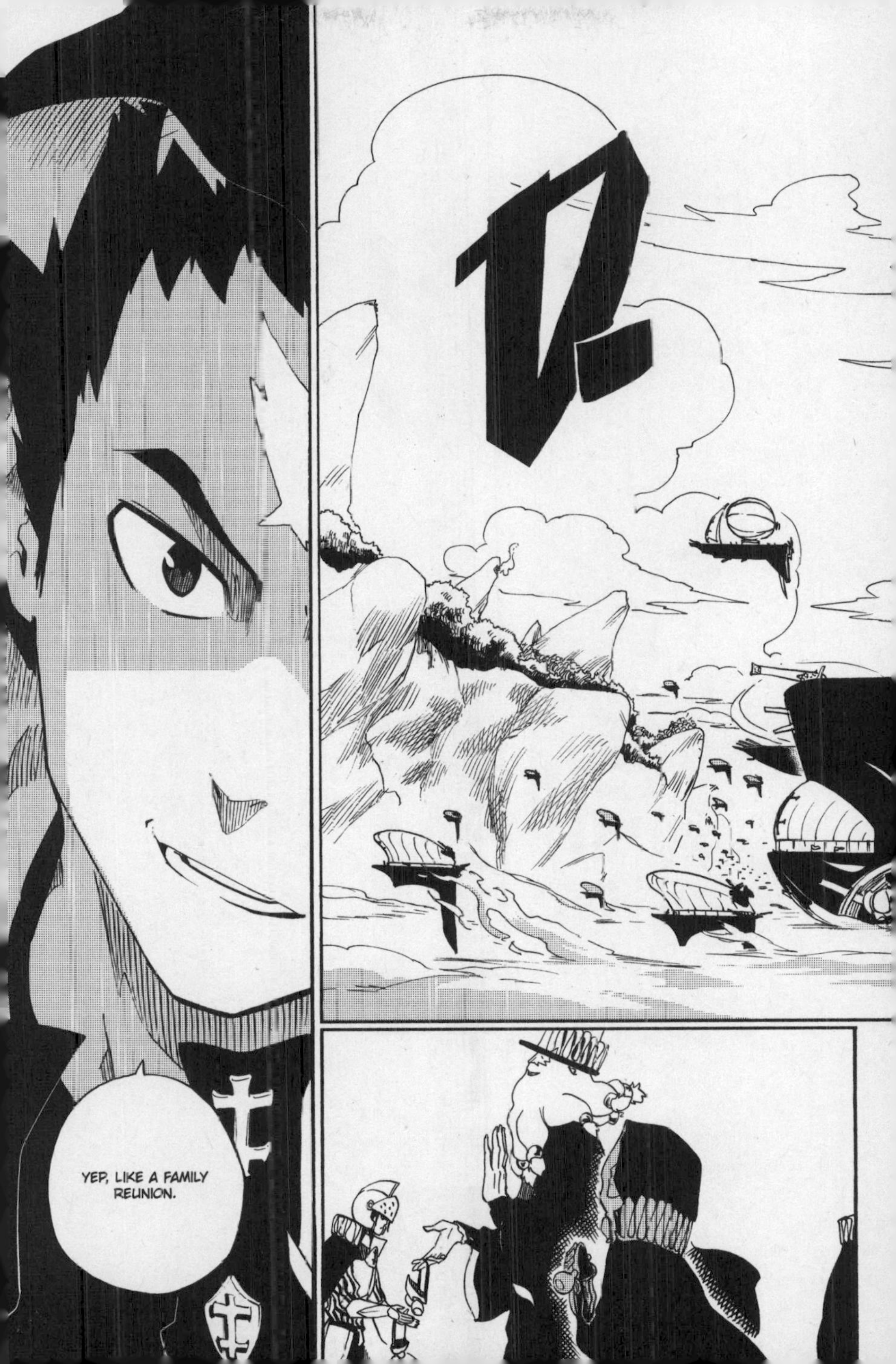
YEP, LIKE A FAMILY REUNION.

TO BE CONTINUED...

Toum? STAK!!

QUESTIONS...

ANSWERS!!

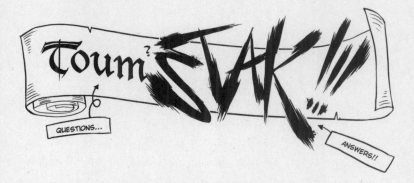

<u>Kaour Salph:</u> Toum! Greetings, Tony-sensei, you have a message.
***Click* Wiener Lock! Okay, now that I have your attention, I have two, three questions to ask you.**
<u>Tony Valente:</u> That wasn't me, I don't walk around with mine out in the open. But you can go ahead and ask me your questions anyway. Just let the other poor guy go.

- If the unipig is really so mythical, how come we can see two of them flying around above the Artemis at the beginning of volume 5? Did they escape from the Institute's zoo?
That is because of their migration trajectory. They always pass by the Artemis after mating season. And although they're pigs, they hump like rabbits and end up reproducing way too much, which ruins their environment, and puts their entire species, which is already at a bit of a crossroads, completely in jeopardy. So after egg-laying season, they come to drop off a few baby unipiglets and go back south. So where do the piglets end up then? Well, that actually depends... In pasta, sausages, ham and salami... Why not as pets, you say? Oh no, they're too mythical for that! Come on, show a little respect!

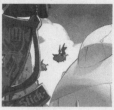

- And lastly! When Baron Cristolom drinks his two potions, one is for his turbo-hams, but what is the other one for? Anti-magic?
Nice! That is exactly it! That's what the symbol on the bottle means.

<u>Hugo Pelletier:</u> Is Verdoux a reference to Charlie Chaplin?

<u>Tony Valente:</u> Yup!

- I also wanted to know something else. You talked about the references in certain characters' names, but not yet Grimm's. Is he a reference to the Brothers Grimm? I really hope so :3
A little bit, but there're also some other reasons that I will explain throughout the story. Although, if you really want to know, at first he had this long, far-fetched name: Shun Napoleon Spencer. Why's that you say? No idea! The man used to be full of mysteries, even for me! Then that changed to Grimm Napoleon Spencer, then just Grimm. And I learned very recently that the figure that personifies Death, that giant skeleton with a hoodie, holding a scythe, is called the "Grim Reaper" in English... So yup, I did not do that on purpose! Seriously, this man has so many mysteries surrounding him... So...many...

Berat Adl: Is there anything you do to draw so well? Do you have any techniques and if so, could you show them to us?

Tony Valente: Of course! So there's the really classic technique where you hold a pencil, like this and *fwoop fwoop fwoop*, you're drawing. Then there's also a technique where I hold the pencil like this, and bam! I do that! Another one I like is when I take eight pencils, but you have to warm up a bit beforehand... But my favorite one is the secret technique of the "Wise Sheep." Look closely, this is going to go quickly... And... There! Okay, with all this, you should be all set to draw a manga now.

....

Fanilo Rakotomalala: Li'l question that's been bugging me: is Doc's infection that he's an immortal wizard °-°?

Tony Valente: Li'l answer that's really confusing: Is Doc a wizard? -(°0°)-

....

Valentin Lopez: After reading *Radiant*, I noticed something: Grimm is *really* mysterious, so I just need to ask this question: does he like chocolate croissants?

Tony Valente: He doesn't know what those are, but if it helps, he like vroissants and pioches!

....

Deusty L: Hey Tony! I would really like to become a manga author and illustrator! *.* So I'd like to know your secret and get your advice on how to draw amazing backgrounds like yours! And the characters! Any special training with books, images or otherwise? Anyway, hope everything continues to go well, I'm a fan of *Radiant*! **

Tony Valente: Okay, so my advice is the following: draw and tell whatever story you like! Characters, backgrounds... As long as **you're** invested in it, there's a high probability that you'll put in a **lot** of time working on them. As for references, even if I make up my own backgrounds, I take a lot of my ideas from all kinds of books I find in the library: travel books, pictures, documentaries related to subjects that interest me... I like to go through a book I enjoy and take notes in the form of small sketches, so that way I'm already digesting that info. With the internet nowadays, you can silently store thousands of images related to a subject to the point you feel like you'll never really be able to go through all of them. It's amazing! But it's also a poison to my creativity! With that, what's important is exercise. If you want to write and draw, start by writing and drawing. A drawing isn't a drawing until the moment you actually have it jotted down on paper. It's the same for a story: as long as it's in your head, it's maybe even a couple of stories at the same time and it doesn't help you gain any experience... So exercise and try to better yourself!!

And there we have it, I was able to give an actual response without joking. I didn't even mention pee or anything similar once!

Crap, now I just ruined my own answer!

....

Benji the Lizard: The incantations and symbols the wizards use when blurting out their spells are like mnemonic devices, right? Ideas they associate to a specific usage of the Fantasia in order to more instinctively be able to use them in full combat. Are there any wizard that don't need to resort to these types of tricks and can bend Fantasia to their will?

Tony Valente: Nobody *really* needs them, but it makes the learning process go smoother so everyone uses them. It'd be like running on your knees: at first we can all do it, but it's just hard to. But if someone were to start jogging like that every morning they'd end up convincing a few more people to do the same, even if it does seem difficult to do. Everyone uses their feet to run, it's more practical. Running on your knees doesn't help you go that fast. And it hurts! I just tried it.

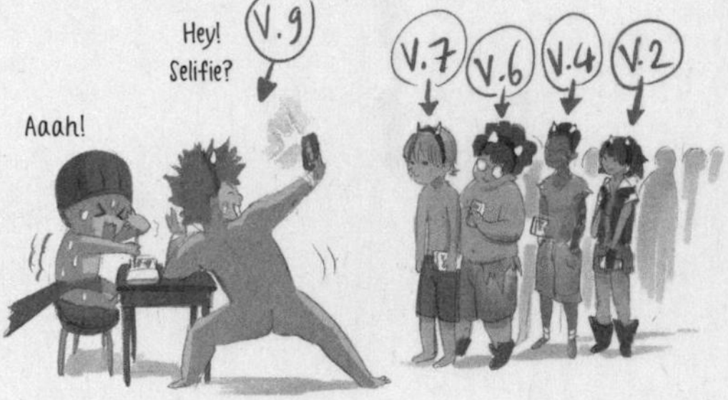
Aaah!
Hey! Selifie?
V.9
V.7
V.6
V.4
V.2

At first, I thought Seth was going to accumulate all these Wizard's accessories like parchments, potions, brooms, wands, grimoires... but in the end, nothing! He keeps losing everything and even keeps ending up undressed more and more! At this rate, in one or two volumes, I'll risk seeing unseemly cosplays at signings.

–Tony Valente

Tony Valente began working as a comic artist with the series *The Four Princes of Ganahan*, written by Raphael Drommelschlager. He then launched a new three-volume project, *Hana Attori*, after which he produced *S.P.E.E.D. Angels*, a series written by Didier Tarquin and colored by Pop.

In preparation for *Radiant*, he relocated to Canada. Through confronting caribou and grizzlies, he gained the wherewithal to train in obscure manga techniques. Since then, his eating habits have changed, his lifestyle became completely different and even his singing voice has changed a bit!

RADIANT

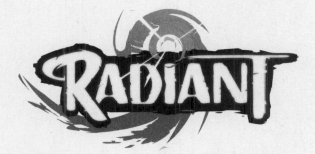

RADIANT VOL. 7
VIZ MEDIA Manga Edition

STORY AND ART BY **TONY VALENTE**

Translation/**(´・∀・`)ｻｧ?**
Touch-Up Art & Lettering/**Erika Terriquez**
Design/**Julian [JR] Robinson**
Editor/**Gary Leach**

Published by arrangement with MEDIATOON LICENSING/Ankama.
RADIANT T07

Printed in the U.S.A.

Published by VIZ Media, LLC
P.O. Box 77010
San Francisco, CA 94107

10 9 8 7 6 5 4 3 2 1
First printing, September 2019

VIZ MEDIA
viz.com

ratings.viz.com RATED T TEEN

PARENTAL ADVISORY
RADIANT is rated T for Teen and is recommended for ages 13 and up. This volume contains fantasy violence.

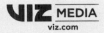

Ruby, Weiss, Blake and Yang are students at Beacon Academy, learning to protect the world of Remnant from the fearsome Grimm!

RWBY

MANGA BY **Shirow Miwa**

BASED ON THE ROOSTER TEETH SERIES
CREATED BY **Monty Oum**

viz.com

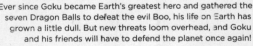

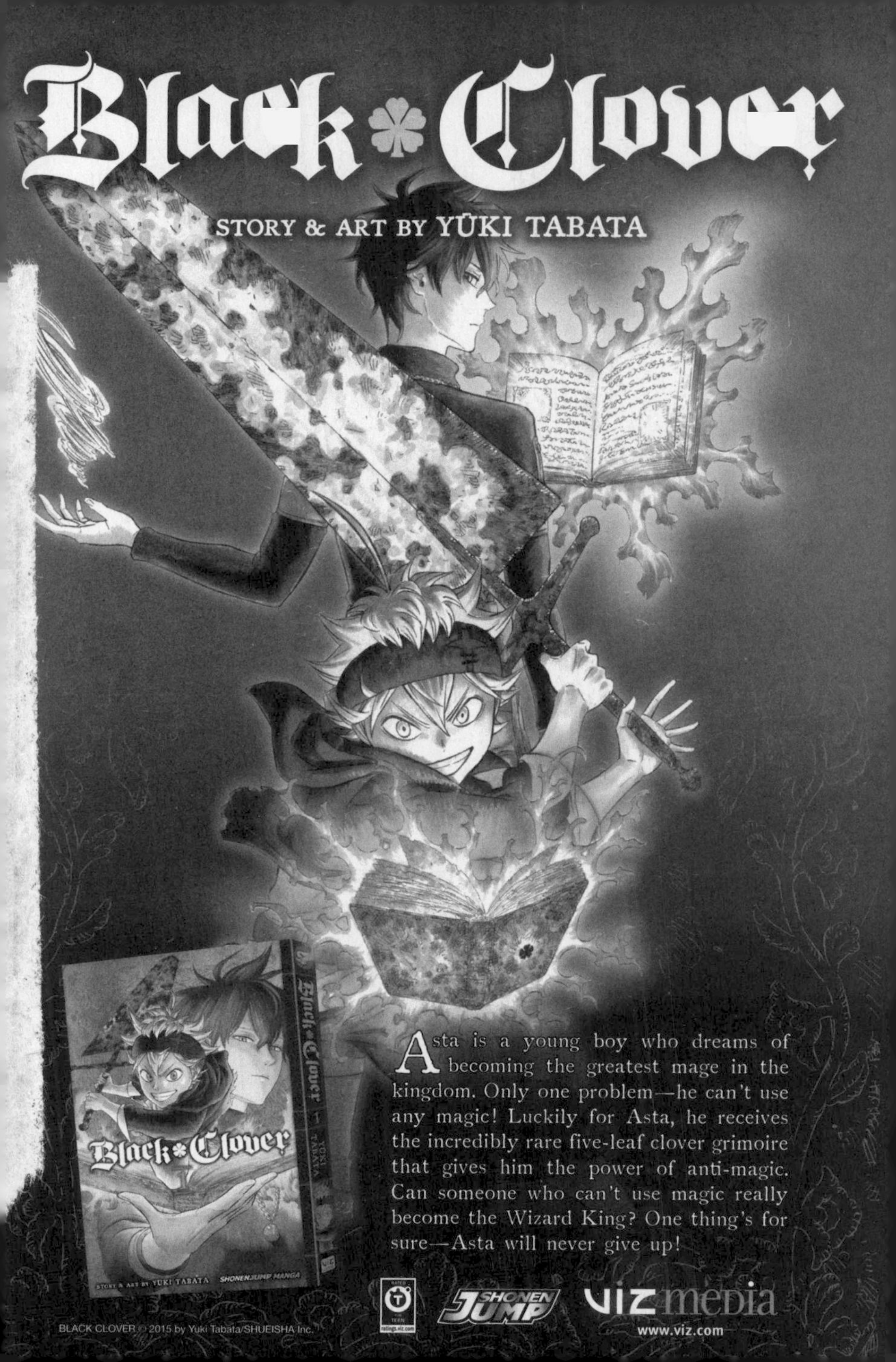
Black Clover
STORY & ART BY YŪKI TABATA
Black Clover
STORY & ART BY YUKI TABATA
SHONENJUMP MANGA
Asta is a young boy who dreams of becoming the greatest mage in the kingdom. Only one problem—he can't use any magic! Luckily for Asta, he receives the incredibly rare five-leaf clover grimoire that gives him the power of anti-magic. Can someone who can't use magic really become the Wizard King? One thing's for sure—Asta will never give up!
SHONEN JUMP
VIZ media
www.viz.com
BLACK CLOVER © 2015 by Yuki Tabata/SHUEISHA Inc.

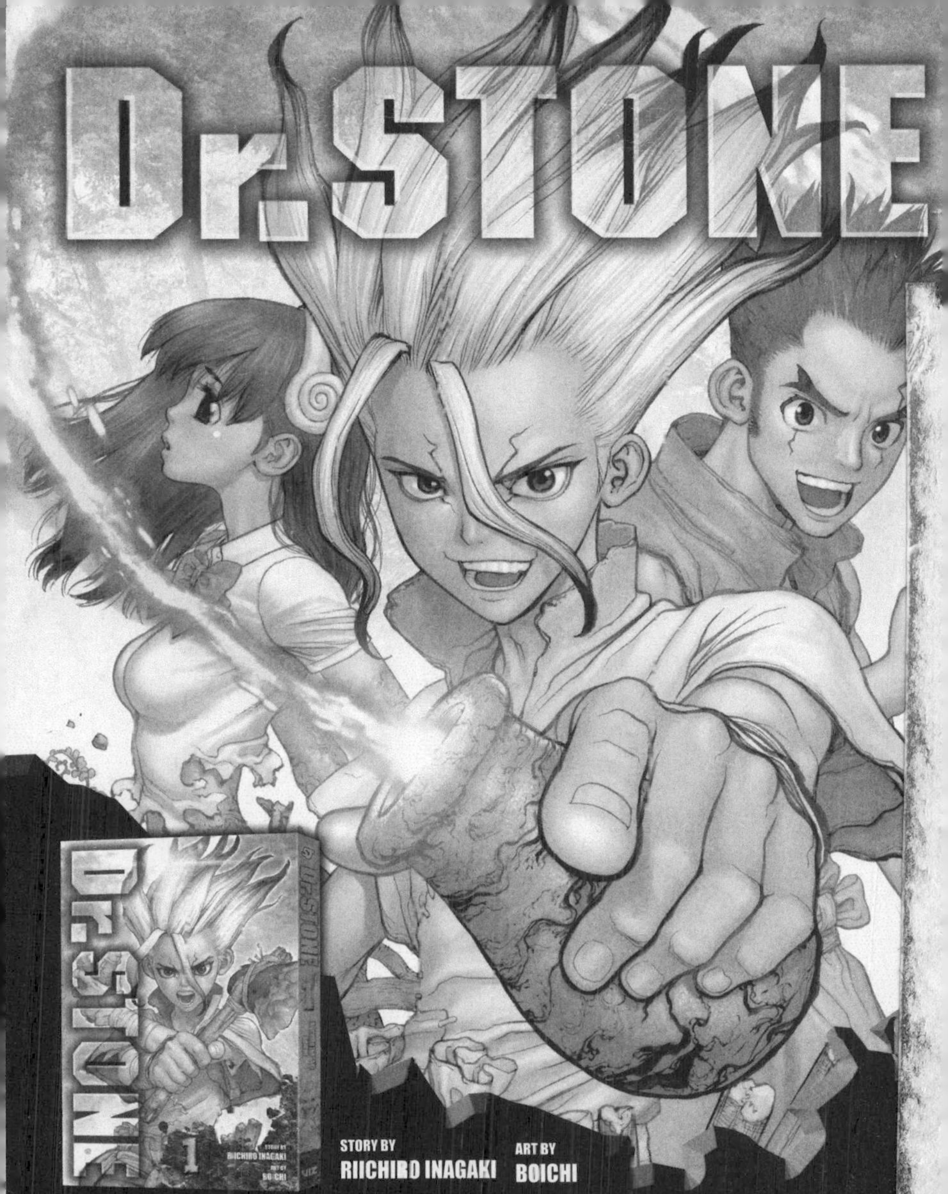

Dr. STONE

STORY BY
RIICHIRO INAGAKI

ART BY
BOICHI

One fateful day, all of humanity turned to stone. Many millen
later, Taiju frees himself from petrification and finds himse
surrounded by statues. The situation looks grim—until he runs
into his science-loving friend Senku! Together they plan to restart
civilization with the power of science!

YOU'RE READING THE WRONG WAY

RADIANT reads from right to left, starting in the upper-right corner, meaning that action, sound effects, and word-balloon order are completely reversed from English order.

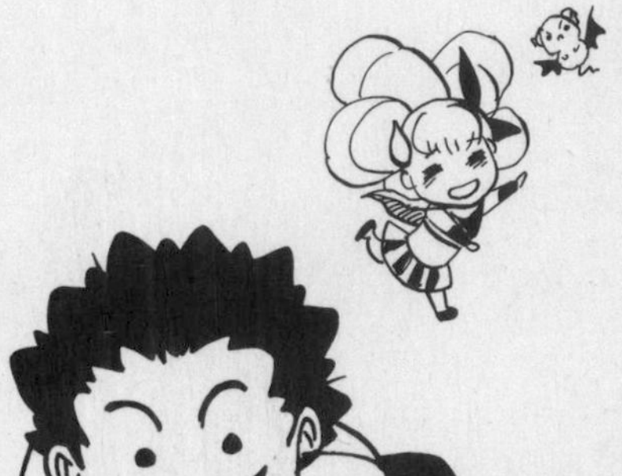

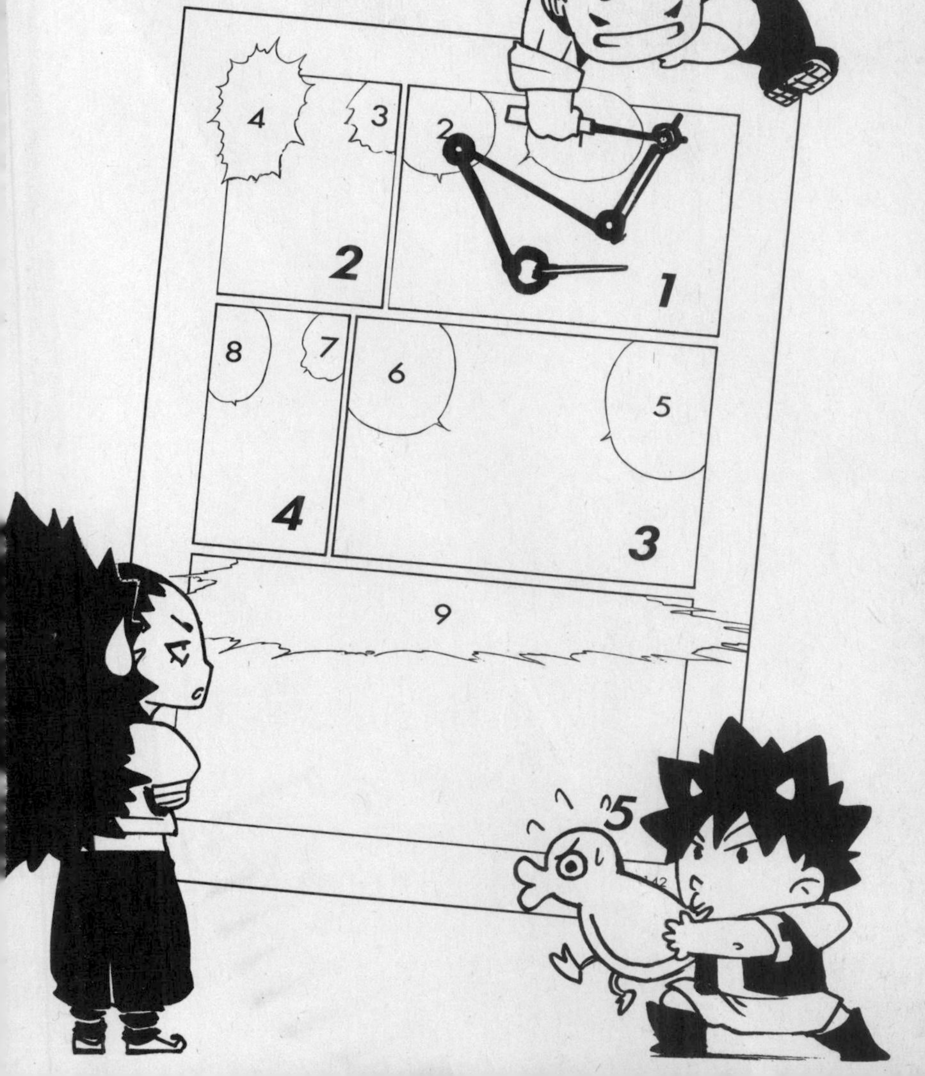
1
1
2
2
3
4
3
5
6
4
7
8
5
9